THE HISTORY OF INDIANA LAW

Ohio University Press Series on Law, Society, and Politics in the Midwest

Series Editor: Paul Finkelman

The History of Ohio Law, edited by Michael Les Benedict and John F. Winkler

Frontiers of Freedom: Cincinnati's Black Community, 1802–1868, by Nikki M. Taylor

A Place of Recourse: A History of the U.S. District Court for the Southern District of Ohio, 1803–2003, by Roberta Sue Alexander

The Black Laws: Race and the Legal Process in Early Ohio, by Stephen Middleton

The History of Indiana Law, edited by David J. Bodenhamer and Hon. Randall T. Shepard

THE HISTORY OF
INDIANA LAW

Edited by David J. Bodenhamer
and Hon. Randall T. Shepard

Ohio University Press Athens
In association with the Indiana Bar Foundation

Ohio University Press, Athens, Ohio 45701

www.ohio.edu/oupress/

Printed in the United States of America

Ohio University Press books are printed on acid-free paper ∞ ™

14 13 12 11 10 09 08 07 06 5 4 3 2 1

Library of Congress Cataloging-in-Publication Data

The history of Indiana law / edited by David J. Bodenhamer and Randall T. Shepard.

p. cm. — (Ohio University Press series on law, society, and politics in the Midwest)

Includes bibliographical references and index.

ISBN-13: 978-0-8214-1637-2 (cloth : alk. paper)

ISBN-10: 0-8214-1637-5 (cloth : alk. paper)

1. Law—Indiana—History. 2. Courts—Indiana—History. 3. Justice, Administration of—Indiana—History. I. Bodenhamer, David J. II. Shepard, Randall T., 1946– III. Series.

KFI3078.H57 2006

349.77209—dc22

2006005955

INDIANA BAR
FOUNDATION

Publication of *The History of Indiana Law* has been made possible by the generous support of the Indiana Bar Foundation

CONTENTS

PREFACE AND ACKNOWLEDGMENTS

Indiana has a rich history. It is well documented by scholars and others who have written with grace and insight about the state frequently touted as the Crossroads of America. Its contributions, foibles, personalities, legends, and myths are fodder for the state's residents, taught in the state's schools, and framed in countless images and stories. Whatever else they may think of their state, Hoosiers generally know its story and recognize it as their own.

Indiana legal history can claim no such legacy. State law touches the lives of Indiana citizens intimately and in every facet of daily life, yet its story is unknown to all but a few students. The governor's face and biography are familiar even to small children; many people struggle to name his constitutional peer, the chief of the state's highest court. No riveting case exists in popular memory to rival the dramatic elections of Indiana history; no legal personality has seized the public stage as decidedly as have numerous political or business figures; no event in law symbolizes the state's culture in the public mind. There is no Milan in the state's legal past.[1]

These essays aim to remedy this oversight, if only in part. We regard *The History of Indiana Law* as an overly ambitious title because no single volume can address the complex development of the state's law. But in many ways this volume sets the contours of Indiana's legal heritage. Its chapters provoke a deeper appreciation of law's often seminal role in Indiana history and a heightened appreciation for the contributions of its practitioners.

Certain themes shape an understanding of Indiana legal history. The state came into being—and its law formed—in a postrevolutionary world marked by a deep skepticism of central authority and a new theory of sovereignty that vested ultimate power outside of government. This philosophy contained within it a powerful drift toward limited government, one reinforced in Indiana and elsewhere by the triumph of Jacksonian democracy in the mid-nineteenth century. A Hoosier preference for localism, an emphasis on the virtue of community and consensus, and a failed fiscal experiment (the canal debacle of the 1830s) further restrained any desire to use law as an instrument for change. The growth of corporate power in the late nineteenth and early twentieth centuries witnessed a small shift toward legal intervention to address social ills and introduced a theme that marked Indiana law in the twentieth century—early adoption of successful progressive reforms pioneered by other states, many of them in the Midwest. The state has rarely led a legal reform movement, but it has been quick to adopt changes enacted elsewhere. The last half of the twentieth century witnessed another shift, as judges assumed ascendancy in setting the terms of the state's legal culture.

None of these themes is unique to Indiana, but it is worth noting how completely the state's experience fits the nation's legal development, at least for states outside the commercial centers. In this sense, Indiana is indeed representative of much of American legal history—cautiously progressive, with a commitment to instrumental change consistent with ideals of local control and egalitarian democracy. Change has been pragmatic and incremental, sometimes responding to forces within the state and sometimes to pressures outside of it. Hoosier law has not always been on the side of justice—witness the legal discrimination visited in past decades upon both blacks and women—but ultimately it has promoted the society Hoosiers claim to prize most, one that fosters the realization of individual ambition. In this fundamental sense, Indiana has been in the mainstream of American law.

The essays in this book examine the themes of Indiana legal history in a wide variety of areas—race, family, crime, juvenile justice, women's rights, education, and civil liberties, among others. Important legal figures and cases receive attention, as do the larger themes that connect legal history to Indiana and American history more broadly. The authors, all experts in their fields, represent equally the community of scholars and the community of practitioners. Each chapter is a significant contribution to what is, at present, a scanty secondary literature. Both the editors and the authors trust this volume will stimulate a recognition of the role law has played in making the state what it has been. More important, we hope it will spur reflection on how we can use law still to help Indiana achieve its noblest ambitions.

It always is important to acknowledge the contributions of others in making a book possible. This volume began with an invitation from Paul Finkelman, Chapman Distinguished Professor of Law at the University of

Tulsa College of Law, and Gillian Berchowitz, senior editor at Ohio University Press, to consider a book on Indiana as the second publication in its new Series on Law, Society, and Politics in the Midwest. We are grateful for their support and patience. We also acknowledge Rick Huard for his expert guidance of this project and thank him for his judicious editing of the manuscript.

The Indiana Bar Foundation deserves thanks for a grant that underwrote work on this project. Its interest in the legal history of Indiana is not new, and its generosity in supporting this volume did much to affirm both the editors and authors in the importance of their research and writing.

Few books would come into being without the support of individuals who were willing to check facts, prepare manuscripts, and ensure the volume met the standards for a professional submission. The following people contributed in various ways to these tasks: Sherri Wilson, Jamie Kojetin, Tabitha Maxwell, and Deborah Baumer.

The editors and authors assume responsibility for all errors of fact. For misinterpretations we are prepared to argue the case, but for egregious mistakes we only seek pardon.

We dedicate this work with love to Amy McDonell and Penny Bodenhamer.

RTS and DJB
Indianapolis
November 2004

Note

1. Milan is the small town in southeast Indiana whose high school basketball team captured the state's imagination when it defeated a heavily favored big-city team for the state basketball championship in 1954, a victory memorialized by the movie *Hoosiers.* The victory captured in a moment the virtues of teamwork, hard work, commitment, and community that enthusiasts tout as emblematic Indiana values.

PART I

Constructing the Framework

ONE

David J. Bodenhamer and Randall T. Shepard

THE NARRATIVES AND COUNTERNARRATIVES OF INDIANA LEGAL HISTORY

Every state has a story its citizens tell to identify where they are from and who they are.[1] Indiana's narrative is both American and midwestern. Hoosiers are the most representative of Americans, or so we believe. Indiana is the home of Middletown, the name sociologists Robert and Helen Lynn gave to Muncie, the site for their famous study in the 1920s and 1930s. We are literally and metaphorically residents of the "Crossroads of America," the tag cited most often by the state's tourism and economic development offices. We live in the nation's heartland, a broad middle ground from Ohio to Kansas where the values that made a country great find their strongest and most fruitful expression. Like all midwesterners, but more so, we Hoosiers are authentically American.

Of course, there is a counternarrative of the Indiana story. This version emphasizes the middling nature of our history. In this telling, we are stifled by consensus and marked by mediocrity. We are followers, not leaders; the state of vice presidents, not presidents. We are the "booboisie": small-minded shopkeepers, farmers, and mill workers who are always placing respectability before creativity, petty morality before progressive ideas. Our motto in this counternarrative is "Good enough is good enough."

In both versions of the Indiana story, law plays a role. In them, as in all variants of the American story, law is an embodiment of values. We are a nation—and a state—of laws. In our national mythology, law is the instrument of popular will and the protector of individual liberties. Stemming from fundamental compacts, national and state constitutions, these laws reflect who we are and shape the society we are becoming. The preferred narrative casts law as forward-looking or progressive. Law has enabled a polyglot society to meld and has provided both ballast and impetus to an economy that rapidly moved from agriculture to industry to service activities over a brief 150-year history. The counternarrative is darker in its portrait, seeing law as discriminatory and protective of entrenched interests. In this story, law is oppressive and moralistic, the stern guardian of small-town values that kept Indiana benighted and backward, an obstacle to progress rather than its aide.

Neither story is correct, but what is striking about both is their inability to speak with discernment or detail about the role of law in Indiana's history. A cursory glance through our primers reveals why. For most of our chroniclers, law is present primarily during the foundational moments in our past—the Northwest Ordinance of 1787, the constitution of 1816, and the constitution of 1851. During these events, law is seminal: it is the expression of our highest aspirations and sometimes—as with the 1851 prohibition of African American immigration—it reveals our deeper shame. At other times, law is largely the result of politics, the true central actor in both versions of the Indiana story. It is the exercise of power—sometimes for good cause, sometimes not—wielded by the legislature or by the governor but only rarely by its chief guardian, the state's courts.

In truth, the role of law in Indiana's story is complex. It has been progressive and conservative, enlightened and reactionary, influenced by law elsewhere and isolated from the larger national legal culture. Dominant political and economic interests have wielded it to serve their purposes, but its basic thrust has been democratic, not hegemonic. In a state not known for innovation, Indiana law has been cautiously progressive.

Legal culture, by definition, is the formal and informal expression of values, attitudes, and assumptions that have shaped both the operation and perception of law. It is the matrix of ideas that expresses how the world should operate; these ideas reflect, as well, beliefs about how the world operates in fact. Legal culture also is the response of law, in its structure and substance, to individual and group interests. It is both an expression of power and an attempt to find an acceptable compromise among diverse and competing interests within the larger society.[2]

American society, past and present, is marked by diversity and conflict. One measure of the law's success and vitality is the degree to which it promotes consensus. By this standard, Indiana's legal culture demonstrates a remarkable agreement on values that continues to shape the state's response to contemporary issues. These values include gradual change, accommodation, public-private cooperation, and economy in government. Indiana's legal history reflects that of the nation and makes real the oft-repeated claim of the state's representative character. But to rely too heavily on this theme is to obscure the nature of Hoosier jurisprudence. It fails to acknowledge how Indiana law fits squarely with the national paradigm—and, at times, how it does not. Indiana legal history may exist at the crossroads of the history of American law, but more than once the state has taken a road less traveled.

Three cultural moments in the state's past help us to understand the contours of Indiana's legal heritage—its birth in an age of revolutionary republicanism, its growth in a democratic and entrepreneurial society, and its maturity in an environment of corporate and national power. The story that emerges is one of transition from law as an instrument to create the good society to law as the protector of a society deemed good by its residents.

An accident of timing shaped the initial nature of Indiana law. The state was the sixth created after the American Revolution and the first admitted after the War of 1812, the so-called second war for independence that secured the nation's revolutionary character. Equally important, Indiana was the second state developed out of the Northwest Territory established by the Northwest Ordinance of 1787. This charter document was seminal in establishing a midwestern legal culture. Not only did it set forth a common framework for territorial expansion based on the principles and ideas of revolutionary republicanism but it represented a "heroic effort to guarantee the nation's future prosperity and power by defining the rules of everyday conduct on both the private and public levels."[3] The influence of the Ordinance persisted long after pioneer settlements had become prosperous and stable communities.

The values embraced by the Northwest Ordinance included widespread ownership of property as a guarantor of social stability, the use of agriculture to promote prosperity, and a commitment to moral and material development. It was a Jeffersonian vision that emphasized public virtue, civic engagement, and interdependence as antidotes to the rampant individualism and selfishness associated with frontier societies. In its recipe for an orderly march to statehood, the Ordinance sought to link material and moral progress. Encouraging the establishment of courts, schools, and churches or banning slavery from the territory, for example, promoted public morality and good citizenship and made possible a "new republican order of prosperity, peace, and decorum."[4]

Although the specific provisions ceased to possess legal authority after statehood, much of Indiana's early law reflects the Ordinance's continuing influence. The constitution of 1816, for example, created a state obligation to encourage educational progress by free and open public schools and by publicly funded libraries. It required the state's laws "to countenance and encourage the principles of humanity, honesty, industry, and morality," virtues that were at once both republican and midwestern. Indiana's penal code was to be "founded on the principles of reformation, and not of vindictive justice," and the General Assembly was charged with establishing asylums for the aged, infirm, or other persons who needed the "aid and beneficence of society" to become productive citizens and "lose, by usefulness, the degrading sense of dependence."[5]

Statute law and judicial opinion often, although not always, mirrored these constitutional injunctions. Legislators early abolished whipping as a permissible form of punishment. Debates on the abolition of the death penalty were a staple of General Assembly sessions during the middle decades of the nineteenth century, but reformers succeeded only in shifting from public hangings to executions held behind prison walls. Establishment of a penitentiary also found support, and a state-funded institution founded on reformative ideals was established in 1821. Missing from this list of progressive acts were public schools. The legislature created Indiana University in 1820, but the free and open schools mandated for the lower grades never materialized. Public libraries, too, were more promise than reality.

The use of law to create the good society also found expression in measures to regulate morality through criminal law. The code itself—actually the criminal statutes taken as a whole—doubled in size between 1816 and the Civil War, and most violations were classified as misdemeanors or minor crimes that threatened the good order of society more than life or property. Although economic crimes such as theft were a central concern of lawmakers, an increasing number of laws focused on preserving public morality. Hoosier lawmakers targeted sexual deviance, intemperance, and especially gambling; one-seventh of the substantive sections of the state's 1817 code, for instance, addressed gaming.[6] These laws, along with others that focused on violations of public order such as affrays and riots, provide an index to the values most important to Indiana residents. The good society fostered responsible citizens, civic order, and public morality.

In their attempt to shape the infant state through the adoption of law, legislators and judges were responding both to their environment and to ideals that sprang from the revolutionary experience. Early Indiana was a pioneer state, sparsely settled, with untamed lands and poor transportation. Like all frontier states, it appealed to immigrants who sought new opportunities and the chance for a new life. Exploiting the imagined riches of an untapped landscape required, above all, the protection of private property and the stability of economic transactions. But society was more than an economy; it was community, as well, and here lawmakers accepted the American Revolution's embrace of communal norms and a publicly virtuous citizenry as essential for the advancement of liberty itself. Not surprisingly, many of the state's laws, civil and criminal, sought to advance these goals, which, after all, were central to the concept of a triumphant new American society, radically different from the corrupt order of ancient Europe.

Out of this conception of Indiana as a commonwealth, the General Assembly acted to promote the state's interests. An early example was the 1821 act creating an ambitious state highway system: two dozen roads to link all parts of Indiana to the new capital at Indianapolis, paid for by the sale of public lands. The law's purpose was both democratic and economic. Roads were necessary to allow all citizens the opportunity to participate in state government; they also were required to move goods to market. Other states sought to attract private investment for such public purposes through monopoly charters, but Indiana chose instead to use public funds to advance a public good. It followed the same path when it floated state-backed bonds to finance the construction of a statewide canal network in the 1830s. The impulse to use public funds to promote the general welfare was short-lived, running afoul of a preference for local control and decentralized administration in the construction of roads and a depression that rendered the state insolvent and forced it to jettison the canal project. The lessons in these uses of law were instructive for Hoosiers, even if scholars have labeled the projects as misguided: private initiative, not public action, was a safer way to promote the public good.[7]

Another contradiction between constitutional ideals and the law in practice emerged early in the state's history. An aversion to taxes, still a hallmark of Indiana culture, forced numerous compromises with the lofty sentiments expressed in the 1816 constitution. A statewide system of public schools was stillborn, starved by lack of funding and a fear of losing local control. By the 1840s, the visions of reforming criminals in a state penitentiary had become a cost-saving system of private prisons and convict labor. In other ways not affected by public funding, lawmakers set a course at odds with the state's formally ascribed aspirations. The constitution of 1816 banned slavery in the state—and, in unambiguous language, the Indiana Supreme Court decided in *State v. Lasselle* (1 Blackf. 59 [1820]) that the few slaves still in the state were free—but neither this prohibition nor the constitution's assertion that all men were born free and equal blocked the spate of antiblack legislation passed during the first five decades of statehood. Even the promise of stable communities anchored by strong families came under assault in the scandal of easy divorce laws in the 1850s.

The development of such tensions precipitated the rise in Indiana of a new ethic—one that emphasized individual autonomy more than communal values. Individualism and equality had emerged as dominant themes in American culture by the 1830s, as witnessed by the triumph of free-market capitalism and Jacksonian democracy. Both developments emphasized limited government as a condition of liberty. The lineage of this belief ran to the Revolution, but it achieved new language and new force in the middle decades of the nineteenth century. The contemporary French visitor Alexis de Tocqueville had observed that the quest for profit was the quintessential characteristic of the American people, and now a majority of Americans, including Hoosiers, believed that the surest road to profit was through privatizing the marketplace.

Under this new creed, the signal role of government—and, therefore, of law—was to remove barriers that prevented men from competing as equals in the political arena and economic marketplace. Universal white adult male suffrage and general incorporation statutes were only two of the numerous legal reforms embraced by Indiana and other states to achieve this end. Both legislators and jurists demonstrated a keen awareness of the course of legal reform nationally and acted to bring state law into a closer correspondence with national norms. Initiatives to codify the law in the 1830s and 1840s followed templates established by the nation's leading commercial states, especially in banking, creditor-debtor, and contract law.[8] The respected supreme court reports compiled by Isaac Blackford, the leading Indiana jurist of his day, also promoted the notion that the state's case law aligned with the national legal culture.

This awareness of events in other states provided the context for a new constitution, even though the immediate impetus came from the fiscal crisis that followed the canal debacle. A wave of state constitutional reform had begun in the 1820s and had reached its zenith by the 1840s, with one-half of the states revising or rewriting their constitutions by 1861. After several false starts earlier in the decade, Hoosier leaders in 1848 agreed that Indiana required a new constitution to make government more responsive to changing social and economic conditions. The Indiana constitution of 1851 largely reflected the same impulses that drove the creation of new state constitutions throughout the Midwest. The result of market-oriented Jacksonian democracy, it captured the popular wariness of government by limiting its role, especially in matters relating to the economy, taxation, legislative authority, and individual liberties.[9] The constitution also included darker language from the state's counternarrative: it banned black migration, making Indiana the only midwestern state to do so in its fundamental charter.

The ethic of individualism and the distrust of governmental power embodied by the 1851 constitution promoted a conception of criminal law that was more liberal than the national norm. The new charter, for example, granted authority to the legislature to modify or abolish the grand jury. To its defenders, the grand jury was an ancient and essential instrument in the continuing battle to maintain public order and promote public virtue. Opponents, who proposed an alternate system of public examination and presentment, viewed the institution as inimical to individual liberty because of its secret, ex parte proceedings. Three midwestern states—Michigan, Ohio, and Indiana—debated the abolition of the grand jury in constitutional conventions in the late 1840s and early 1850s, but Indiana was the only state to include a clause permitting the legislature to abolish it.[10] Three years later, the state supreme court also embraced the philosophy of restraint on governmental power by interpreting the new constitution's promise of right to counsel to mean that the state had to provide an attorney at public expense for indigent defendants in felony cases, a result the U.S. Supreme Court did not reach until the 1960s.[11]

Two particular constitutional provisions strongly influenced the future development of Indiana legal culture—the prohibition on state debt and the popular election of state judges. Unlike the new constitutions in sister states, Indiana's constitution did not place a limit on state indebtedness: it banned it outright. Though a reasonable response to the unfulfilled promises of the failed internal improvement scheme, the ban inhibited the pace of change by forcing Indiana lawmakers into extraordinary measures to keep state government responsive to new needs. The popular election of judges had a similar effect, though in a different direction. Not only were all levels of state courts elective, but the new constitution expanded the number of lower courts and required circuit judges to live in a county within the circuit. When coupled with other mandates reflective of Indiana culture but at odds with national trends—for instance, that juries be arbiters of both fact and law in criminal cases and that any adult male of good moral character could be admitted to the bar—the election of judges reinforced the state's insular and localist tendencies and inhibited the development of a consistent and cohesive common law.

As has often been the case in Indiana history, outside forces provided a counterbalance to the particularistic impulses of Indiana lawmakers. The Civil War strengthened the role of the national government and blunted the political claims of Democrats, who not only ardently advocated limited government and local control but also lent lukewarm support to the Union and completely rejected emancipation. The industrialization spurred by the Civil War and the emergence of a national market drew the state headlong into a new economic order, but the depression of the 1870s reinforced the localism and hostility to government that had marked the state's late antebellum years.[12] The legal response fit the dominant laissez-faire economic theory of the period, which advocated a limited role for government in the market and no restrictions on the free flow of capital. Lax banking laws, a favorable tort environment, and the absence of corporate regulation were hallmarks of late nineteenth-century Indiana law. The state trailed other midwestern states in passing labor and welfare legislation, not from a lack of concern about the conditions of the industrial workplace but because its blended creed of individualism and social Darwinism found value in unrestrained competition. In a legal culture that favored limited government interference in the economy, the absence of regulation extended as well to the struggle between labor and management. For this reason, perhaps, labor unions found a home in Indiana.

Late nineteenth-century Indianans did not use law aggressively to redeem constitutional pledges or to address social issues. Consider child labor. In this area, Hoosiers uniformly expressed concern—it was not uncommon for children as young as ten years of age to perform heavy work for long hours in Indiana factories—but the state lagged behind others in providing a legal remedy. The General Assembly began debating the issue shortly after the Civil War, but not until 1897 did it prohibit the employment of children under fourteen in manufacturing or limit the work day of any child under sixteen to ten hours. Even then, the law was not enforced vigorously. A 1910 survey revealed that Indiana had a higher percentage of child labor than all but two northern states. The regulation of working conditions for women was slower still in coming, despite documentation of low wages and dismal working conditions.[13]

When working conditions led to injuries, workers had little prospect of obtaining compensation through the courts. Like most other states in the nineteenth century, Indiana had adopted various common-law doctrines that, taken together, made recovery extremely difficult. One of these, the fellow-servant rule, held that employers were not vicariously liable for injuries to one worker caused by the negligence of another worker. Courts also recognized assumption of risk as a defense available to employers, saying that an employee fit for the job could be deemed to understand and assume the risks that came with it and might indeed be better informed about the details of those risks than the employer. Finally, an employee's contributory negligence, even if it played a lesser role in the injury than the negligence of the employer, commonly barred recovery. The General Assembly attempted to open the door to recovery by workers in 1893, but the judiciary held unconstitutional enough of the law's provisions that the effort went for naught. It was only when Indiana adopted a comprehensive workers' compensation scheme in 1915 that the deadly trio of common-law doctrines finally was put to the sword.[14]

The law of contract also proceeded in classic formulas, much influenced by the growing importance of business transactions among expanding commercial organizations. The courts recognized regular defenses to contract claims, like duress and mistake, but always attached substantial importance to the notion that people could make their own agreements and expect them to be vindicated at law. This notion found such a robust and lengthy life in the state that a federal appellate court in Chicago in the late twentieth century observed, "Freedom of contract is alive and well and it is living in Indiana."[15]

The democratic zeal for local control that marked Indiana's legal culture began to lessen, albeit slowly, during the first decades of the twentieth century as Hoosiers wrestled with the transition from a rural agricultural society to an urban industrial one. The harsh consequences of laissez-faire economics finally provoked a progressive response from both major political parties that mimicked the reform platforms from other midwestern states, especially Wisconsin. Child labor and workers' compensation laws, a state income tax, a central highway commission, health and safety regulations, and a host of other bills appeared routinely before the General Assembly in the late nineteenth and early twentieth centuries. The result—hesitant, moderate reform—was true to the state's character. Enacted measures included a strengthened child labor law, the establishment of an inheritance tax, the creation of state railroad and public service commissions, and the second juvenile court system in the United States. Other progressive reforms came from energetic efforts by leaders of long-established agencies, such as the successful efforts by the state board of health to combat disease and protect the purity and food and water. But the state was too divided politically and its cultural divisions too stark, as seen in the campaigns to enact prohibition, to bring much change. "Conservative resistance among citizenry and political leadership," historian Jim Madison observed, "combined with a cautious state supreme court and difficulties of amending the state constitution to defeat or postpone many of the progressive proposals."[16]

The progressive movement in Indiana found its strongest voice during the 1910s and 1920s in Congressman Charles LaFollette, of Evansville, a member of the family whose very name represented progressivism in the national mind. Indiana adopted most of the prominent measures of the age, addressing the working conditions of women and children and enacting a workers' compensation system that wiped out the unholy trinity of legal doctrines—the fellow-servant rule, assumption of risk, and contributory negligence—that had usually barred injured employees from receiving any damage awards for injuries on the job. The state dithered on other progressive issues until federal action forced a change. Woman suffrage finally won favor in the General Assembly in 1917, but the difficulty of amending the state constitution and an adverse decision by the Indiana Supreme Court kept women from the ballot box until the ratification of the Nineteenth Amendment to the U.S. Constitution in 1920. The next year Indiana voters approved an amendment to keep the Indiana constitution consistent with the U.S. Constitution.

In the counternarrative of Indiana legal history, the decades of progressive reform also witnessed the triumph of prohibition in the state and the ascendancy of the Ku Klux Klan. Adopted by the legislature in 1917, two years before a federal constitutional amendment made the nation legally dry, prohibition was a middle-class reform aimed at what many perceived to be a lower-class and ethnic problem. The Klan also took aim at these groups in its anti-Catholic, anti-Semitic, antiblack rhetoric of superpatriotism and 100 percent Americanism. The influence of the Ku Klux Klan was enormous, reaching city halls and the State House itself. Mercifully, the Klan's reign was brief, and its impact on the state's legal culture was slight. The end came quickly in 1925, when Klan leader D. C. Stephenson was convicted of kidnapping and murdering a young woman, a conviction finally upheld on appeal by the Indiana Supreme Court in 1932.

The role of the Indiana Supreme Court—and, by extension, of the state's judiciary—during this period of hesitant reform is instructive in understanding the development of Hoosier law. From the beginning of statehood, the General Assembly was the dominant force in shaping Indiana law. The democratic impulse that fostered ratification of the 1851 constitution simultaneously expanded the number of judicial offices dramatically and circumscribed judicial authority, at least notionally, by making judges elective and therefore accountable to voters. Although this change fit accepted notions of popular sovereignty, it inhibited the development of a truly independent judiciary, at least as measured by the norms of its federal counterpart. Judges were politicians in Indiana, and they approached lawmaking in ways both idiosyncratic and conservative. They deferred to the legislature and, at the appellate levels, did little to advance new rights or powers under the broad language of the Indiana constitution, except in the area of individual rights. In fairness, their formalistic approach differed little from that of their brethren elsewhere during much of this period.[17] Not until the advent of the Progressive Era at the national level in the early twentieth century did theories of legal realism begin to move the judicial firmament to any great degree. Indiana was no leader in this shift, either.

The judiciary's influence on law during these decades was largely to confirm the changes wrought by legislative action. There were but two moments when the courts stepped in to thwart the will of the other branches. The first occurred in 1911–12, when the state's popular Democratic governor, Thomas R. Marshall, placed sweeping constitutional changes before the legislature. Marshall's plan called for a line-item veto of appropriations, raised the veto override threshold to three-fifths, expanded both houses of the General Assembly and the supreme court, and provided for nearly every known populist tool of the age: initiative, referendum, and recall. The changes were so far-reaching that they became known as the

"Marshall Constitution." The governor and legislature agreed to submit the "new constitution" to the voters immediately, without waiting for the approval of a second General Assembly, as required by the 1851 constitution. There was, of course, some American precedent for such a maneuver; the framers of the federal Constitution submitted their work in 1787 directly to the states without pausing to comply with the amending procedure embodied in the Articles of Confederation.

Opponents of the new constitution cried foul and obtained an injunction preventing presentation of the Marshall Constitution to the voters at the 1912 general election. Although the Indiana Supreme Court had recently acquired a Democratic majority, it affirmed the injunction by a 3-to-2 vote when one of the Democratic members joined with the two Republicans to affirm the amending processes adopted in 1851 as the sole means of changing the state's organic law.[18] Governor Marshall railed at the court's interference with the democratic process, but he eventually withdrew his proposals and soon pursued progressive policies as vice president to the quintessential progressive, Woodrow Wilson. Tempers had calmed four years later when the wayward Democratic justice came up for reelection; his fellow Democrats renominated him unanimously. That the supreme court would stand in such strenuous opposition to the other branches in the Marshall Constitution case was the exception that proved the rule.

The judiciary's second moment of note in the first half of the twentieth century was more typical. Republicans had spent the entire Great Depression in the wilderness, even in Indiana. During the Democratic ascendancy, both nationally and in the state, government became more active and more expansive, a result embraced by Hoosiers. Paul McNutt, elected governor in the Democratic landslide of 1932, reorganized state government, placing more power in the executive branch—and more patronage in the hands of the governor—and effectively diminishing the authority of local officials. Eight years later, power shifted back to Republicans, who swept both houses of the legislature, elected a Republican to the supreme court for the first time since 1928, and carried nearly the entire list of their nominees, except for governor, for the executive branch. With a State House full of newly elected Republicans, the party decided to grab what patronage it could by reorganizing the executive branch. It advanced a plan to rearrange the government into a series of large units patterned on the McNutt proposals. Under this arrangement, the directors of each unit were to be chosen by commissions consisting of the governor and two other executive officers who almost always were Republicans. The effect would have been to strip the governor of effective control over the personnel of the executive department. With the four Democratic justices from the 1930s still in the majority, the state supreme court invalidated these statutes on a party-line vote of 4 to 1.[19]

As they had been since the 1850s, judges still were brothers in the same political club with governors and legislators, although they were the least among equals in this regime. State parties chose both executive and judicial nominees through state conventions in which the big political prizes were the executive offices. Nominations for the supreme court frequently became occasions for balancing the ticket or for trading votes with some small county delegation to achieve victory on a more important office. This bias for relatively rural judges, of course, affected the outlook of the court itself, reinforcing the localism of Indiana legal culture. The political system also produced a high level of turnover because judges occupied "down-ballot" offices most susceptible to shifts in the political winds and because low judicial salaries led to frequent midterm resignations. The nadir of the supreme court's status under this system undoubtedly occurred in 1955. The resignation of an incumbent justice prompted a series of temporary appointments by Governor George N. Craig. In a period of less than five months, Craig appointed four different justices du jour. One of these had the bad manners to tell the press that the "last thing in my life I would do" was to stay on the highest bench, but that serving for a few months "would allow my grandchildren to say that grand-daddy served on the Supreme Court."[20]

The election of 1960 set the stage for changes that would create a third cultural moment in Indiana's legal history. It was, as presidential years usually are in Indiana, a Republican year. The leading exception was the young and energetic Democratic lawyer Matthew Welsh, who won the governor's office. Welsh aligned himself with the fresh approach of the Kennedy administration and with the blizzard of policy initiatives that were the hallmark of the Johnson years. He pushed reforms through the General Assembly on policies from the sales tax to civil rights remedies to protecting the environment.

With the exception of New Deal relief, Indiana had never been hospitable territory for federal initiatives; the state became famous during the 1950s and 1960s by turning down offers of federal money for various social programs. The Welsh years ran only modestly against this Hoosier wariness of things federal, but the election of Richard Nixon in 1968 altered more dramatically Indiana's idea of the role it should play in relation to the national government. President Nixon believed that the initiatives of the Kennedy-Johnson years had placed too much emphasis on direct federal action. He devised a "New Federalism" in which state governments became the principal implementers of new federal initiatives. Although these new partnerships relied on state agreement to participate, it was usually plain that if the state government did not agree the federal government would proceed through direct regulation. In fields such as worker safety, mining, and air and water pollution, even relatively conservative Hoosiers preferred local management of day-to-day activities, even if it meant entanglement with federal agencies. It did not hurt that some of the Nixon administration's new initiatives were especially popular with Hoosiers, grants to state and local law enforcement agencies to wage the "war on crime" being a prime example.

Even though obvious changes occurred only later, the Welsh momentum created an environment favorable to a host of constitutional reforms sent to the voters after he left office. Constitutional measures approved by the voters in 1970 and 1972 proved to be momentous shifts, altering in important ways the relative roles of the three branches. One clear result was an increase in the influence of the state's appellate judiciary, especially the supreme court.

In the first set of reforms, voters approved annual sessions of the legislature, which had been meeting only every other year since the adoption of the 1851 constitution.[21] This amendment put the General Assembly in a position to make law more quickly than had been the case. To sustain this new role, the legislature created a permanent office of legislative services that vastly improved the drafting of proposed legislation, a necessary legal craftsmanship that resulted in technically sound bills. Annual sessions also gave legislative leadership a higher visibility in the public arena than had been the case in the days when the General Assembly was only in the capital for a few months every two years.

Also in 1970, voters agreed to abandon partisan contests for the appellate bench, even as they were selecting judicial candidates in the traditional manner. They approved a system modeled after the so-called Missouri Plan, in which the governor appointed appellate judges from a list fashioned by a constitutional commission of lawyers and nonlawyer citizen members. The governor's appointees were subject to periodic retention votes.[22] This amendment led to dramatic changes in the courts as institutions. Because the referenda occurred only once every ten years, the average time in service by the state's appellate judges increased dramatically. Six of the ten longest-serving justices in Indiana Supreme Court history have served since 1970. This stability both raised the public profile of the appellate courts and made sustained judicial initiatives possible. Longer tenures also became the norm in the chief executive's office when voters agreed to permit the reelection of governors in 1972. Since this change, all four of the state's elected governors—Otis Bowen, Robert Orr, Evan Bayh, and Frank O'Bannon—have won two terms.

These organic changes altered the roles of the players in developing Indiana law. A series of governors with longer tenure and larger political clout left landmark policy initiatives embedded in Indiana law—for example, the Bowen tax package designed to give property tax relief and the Orr "A+ Program" that increased spending and raised the level of accountability in education. The legislature became a more professional body in which members served multiple terms, thanks to skillfully gerrymandered districts. Myriad interim study committees emerged to consider legislative remedies to a wide variety of issues. The permanent legislative services staff and the members' own staffs soon outnumbered the senators and representatives.

The impact of these changes is evident in two ways that most voters rarely notice. First, the Indiana General Assembly regularly adopts statutes devised by the National Conference of Commissioners on Uniform State Laws, a body providing nonpartisan, well-drafted legislation that brings clarity and stability to state statutory law. Although some of these acts directly and frequently affect the lives of citizens (like Indiana's early adoption of the Uniform Dissolution of Marriage Act in 1973), they more often bring Indiana law into conformity with national economic and legal norms in ways that make the Hoosier economy a complementary part of the national enterprise without prompting any notice among the citizenry. Second, the Indiana General Assembly began a thorough and continuing examination of the form of the state's law when it adopted an official Indiana Code in 1971; since then it has sustained the effort through a routine and well-developed system of recodification. These important processes make for a sounder body of law but rarely reach public attention.

The most dramatic effect of the 1970 constitutional amendments has been in the role the state's judiciary plays as a source of law reform. When the Indiana Supreme Court adopted nearly wholesale the federal rules of civil procedure, the court and the legislature agreed that both bodies would adopt the same rules (one embodied in statute, the other by court order). The pace of such reforms has quickened in the intervening years. At the beginning of the 1970s, the justices took bar discipline under their wing and assumed greater authority over the rules of practice. Mandatory continuing legal education for lawyers followed, imposed by court rule. This action paralleled the development of a new institution under the court's umbrella, the Indiana Judicial Center, which bears responsibility for mandatory continuing judicial education and a host of other voluntary programs aimed at strengthening the trial bench. By the 1990s, the supreme court deployed its rulemaking authority for projects that seemed rather substantive. The court issued Indiana's first codified rules of evidence. It issued mandatory guidelines for the calculation of child support and then guidelines for "parenting time" in divorced families and paternity cases. By rule, it revised the conduct of jury trials.

The judiciary's appellate functions grew as the Indiana Court of Appeals expanded and as the supreme court shed most of its mandatory criminal jurisdiction, thus permitting more attention to developments in the civil law. More important, the judiciary became a branch that was "always open for business" as the appellate courts applied the techniques of legal reasoning to the substantial flow of disputes in fields such as corporate governance, collective bargaining, environmental cleanup, marriage and children—not to mention the old standbys of tort and contract. This collective outpouring of law and legal interpretation, bolstered by aggressive use of new electronic tools, became a leading source of law for practitioners and citizens.

Such aggressiveness brought increased public visibility, especially when the court forced action from the other two branches of government. In no instance was this more true than in the tax reassessment cases. At the turn of the millennium, newspapers regularly reported the ongoing political debate about how to handle what was usually called the "court-ordered reassessment crisis." During the previous decade, both the Indiana Tax Court and the Indiana Supreme Court had declared unconstitutional the system long used for assessing local property taxes. The early twentieth-first century has witnessed a widespread alteration of values and a realignment of the state's budget to accommodate the new fiscal reality, both occasioned by the sweeping property tax decisions.

Whether these structural changes mark the emergence of a new narrative in Indiana legal history, the judiciary has gained parity with the legislature and governor as one of the prime actors in the state's legal culture. In some ways, this shift seems inevitable, given the twentieth century's emphasis on national standards in law (and elsewhere) as seen in the development of national law schools, uniform codes, and large law firms that practiced far beyond the borders of their home state. Even the countervailing forces in the nation's legal culture served to strengthen the role of the state bench; for example, the Rehnquist Court's rediscovery of federalism increased the visibility and role of state constitutions and supreme courts, including those of Indiana.

Whatever the outcome of recent changes, Indiana legal culture will continue to reflect the larger social and political culture of the state itself. Here the historical record is certain: moderation is the Indiana way. At times, the narrative of Indiana law has been remarkably progressive in its embrace of the highest ideals of American constitutionalism, whether in nineteenth-century criminal justice reforms or in the professional legal standards advanced by the judiciary in the late twentieth century. But as often as the dominant theme appears, a subterranean narrative surfaces in counterpoise. Localism, parsimony, prejudice have all worked at various times to defeat the fullest expressions of constitutional mandates ratified by Indiana voters. This story, of course, is familiar to more places than Indiana. Indeed, it is an American story, one that Indiana, true to its motto, expresses as completely as any of its sister states.

Notes

1. The idea of narratives used in this essay is borrowed from Andrew R. L. Cayton and Susan E. Gray, eds., *The American Midwest: Essays on Regional History* (Bloomington: Indiana University Press, 2001).

2. Kermit L. Hall, *The Magic Mirror: Law in American History* (New York: Oxford University Press, 1989), 6.

3. Andrew R. L. Cayton and Peter S. Onuf, *The Midwest and the Nation: Rethinking the History of an American Region* (Bloomington: Indiana University Press, 1990), 3; Peter S. Onuf, *Statehood and Union: A History of the Northwest Ordinance* (Bloomington: Indiana University Press, 1987), chaps. 4–7.

4. Cayton and Onuf, *Midwest and the Nation*, 9.

5. Ind. const. of 1816, art. IX, §§ 1, 2, 4, 5.

6. David J. Bodenhamer, *The Pursuit of Justice: Crime and Law in Antebellum Indiana* (New York: Garland, 1986), 26.

7. James H. Madison, *The Indiana Way: A State History* (Bloomington: Indiana University Press, 1986), 86. On the Internal Improvements Act, see Donald F. Carmony, *Indiana, 1816–1850: The Pioneer Era* (Indianapolis: Indiana Historical Society, 1998), 185–201.

8. See generally Morton J. Horowitz, *The Transformation of American Law, 1780–1860* (Cambridge, Mass.: Harvard University Press, 1977).

9. Hall, *Magic Mirror,* 103–5. On the constitution of 1851, see Carmony, *Indiana, 1816–1850,* 403–51. For a comparison with Ohio's constitution of 1851, see Barbara A. Terzian, "Ohio's Constitutional Conventions and Constitutions," in *The History of Ohio Law,* ed. Michael Les Benedict and John F. Winkler (Athens: Ohio University Press, 2004), 1:50–60. Significantly, the framers of Indiana's new constitution saw the legislature, not the executive, as the primary threat to liberty, or so the president of the convention believed, as noted in his closing remarks: "[O]f the three departments . . . the legislative or law making department or power, is the one above all others most likely to encroach upon the rights of the citizen and to subvert the liberties of the mass of the people; hence the necessity to restrain, (within proper and safe limits) not the people themselves, but those to whom their power for a time may be delegated, for the purpose of making laws for their government." *Journal of the Convention of the People of Indiana* (1851; Indianapolis: Indiana Historical Bureau, repr. 1936), 997.

10. David J. Bodenhamer, "Criminal Justice and Democratic Theory in Antebellum America: The Grand Jury Debate in Indiana," *Journal of the Early Republic* 5 (Winter 1985): 481–502.

11. Webb v. Baird, 6 Ind. 13 (1854).

12. Indiana was not alone in its retreat from the more activist government of the Civil War period. See Morton Keller, *Affairs of State: Public Life in Late Nineteenth Century America* (Cambridge, Mass.: Harvard University Press, 1977), 318–20.

13. Madison, *Indiana Way,* 165–67. Clifton J. Phillips, *Indiana in Transition: The Emergence of an Industrial Commonwealth, 1880–1920* (Indianapolis: Indiana Historical Society, 1968), 327–36.

14. 1915 Ind. Acts 392.

15. U.S. v. Stump Home Specialties Mfg., Inc., 905 F.2d 1117 (7th Cir. 1990).

16. Madison, *Indiana Way,* 222; Phillips, *Indiana in Transition,* 469–502.

17. Hall, *Magic Mirror,* 230.

18. Ellingham v. Dye, 178 Ind. 336, 99 N.E. 1 (1912).

19. Tucker v. State, 218 Ind. 614, 35 N.E.2d 270 (1941).

20. Jerome L. Withered, *Hoosier Justice: A History of the Supreme Court of Indiana* (Lafayette, Ind.: privately printed, 1998), 94.

21. Ind. const. art. IV, § 9. The schedule for legislative sessions approved by voters as part of the amendment was removed by amendment in 1984.

22. Ibid., art. VII, §§ 9–11.

TWO

Patrick Baude

INDIANA'S CONSTITUTION IN A NATION OF CONSTITUTIONS

It is still possible to visit Corydon, where Indiana's first constitution was written. Visitors will be directed not to a building, for it no longer stands, but to the elongated stump of an elm tree. Here, they will be told, the drafters did most of their work, in the easy shade near a fresh stream where jugs could be cooled. What a contrast this is to visiting Independence Hall in Philadelphia, where the national constitution was written but twenty-nine years earlier. The site in Philadelphia rings with self-importance, blending the lingering sense of a great historical moment with contemporary entrepreneurial exhibitionism. Every citizen, indeed every foreign visitor to Philadelphia, will know the general outline of what was done there and how and why the world was changed. Even a history buff, or perhaps a political scholar, will contemplate the remnant of Corydon's constitutional elm with unanswered questions about what happened there and why it should matter.

Making sense of one state's constitution is never an easy task. Of course, there was a historical goal: the establishment of a government. Certainly, too, this founding document and its sequel needed to locate boundaries between change and continuity, between collective power and individual right. But more than that, the observer will want to know something about the specialness of what happened there, about how the life and history of the state of Indiana were called forth. This elusive inquiry is the dangerous temptation of studying state constitutional law.

The meaning of the federal Constitution does not inhere in how it allocates the might of the United States. The exact words of the provisions in that document have been shunned, quietly, for more than two centuries. The Electoral College, for example, works in mysterious ways. The public assumes that presidential electors are bound by law to vote for the candidate with whom they are listed on the ballot, but in reality they are not so bound at all. The limited list of congressional powers in Article I, Section 8, bears little resemblance to the actual agenda of any recent Congress. And the rights of privacy, autonomy, and identity that have dominated recent constitutional debates about abortion, marriage, or euthanasia are nowhere to be found in the work product of Independence Hall. What has given the federal constitution its iconic status is not the historic document itself but the "constitutional culture" that has grown up around it. Even the words of aging Supreme Court decisions—"color blind," "clear and present danger," "contemporary community standards," or "diversity"—have passed into the everyday language in which Americans discuss ethical and social issues.

But state constitutions and the decisions interpreting them simply have not passed into the culture. For example, practically the entire nation is aware that, in 2004, the Supreme Judicial Court of Massachusetts decided that a ban on marriage between persons of the same sex is invalid—but probably fewer than two hundred people in the entire country could explain what language or clauses or preceding decisions underlie that decision. Forced to guess, most citizens probably would mutter something about "equal protection"—and would be surprised to learn that there is nothing of the sort in the Massachusetts constitution (or in that of Indiana). Indeed, one of the most striking examples of this lack of cultural grasp of the constitutions of individual states is the Indiana Court of Appeals's onetime impression that its state constitution contained an equal protection clause; in fact, rather than guaranteeing the equal treatment of African Americans, the 1851 state constitution essentially outlawed their entry into the state.[1]

Some scholars attempt to find the meaning of the Indiana constitution in the particular facts of Indiana's history or geography. Justice Roger DeBruler, in the course of explaining a disposition to limit automobile searches more strictly under the state constitution than under the federal, wrote that "Americans in general love their cars. It is, however, particularly important, in the state which hosts the Indy 500 automobile race, to recognize that cars are sources of pride, status, and identity that transcend their objective attributes. We are extremely hesitant to countenance their casual violation, even by law enforcement officers who are attempting to solve serious crimes."[2]

Evoking a somewhat larger sense of history, Chief Justice Randall Shepard in another case characterized the Indiana constitution as one dominated particularly by a rejection of elitism. In *Price v. State,* he wrote that

> Indiana's drive toward statehood saw its territorial leadership, comprised predominately of southern planters, pitted against comparatively poor frontiersmen. The former group generally considered the "common citizen" to be "unworthy . . . of presuming to criticize the conduct of officials." The frontiersmen agitated for greater popular participation, holding that "even the poorest had a right to a voice in the determination of the policies which affected his life as well as the career of the richest." The frontier democrats who dominated the first Constitutional Convention countered the risk that reactionary elements might fashion a nonmajoritarian government by adopting measures to guarantee popular participation and protect scrutiny of public affairs. . . . Thus, while the delegates relied heavily on the constitutions of the Ohio Valley and southeastern states, they generally borrowed only those features which promoted political inclusion, eschewing the elitist provisions favored by territorial federalists, such as tax requirement for voting, property qualifications for officeholders, unequal apportionment of representation and protection of slavery.[3]

Giving practical meaning to this view of the state constitution as an antielitist statement for the frontier, the chief justice went on to reverse the disorderly conduct conviction of a woman who had made a good deal of unpleasant noise, on the ground that the "political expression of Hoosiers" should not be subjected "to this standard of gentility."[4] Justice Brent Dickson, who had dissented in *Price* and would have upheld at least the standard of gentility in the criminal statute, later delivered his own view of the state constitution—in a paper alluding to the populist sentiments important to the majority but also discussing the higher-law background and, particularly, pointing out the state constitutional emphasis on education and the considerable number of legally trained delegates to the 1850–51 constitutional convention. The document Justice Dickson sees is far more genteel.[5] Perhaps the search for a distinctive Hoosier constitutional philosophy may prove to be as elusive as the etymology of the word "Hoosier," a derivation that has been given official but inconclusive consideration by the U.S. Senate.[6]

As a factual matter, the Indiana constitution of 1816 borrowed much of its language from the then recently adopted constitutions of Kentucky and Ohio. The constitution of 1851 drew much from the constitutions of Illinois and Wisconsin. Perhaps more important, the founders were seriously limited in their choices because the Northwest Ordinance, in adding to the United States the Northwest Territory—a part of which became the state of Indiana—imposed a number of conditions on the state governments to be formed. The Northwest Ordinance set Indiana's constitution on a course notably different from that of the federal constitution. The Ordinance, written during the same year as the federal constitution, is fundamentally different in its philosophy. Perhaps most famously, the Ordinance outlawed slavery, the very same legal institution to which the national constitution gave positive protection. In a more subtle way, the Ordinance also rejected the model of limited government adopted by the federal constitution. The federal Bill of Rights, for example, is simply a set of things the national government may not do—citizens are not given any positive rights to government action. The main positive guarantee in the federal constitution is the right to get one's slaves back from another state. The Ordinance, on the other hand, created the right to education, a right that to this day does not exist at the federal level. And finally, the Northwest Ordinance provided for comprehensive religious liberty at a time when some of the seaboard states had established churches.

In general, the Indiana constitutions of 1816 and 1851 share most of their attitudes with the other midwestern constitutions of the nineteenth century. These constitutions, as a class, differ from the federal constitution and from the earlier state documents in three ways.[7]

First, they were concerned with public debt and the related issue of subsidies for private corporations. In Indiana, for example, vast and shortsighted borrowing for canals in 1836—on the eve of the railroad age—left the state essentially bankrupt. So the 1851 constitution, following Wisconsin's 1848 example, outlawed public debt in article X, section 5, except in emergency or short-term cases. And article I, section 23, prohibits granting special privileges for the few. This section is often, but erroneously, cast as something like the equal protection clause of the Fourteenth Amendment to the U.S. Constitution. But the difference is striking. The purpose of the equal protection clause is to prevent harm to the weak, whereas the Indiana provision is aimed at stopping the corruptive practice of favoring the powerful.[8]

Second, these midwestern constitutions for the first time guaranteed some versions of what one now might call social rights:[9] affirmative claims for services, rather than the purely political rights of governmental nonintervention found in the federal Bill of Rights. Thus, Indiana's article VIII provides for a free system of common schools, and article IX imposes a "duty" on the General Assembly to support institutions for the deaf, mute, blind, and insane, and requires institutions for the "correction and reformation of juvenile offenders." Article IX authorizes the counties to provide for "those persons who, by reason of age, infirmity, or other misfortune, have claims upon the sympathies and aid of society."

Third, these constitutions reflected a view that power should come from the bottom up, rather than be imposed from the top. Although historians often think of the popular referendum as an innovation from the western states at the beginning of the twentieth century, the Indiana constitution of 1851 provided that the voters, in approving the constitution, should vote both on the general instrument and, independently, on the status of African Americans.[10] These distinctive historical features of the midwestern constitutions sometimes have been attenuated in contemporary doctrine.[11] The provisions on debt have not prevented the state from discovering bonding authority to fund improvements.[12] The article IX rights of juveniles have been limited greatly by the interpretation that, although the legislature may be required to create the institutions, juvenile offenders do not have a right to be placed in them.[13] And the early practice of referendum has not picked up its pace in Indiana.

But the dominant relationship, of course, was with the federal Constitution. The basic structure of the state government bears an obvious family resemblance to that of the federal government. The first structural provision is article III, which contains only one section and explicitly recognizes the principle of separation of powers. Although the federal Constitution is understood to be based on that principle, the constitution itself does not state it explicitly and leaves it to inference. And nothing in the federal Constitution obligates the states to follow the principle.[14] Such explicit provisions are fairly common in state constitutions. In a leading decision, the North Carolina Supreme Court reviewed opinions on similar clauses around the country, finding their interpretation lax in some states but particularly approving the seriousness with which the Indiana Supreme Court construed article III.[15] In recent years, some state courts have used similar language to draw a sharp distinction between the implicit federal doctrine and the explicit state constitutional provisions,[16] while others have been at some pains to say that making the doctrine explicit does not make its substance different from the federal principle.[17] The Indiana Supreme Court usually has cited federal separation of powers decisions with evident approval, once referring to a "similar separation of power doctrine premised on the national constitution," thus not seeming to place great significance on the fact that the principle is explicit in the state constitution.[18]

Article IV establishes an elected bicameral legislature. The subject matter power of the legislature, unlike that of the national Congress, is not limited—that is, rather than being restricted to commerce, copyright, bankruptcy, and the like (as Article I, Section 8, of the federal Constitution limits the Congress), the Indiana legislature is fully empowered in article IV, section 16: "Each house shall have all the powers necessary for a branch of the Legislative department of a free and independent State." In its time, there was a serious debate about including such explicit language in state constitutions. Some held that legislative power was inherent and needed no explicit vesting, whereas others, embracing what one today might call a libertarian tradition, believed that no powers were inherent in any part of government.[19] Consistent with its roots of opposition to powerful government, Indiana declined to embrace the inherent power theory. Of greater practical significance, the remainder of article IV contains significant procedural limits on legislative power.

Such limits are nearly universal in this country, having been adopted during the nineteenth century in response to both an emerging populist sensibility and various corruption scandals. Most scholars and students of administration find these provisions ineffectual and inefficient, but they have not succeeded in persuading constitutional drafters to abandon them.[20] Most of the procedural provisions in article IV concern details like quorums, reading of bills, filling of vacancies, and the like. The two important substantive measures in the article are section 19, requiring "one subject" and sections 22 and 23, requiring "a general law." Taken together, these provisions seem intended to outlaw the particular kind of political compromise denounced as "logrolling." The Indiana Supreme Court's decision in *City of South Bend v. Kimsey* is instructive.[21] Justice Theodore Boehm's majority recognized that the prohibition on special legislation had not always been justiciable in Indiana and that there was substantial disagreement among the states about the role courts should play in its enforcement. But, in the end, the court found that "[w]hether Article IV, Section 23's effort to limit logrolling is wise is not the issue. The Constitution makes that call for us."[22] The Indiana Supreme Court, on the other hand, has shown less severity in enforcing the one-subject rule.[23]

Article V establishes the executive branch, and there is nothing unusual about it. The executive power is vested in the governor, who, as in most states, is elected to a four-year term and can serve only two terms in a row. States vary somewhat in the detail with which gubernatorial powers are specified. Indiana's language seems to have been influenced heavily by Article II of the U.S. Constitution, charging the governor to "take care that the laws are faithfully executed" and, even, specifying that he shall be "commander-in-chief of the armed forces." Otherwise, the executive power is weaker than it is in the federal constitution because the governor has only limited power to appoint judges and no power at all over local officers, some of whom, especially prosecutors, have a good deal of authority. These limits are common in other states as well. More unusual is the fact that the veto can be overruled by a simple majority of each legislative house: most states require a larger majority or, at least, an absolute majority of the whole membership. Whatever the language of article V, an important 1941 case speaks strongly of implied executive power in matters of removal and appointment and seems still to reflect the view that the governor's powers over statewide executive and administrative functions are substantially independent of the legislature.[24]

The judicial branch has been the structural feature most altered over the years. In the 1816 constitution, judges were appointed by the governor and confirmed by the Senate—the federal model. Indeed, only in the Mississippi constitution of 1832 were elected judges introduced to the United States (or, to all appearances, anywhere else in the world). This idea of the elected judge rapidly gained favor with the populists of the nineteenth century and was embraced by the drafters of the 1851 Indiana constitution. But in major 1970 amendments to article VII, Indiana adopted what is often called "the Missouri plan" for the supreme court and appeals courts. Under the Missouri plan, a nominating commission composed of the chief justice, three lawyers elected by the bar, and three nonlawyers appointed by the governor sends up three names, from which the governor picks the appointee, who thereafter runs periodically in a yes–no referendum. About one-fourth of the states follow some version of the Missouri plan, about one-fourth still have a significant number of appointed and confirmed judges, and about half have completely elected judiciaries.[25] The 1970 amendments give the legislature general power over the architecture of the branch, without defining in the sort of detail one finds in Article III of the federal Constitution the jurisdiction of the individual courts. Article VII, section 4, recognizes explicitly the power of the supreme court over the practice of law, discipline of judges, and lower court jurisdiction. Indiana, like most states, has long recognized an inherent judicial power not necessarily identified in the language of the judicial article.[26] Perhaps the most notable feature of judicial power in Indiana concerns the doctrine of standing. In federal court, it is an absolute rule that a plaintiff must show some personal harm to invoke the jurisdiction of any court exercising power under Article III of the Constitution, although the exact contours of that personal stake may sometimes be difficult to identify concretely.[27] In Indiana, on the other hand, the court has long recognized that a personal stake in the outcome is not necessary to seek judicial relief for vindication of a "public right."[28]

Traditionally, the greatest scholarly interest in state constitutional law has been in the individual rights provisions.[29] Indeed, unlike the federal Constitution, Indiana's begins with its bill of rights. At the very beginning is a powerful statement, partly adopted from the Declaration of Independence, recognizing the inalienable rights of "life, liberty, and the pursuit of happiness" and the indefeasible right of the people "to alter and reform their government." One of the great battlegrounds of federal Constitutional law in the last century has been the question of rights not enumerated in the Bill of Rights; but the Indiana language, with its reference to "pursuit of happiness," seems broad enough to include all aspects of autonomy and was in fact cited in an important case involving end-of-life decisions.[30]

Sections 2 through 9 of article I provide various protections of religious liberty, outlawing religious tests for public office and competency of witnesses, prohibiting preference for any creed, and securing free exercise of religious opinions and "the rights of conscience." These religious guarantees seem essentially like the federal clauses in the First Amendment, if somewhat different in wording. In an important 2001 case involving the power of eminent domain over church property, a majority of the Indiana Supreme Court held that these clauses, considered together, protect not only individual religious conscience but also the collective organization of those practices, that is, religious institutions.[31] Philosophically considered, this may be an important distinction between the current federal interpretation of the First Amendment, which is reluctant to find higher protection for religious interests than for secular ones.[32] Although the court did not rely on this part of the text, the result is perhaps consistent with article I, section 2, which protects the "natural right to worship *Almighty God*" (italics in original) rather than "worship *or not.*" Rather than rely on this preference for religion, the court was careful to note that freethinking was abroad in nineteenth-century Indiana and that at least two freethinkers were delegates to the constitutional convention. As a practical matter, the court's repeated statements about the high burden of proof on the church in such cases may erode the significance of any difference. Article I, section 6, provides that "[n]o money shall be drawn from the treasury, for the benefit of any religious or theological institution." In 2003, the Indiana Supreme Court found that this language did not prohibit public services provided in parochial schools but did not resolve how, otherwise, this language common to many state constitutions might affect religious aid to church schools.[33]

Elsewhere in article I, the constitution contains a variety of protections for criminal defendants, largely tracking the protections of the federal Constitution in substance, but with differences in wording and sometimes in the tests articulated by the Indiana courts. Article I, section 14, prohibits double jeopardy, for example. For a time, it appeared that the "same evidence" test applied in Indiana might lead to a result different from that reached under the "same elements" test of federal law; but the divided decision of the court in *Guyton v. State* left the situation still unsettled.[34] The search and seizure provisions in article I, section 11, track the federal Fourth Amendment closely.[35] Two sections concerning criminal law seem on their face to introduce significant departures from the federal Constitution. According to section 18, "The penal code shall be founded on the principles of reformation, and not of vindictive justice." The reader may be forgiven for thinking that this section bans capital punishment, as it would be hard to describe being dead as being reformed. This interpretation, however, has been rejected consistently on the ground that the code as a whole is reformative, even though individual parts may be vindictive.[36] Similarly striking in its wording is section 19, which says: "In all criminal cases whatever, the jury shall have the right to determine the law and the facts." The reader may be forgiven for thinking that this provision would prohibit a judge from sentencing to death a defendant for whom the jury had not found the aggravating factors to outweigh the mitigating factors: but, again, the answer is no, this time because a "sentence" is neither fact nor law.[37]

In other sections of the bill of rights, the court has developed distinct tests for the application of the state guarantees, although it is not clear that these analyses have led the court to strike down laws that would be upheld under the federal provisions. With similar effect, the Indiana constitution contains several clauses that seem, by their terms, to provide some limits on legislative power to restrict individual civil remedies. Although some state courts have used comparable language to protect common-law rights, Indiana has not done so to any significant degree.[38] The overarching practical question is the burden of proof. As a matter of federal law, the presumption of validity typically disappears once a law is shown to limit a right explicitly protected by a specific guarantee. Indeed, this principle is probably the central reality of federal constitutional law, expressed in the famous footnote four: "There may be narrower scope for operation of the presumption of constitutionality when legislation appears on its face to be within a specific prohibition of the Constitution, such as those of the first ten Amendments, which are deemed equally specific when held to be embraced within the 14th."[39] In Indiana, however, the presumption of validity always applies, and the burden of proof is always on the party asserting the constitutional right: "We will presume a statute to be constitutional, and a challenger, against whom all doubts are resolved, must overcome that presumption by clearly demonstrating the provision to be invalid."[40]

Judge John Baker, in a court of appeals opinion later superseded by the supreme court, wrote in 1992: "Although the constitutional elm tree towering above the grounds at Corydon in the early years of our statehood may have passed from this earth, the sentiment expressed by our first lawmakers in its shade continues to this day."[41] But channeling that sentiment is no easy task. As is true of all sorts of spiritualism, much will depend on the questions put to the departed.

Some, especially lawyers on a case, ask mainly that the state constitution help them attack a law that has somehow escaped federal invalidation. It was mainly in this exercise that Justice William Brennan used his great prestige to push lawyers into state constitutional arguments, hoping to implement the visions that were lost when the Warren Court died.[42] And so tort lawyers, civil libertarians, and social activists around the country renewed their acquaintance with their states' high courts. In Indiana, nothing has come of this. The state constitution has not brought back the exclusionary rule, equalized school funding, or reformed the penitentiary. Others sought to find the iconic meaning of the community in its founding documents.[43] In Indiana, anyway, only Justices Dickson and Shepard seem drawn to this process, and they often seem to be seeing different worlds—perhaps it is no accident that Chief Justice Shepard seems to invoke the rougher spirit of Corydon in 1816 and Justice Dickson prefers to seek out the views of the lawyers in Indianapolis in 1850—perhaps in the same way that some national patriots connect with the Jeffersonian fire of the Declaration of Independence and others seek the prudent counsel of James Madison at the constitutional convention. Whatever the reason, no clear epic emerges.

In the end, however, if lawyers and scholars miss the message of the elm, it is because they are asking questions that have been conditioned by the long domination of the federal model of thinking about the purposes of a constitution. Whatever the details of federal constitutional law, its underlying reality is the tension between life-tenured and insulated judges and the idea of democracy. Society has come to ask of the federal courts that they tell the truth to power, that they preserve the great principles of freedom and equality from the shifting values and mores of the impatient but temporary majority down at city hall or up on Capitol Hill. Judged by this standard, the Indiana constitution has not done much. It has not transformed education, attacked racism, or stopped executions. It has done little to thwart the will of the majority; it lacks its *Brown v. Board* or *Steel Seizure* moments.

It is instructive, instead, to look at cases about issues on which sentiment and ideology are less engaged. There is no better example than the long course of litigation concerning Indiana's property tax.[44] In the end—if an end there is—the Indiana Supreme Court has transformed the tax from a complex and arbitrary set of political and historical judgments to a potentially simpler and more reasonable one. This is exactly the sort of work the U.S. Supreme Court turns down on principle, because it does not call for great value judgments or countermajoritarian courage or republican vision. Similar, perhaps, is the *Kimsey* case discussed earlier in this essay, dealing with the problem of special legislation. These are not decisions driven by the tension between democracy and individual rights, and particularly not in the framework of the federal model, which equates legislative decisions with majority rule. They are driven instead by the likelihood that the political branches themselves have failed to deliberate on the popular will.

It should not seem surprising to discover that judges without life tenure or political insulation do not define their role as thwarting the popular will. The political process that Indiana uses, the Missouri plan, makes judges political, but in a way that is longer in term and different in nature from the politics of legislators. It seems reasonable, in other words, that the lasting contribution of the Indiana constitution is the expression of the popular will rather than its frustration. Judges are, of course, inescapably deliberative by nature, but they can deliberate about the public will as much as they could on its defects. (Of course, a constitutional system that had only the "deliberated popular will" would soon turn to the dark side. But the federal courts will always be with us too.)

In Philadelphia, James Madison and his planter friends were occupied with reflections on how to make sure the republic would not succumb to the mob. But in Corydon, they knew that they *were* the mob and were determined to make themselves heard too.

Notes

1. O'Brien v. State, 422 N.E.2d 1266, 1270 (Ind. Ct. App. 1981); see Patrick Baude, "Is There Independent Life in the Indiana Constitution?" *Indiana Law Journal* 62 (Spring 1987): 263, 264.

2. Brown v. State, 653 N.E.2d 77, 80n3 (Ind. 1995).

3. Price v. State, 622 N.E.2d 954, 961–62 and 962n10 (Ind. 1993) (citations omitted and textual footnote combined with text). See Patrick Baude, "Has the Indiana Constitution Found Its Epic?" *Indiana Law Journal* 69 (Summer 1994): 849.

4. Price v. State, 622 N.E.2d at 963.

5. Brent E. Dickson, "Indiana's Constitutional Past" (remarks at the Indiana State Library and Historical Building, Indianapolis, December 8, 1996). Because much of the work in the Indianapolis convention ratified the essential plan of the Corydon convention, it is not clear which one should be the "context."

6. Paul Dickson, "Who's Who in the Hoosier Debates: *Quayle v. Webster* over True Meaning of a Sacred Word," *Los Angeles Times,* November 10, 1988, pt. 5, 4.

7. See generally Patrick Baude, "State Constitutions," in *Encyclopedia of the Midwest,* (Bloomington: Indiana University Press, forthcoming 2005).

8. The current test is *Collins v. Day,* 644 N.E.2d 72 (Ind. 1994). See the excellent discussion of various meanings of equality in Michael J. DeBoer, "Equality as a Fundamental Value in the Indiana Constitution," *Valparaiso University Law Review* 38 (Spring 2004): 489.

9. See the general discussion in Helen Hershkoff, "Positive Rights and State Constitutions: The Limits of Rationality Review," *Harvard Law Review* 112 (April 1999): 1131.

10. Patrick Baude, "A Comment on the Evolution of Direct Democracy in Western State Constitutions," *New Mexico Law Review* 28 (Spring 1998): 343.

11. See Jon Laramore, "Indiana Constitutional Developments: The Wind Shifts," 36 *Indiana Law Review* 36, no. 4 (2003): 961, 986–89. Laramore suggests that the irony in question results from the court's retreat from a specific reliance on the original intention of Indiana's framers to a more general reliance on how other jurisdictions have interpreted similar language.

12. The state cannot simply borrow money to build an office building. It can, however, create a separate corporation that will borrow the money, build the building, and repay the "debt" with "rent" from the state. Book v. State Office Bldg. Comm'n, 238 Ind. 120, 149 N.E.2d 273 (Ind. 1958).

13. Ratliff v. Cohn, 693 N.E.2d 530 (Ind. 1998).

14. Prentis v. Atl. Coast Line R.R., 211 U.S. 210 (1908).

15. State ex rel. Wallace v. Bone, 304 N.C. 591, 286 S.E.2d 79 (1982). See John V. Orth, "Forever Separate and Distinct: Separation of Powers in North Carolina," *North Carolina Law Review* 62 (August 1983): 1. The Indiana decision specifically supported by the North Carolina court was *Book,* barring legislative appointments to an administrative body (see note 12, *supra*).

16. E.g., Dept. of Bus. Regulation v. Nat'l Mfd. Housing Fed'n, 370 So. 2d 1132 (Fla. 1979).

17. E.g., Brown v. Heymann, 61 N.J. 1, 297 A.2d 572 (1972).

18. Barco Beverage Corp. v. Indiana Alcoholic Beverage Comm'n, 595 N.E.2d 250, 254 (Ind. 1992).

19. The classic article is Walter F. Dodd, "The Function of a State Constitution," *Political Science Quarterly* 30 (1915): 201–21.

20. Robert F. Williams, "State Constitutional Limits on Legislative Procedure: Legislative Compliance and Judicial Enforcement," *Publius: The Journal of Federalism* 17 (Winter 1987): 91.

21. City of South Bend v. Kimsey, 781 N.E.2d 683 (Ind. 2003).

22. Ibid., 686n4. Decades before the television program made the term common, a distinguished scholar referred to the definition of special legislation as a "twilight zone." Frank E. Horack, "Special Legislation: Another Twilight Zone," *Indiana Law Journal* 12 (December 1936): 108, 183.

23. See Bayh v. Indiana State Bldg. and Const. Trades Council, 674 N.E.2d 176 (Ind. 1996).

24. Tucker v. State, 218 Ind. 614, 35 N.E.2d 270 (1941).

25. The numbers in the text are given loosely; the classifications themselves are not sharply distinct because many states use some sort of combination. The reader who wants more exact detail and a provocative analysis should consult Steven P. Croley, "The Majoritarian Difficulty: Elective Judiciaries and the Rule of Law," *University of Chicago Law Review* 62 (Spring 1995): 689.

26. Noble County v. Rogers, 745 N.E.2d 194 (Ind. 2001). See generally Carl Baar, "Judicial Activism in State Courts: The Inherent Powers Doctrine," in *State Supreme Courts: Policymakers in the Federal System,* ed. Mary Cornelia Porter and G. Alan Tarr (Westport, Conn.: Greenwood, 1982), 129.

27. Friends of the Earth v. Laidlaw, 528 U.S. 167 (2000).

28. Cittadine v. Ind. DOT, 790 N.E.2d 978 (Ind. 2003).

29. E.g., Randall T. Shepard, "Second Wind for the Indiana Bill of Rights," *Indiana Law Review* 22, no. 2 (1989): 575.

30. In re Lawrance, 579 N.E.2d 32 (Ind. 1991).

31. City Chapel Evangelical Free, Inc. v. City of South Bend, 744 N.E.2d 443 (Ind. 2001).

32. At least, this is one way of reading the highly controversial decision in *Employment Div. v. Smith,* 494 U.S. 872 (1990). The *Smith* decision has been unpopular with Congress, which unsuccessfully attempted to eliminate it (see *City of Boerne v. Flores,* 521 U.S. 507 (1997), and has also been under attack in litigation under other state constitutions. Humphrey v. Lane, 89 Ohio St. 3d 62, 728 N.E.2d 1039 (2000).

33. Embry v. O'Brien, 798 N.E.2d 157 (Ind. 2003).

34. Guyton v. State, 771 N.E.2d 1141 (Ind. 2002). See the incisive analysis in Laramore, "Indiana Constitutional Developments," 976–79.

35. The most recent important case, *Linke v. Northwestern Sch. Corp.,* 763 N.E.2d 972 (Ind. 2002), at first seemed to depart somewhat from the federal standards for drug testing, but a subsequent decision by the U.S. Supreme Court in effect realigned the two. Bd. of Educ. v. Earls, 563 U.S. 822 (2002).

36. E.g., Harrison v. State, 644 N.E.2d 1243 (Ind. 1995).

37. Peterson v. State, 674 N.E.2d 528 (Ind. 1996).

38. See generally David Schuman, "The Right to a Remedy," *Temple Law Review* 65 (Winter 1992): 1197. For an excellent review of the Indiana cases, see Rosalie Berger Levinson, "State and Federal Constitutional Law Developments," *Indiana Law Review* 35, no. 4 (2002): 1263, 1291–95.

39. Carolene Prods. v. U.S., 304 U.S. 144, 152n4 (1938). See Peter Linzer, "The Carolene Products Footnote and the Preferred Position of Individual Rights: Louis Lusky and John Hart Ely vs. Harlan Fiske Stone," *Constitutional Commentary* 12 (Summer 1995): 277.

40. State v. Hoovler, 668 N.E.2d 1229 (Ind. 1996).

41. Campbell v. Criterion Group, 588 N.E.2d 511, 518 (Ind. App. 1992).

42. William J. Brennan Jr., "State Constitutions and the Protection of Individual Rights," *Harvard Law Review* 90 (January 1977): 489.

43. Patrick Baude, "Interstate Dialogue in State Constitutional Law," *Rutgers Law Journal* 28 (Summer 1997): 835.

44. The latest chapter is State Bd. of Tax Comm'rs v. Town of St. John, 751 N.E.2d 657 (Ind. 2001).

PART II

The Law of Personal Status

THREE

James H. Madison

RACE, LAW, AND THE BURDENS OF INDIANA HISTORY

Indiana never has been color-blind. For a very long time, the state's constitution, laws, courts, and majority white voice placed black Hoosiers in a separate and unequal place. White settlers had created a color line in the territorial period and had affirmed it by 1816, the year of Indiana's birth as a state. Twists and turns brought some legal modifications by the centennial year of 1916, but separation and discrimination, whether legal or extralegal, were the patterns of public life for African Americans. Substantial change came in the 1960s, with the so-called civil rights revolution. But establishment of equality before the law was more gradual than revolutionary in Indiana and did not bring true equality, even as Hoosiers moved toward their bicentennial year of 2016. In the long struggle toward America's highest ideals, Indiana seldom had marched in the forefront and often had lagged behind other northern states. The burden of a past colored by color remained part of twenty-first-century life.[1]

America's harshest expression of racial injustice took root soon after the first European settlers arrived. A 1746 report described the French settlement of Vincennes as composed of forty citizens and five slaves. French black codes regulated slave conduct on the banks of the Wabash and gave slaves some rights, including due process in criminal cases, but also defined them as moveable goods similar to horses or pigs. When the area became part of the British Empire in 1763, authorities assured French inhabitants they would continue their property rights, including those of slave ownership. Two decades later, when the American Revolution produced a new nation, the question of slavery again required a response.[2]

The answer came in 1787 in the Northwest Ordinance, in which the Continental Congress set out a form of government and law for the territory north and west of the Ohio River. Article VI stated: "There shall be neither slavery nor involuntary servitude in the said territory." Although seemingly clear and direct, this prohibition proved to be (as any good judge, lawyer, or historian might suspect) ambiguous in meaning and contested in operation.[3]

Part of the problem was the article's origins. Just why congressional delegates from the slaveholding South would agree to such a prohibition remains a mystery. Doubtless there were compromises and agreed-upon ambiguities not recorded for later historians. In particular, the Ordinance was not clear on the status of slaves then living in the Northwest Territory. On several occasions, the 1787 document used the words "free male inhabitants," implying, some thought, that unfree men, that is, slaves, were excluded from the rights of free men. In addition, the Ordinance gave French inhabitants "their laws and customs now in force among them, relative to the descent and conveyance of property." Such property might well include slaves. More generally, while the Ordinance would no longer allow slave owners to bring their human property north of the Ohio River, it did not specify the status of slaves already resident there and owned by American settlers. There was widespread assumption that article VI was not retroactive and that slaves already held in the territory would continue in bondage, an assumption consistently upheld by territorial courts.

Congress refused to step in and clarify the ambiguities—such federal discretion was not unusual in contentious matters of slavery or race. It remained for the people of the Indiana Territory to work out policy. The initial thrust in the debate came from Indiana Territorial Governor William Henry Harrison, who served from 1800 to 1812. Harrison and many of his political allies were slaveholders. They were acutely aware of the shortage of labor and investment on the Indiana frontier and believed that slavery was essential to both their own prosperity and that of the new territory. Slavery was as natural to a Virginian like Harrison as his own status near the top of the social and political hierarchy.

Soon after Indiana became a territory, in 1800, proslavery activists began to petition Congress for an amendment to the Northwest Ordinance that would allow slaves to be brought into the territory for a period of ten years. Congress refused to act. The proslavery movement then turned to subterfuge in the form of indenture. In 1805, the newly established territorial legislature passed "An Act concerning the Introduction of Negroes and Mulattoes into This Territory." "Slaves" became "servants" by signing a contract agreeing to work for their former owners for a set term, one that was often beyond the individual's life expectancy. In 1805, the clerk of common pleas in Knox County recorded a typical indenture:

> Be it remembered that . . . personally came Eli Hawkins of the said county and a negro lad of the age of sixteen years being a slave named Jacob belonging to the said Eli Hawkins and by him brought into this Territory from the state of South Carolina, which said Hawkins and the said Jacob . . . agreed among themselves . . . that said Jacob shall and will serve the said Eli Hawkins and his assigns for term of Ninety years from the day of the date hereof, he, the said Eli Hawkins and his assigns providing the said Jacob with necessary and sufficient provisions and clothing, washing and lodging, according to his degree and station. From and after the expiration of said term the said Jacob shall be free to all intents and purposes.[4]

Jacob would be free at age 106. Indentures were not usually so long, the most common periods being twenty to forty years, thereby covering the most productive working years of the servant's life while avoiding the master's obligation to care for the aged servant once free. Even children born of these servants in the Indiana Territory were bound to their masters until the age of thirty for sons and twenty-eight for daughters. Thus did Governor Harrison, his successor, Governor Thomas Posey, and others of the territory's best men use the law to gain the benefits of slavery and to subvert the federal prohibition of the 1787 Ordinance. Indiana has few legal precedents more troubling.

Even as indentured servitude took form, a growing number of Hoosiers argued against it. Indiana must attract free white settlers, whose labor would be their own and whose voices would be democratic, they asserted. Free white Americans would not move to a land dominated by a slaveholding aristocracy nor would they compete with slave labor. The slave system was corrupt and lazy and a barrier to a prosperous future. Slavery was anathema to proper democracy, good order, and civilization. Many of Indiana's pioneers came from the South, but they were upland southerners who were too poor to own slaves and who resented those elites who did. Like Thomas Lincoln, they did not want to compete with slave labor, whether in Kentucky or Indiana. A small minority among the growing antislavery faction even asserted that slaves had human rights and that slavery was a moral outrage in a land of liberty. Indiana's Quaker pioneers were most vociferous in this argument. But these more determined antislavery Hoosiers were relatively few in number compared to their confreres in other northern states, such as neighboring Ohio, where more New Englanders had settled with their dairy cows and their stronger antislavery prejudices.[5]

Growth of antislavery sentiment was sufficient by 1810 to effect repeal of the Indiana Territory's 1805 indenture law. Yet the status of African Americans remained uncertain even after repeal: indentures made before 1810 remained legal, and the masters of newly arriving African Americans continued to bind them to service in ways that approached the grim reality of slavery. Whether as slave property or as indentures with a set term of service, African Americans were bought, sold, and bequeathed in wills throughout the territorial period. The will that Governor Posey made in 1816 gave two servants to each of his three children.

The Indiana Territory also endorsed slavery by providing masters with legal mechanisms of control that emulated the notorious black codes of the South. Territorial laws allowed for public whippings of slaves and servants caught traveling without passes, prohibited the sale of liquor to them, and made it unlawful for three or more slaves or servants to gather "for the purpose of dancing or reveling, either by night, or by day."[6]

In the end, the American people decided the slavery question with their feet, by moving or not moving to the Indiana Territory. Americans who owned slaves or wished to own slaves could see that prospects in Indiana were increasingly risky. They went elsewhere, to Alabama and Mississippi, for example, where the law was clearer and the future more certain. Those committed to free labor took up their land in Indiana and became the growing majority that organized against Harrison and his proslavery allies. They took control of the territorial legislature by 1810. The consequences for the future of Indiana and the nation were momentous. The French visitor Alexis de Tocqueville could see some of those consequences when traveling by steamboat down the Ohio River in 1831:

> The traveler who lets the current carry him down the Ohio till it joins the Mississippi sails, so to say, between freedom and slavery; and he has only to glance around him to see instantly which is best for mankind.
>
> On the left bank of the river the population is sparse; . . . society has gone to sleep; it is nature that seems active and alive, whereas man is idle.
>
> But on the right bank a confused hum proclaims from afar that men are busily at work.

Tocqueville could not see thirty years ahead, when Indiana joined the Union against the slave South in the state and nation's most critical trial, but his observation illustrates the great divide that led to the war.[7]

Any remaining doubt about the future of slavery in Indiana was settled by the state's new constitution. In 1816, forty-three delegates gathered in the summer heat of Corydon and wrote a document of astonishing interest even today. Among its most important provisions was the commitment, in language similar to that of the Northwest Ordinance, that "[t]here shall be neither slavery nor involuntary servitude in this state, otherwise than for the punishment of crimes, whereof the Party shall have been duly convicted." To this the drafters added: "Nor shall any indenture of any negro or mulatto hereafter made, and executed out of the bound of this state be of any validity within the state." To ensure that they made clear their antislavery convictions, the delegates added to article VIII (which otherwise provided for easy revision of the document) this lock against slavery: "As the holding any part of the human Creation in slavery, or involuntary servitude, can only originate in usurpation and tyranny, no alteration of this constitution shall ever take place so as to introduce slavery or involuntary servitude in this State, otherwise than for the punishment of crimes, whereof the Party shall have been duly convicted."[8]

The constitution of 1816 locked the door on slavery, though there were still some attempts to pry it open. Most of the 190 slaves counted in the 1820 census lived in Knox County, where masters of slaves and indentured servants argued that the constitution of 1816 was not retroactive and applied only to contracts or arrangements made after 1816. At least seven suits were brought in 1817 and 1818 in the Knox County Circuit Court seeking freedom for slaves or indentured servants. In all but one case, the court denied freedom.

It took the Indiana Supreme Court to tell the local court the meaning of the new constitution. The landmark case concerned the freedom of Polly, the daughter of a woman bound to slavery prior to the Northwest Ordinance and now the property of Hyacinthe Lasselle, a prominent descendant of French settlers in Vincennes. Lasselle claimed that the guarantees made in 1787 to French property owners included not only Polly's mother but Polly herself. The Knox County Circuit Court agreed. In its 1820 decision in *State v. Lasselle,* the Indiana Supreme Court rejected that argument. Ignoring questions of the 1787 Ordinance, the court decided that "the framers of our constitution intended a total and entire prohibition of slavery in this State; and we can conceive of no form of words in which that intention could have been more clearly expressed."[9]

Indentured servants raised more complicated questions, but here, too, the Indiana Supreme Court moved toward freedom. Masters continued to buy and sell indentured servants after 1816 by arguing that the constitutional prohibition applied only to indentures made outside the state after its adoption. Then, in 1821, the Indiana Supreme Court held that an indentured servant named Mary Clark was in fact "in a state of involuntary servitude; and we are bound by the constitution, the supreme law of the land, to discharge her therefrom." There still were thirty-two slaves counted in a Vincennes local census in 1830 and doubtless a few elsewhere, but the institution was breathing its last, ended by the state constitution and supreme court.[10]

Indiana's pioneer democracy had destroyed slavery. But in one of its more complex and important legacies, that democracy allowed scant room for expectations of equality between black and white Hoosiers. Most white Hoosiers were convinced that African Americans, slave or free, were inferior beings and not entitled to equality before the law. Indiana was an antislavery state; and it was an antiblack state. These two notions were widely held and not at all contradictory; they ran as major threads through the state's history. White Hoosiers wanted no slaves and no African Americans. In the straightforward language of pioneers, settlers in Harrison County petitioned Governor Posey just before statehood: "We are opposed to the introduction of slaves or free Negroes in any shape. . . . Our corn Houses, Kitchens, Smoke Houses . . . may no doubt be robbed and our wives, children and daughters may and no doubt will be insulted and abused by those Africans. We feel for our property, wives and daughters. We do not wish to be saddled with them in any way."[11] The laws pioneer Hoosiers made reflected that antislavery, antiblack conviction.

Indiana's 1816 constitution asserted that "all men are born equally free and independent, and have certain natural, inherent, and unalienable rights." Racial (and gender) distinctions nonetheless followed. The constitution granted the vote only to adult white males and apportioned representation in the General Assembly on the basis of adult white male population. It required state militia service of "all free able bodied male persons; Negroes, Mulattoes and Indians excepted."[12]

The Indiana General Assembly followed with laws further excluding African Americans. In 1818, the legislature excluded blacks from testifying in courts of law. And in the ongoing struggle to define who was "black" and who was "white," the legislature first excluded Hoosiers with one-quarter black ancestry and then, in 1853, revised the definition so that "[n]o Indian, or person having one-eighth or more of Negro blood, shall be permitted to testify as a witness in any cause in which any white person is a Party in interest." Illinois, California, and Iowa had similar laws, as, of course, did the slave states, but Indiana was the last northern state to remove this ban on testimony, in 1865.[13]

The 1818 General Assembly also prohibited marriages across the color line. In 1840, the legislature extended penalties in a new law "to prohibit the amalgamation of whites and blacks," which defined blacks by the one-eighth rule and imposed heavy fines and prison terms. Indiana did not repeal the antimiscegenation law until 1965 and was among the northern states with the longest history of legal prohibition of "race mixing."[14]

Such restrictions before the law were indicative of a deep and intense racism in Indiana, one that had its highest legal expression in efforts to exclude entirely African Americans from the state. As so-called Jacksonian democracy was rising, the 1831 General Assembly discouraged migration by passing a bill that required blacks settling in Indiana to post a bond of $500 as guarantee that they would not become paupers or criminals. The Indiana Supreme Court upheld the law in three different decisions in the 1830s, although, as a later chief justice would argue, "it did so in most reluctant of tones." Local officials seldom enforced the 1831 law, but it sent a clear message about race that long endured.[15]

An even stronger message about race and law emanated from the state's second constitution, enacted in 1851. This document specified numerous privileges and prohibitions on the basis of color. No convention delegate argued for full equality. The framers continued to grant the right to vote only to white male citizens and, to be certain, added a provision that "[n]o Negro or Mulatto shall have the right of suffrage." Service in the state militia was open only to "white male persons." Most important, in article XIII the new constitution set out prohibitions that rank among the most vicious in the state's history. Article XIII, section 1, read: "No negro or mulatto shall come into or settle in the State, after the adoption of this Constitution." Section 2 voided any contracts made with black newcomers and fined anyone who employed them.

Article XIII was a constitutional wall surrounding the state and papered with signs reading "Whites Only." To make their point clear, the 1851 constitution makers required that article XIII be sent to the people for approval or rejection; it was the only provision submitted to a separate popular vote. Indiana voters spoke loudly in endorsement of article XIII: 113,828 in favor (slightly more than voted for the ratification of the whole of the constitution) and only 21,873 against. An even more precise public opinion poll came from reports of the vote by county. Only four counties (Randolph, Elkhart, Lagrange, and Steuben) offered a majority against the article. Knox County, for example, voted in favor, 1,461 to 89; Marion County, 2,505 to 308; Hamilton County, 1,135 to 597.[16]

The Indiana Supreme Court upheld article XIII, most notably in *Barkshire v. State,* an 1856 decision that exemplified the court's tendency to endorse restrictions on the rights of African Americans. Arthur Barkshire brought Elizabeth Keith from Ohio to Indiana in order to marry her. Both were black. The court upheld Barkshire's conviction for violating article XIII by aiding a black person to move into Indiana: "A constitutional policy so decisively adopted, and so clearly conducive to the separation and ultimate good of both races, should be rigidly enforced," the court asserted. Even Barkshire's goal of marriage did not change the constitutional exclusion of blacks; indeed that contract of "marriage itself, solemnized in contravention of both [constitution and law], must be regarded as void."[17]

Of course, it was impractical to enforce article XIII. But by reflecting harsh racial notions, exclusion sent a chill across Indiana and beyond, doubtless having some influence in the very small numbers of black newcomers in the 1850s and in the increase in bitter race politics that emerged in that troubled decade and after.

A sidekick to exclusion was colonization. The solution to America's challenge of slavery and race, colonizers believed, was to encourage African Americans to move to Africa. Colonization would benefit both black and white Americans, proponents argued. Governor Joseph A. Wright in his biennial message of 1855 expressed the sentiments of many: colonization "is practicable, and no enterprise of the age holds out greater promise of good to the colored race." Article XIII of the 1851 constitution provided that fines gathered from violators of the exclusion provision, such as Arthur Barkshire, were to go to a colonization fund. In the 1850s, the General Assembly appropriated additional state money to encourage Hoosier immigration to Africa. Very few blacks were interested.[18]

As Hoosiers debated exclusion and colonization, the primary lightning rod of the racial struggle in the 1850s became fugitive slaves. Indiana had long attracted runaway slaves, whose owners came chasing after them across the Ohio River. In this unseemly enterprise, free blacks in Indiana were sometimes victims of unscrupulous or ignorant slave catchers. Federal and state laws, court decisions, and citizen responses varied through the decades before the Civil War. Initially, there was some effort to protect free African Americans from kidnappers falsely claiming rights of slave owners, but kidnapping remained a fear for all black Hoosiers, whether free men and women or escaped slaves.[19] The Fugitive Slave Act of 1850 was the federal government's effort to provide clarity by protecting the property rights of southern slave owners. Indiana's legislature and courts in the 1850s tended to uphold this vexing federal law; they deferred to the authority of the federal government, unlike their counterparts in many other northern states, which resisted and obstructed slave catchers.

One exception was the case of John Freeman, a longtime, respected resident of Indianapolis, perhaps the wealthiest black man in the city. In 1853, a Missouri slave owner claimed before the U.S. commissioner that Freeman was his property. Freeman spent nine weeks in jail, where he was forced even to pay the costs of his own guard while his lawyers sought witnesses to prove that he was not a runaway slave. He eventually won his freedom and even a technical victory before the Indiana Supreme Court in the case of *Freeman v. Robinson,* decided in 1855. But the lesson was clear, as a Fort Wayne newspaper noted: "If Freeman had not had money and friends he must inevitably have been taken off into bondage." Even so, Freeman no longer trusted the law to protect him: he left his Indiana home for Canada, where there was a guarantee of safety from slave catchers.[20]

The fact that John Freeman had white champions should not obscure the dominant white attitude toward blacks. In Indiana of the 1850s, as in neighboring Illinois and Ohio, there existed "a race prejudice so visceral and powerful," one historian has written, "that it often required no justification, no supporting reasoning, at all." The prejudice varied but was strongest in southern Indiana and in the Democratic Party, a party that from the 1850s to the early twentieth century took every opportunity to play the race card by reminding whites of their fears.[21]

At the other extreme, there were antislavery advocates in Indiana, though they were few in number. Antislavery Quakers were among the most active, engaging in the Underground Railroad as well as providing education for black children and condemning the state's black codes. A newspaper editor in Salem condemned Quakers by asserting that "their *tenacious* and *universal* adherence to negro equality is the rotten spot that has marked them since the days of the Revolution."[22]

A few newspapers, such as the *Fort Wayne Standard,* condemned the Fugitive Slave Act, Kentucky slave hunters, and Indiana's own constitution. Antislavery Hoosiers struggled with the challenge whether to resist or to obey a law that conflicted with their consciences. One such troubled conscience was that of Calvin Fletcher, a noted Indianapolis lawyer and banker. Fletcher assisted in keeping John Freeman from the slave catchers. He struggled with the question whether to obey the Fugitive Slave Act, writing his wife in mid-1853: "I feel like resistance but I love the union[.] I love its institutions all except the recognition of slavery. When I think of this great wrong I am almost ready to forego the greatest blessing that ever was conferred on a nation, the union of our states."[23]

Among antislavery forces were African Americans who played a large role in the Underground Railroad and who used their meager political strength to fight for equality. They organized black state conventions, such as the one held in Indianapolis in 1851, to condemn the new constitution's proposed article XIII and to assert that blacks "as Americans . . . are entitled to all the rights, privileges, and immunities of citizenship." Another black convention, in 1857, petitioned the state legislature to remove the restrictions on testimony in courts. There was always a black voice of opposition to the dominant legal and constitutional form, but it was small and of slight effect.[24]

The Civil War and Reconstruction created possibilities for momentous change. A gathering of African American Baptist Hoosiers in 1867 announced that "hatred on account of color or race is rapidly disappearing, [and] mean, low black laws are being erased from almost every statute book of the different States of the Union, and laws enacted in their stead built upon truth, justice and liberty." The newly formed Republican Party had grown rapidly on its strong antislavery policies to win state and national offices in the election of 1860. The Indiana Republican Party's most powerful member was Oliver P. Morton, governor during the Civil War years and U.S. senator during Reconstruction. The hard politics of Civil War and Reconstruction pushed Morton and other Republicans to support emancipation and even to consider possibilities of legal equality for African Americans. By 1867, Morton was urging ratification of the Fourteenth Amendment to the U.S. Constitution, guaranteeing due process and equal protection of the laws. He led the drive for Indiana's ratification of the Fifteenth Amendment, guaranteeing black men the right to vote. Passage of these Reconstruction amendments substantially changed the legal status of African American Hoosiers, most notably by giving them a formal political voice. In 1870, for the first time, black male Hoosiers voted.[25]

The Indiana Supreme Court in 1866 ratified the new possibilities when, in *Smith v. Moody,* it held void article XIII of Indiana's constitution. African Americans were citizens of the United States, the court decided, and could not be excluded from the state. The state did not actually remove article XIII or the racial distinctions regarding suffrage from its constitution until 1881, a delay resulting from complexities of the amendment process and from disinterest. After 1881, the only remaining constitutional racial distinction was the prohibition on service in the state militia, a qualification not removed until 1936.[26]

Despite constitutional change, the politics of Civil War and Reconstruction brought more intense racist language to the political arena. The Democratic Party, with its base in the former Confederate states, seldom missed an opportunity to appeal to whites' meanest fears. In 1864, Democrats had called for stronger laws to enforce article XIII, on grounds that "the soil of Indiana belongs to the white man." In denigrating language that accused Republicans of advocating racial equality—or even encouraging black men to marry white women—Democrats made clear their opposition to arming African American troops, emancipating slaves, and passing the Thirteenth Amendment to end slavery. Challenging Republican Reconstruction in the South, Indiana Democrats returned to power in the early 1870s, earlier than in most other northern states. They determined that, whatever the law, African Americans would be second-class citizens.[27]

As the years passed, Republicans lost interest in progress toward equality. By the end of the nineteenth century, nearly all whites pretended to forget that slavery and emancipation had been at the center of the Civil War, that Reconstruction had offered unprecedented opportunity for change, and that some white Americans even had talked of equality in those years. Instead, most white Hoosiers joined in tacit or active endorsement of the rising tide of discrimination and segregation that washed over the nation in the last decades of the century. Commonly labeled "Jim Crow," this hardening of the color line reached every nook and cranny of the state and nation.[28]

One small exception to the rise of Jim Crow came in 1885 when the General Assembly enacted a civil rights law. The law provided for equal accommodations in hotels, restaurants, theaters, public transportation, and other public places "regardless of color or race." The 1885 law was rarely enforced, however, and doubtless had been intended only as an enticement to black voters. In most of the few instances when African Americans attempted to bring suit under its provisions, they lost. The Indiana Supreme Court never offered an interpretation of its meaning. In one appellate court decision, *Fruchey v. Eagleson* (1895), an Indiana University football player was awarded one hundred dollars after the court agreed that he had been denied hotel accommodations in Crawfordsville because of his color. More typical, however, was the appellate court's very narrow interpretation in 1920 when it denied two African American women the right to eat in a Marion ice cream parlor. The 1885 civil rights law also guaranteed blacks the right to serve on juries. A few did, but most juries in most Indiana communities were all white well into the twentieth century. Nowhere was the gulf between written law and actual practice wider than in relation to this 1885 legislation.[29]

Equal access to public education was another elusive goal. Despite the commitment in the 1816 constitution to provide a free education "equally open to all," pioneer Indiana closed its public schools to black children. A state law in 1843 specifically stated that only white children were eligible for public education, and the Indiana Supreme Court in the 1850 case of *Lewis v. Henley* upheld that exclusion. Private schools supported by black churches and families and by Quakers and other religious groups provided some opportunities. Many black Hoosiers recognized the significance of education and agitated for access. Finally, in 1869, the General Assembly enacted a law that required creation of schools for African American children, so long as there were sufficient numbers of black children in the community. A half dozen years later, 68 percent of school-aged black children were enrolled in public schools, compared to about 76 percent of white children. After a narrow interpretation of the 1869 law by the Indiana Supreme Court in *Cory v. Carter* (1874), the legislature in 1877 stipulated that, should a school district refuse to create a school for black children, then those children could attend the local white school. Thus some black children had access to good, integrated schools; some continued to have no access; and many attended segregated schools in which conditions remained almost universally unequal, often pitifully so. Per capita expenditures in Evansville's white public schools in 1897–98, for example, were $24 compared to $13 in the city's black schools. Indiana courts before the middle of the twentieth century offered no assistance to blacks seeking equality in education.[30]

By the beginning of the twentieth century, there remained few legal restrictions on African Americans in Indiana. State law still prohibited marriage to a white person, attending a white school if local authorities insisted on providing a segregated school, or serving in the state militia. Despite this significant legal progress, the reality of everyday life for black Hoosiers was one of segregation and discrimination.

Conditions varied, usually worse in southern Indiana than northern. Nowhere in Indiana were blacks equal. Good jobs were virtually impossible. Restaurants, theaters, hospitals, swimming pools, and hotels were usually closed. Booker T. Washington, the best-known African American in the nation, was denied a hotel room in Anderson in 1900. Many small- and medium-sized towns had "sunset laws"—not posted usually, and often not even laws, but rather understandings that blacks, especially those who were strangers, should be gone before sunset. Churches tended to separate along the color line, as did most social organizations: there were black Methodist congregations and white Methodist congregations, black women's clubs and white women's clubs, black baseball teams and white baseball teams. This sort of segregation and discrimination actually worsened in Indiana in the late nineteenth century and the first decades of the twentieth century. For Africans Americans seeking a level playing field, Indiana's laws and courts had but slight relevance.[31]

There was violence, too—a violence that seemed to worsen as whites drew the color line that circumscribed the lives of black citizens ever more tightly. Its most vicious form was lynching, which challenged the rule of law more harshly than any other feature of America's history. Indiana's vigilante justice claimed white as well as black victims, but blacks in far larger proportion. Lynching statistics are incomplete, perhaps grossly so, but blacks, who accounted for about 2 percent of the state's population, were nearly a third (twenty) of the known sixty-one victims of Indiana lynch mobs in the years from 1865 to 1903. White mobs lynched blacks for many reasons, but most common were allegations of murder or rape of a white person. Sometimes local authorities resisted, as in the case of the heroic Grant County sheriff who stood against a lynch mob in 1885. More often they cooperated with the mob.[32]

Indiana's growing reputation as a northern lynching state became sufficiently embarrassing that the legislature in 1899 passed an antilynching bill, and a new governor, Winfield Durbin, determined to enforce it. Durbin responded to a lynching in Sullivan County in 1902 not by ignoring the violence, as his predecessors had done, but by forcing an investigation and then removing from office the sheriff who had permitted the victim to be taken from his jail. And when, on July 4, 1903, a race riot erupted in Evansville, Durbin sent the state militia to bring order. Durbin was the first Indiana governor to take such strong measures against racial violence. He was less interested in matters of race, however, than in replacing the vigilante tradition and mob rule with a commitment to jury trials and law and order.[33]

Durbin's decisive action seemed to mark the end of lynching in Indiana. When, for example, an Indianapolis mob of six hundred men attempted to remove a black prisoner from the Marion County Jail in 1920, they met the city's police force, well equipped and standing their ground. Such was the norm, with one exception. In 1930, the "monster with many hands and no brains," as Benjamin Franklin long ago had labeled mobs, once again reared its head in Indiana.[34]

The mob that lynched Thomas Shipp and Abe Smith in Marion on August 7, 1930, committed a heinous crime. Even more troubling was the failure of justice that followed. The Grant County sheriff offered only slight resistance as the lynch mob broke into his jail, removed three black teenagers accused of murder and rape, and lynched two of them from a tree on the courthouse square. The brutal violence, the infamous photograph, and the majority community reaction exposed some of the worst of white America's racism. The law failed. Local authorities declined to prosecute any of the mob leaders. Governor Harry Leslie endorsed that sentiment. Indiana's attorney general, James Ogden, then entered the case and pushed for justice. Ogden brought indictments against alleged mob leaders, but local juries refused to convict. It was Indiana's last lynching, but it left scars that endure to the present.[35]

The violence and lawlessness of lynching are not sidebars but are central to understanding Indiana's struggles with race and justice. By the twentieth century, however, the immediate danger for most African Americans was not lynching but discrimination and segregation in public accommodations, housing, jobs, health care, education, and all aspects of life, extending even to segregated burials in some cemeteries. Only in the last half of the twentieth century did the law and the changing culture begin to address such issues.[36]

During the first decades of the twentieth century, the lines of color continued to tighten, especially during the 1920s. Courts and law enforcement did very little to impede the process. White fears intensified as blacks migrated from the South to Indiana's growing cities. One response was to create new all-black high schools in Gary (Roosevelt) and Indianapolis (Crispus Attucks). In 1926, in the case of *Greathouse v. Board of School Commissioners of City of Indianapolis,* the Indiana Supreme Court refused to stop construction of the new, segregated Attucks High School. Another response to growing African American populations was to keep white neighborhoods white. Racial covenants appeared in property deeds. A 1927 Bloomington plat for a new subdivision, for example, repeated the word "white" half a dozen times, beginning with, "the ownership and occupancy of lots or buildings in this sub-division are forever restricted to members of the pure white race." In Indianapolis, neighborhood associations formed to prevent the growing black population from moving next door. In 1926, the Indianapolis City Council passed a zoning ordinance intended to maintain segregated neighborhoods. The Marion County Circuit Court in the case of *Gaillard v. Grant* (1926) decided that the ordinance violated the Fourteenth Amendment. The ruling was the only significant legal blow to segregationists in the 1920s, but it did not prevent white realtors, neighborhood associations, and other forces in Indianapolis and elsewhere from continuing to keep blacks out of white neighborhoods. The tradition was perpetuated in segregated federal housing projects built in the 1930s.[37]

The Ku Klux Klan of the 1920s included African Americans on its enemies list, though (contrary to present-day assumptions) they were not nearly as high in priority as Catholics. The Klan's control of the General Assembly in 1925 produced efforts to restrict alcohol consumption and Catholic influence but no attempted legislation directed against blacks. Still, the Klan's brand of narrow patriotism and white Protestantism exacerbated lines of division among all Hoosiers, including those between whites and blacks.[38]

African Americans responded in various ways to white restrictions. Many sought accommodation, making the best of a situation that often seemed beyond their control. Many helped create black community organizations, such as churches and women's clubs, that provided aid and comfort. Some lived in all-black rural settlements, such as Hamilton County's Roberts Settlement.

Some African Americans resisted in subtle ways. Others challenged directly. The most effective of direct challenges came from those who organized branches of the National Association for the Advancement of Colored People (NAACP), the most important national and state civil rights organization of the twentieth century. Together with some white members, African Americans created NAACP branches in Indianapolis, Terre Haute, Evansville, Gary, and elsewhere in the early decades of the century. Members and leaders were often ordinary people, sometimes possessed of extraordinary courage, such as Katherine (Flossie) Bailey, the homemaker and mother who was the most visible and outspoken voice for justice following the Marion lynchings of 1930. The NAACP's most distinguished members were black lawyers. Indeed, no other group of Hoosiers challenged the color line as boldly as did black lawyers. In Indianapolis, black attorneys Robert Lee Brokenburr, Freeman Ransom, and Robert Lee Bailey were among the best, and they engaged in the hard struggle at a time when victories were few, long before the civil rights movement of the 1960s.[39]

The Jim Crow patterns that hardened during the 1910s and 1920s did not change during the Great Depression. One exception was the removal in 1936 of the constitutional provision that had allowed only whites to serve in the state militia. Another change, with a significance realized only later, came as African Americans moved from their traditional Republican vote to the Democratic Party, where they sometimes found more effective political voices.[40]

It was World War II that really challenged the color line. Many whites could see the necessity for national unity, including the practical need for black workers and soldiers. Some whites and nearly all blacks also saw the ideological incongruity of fighting as a segregated nation against Hitler's Germany. The necessities of victory required increased opportunity for African Americans, even if some white Americans did not will it. At the start of the war, employers still closed most good jobs to black workers. Legislation introduced in the General Assembly in 1941 to force fuller employment opportunities failed to pass. Indiana then moved to a voluntary state plan designed to encourage but not require employment of qualified black workers. The war years brought significant numbers of African American workers to better jobs, including semiskilled labor in factories. Obstacles to equal employment remained, and segregation and discrimination continued, even against blacks in military uniform, but the war gave impetus to the handful of civil rights activists and produced returning veterans determined to change the status quo.[41]

The first success came in 1949, when the General Assembly passed the Indiana School Desegregation Act, which mandated an end to separate schools. The Indiana law preceded the 1954 U.S. Supreme Court desegregation decision in *Brown v. Board of Education*. White Hoosiers offered none of the massive resistance that characterized responses to the *Brown* decision across the South. At the same time, Indiana was among the last of northern states to abandon segregated schools. The 1949 state law did not bring immediate integration everywhere. Most of the state's traditional "colored" schools closed in the 1950s. But, in many large cities, segregation continued in other forms, derived from housing patterns, attendance zones, and school transfers. In such instances, change often came, if at all, only with court action or the threat of action.[42]

As it became clear that neither state law nor the federal *Brown* decision would automatically produce integrated schools, parents and NAACP leaders took legal action. In Gary, South Bend, and Kokomo, black parents went to federal district court in the 1960s but received little or no assistance in integration. By the 1970s, the federal courts were more inclined to require desegregation, as in the school cases in Evansville, Fort Wayne, Indianapolis, and South Bend. Consequences were ambiguous and troubled, including white flight from center cities, but by the 1990s most Indiana schools met federal guidelines for racial balance.

The Indianapolis case was the most prolonged and difficult. The city had long resisted integration, both before and after passage of the 1949 law. Some saw the creation of Uni-Gov in 1969—which moved most government functions from citywide to countywide scope but excluded schools—as a means of continuing all-white suburban schools. In a suit pushed by the NAACP and initiated by the Department of Justice under the federal Civil Rights Act of 1964, Judge S. Hugh Dillin in 1971 found that the Indianapolis School Board, "through the years, consistently had employed policies and practices causing and maintaining racial segregation." Judge Dillin ordered desegregation of the Indianapolis Public Schools (IPS) with a plan that included busing black students to Marion County township schools outside of the IPS. Intense resistance and controversy followed, but in 1981 the first buses carried black students to the suburbs, although white students were not bused the other way. Whether the Indianapolis plan improved education or race relations in Marion County remains the subject of very different opinions.[43]

Schools were the place of greatest challenge in equality of access and opportunity. Opening Indiana's public places to all races proved difficult as well. Efforts by NAACP lawyers and others to bring about enforcement of Indiana's 1885 civil rights law in the immediate post–World War II years proved unsuccessful. Hotels, theaters, and restaurants in many towns and cities remained closed to blacks. African American members of the General Assembly were barred from downtown hotels and restaurants, which only gradually opened their doors in the late 1950s and 1960s. In Indianapolis in the late 1940s, both black and white citizens from the NAACP, church groups, and labor unions distributed copies of the 1885 law to restaurants but to little effect. Civil rights proponents introduced public accommodation bills in the General Assembly every year beginning in 1949, but they met with failure, as did their attempts to enact an effective Fair Employment Practices bill in the 1950s.

There were scattered signs of protest and progress across the state, as in the fight to open the city's public swimming pool in Marion to African Americans. This local struggle eventually reached the U.S. District Court for the Northern District of Indiana, which decided in 1954 that the Fourteenth Amendment entitled all citizens to full and equal access to this public facility.[44]

The 1960s brought the full force of the civil rights movement to Indiana as well as the nation. In 1960, Hoosier voters elected Matthew Welsh, a liberal Democrat, to the governor's office, joined by some state legislators committed to action, such as Birch Bayh. More and more citizens began to wake up to the nation's ideals, evidenced, for example, in the work of numerous church groups and in the voters' rejection of the Alabama segregationist George Wallace in the state's 1964 presidential primary election.

In 1961 and 1963, the General Assembly passed civil rights bills that allowed individuals to bring charges, provided penalties for violations, and gave power to a state civil rights commission. This state legislation preceded the federal Civil Rights Act of 1964 and made Indiana among the more progressive states in matters of law. In 1965, the legislature repealed the state's prohibition of marriage between blacks and whites, the last legal restriction regarding race. In the late 1960s, the legislature added laws that affected housing discrimination, in some ways stronger than the federal law. In addition, most Indiana cities and towns created human relations commissions to assess complaints and propose remedies. It was nearly impossible to ignore the new legal environment and the new optimism. Harriet Wells later recalled her participation in the 1960s lunch counter sit-ins at one of Madison's drugstores: "We went back every day for a week. They knew we were determined. And we had the law on our side—they knew that, too."[45]

The successes of the civil rights movement of the 1960s were substantial in any context and particularly so in light of Indiana's long and stubborn reluctance to embrace racial equality. The achievement of equality before the law and the demonstrable improvements in the quality of life for many African Americans were worthy of accolades.

By the twenty-first century, nearly all Hoosiers proclaimed an abhorrence of active racism. The occasional gathering of a few ignorant whites in Ku Klux Klan regalia sparked much larger counterdemonstrations. The sort of narrow Americanism and vicious prejudice that fueled the Klan of the 1920s were largely gone. Indiana was not a "Klan state."[46]

Yet full equality and justice for all remained unrealized. Access to quality education, housing, and jobs still depended on color, even if many whites pretended otherwise. The heritage of the past lurked in such forms as the Marion lynching of 1930, the colored schools of the 1890s, the unenforced Civil Rights Act of 1885, article XIII of the 1851 constitution, and territorial indenture laws that were subterfuges for slavery. That such bold expressions of the dominant white culture's notions of race no longer existed did not mean that their consequences were dead and gone. Indiana's particular past placed a special burden on twenty-first-century lawmakers, courts, and citizens to check and then double-check to be sure that America's ideals were always fully engaged in matters of race.

Notes

1. For an excellent short overview, see Richard B. Pierce, "Negotiating Freedom: African Americans in Indiana," in *The State of Indiana History 2000,* ed. Robert M. Taylor Jr. (Indianapolis: Indiana Historical Society, 2001), 319–41.

2. Emma Lou Thornbrough, *The Negro in Indiana: A Study of a Minority* (Indianapolis: Indiana Historical Bureau, 1957), 1–5; Andrew R. L. Cayton, *Frontier Indiana* (Bloomington: Indiana University Press, 1996), 51.

3. The following discussion of the Northwest Ordinance and Indiana Territory draws largely from David Brion Davis, "The Significance of Excluding Slavery from the Old Northwest in 1787," *Indiana Magazine of History* 84 (March 1988): 75–89; Robert M. Taylor Jr., ed., *The Northwest Ordinance, 1787: A Bicentennial Handbook* (Indianapolis: Indiana Historical Society, 1987), especially 72–76; John D. Barnhart and Dorothy L. Riker, *Indiana to 1816: The Colonial Period* (Indianapolis: Indiana Historical Bureau and Indiana Historical Society, 1971), 333–35, 346–49, 352, 354; Andrew R. L. Cayton, "Race, Democracy, and the Multiple Meanings of the Indiana Frontier,"

in *The Indiana Territory, 1800–2000,* ed. Darrel E. Bigham (Indianapolis: Indiana Historical Society, 2001), 47–70; Cayton, *Frontier Indiana,* 187–93, 246–47; Thornbrough, *Negro in Indiana,* 5–21; Paul Finkelman, "Slavery and the Northwest Ordinance: A Study in Ambiguity," *Journal of the Early Republic* 6 (Winter 1986): 343–70.

4. Quoted in Thornbrough, *Negro in Indiana,* 10–11.

5. Nicole Etcheson, *The Emerging Midwest: Upland Southerners and the Political Culture of the Old Northwest, 1787–1861* (Bloomington: Indiana University Press, 1996), 67–71; Thomas D. Hamm, April Beckman, Marissa Florio, Kristi Giles, and Marie Hopper, "'A Great and Good People': Midwestern Quakers and the Struggle against Slavery," *Indiana Magazine of History* 100 (March 2004): 3–25.

6. Quoted in Thornbrough, *Negro in Indiana,* 16.

7. Alexis de Tocqueville, *Democracy in America,* ed. J. P. Mayer (New York: Harper and Row, 1969), 345–46. The numbers of black Hoosiers were small: census takers in 1810 counted 630 African Americans, of whom 237 were listed as slaves. Almost certainly many of the other 393 were indentured servants. Such small numbers should not obscure the large significance of Indiana's choice, the consequences of which were clear to all by 1861.

8. Charles Kettleborough, *Constitution Making in Indiana: A Source Book of Constitutional Documents with Historical Introduction and Critical Notes* (Indianapolis: Indiana Historical Commission, 1916), 1:117, 112.

9. State v. Lasselle, 1 Blackf. 60, 62 (1820); Sandra Boyd Williams, "The Indiana Supreme Court and the Struggle against Slavery," *Indiana Law Review* 30, no. 1 (1997): 306. See the Indiana Supreme Court Web site on slave cases for some of the essential documents: http://www.in.gov/judiciary/education/special/railroad.html.

10. The Case of Mary Clark, a Woman of Color, 1 Blackf. 122, 126 (1821); Thornbrough, *Negro in Indiana,* 27–30; Randall T. Shepard, "For Human Rights: Slave Cases and the Indiana Supreme Court," *Traces of Indiana and Midwestern History* 15 (Summer 2003): 34–41. For a good discussion of the legal twists and turns over slavery and indenture in the years immediately after adoption of the new constitution, see Merrily Pierce, "Luke Decker and Slavery: His Cases with Bob and Anthony, 1817–1822," *Indiana Magazine of History* 85 (March 1989): 31–49.

11. Thornbrough, *Negro in Indiana,* 20.

12. Kettleborough, *Constitution Making in Indiana,* 1:109.

13. Thornbrough, *Negro in Indiana,* 121–23, 204, 233. Many of Indiana's relevant laws are gathered in Stephen Middleton, comp., *The Black Laws in the Old Northwest: A Documentary History* (Westport, Conn.: Greenwood, 1993), 157–268.

14. Thornbrough, *Negro in Indiana,* 125–26, 394.

15. Ibid., 58–63; Shepard, "For Human Rights: Slave Cases and the Indiana Supreme Court," 37.

16. Kettleborough, *Constitution Making in Indiana,* 1:305, 360–63, 373; 2:617–18; Donald F. Carmony, *Indiana, 1816–1850: The Pioneer Era* (Indianapolis: Indiana Historical Bureau and Indiana Historical Society), 442–47. Illinois and Oregon adopted similar exclusion provisions in their state constitutions. Justin E. Walsh, *The Centennial History of the Indiana General Assembly* (Indianapolis: Indiana Historical Bureau, 1987), 151n.

17. Barkshire v. State, 7 Ind. 389, 391 (1856); Shepard, "For Human Rights: Slave Cases and the Indiana Supreme Court," 37–38.

18. Thornbrough, *Negro in Indiana,* 73–91; Walsh, *Centennial History of the Indiana General Assembly,* 154.

19. Carmony, *Indiana, 1816–1850,* 467–70, 565–66.

20. Freeman v. Robinson, 7 Ind. 321 (1855); Emma Lou Thornbrough, "Indiana and Fugitive Slave Legislation," *Indiana Magazine of History* 50 (September 1954): 201–28; Thornbrough, *Negro in Indiana,* 94–118; Patrick J. Furlong, "The South Bend Fugitive Slave Case," in *We the People: Indiana and the United States Constitution; Lectures in Observance of the Bicentennial of the Constitution* (Indianapolis: Indiana Historical Society, 1987), 6–24; Williams, "Indiana Supreme Court and the Struggle against Slavery," 310–16.

21. Etcheson, *Emerging Midwest,* 94.

22. Hamm, Beckman, Florio, Giles, and Hopper, "Great and Good People," 3–25 (quote at 13).

23. Peggy Seigel, "The *Fort Wayne Standard:* A Reform Newspaper in the 1850s Storm," *Indiana Magazine of History* 97 (September 2001): 169–80; Calvin Fletcher to Sarah Hill Fletcher, June 22, 1853, in *The Diary of Calvin Fletcher,* vol. 5, *1853–1856,* ed. Gayle Thornbrough, Dorothy L. Riker, and Paula Corpuz (Indianapolis: Indiana Historical Society, 1977), 81n.

24. Thornbrough, *Negro in Indiana,* 145–46.

25. James H. Madison, *The Indiana Way: A State History* (Bloomington: Indiana University Press, 1986), 193–207; Emma Lou Thornbrough, *Indiana in the Civil War Era* (Indianapolis: Indiana Historical Bureau and Indiana Historical Society, 1965), 85–123, 180–273 (quote at 231). For glimpses into the lives of former slaves, see Ronald L. Baker, *Homeless, Friendless, and Penniless: The WPA Interviews with Former Slaves Living in Indiana* (Bloomington: Indiana University Press, 2000).

26. Smith v. Moody, 26 Ind. 299 (1866); Thornbrough, *Negro in Indiana,* 234–36, 249–50; Williams, "Indiana Supreme Court and the Struggle against Slavery," 316–17.

27. Thornbrough, *Indiana in the Civil War Era,* 180–273; Thornbrough, *Negro in Indiana* (quote at 190).

28. James H. Madison, "Civil War Memories and 'Pardnership Forgittin,' 1865–1913," *Indiana Magazine of History* 99 (September 2003): 198–230.

29. Fruchey v. Eagleson, 15 Ind. App. 88, 43 N.E. 146 (1896); Thornbrough, *Negro in Indiana,* 257–66, 271–72. For a detailed discussion of the 1920 case, *Chochos v. Burden,* 74 Ind. App. 242, 128 N.E. 696 (1920), see James H. Madison, *A Lynching in the Heartland: Race and Memory in America* (New York: Palgrave, 2001), 43–47.

30. Thornbrough, *Negro in Indiana,* 160–82, 317–45; Maureen A. Reynolds, "The Challenge of Racial Equality," in *Hoosier Schools: Past and Present,* ed. William J. Reese (Bloomington: Indiana University Press, 1998), 173–77; Darrel E. Bigham, *We Ask Only a Fair Trial: A History of the Black Community of Evansville, Indiana* (Bloomington: Indiana University Press, 1987), 44; Clifton J. Phillips, *Indiana in Transition: The Emergence of an Industrial Commonwealth, 1880–1920* (Indianapolis: Indiana Historical Bureau and Indiana Historical Society, 1968), 400–402.

31. Emma Lou Thornbrough and Lana Ruegamer, *Indiana Blacks in the Twentieth Century* (Bloomington: Indiana University Press, 2000), 2–32; Madison, *Indiana Way,* 170–73.

32. Thornbrough, *Negro in Indiana,* 276–83; Madison, *Lynching in the Heartland,* 13–18, 20–25.

33. Thornbrough, *Negro in Indiana,* 283–87; Madison, *Lynching in the Heartland,* 18–20.

34. Madison, *Lynching in the Heartland,* 19–20.

35. Ibid., passim.

36. Madison, *Indiana Way,* 241–43.

37. Thornbrough and Ruegamer, *Indiana Blacks in the Twentieth Century,* 51–62; James H. Madison, *Indiana through Tradition and Change: A History of the Hoosier State and Its People, 1920–1945* (Indianapolis: Indiana Historical Society, 1982), 8–13; Stanley Warren, "The Evolution of Secondary Schooling for Blacks in Indianapolis, 1869–1930," in *Indiana's African-American Heritage: Essays from Black History News & Notes,* ed. Wilma L. Gibbs (Indianapolis: Indiana Historical Society, 1993), 29–35; Maxwell Manors Incorporated, September 6, 1927, Monroe County Plat Book 3, page 70, copy in author's possession.

38. Leonard J. Moore, *Citizen Klansmen: The Ku Klux Klan in Indiana, 1921–1928* (Chapel Hill: University of North Carolina Press, 1991).

39. Thornbrough and Ruegamer, *Indiana Blacks in the Twentieth Century,* 15, 49–53, 57–58, 63; Stephen A. Vincent, *Southern Seed, Northern Soil: African-American Farm Communities in the Midwest, 1765–1900* (Bloomington: Indiana University Press, 1999); Madison, *Lynching in the Heartland,* 58–60, 103–9.

40. Madison, *Indiana through Tradition and Change,* 138–39; William W. Giffin, "The Political Realignment of Black Voters in Indianapolis, 1924," *Indiana Magazine of History* 74 (June 1983): 133–66.

41. Madison, *Indiana through Tradition and Change,* 384–89; Max Parvin Cavnes, *The Hoosier Community at War* (Bloomington: Indiana University Press, 1961), 120–37.

42. Reynolds, "Challenge of Racial Equality," 173–79; Thornbrough and Ruegamer, *Indiana Blacks in the Twentieth Century,* 144–47; Iwan W. Morgan, "Latecomers to the Industrial City: African Americans, Jobs, and Housing in Fort Wayne, Indiana, 1940–1960," *Indiana Magazine of History* 95 (March 1999): 31–57.

43. U.S. v. Bd. of Sch. Comm'rs of the City of Indianapolis, Indiana, 332 F. Supp. 655, 672 (1971); Thornbrough and Ruegamer, *Indiana Blacks in the Twentieth Century,* 147–61, 196–97; Emma Lou Thornbrough, "The Indianapolis School Busing Case," in *We the People,* 67–92; Reynolds, "Challenge of Racial Equality," 180–90; Ronald D. Cohen, "The Dilemma of School Integration in the North: Gary, Indiana, 1945–1960," *Indiana Magazine of History* 82 (June 1986): 161–84.

44. Emma Lou Thornbrough, "Breaking Racial Barriers to Public Accommodations in Indiana, 1935–1963," *Indiana Magazine of History* 83 (December 1987): 301–29; Thornbrough and Ruegamer, *Indiana Blacks in the Twentieth Century,* 123–32; Alan F. January and Justin E. Walsh, *A Century of Achievement: Black Hoosiers in the Indiana General Assembly, 1881–1986* (Indianapolis: Indiana Historical Bureau, 1986), 10–11; Madison, *Lynching in the Heartland,* 130–37.

45. Thornbrough, "Breaking Racial Barriers to Public Accommodations in Indiana," 329–43; Thornbrough and Ruegamer, *Indiana Blacks in the Twentieth Century,* 167–72, 179; Matthew E. Welsh, *View from the State House: Recollections and Reflections, 1961–1965* (Indianapolis: Indiana Historical Bureau, 1981), 191–225; Madison, *Indiana Way,* 245–47; Don Wallis, ed., *All We Had Was Each Other: The Black Community of Madison, Indiana* (Bloomington: Indiana University Press, 1998), 78.

46. There were occasional outbursts. Those in Martinsville tended to attract most attention. See Stephen Stuebner, "In Hate's Wake," *Southern Poverty Law Center Intelligence Report* 107 (Fall 2002): 44–49; Sara Rimer, "After Arrest, Town Shamed by '68 Killing Seeks Renewal," *New York Times,* May 17, 2002, A16.

FOUR

Michael Grossberg and Amy Elson

FAMILY LAW IN INDIANA

A Domestic Relations Crossroads

Indiana has long been considered a crossroads state. The label suggests the Hoosier state's geographic centrality as part of the American heartland, but it also denotes the representative character of its policies. Family law—the body of rules, practices, and beliefs that govern the home—is a case in point. Its policies oversee all aspects of family life, from courtship and child rearing to spousal violence and inheritance. With a few notable exceptions, the rules Hoosiers have devised to govern their households have been in accord with major national trends since statehood in 1816. This has been true even though American federalism assigns control of family law to the states. Like citizens of other states, Hoosiers have always guarded this right jealously.

The history of Indiana family law reveals that commonality, not diversity, has been the major theme of American family law. From nineteenth-century acceptance of adoption to early twenty-first-century resistance to same-sex marriage, Indiana, like most states, has usually embraced the common policies dominant at particular moments. Its past demonstrates that family law innovations either have spread and become national or have withered away and become historical anomalies.[1]

The representative nature of Indiana family law is best understood by dividing the past into distinct eras. This period approach reveals both the time-bound construction of the state's policies and the ways in which domestic relations rules changed over time. Illustrative examples within each era demonstrate how the state's laws reflected national debates over the nature and function of American households. Examining the creation of national family laws through individual state actions also helps in understanding the pressures of conformity in the law as well as the possibilities of distinctiveness. It thus gives meaning to Indiana as a domestic relations crossroads.

Creating Indiana Family Law

Indiana entered the American union in the midst of a transformation in family law. Although Anglo-American law had long governed households, family law as a distinct legal category was a postrevolutionary creation. In colonial America, rules governing families were strewn across the legal landscape. Although provincial codes sometimes deviated from English practices in their acceptance of partible inheritance and divorce and in their greater toleration for informal marriages, none of the colonies considered family governance a distinct legal activity or its laws a separate body of rules. After the Revolution, however, a dual transformation occurred: families and family law underwent fundamental and reciprocal changes. The American family became, more than ever before, a haven for marital fulfillment and child nurture. At the same time, lawyers, litigants, judges, and legislators crafted a specialized body of legal rules to govern the home, family law. It contained a basic division of legal relationships—husband and wife, parent and child—and established some of the law's fundamental ideological commitments, such as the primacy of individual choice in marriage and parental control of child rearing.

By 1816, when Hoosiers organized their new state government, this process of change was well underway. As a result, Indiana created a body of domestic relations rules and practices that included the major innovations of the era. Like the citizens of other newly formed—or even established—states, Hoosiers borrowed freely and heavily from other jurisdictions. Although statehood secured family law autonomy for Indiana, the state's voluntary adoption of newly emerging policies illustrates the dynamics of family law diffusion in an era when the states had their greatest jurisdictional independence.

Like most Americans, Hoosiers regarded marriage as the most important relationship in their society. What was new in the years after the

Revolution was the way in which people thought about marriage and acted upon it. Although marriage for life remained the social ideal, a new sense of the importance of individual happiness and fulfillment and of marriage as a partnership led to new ideas of marital freedom. There was wide recognition of the basic regulatory issue posed by matrimony: balancing the individual right to wed against the state interest in marriage. That balancing act found legal expression in the definition of marriage as a *civil contract,* and the emphasis began to shift from the first to the second word. Requirements for parental consent, formal celebrations, public notices of impending marriages, restrictions on age, and countless other controls became looser or voluntary. The creation and widespread adoption of common-law marriage—a legally binding union based on whether a couple lived together as man and wife rather than whether they had participated in a formal marriage ceremony—epitomized the changes of the era. These changes tilted the new American law of marriage toward individual choice, contractualism, and limited family and public control.[2]

Hoosiers fully embraced these new marital priorities. State lawmakers accepted the definition of marriage as a "civil contract" and added that "this contract creates a status or relation with which the courts can interfere only to the extent and in the manner prescribed by statute."[3] In 1857, the state supreme court expanded on that declaration in a widely cited definition of marriage: "In this light marriage is more than a contract. . . . It is a great public institution, giving character to our whole civil polity. Hence, as between husband and wife, there is no constitutional provision protecting the marriage itself, or the property incident to it, from legislative control, by general law, upon such terms as public policy may dictate. The sovereign power may, by general enactment, regulate and mold their relative rights and duties at pleasure."[4] On this basis, the state's marriage code reflected Hoosier variants of a national consensus.[5] Legislators, for instance, constantly tinkered with the age of marriage, gradually raising it from the old common-law ages of twelve for females and fourteen for males to eighteen for both sexes by the century's end.[6] But the most important marital policy was expressed clearly in an 1884 state supreme court ruling that a marriage remained valid even if the parties had not followed all of the statutory prescriptions.[7] Thus, as historian Nancy Cott has noted, "Indiana laws of the 1840s and 1850s, for example, allowed any form of marriage ceremony whatsoever, so long as the couple consented before an authorized official; even a fraudulent ceremony could serve if the couple believed it to be legitimate."[8] Interpreting the law as guiding or directing rather than mandating the forms of marriage ensured state recognition of common-law unions.

Hoosiers similarly applied the ideas and practices of contract law to the dissolution of marriages. English law made divorce very rare. Americans rejected this policy. In the early nineteenth century, most states transformed divorce from a legislative responsibility to a judicial responsibility. At the same time, legislators expanded the grounds for divorce beyond the traditional bases of adultery and desertion to a growing number of other reasons, such as drunkenness and mental cruelty. Like the legal changes in marriage, new divorce laws were the result of the era's debates about marital happiness and responsibility. Despite the new access to divorce and changed attitudes about its availability, divorce retained a strong stigma that made it a very hazardous step for any woman or man. The reliance on fault heightened that reality: a marriage would be dissolved only if one spouse proved the other had committed a marital crime.

Yet the possibility of starting over through the formal dissolution of a marriage proved alluring for many Hoosiers and other Americans. As a result, the state's divorce law, first enacted in 1818, mimicked most other jurisdictions by providing an ever-growing number of grounds for ending a marriage.[9] For example, legislative revisions in 1838 granted a wife the right to a divorce if her spouse had been a habitual drunkard for more than two years or had failed for "any reasonable length of time to make provision for his family."[10]

As in many states, the most contentious issue was not spousal conflict but separation of powers. Following English practice, the Indiana legislature had the power to dissolve marriages through special acts. This residual legislative power clashed, however, with a growing sense of divorce as a private action that properly fell within the courts' power to resolve disputes.[11] Thus, Hoosiers attending an 1846 public meeting in Marion County passed a resolution declaring:

> Inasmuch as a great deal of time is consumed and constant expense incurred by the General Assembly's constructively usurping judicial power on the subject of divorces, in defiance of the proper division of the powers of sovereignty between the three great departments of government: Is it not necessary that the General Assembly should be expressly prohibited by the constitution from granting divorces? We think there should be such a prohibition.[12]

That same year, the legislature issued forty-one divorces.[13] Only a ban on legislative divorce in the constitution of 1851 brought an end to the practice.

Indiana did enact one divorce law that took family law down a road not traveled by most other states. In 1824, legislators adopted an "omnibus" clause that permitted divorce for "any misconduct that resulted in unhappiness and destroyed the marriage relationship."[14] In 1831, they revised the law to grant judges the power to grant a divorce "for any other cause, and in any other case, where the court, in their discretion, shall consider it reasonable and proper that a divorce should be granted."[15] Eight years later, the state supreme court upheld the law against claims that it violated the constitution by giving judges legislative powers. The justices declared that the "statute requires a *cause* of divorce, on which the discretion of the Court is to be exercised. The conclusion of the judgment that that cause is reasonable, and such a one as forfeits the marriage contract on the part of the wrong-doer, or otherwise, is not an act of legislation. It prescribes no rule." The court also explained that the discretionary power was not limitless because of the requirement that it be "exercised in a sound and legal manner."[16] In a few years, however, the omnibus clause would help earn Indiana family law notoriety.

Far more typically, Indiana joined the midcentury campaign to grant property rights to married women. Hoosiers rejected traditional common-law restrictions based on the concept of coverture, which created the legal fiction of marital unity and imposed significant legal disabilities on married women. For example, a wife could not control any personal property that she brought to the marriage, sue or be sued in her own name, or even write a will. Once married and under her husband's coercion, she was no longer responsible for herself even in matters of criminal law, although she could act as an agent for her husband and contract with third parties for necessities. Under common law, husband's responsibilities were as great as wife's disabilities.

Following the lead of Mississippi in 1839, and, most influentially, that of New York in 1848, states began to endow women with property rights and thus to revise the legal relationship of man and wife.[17] Indiana joined the crusade early. Utopian reformer Robert Dale Owen led the effort at the 1850 constitutional convention. He successfully proposed that women "hereafter married in this State, shall have the right to acquire and possess property to their sole use and disposal; and laws shall be passed securing to them, under equitable conditions, all property, real and personal, whether owned by them before marriage or acquired afterwards by purchase, gift, devise, descent, or in any other way, and also providing for the registration of the wife's separate property." He argued that gender fairness and women's protection demanded these changes and insisted that reform would support rather than disrupt families.[18] Nevertheless, Indiana, like other states, granted women property rights in a piecemeal fashion because legislators feared that extensive property rights for wives would generate spousal conflict and undermine the unity of the home.[19]

Laws governing parents and children also underwent a transformation. In Indiana, as in the rest of the nation, legal change was both a cause and a product of the changing role of children. Changing family beliefs and practices fostered a new view of children as a particular kind of person with distinct rights and duties and a relationship with the state. Determining a new legal place for the young became a major challenge for the antebellum legal order. State judges and legislators struggled to find a way to treat children as distinct individuals without treating them as adults in a system that tied legal power to individual autonomy. The most revealing result was a new doctrine—the best interests of the child—that would dominate legal debates about children into the twenty-first century. Early in the nineteenth century, judges and other policymakers developed this doctrine by reinterpreting the state's power of parens patriae to include a newfound acknowledgment of children as having distinct interests recognizable by the law. At the same time, by deferring to family privacy and parental rights, the doctrine supported the emerging notion of the family as a private institution possessing significant autonomy. In this way, the new rule sanctioned broad discretionary authority to determine the interests of children in the event of family conflict or failure.[20]

The best interests of the child doctrine emerged most directly out of child custody disputes between warring parents, in which each sought to take advantage of the new divorce laws. Those disputes, in turn, were fueled by new ideas of child rearing and gender roles, particularly a growing faith in the nurturing power of mothers, which challenged the traditional superiority of paternal custody rights. More and more women fought to keep their children when their marriages failed, and judges used the best interests of the child to establish maternal preference as the basic rule of American custody law. Indiana judges and legislators embedded the new policy in the state's family law decisions and legislation. The supreme court expressed that reality in 1901 with the declaration: "The tendency of the modern decisions of our courts has been to affirm that the father's right to custody of his minor child is not absolute, but that it is secondary or subordinate to the welfare and happiness of the child, and that such welfare is the paramount or controlling question to be determined in providing for the infant's custody and control."[21]

The creation of legal adoption was the most dramatic example of the radical potential of the new ideas about children and parents. English law, with its priorities of family preservation and property protection, had never recognized the possibility of such a change. Indeed, the English did not accept adoption until 1926. However, the new American custody regimes of the nineteenth century encouraged this radical innovation of parent-child relations based on choice, not birth. Massachusetts launched this change in 1851, and, by the end of the century, almost every state had added adoption to its children's code. Indiana joined the ranks quickly, passing its first statute in 1855.[22] Adoption remained a secondary form of family formation, however, and adopted children and their new parents received greater rights only gradually. In Indiana, as in most states, inheritance was the most litigated adoption issue because the major point of contention for most litigants was property, not child care. By 1911, the state appellate court held that an adopted child was a legal heir, a lineal descendent, the same as if born in lawful wedlock: "The manifest purpose of the statutes relating to the adoption of children cannot be construed to impose duties and obligations alone upon the adopting parents, but should be held to establish a reciprocal relation between adoptive parents and adopted children." It insisted there was no distinction "between the rights of an adopted child in the estate of the adopting father or mother and a natural child."[23]

The basic rules embedded in Indiana family law in the decades after statehood were both representative and long-lasting. Most policies remained in place until the mid-twentieth century, or later. These Hoosier variants of mainline national policies illustrate the basic features of American family law constructed during this era of transformation. The diffusion of basic policies throughout the nation also illustrates what legal historian James Willard Hurst called "drift." By drift, Hurst meant the ongoing elaboration of dominant legal trends in jurisdictions around the nation. Indiana's domestic relations policies demonstrate that power of drift even in an era of transforming change.[24]

Nineteenth-Century Departures

There was one era when Indiana took a major detour from the main roads of American family law. In the middle decades of the nineteenth century,

Hoosiers veered down two radical paths. One of these detours later became commonplace and merged into the main thoroughfares of American family law; the other remained anomalous, and its radicalism compelled state policymakers to abandon it. These departures illustrate some of the possibilities and some of the limits of state autonomy in domestic relations.

The first departure expressed the state's deep-seated racism. Though Indiana sprang from the Northwest Territory and its path-breaking ban on slavery, the state long followed policies of racial exclusion and subordination.[25] The determination to impose de jure racial barriers instead of relying on de facto ones—as most other northern states did—carried over to family law. In 1818, the state prohibited intermarriage between whites and blacks: "If any white person shall have sexual intercourse with any negro within this state, he or she so offending, shall, on conviction by presentment or indictment, if a male, be fined in any sum not exceeding one hundred dollars, and if a female, be imprisoned not exceeding ten days; and it shall not hereafter be lawful for any white person to intermarry with any negro in this state."[26] The ban had a checkered statutory history but remained basic state policy throughout the nineteenth century and into the twentieth.[27]

In 1840, news of a marriage between a white Indianapolis woman and her black servant led legislators to change the penalties to mandate "fines of $1,000 to $5,000 for the offending parties along with ten to twenty years in prison; [and] a fine of $1,000 to $10,000 for the person officiating, who would also be removed from his job. At a time when a master artisan's home, workshops, and outbuildings might be worth $4,000 at most, these fines were stupendous, the equivalent of many millions of dollars today." Although lawmakers lowered those fines the next year out of fear that juries would not convict violators, the episode reveals both the intense racial antipathies finding expression in the marriage code and the limits of the state's commitment to nuptial contractualism.[28]

The ban on interracial marriages survived a major legal challenge after the Civil War. In *State v. Gibson,* the state supreme court rejected a black Hoosier's claim that the Fourteenth Amendment to the federal Constitution and 1866 federal Civil Rights Act abrogated the state law. Turning away his attempt to legitimate his marriage to a white woman, the justices asserted the power of the states over domestic relations law:

> The right, in the states, to regulate and control, to guard, protect, and preserve this God-given, civilizing, and Christianizing

> institution is of inestimable importance, and cannot be surrendered, nor can the states suffer or permit any interference therewith. If the federal government can determine who may marry in a state, there is no limit to its power. It can legislate upon all subjects connected with, or growing out of this relation. It can determine the rights, duties, and obligations of husband and wife, parent and child, guardian and ward. It may pass laws regulating the granting of divorces. It may assume, exercise, and absorb all the powers of a local and domestic character. This would result in the destruction of the states.[29]

Ignoring the basic uniformity of American family law, the justices also insisted that the "customs, habits, and thoughts of the people in one state differ widely from those of the people in another state, and this results in different laws." After these declarations of states rights and dual federalism, the court then gave its blessing to the ban: "The people of this State have declared that they are opposed to the intermixture of races and all amalgamation. If the people of other states desire to permit a corruption of blood, and a mixture of races, they have the power to adopt such a policy. When the legislature of the State shall declare such policy by positive enactment, we will enforce it, but until thus required we shall not give such policy our sanction."[30]

Although anomalous when first adopted, such bans on interracial marriage became increasingly commonplace in the corrosive racial environment of late nineteenth- and early twentieth-century America. By 1916, twenty-eight states and territories prohibited interracial marriage.[31] Indiana's antebellum family law innovation thus had helped set the stage for what would be the most racist marriage code in American history.

Indiana's second midcentury domestic relations deviation ended much more quickly. In 1852, state lawmakers took advantage of technological change—particularly the railroad—and jurisdictional diversity to make Indiana the nation's first divorce mill. They adopted a lax residency requirement, which, when combined with the state's omnibus grounds for divorce, made migratory divorce a lucrative business.[32] Enterprising lawyers began drumming up business by placing newspaper ads in other states, for example, New York. Thus, soon after railroad lines were united in a depot in Indianapolis, the clerk of the Marion County court claimed that he received at least one letter a day inquiring whether a disappearing spouse had applied there for a decree.[33] One study later concluded that, in

1858, more than two-thirds of all divorce actions in Marion County had been filed by nonresidents.[34]

The state's judiciary lent its support to the new policy. In 1859, the state supreme court turned back the charge of a New York wife that her husband had fraudulently established residency in Indianapolis for the sole purpose of divorcing her and then immediately had returned to the Empire State and his paramour. Despite a contrary ruling by a lower court, the court held that a divorce proceeding, once finalized, could not be reopened. "The policy of our state seems to have been, and to still be, against disturbing divorces granted," the justices ruled. "This has been induced by a consideration of the consequences necessarily incident to an opposite policy. This case affords an illustration. Within the three years between the granting of the divorce, and the setting of it aside, Edmund H. McQuigg had married another woman."[35]

Divorces like McQuigg's soon made Indiana the target of critics around the country who decried the nation's loose morals. The issue was joined most dramatically in an 1860 newspaper debate between Indiana reformer and state legislator Robert Dale Owen and *New York Tribune* editor Horace Greeley. Condemning Indiana as "the paradise of free-lovers," where men and women could "get unmarried at pleasure," Greeley blamed Owen for the lax divorce law. Owen refused responsibility, but contended that Indiana's approach was far more likely to produce sound morality than was New York's rigid, adultery-only divorce law. In New York, he argued, "you have elopements, adultery, which your law virtually encourages, you have free-love, and that most terrible of all social evils, prostitution." Equally important, Owen supported the right to divorce as a salutary action that promoted sound marriages based on love and affection. Greeley rejected such claims and demanded that marriage be indissoluble.[36]

Despite Owen's defense, the pressure to conform proved too great to resist. An 1858 editorial in the *Indianapolis Daily Journal* complained that the city was "overrun by a flock of ill-used, and ill-using, petulant, libidinous, extravagant, ill-fitting husbands and wives as a sink is overrun with the foul water of the whole house."[37] The next year, legislators began tightening residency requirements; when they eliminated the omnibus clause in 1873, the state's days as a divorce colony ended.[38] The courts also jumped on the repeal bandwagon. In an 1865 divorce case, the supreme court bemoaned the by then discredited policy: "Under that act, such monstrous abuses were practiced, to the injury of unsuspecting husbands and wives, in other states, that our statute became a reproach to us abroad." The justices embraced the revision, claiming that it "is due to our character as a state to say that this remedial legislation has put an effectual check upon the preexisting state of affairs, and that it is believed that the judges of our *nisi prius* courts . . . are quite as successful in preventing the fraudulent practices of which we have spoken, as are the tribunals of most of our sister states. If these continue, they will be chargeable, not to our laws, but to those who are intrusted [*sic*] with their administration."[39]

Indiana's long-lasting ban on interracial marriage and its short-lived career as a divorce mill illustrate some of the dynamics of American family law. Jurisdiction over domestic relations gave states the freedom to innovate. They could be, as Supreme Court justice Louis Brandeis put it, laboratories for legal change. But the pressures for conformity were great and fed a tendency toward family law uniformity. With some exceptions, such as South Carolina's refusal to grant divorces at all, state family law variations usually fell within a fairly narrow range. The fate of Indiana's mid-nineteenth-century marriage radicalism suggests why.

Industrial Revisions

Late in the nineteenth century, Indiana merged again with the main roads of American family law, expressing Hoosier variations of national policies. Like their counterparts around the country, state lawmakers increased state regulation of the home. They did so largely in response to fearful reports about the nation's homes: rising divorce rates, juvenile delinquency, falling family size among the native-born through use of abortions and birth control, rising family size among immigrants, the choice of more and more educated women not to marry, child abuse and neglect. A growing sense of family crisis spurred demands for a new balance between public interest in families and individual choice and household autonomy. In Indiana, as in most states, the revisions did not fundamentally alter the basic content of family law. Instead, they increased state regulation of husbands and wives, parents and children in several particular ways.[40]

Increasing restrictions on the right to wed illustrated the new tenor of debate over the laws regulating Indiana families. Indeed, in this era, the Indiana ban on interracial unions not only became a representative American policy, but it also expressed a new determination to curb nuptial freedom and contractual rights. Throughout the nation, calls for greater controls on the right to wed became increasingly common. Although Indiana and most other states continued to define marriage as a civil contract,

Hoosier lawmakers joined the movement to shift emphasis from contract law to civil law, that is, to employ the police power of the state to impose new restrictions on potential brides and grooms. They hiked the age of marriage, demanded that brides and grooms obtain licenses, lengthened waiting periods before couples could wed, and imposed other restrictions.[41]

Indiana's most distinctive contribution to the national campaign came in the first decade of the twentieth century, when legislators took the lead in imposing eugenic controls on marriage. At the instigation of Dr. John N. Hurty, director of the Indiana Board of Health, legislators passed a law in 1905 barring the marriage of "imbeciles," anyone with "transmissible disease," anyone "of unsound mind," or anyone who had been confined in a county asylum. Hurty "espoused the notion that imbecility, criminality, feeblemindedness, alcoholism, immorality, and syphilis were all inherited conditions, passed down the family line through defective genes, and championed the law as a way to rid Indiana of 'undesirables.'"[42]

Two years later, legislators took even more aggressive action. Acting again at Hurty's prodding, they passed the country's first sterilization law. The act "licensed the involuntary asexualization of inmates deemed 'unfit' by superintendents of state hospitals."[43] By 1930, twenty-four states had joined the eugenic crusade. In 1927, the U.S. Supreme Court gave this policy its imprimatur, when Justice Oliver Wendell Holmes Jr. expressed the sentiments of Hoosier marriage law reformers by declaring in a case from Virginia: "Three generations of imbeciles are enough."[44]

In Indiana, as in much of the country, the most far-reaching changes of the era occurred in the regulation of parents and children. Concern about abuse, delinquency, and neglect led to demands for greater state intervention based on parens patriae. The resulting expansion in the role of the state also expressed a growing faith in law as a tool for changing children's lives. In this new relationship among children, parents, and the state, public authorities assumed greater control over the health, welfare, and education of young Hoosiers. The Indiana Supreme Court articulated the ethos of the new policies when it upheld an act expanding state control of neglected, abused, or abandoned children:

> [O]ur constitution, and our laws enacted under it, sanction and confirm the great principle of the sovereign's guardianship of the children within the dominions of the sovereign. But while it is true that this great principle is thus sanctioned and confirmed, it is still true that the equally great principle that natural right vests in

> parents the custody and control of their children is confirmed and enforced. This high and strong natural right yields only when the welfare of society or the children themselves comes into conflict with it; but where there is such conflict the supreme right of guardianship asserts itself for the protection of society and the promotion of the welfare of the wards of the commonwealth.[45]

The determination to regulate Indiana child rearing more closely found expression in a campaign to restrict child labor. As in other states, particularly in northern urban and industrial centers, a new conception of childhood led Hoosier reformers to argue that children belonged in school rather than in factories making glass or steel or on the streets hawking newspapers and artificial flowers. Reformers met resistance from employers, from opponents of state activism, and from working-class and immigrant parents who insisted that their struggling families needed the wages of the young to survive. These opponents recognized that child labor reformers sought to sever the traditional common-law notion of family reciprocity, in which children exchanged their labor for parental support. In a further attempt to entrench child nurture as the fundamental duty of families, child labor legislation restricted parental rights to children's services while continuing to require parental support for the young.

Concern focused on particular forms of youthful employment. For instance, farm work won approval as morally and physically uplifting, while the employment of children in glass manufacturing, coal mining, furniture making, vegetable canning, and retailing was condemned. In 1885, legislators restricted the employment of children under the age of twelve.[46] Statutes like these, however, did not satisfy reformers who wanted a national ban like those enacted in most European countries. None of their efforts passed constitutional muster, however, and state control over child labor remained intact. Equally important, in Indiana as in most states, lax enforcement revealed not only the limits of the state's bureaucratic reach but also a continued reluctance to regulate parents.[47] The new regulations thus exposed a gap between legal rules and family behavior that continued through the era.

Reformers had more immediate success with a companion policy: compelling children to attend school. The campaign took place solely in the states because education was designated a state—indeed a local—concern. Compulsory school laws were championed as another way of taking children out of the work force and prolonging their childhoods. Like many states, Indiana had a history of lax school attendance enforcement. Yet in 1897, as legislators imposed restrictions on child labor they also made school attendance compulsory for all children between the ages of eight and fourteen. They raised the age to sixteen in 1913.[48]

In 1901, the judicial branch sanctioned the new policy, when judges rejected a father's claim that compulsory attendance violated his natural right as a parent to "govern and control his children." The supreme court countered: "The natural rights of a parent to the custody and control of his infant are subordinate to the power of the State, and may be restricted and regulated by municipal laws. One of the most important natural duties of the parent is his obligation to educate his child, and this duty he owes not to the child only, but to the commonwealth. If he neglects to perform it, or willfully refuses to do so, he may be coerced by law to execute such civil obligation."[49] The new policy proved popular in most other states, and, in 1918, Mississippi became the last to enact a compulsory attendance law.

No development as fully epitomized the era's new approaches to children and to the law as did the creation of the juvenile court. Advocates of special courts for children argued that adult standards of criminal responsibility should not be applied to young children because they lacked the moral understanding and judgment of adults. Reformers demanded a separate juvenile justice system that emphasized rehabilitation instead of punishment. They proposed a new legal trade-off: children would forfeit such due process rights as having an attorney and facing a clear charge in exchange for rehabilitative treatment.

The idea proved irresistible. Chicago created the first such court in 1899, and Indiana created the second in 1903. Indianapolis judge George W. Stubbs led the way. Like many juvenile justice reformers of the era, Stubbs first had relied on informal procedures and then had campaigned for a special court. The Hoosier initiative illustrated the process of family law diffusion. As Indiana Supreme Court justice Frank Sullivan notes in his history of the Indiana juvenile court, "Stubbs became aware of the new juvenile court in Chicago. Stubbs apparently made several trips to Chicago."[50] He and his supporters then drafted a bill to submit to the legislature. As Sullivan explains, "It is important to keep in mind that, with the notable exception of the jury trial guarantee and the age of children prohibited from being incarcerated with adults, the Indiana bill, as introduced, was the same as the Illinois act. What is not clear is whether this was the result of the scrivener's use of a sister state's language or the sponsor's concurrence with the policy choices represented by a sister state's act."[51] Either way, Indiana's quick adoption helped legitimate the new, specialized court. Under Indiana's statute, the court dealt with a broad array of children's problems, including delinquency, dependency, and neglect. Soon juvenile courts spread to other Indiana cities while also spreading across the country.

Finally, Hoosier policymakers rearranged the legal relations between children, parents, and state by enacting child protection measures. Fear of child mistreatment and the hope of child saving challenged the age-old assumption that parents knew how best to rear their offspring. Child-savers, as they came to be called, filled state codes with new regulations that substantially enlarged the legal definition of risks facing children and that consequently circumscribed parental rights.[52] Thus, in 1889, Hoosier legislators redefined child cruelty and mandated that "any person who shall cruelly ill-treat, abuse, overwork or inflict unnecessary cruel punishment upon any infant or minor child, and any person having the care, custody or control of any minor child, who shall willfully abandon or neglect the same, shall be guilty of a misdemeanor." They also penalized any adult who employed or hired out a child for wire-walking, acrobatics, obscene purposes, or prostitution.[53] This same belief fueled a successful campaign to raise the age of consent for sexual relations from twelve years to fourteen years, and then to sixteen years.[54]

Early twentieth-century child protection also focused on health. One in ten white children died before his or her first birthday, as did one in four black infants. Still others died from various ailments as they grew older.[55] Concern about children's health reflected the same fears that had spurred eugenic marriage laws. The new concern about child health found a particularly evocative expression in the "Indiana Child Creed," the epigraph to the *Indiana Mothers' Baby Book* published by State Board of Health in 1915 and sent to every Hoosier mother with a newborn:

> Every child has the inalienable right to be born free from disease, free from deformity and with pure blood in its veins and arteries.
>
> Every child has the inalienable right to be loved; to have its individuality respected; to be trained wisely in mind, body, and soul; to be protected from disease, from evil influences and evil persons; and to have a fair chance. In a word, to be brought up in the fear and admonition of the Lord.

> The state is delinquent which does not ceaselessly strive to secure these inalienable rights to its children.[56]

Four years later, such sentiments led to the creation of the Division of Infant and Child Hygiene. Using federal funds and matching grants available to states for educational programs in maternal and infant hygiene under the Shepard-Towner Act (1921), the division promoted better child care through classes for mothers, hygiene films, radio shows on parenting, statistical reports, and, most popularly, "better baby contests" at the Indiana State Fair. The mixture of child health protection with eugenic fears was evident in the belief of the division's director, Dr. Ada E. Schweitzer, that it was "essential to both restrict birth to only the most fit, through marriage and sterilization laws, and then to produce only the most desirable children through scientific child rearing and motherhood."[57]

The campaigns achieved significant successes, particularly declines in the number of underweight babies and in the infant mortality rate. However, as in most states, strong opposition from medical organizations, who challenged the legitimacy of publicly funded medical care, sapped the strength of the movement. The division disbanded in 1933.[58] Its success and its demise demonstrated both the possibilities and problems of child protection.

Indiana's industrial-era family law contained a new set of rules that closely regulated families and significantly altered the balance of power between families and the state. Legal changes also demonstrated how the Hoosier state had reentered the mainstream of American family law. In domestic relations, as in many other aspects of life, Indiana was often cited as the most typical American state. That reputation gained even greater currency at the end of the era, when pioneering sociologists Robert and Helen Lynd cast Muncie as *Middletown: A Study in Modern American Culture.* The Lynds' observations on Hoosier domestic relations realities—from the growing acceptance of divorce to the increasing success of compulsory school laws—amply illustrated how Indiana had become a family law crossroads.[59]

A Second Transformation

Like that of most states, Indiana's nineteenth-century family law regime ended only in the middle of the twentieth century. Lawmakers rewrote the nation's domestic relations rules in many fundamental ways. The federal government and the federal courts assumed powerful new roles in the nation's family law. Although states retained jurisdiction over domestic relations, new legal devices coerced uniformity in family law and reduced even further the possibility that Indiana or any other state could deviate widely from national norms. These changes became evident in every category of Indiana family law.[60]

Indiana's changes in the regulation of nuptials provide particularly revealing examples of the domestic relations transformations of the era. State legislators and judges enlarged individual marital rights by eliminating many restrictions on the right to wed. In the wake of a national civil rights movement, for example, Hoosier lawmakers repealed the antimiscegenation statutes that had been on the books almost since statehood.[61] They also cast aside eugenic restrictions and sterilization laws.[62]

Indiana had already removed regulations on courtship and marital disaffection. Like most states, Indiana had allowed jilted brides and grooms to sue for breaches of promises to marry and had provided husbands the right to sue anyone they thought had alienated their wives' affections. Once regarded as proper means of policing courting couples and as expressions of husbands' property rights in their wives, these provisions were swept away by a 1935 act that condemned them as sources of immoral suits by gold-digging women and as violations of married women's legal autonomy.[63] In 1937, Clarence Pennington discovered the change when the state supreme court rejected the alienation of affection suit he had filed against his father-in-law. Rebuffing his claim of a property right to his wife Ethelene's affection, the justices cited with approval a New York ruling from that same year upholding similar legislation: "In view of the broad and almost unlimited extension of the rights of married women brought about by statutory enactments and social advancement, we think that no court in this State would decide that the rights which a husband has by virtue of the marriage relation constitute property rights. A wife is no longer the property of her husband in the eyes of the law and by the general acceptance of society."[64]

As in every era of Indiana's family law, though, the state's marital changes were not completely consistent. For example, one long-standing form of marital contractual freedom—common-law marriage—fell under attack early in the century. Proponents of greater restrictions on marriage condemned it as a legal sanction for immoral cohabitation and a potent source of illegitimacy and disputes over family property. Indiana judges had accepted common-law marriage early in the state's history, and they likewise had restricted calls for its abolition. Thus, in 1939, the Indiana Supreme Court had echoed the then current state domestic relations code by declaring: "Every marriage in this country if valid is valid for all purposes and is attended with all the civil rights and obligations which the law confers and imposes upon persons who enter into the marriage relation. Hence a common-law marriage, once established, is as valid as a ceremonial or statutory marriage, not only in all civil proceedings but also in that exacting proceeding, a prosecution for bigamy."[65]

The growing chorus condemning common-law marriage proved impossible to ignore. In a 1953 estate dispute, the state appellate court warned: "Common-law marriages should be recognized with caution by courts and should not receive judicial sanction if the conduct of the parties fails to show clearly an honorable, abiding agreement entered into, and that the same existed before the eyes of the community."[66] Three years later, the supreme court added the caution: "There is no occasion to further liberalize the law of this state in favor of common-law marriages. We are not living in a frontier society and there is no hardship on anyone in obtaining a license and having a ceremonial marriage which becomes of record for their protection and the protection of their children. There is always danger of fraud being perpetrated upon the living and the dead as well as employers and their insurance carriers."[67] Heeding such concerns, Hoosier legislators abolished common-law marriage in 1958, and Indiana once again embraced a national family law policy.[68]

In the early 1970s, Indiana quickly enacted one of the most significant family law innovations of the modern era: no-fault divorce. The legitimacy and social utility of divorce had been debated since well before the American Revolution, even though fault and its attendant notions of individual marital morality always had dominated those discussions and the divorce experience. California, however, eliminated the element of fault from its divorce laws in 1969, and every other state quickly did the same. This change brought divorce law into conformity with the way marital dissolution actually functioned at that time. It represented one of the most fundamental redefinitions of legal rules and individual legal responsibility ever attempted in American family law. Equally important, like many family law changes, it occurred throughout Western Europe and North America, not only in the United States.[69]

Indiana was the third state to adopt no-fault divorce. The passage of a 1972 act establishing marital counseling bureaus in the largest metropolitan areas suggested a continuing concern about divorce in the Hoosier state.[70] Nevertheless, the major marriage and divorce innovations of the era produced a new balance between the rights of individual Hoosiers to marry or divorce and state control over those actions.

In the last half of the twentieth century, Indiana's law regarding children underwent an equally dramatic transformation on a scale warranting comparison with the transformations of the early nineteenth century. For instance, prodded by decisions of the federal Supreme Court and by sentiments that children deserve their own set of formal legal rights, Hoosier lawmakers revamped the state juvenile laws by granting youths greater due process rights. Indiana and other states revised the rehabilitative ideal of the juvenile courts and aligned them more closely with adult tribunals. Juvenile justice reform revamped the relationships between children, parents, and the state by expanding the legal autonomy of the young.[71]

A similar process led Hoosier lawmakers to rewrite the laws of illegitimacy. A series of U.S. Supreme Court decisions in the 1960s and 1970s remade the law amid rising rates of illegitimate births, fears of unpaid and uncollectible child support owed by putative fathers, concerns about the psychological impact of illegitimacy on children, increasingly reliable paternity tests, and reevaluations of the social utility of illegitimacy as a means of policing sexual misconduct. The court declared illegitimacy to be a constitutionally suspect classification and granted children the rights to be treated as individuals and not punished for the sins of their parents. Indiana joined this effort.[72] As the Indiana appellate court explained in a 1982 wrongful death suit,

> Numerous cases decided by the Supreme Court of the United States in recent years address the problem of statutorily imposed burdens or statutorily denied rights involving illegitimate children, and the relation of those statutes, rights and burdens to the equal protection clause of the Fourteenth Amendment to the Constitution of the United States. In the interest of brevity, we have distilled from those cases certain general rules which we will summarize. In general, a statute may not deny an illegitimate child rights given to children generally. The rationale for the rule is that a state should not attempt to influence the actions of men and women by imposing sanctions on the children of illicit relationships. Visiting condemnation upon the head of an innocent child who is not responsible for his birth is illegal and unjust, as well as an ineffectual way of deterring parents.

However, as in other states, the jurists refused to eliminate completely the legal designation of illegitimacy. "A state may create statutory classifications, and great respect, deference and latitude is accorded them by the courts," they counseled.[73]

Major alterations in Indiana's child custody law offer revealing evidence about the dynamics of change in family law during the era. Amid broad changes in gender roles and beliefs, the central tenet of custody rules—the primacy of the mother, or maternalism—came under attack as support for the presumed superior ability of mothers to raise children eroded. Advocates of custody law change drafted model acts and then pressured the states to adopt them. Thus, the Uniform Parentage Act of 1973 provided that the custody claims of mothers and fathers should be balanced equally.[74]

Indiana lawmakers enacted the full panoply of custody law reform. The legislature mandated that "neither the father nor the mother has per se a paramount right to the custody of their children on divorce. Indeed, under the Dissolution of Marriage Act, in determining the best interests of the child, there must be no presumption favoring either parent."[75] Following that standard, a state court used its ample discretion under the best interests of the child doctrine to take custody from a mother who had an erratic work schedule and had not taken the time to investigate child care options and to give it to the father who had weekends and evenings free and who had arranged for care during his workday.[76] The Indiana appellate court embraced the state's new custody law when it decreed in 1979 that a lower court had erred in presuming maternal preference. Instead, the court ruled that neither parent had a presumptive right to the custody of their child.[77] Both legislators and judges endorsed joint custody if it seemed in the best interests of the child.[78] While this reorientation of Indiana custody law fundamentally altered the nature of spousal and third party contests over children, it did not alter the reality that judges continued to have broad discretionary authority to determine the fitness of parents and the needs of children. In Indiana, as in the rest of the nation, such continuities imposed institutional limitations on the scope of change.

Few Hoosiers long resisted the family law transformations of the late twentieth century. For example, a 1982 update of the Lynds' Muncie study reported: "Middletown in the late 1970s seems to have come to terms with sex and with mismatching. Even the ministers now maintain that there are many justifiable grounds for divorce, and many ascribe no responsibility to divine providence for the matching of marriage partners. If marriage is still regarded as sacred, it is as a primary social institution and not as an indissoluble bonding of souls. The marital contract is now viewed by those who solemnize marriages as a matter of 'interpersonal adjustment' and 'mutual benefit.'"[79] Yet complacency hardly characterized Hoosier domestic relations. In an era in which fears of a family crisis erupted once again, bitter disagreements flared at times over issues from curfews for teenagers to abortion rights.

As a new millennium began, however, one issue sparked a sustained conflict over the state's family law: homosexuality. Differences over the rights that should be accorded to gays and lesbians deeply divided the state. The conflict found legal expression in two significant ways: fights over same-sex marriage and disputes over the custody rights of homosexual parents.

Debate over same-sex marriage erupted in Indiana after judicial rulings in Hawaii granted legal sanction to such unions.[80] Although later disavowed by the Hawaii legislature, the mere possibility of legalizing such marriages compelled a majority of Hoosier lawmakers to demand an explicit ban.

Most of the state's congressional delegation supported a statute defining marriage as a union of a man and woman and giving states the right to reject out-of-state marriages by their citizens that violated that rule. Indeed, ironically, as historian Cott points out, "Advocates of the bill saw the threat looming from Hawaii the way that opponents of divorce had seen the threat of Indiana's liberality in the 1850s: if any same-sex couple could go to Hawaii to be married, and return to their home state to live, then Hawaii was strong-arming the other states, setting marriage policy for the nation. The Defense of Marriage Act struck preemptively against that possibility."[81]

Indiana state legislators enacted a similar law in 1997 in an attempt to ensure that homosexual Hoosiers could not wed.[82] The 2003 decision of the Massachusetts Supreme Judicial Court declaring that the state constitution compelled the sanctioning of same-sex marriages only strengthened the resolve of most Hoosier lawmakers to resist this form of nuptial freedom.

Such single-minded opposition, however, did not emerge in response to the custody claims of gay and lesbian parents. Instead, Indiana judges used their discretion to make case-by-case determinations. Thus, in 1981, the state appellate court explained that "homosexuality standing alone without evidence of any adverse effect upon the welfare of the child does not render the homosexual parent unfit as a matter of law to have custody of the child."[83] Other decisions held that a mother could not be deemed unfit because she lived in a trailer and had engaged in a previous lesbian relationship and that a court could rationally restrict the visitation rights of a homosexual parent.[84] The contrasting responses to these custodial claims indicated both the nature of the transformation of family law in Indiana during the era and the ways in which those changes continued to frame domestic relations law debates in the new century. They also revealed how in the most recent history of Indiana family law, as in the past, national debates over family governance had been played out within the state's borders.

One of the most famous lines penned by a Hoosier is Hoagy Carmichael's lyric refrain, "Back home again in Indiana." As this chronicle of the state's family law has demonstrated, like Carmichael, most Americans would have felt at home in the state at almost any moment in the past. Except for the anomalies of the mid-nineteenth century, sojourners to the state would have found little unusual in the state's domestic relations laws.

Consequently, the history of family law in Indiana is an apt illustration of the power of policy consensus in the American republic. Despite their freedom in the federal system to exercise autonomy in the law of domestic relations, most states have followed common policies. Variations have existed, but they generally have been variants of common domestic relations themes.[85] Even as Hoosiers embraced policy innovations, from common-law marriage in the nineteenth century to no-fault divorce in the late twentieth, the state's family law codes illustrate the process of legal diffusion. As a result, Indiana continues to be a domestic relations crossroads.

Notes

1. For the full development of this argument, see Michael Grossberg, *Governing the Hearth: Law and the Family in Nineteenth-Century America* (Chapel Hill: University of North Carolina Press, 1985). For arguments about the importance of regionalism in American family law, see Peter W. Bardaglio, *Reconstructing the Household: Families, Sex, and the Law in the Nineteenth-Century South* (Chapel Hill: University of North Carolina Press, 1995); and see Daniel W. Stowell, ed., *In Tender Consideration: Women, Families, and the Law in Abraham Lincoln's Illinois* (Urbana: University of Illinois Press, 2001).

2. For a general overview, see Michael Grossberg, "Broken Promises: Judges and the Law of Courtship," "Nuptial License: The Regulation of Weddings," and "Matrimonial Limitations: Who's Fit to Wed?" in *Governing the Hearth: Law and the Family in Nineteenth-Century America* (Chapel Hill: University of North Carolina Press, 1985), 33–152; and Hendrik Hartog, *Man and Wife in America: A History* (Cambridge, Mass.: Harvard University Press, 2000).

3. George E. Howard, *A History of American Matrimonial Institutions* (Chicago: University of Chicago Press, 1901), 3:470.

4. Noel v. Ewing, 9 Ind. 37, 48 (1857).

5. Act of February 4, 1831, ch. 63, 1831 Revised Laws of Indiana 370 (An Act to Regulate Marriages); Howard, *Matrimonial Institutions,* 3:460, 468.

6. Howard, *Matrimonial Institutions,* 3:460, 468.

7. Teter v. Teter, 101 Ind. 129 (1884); and see Howard, *Matrimonial Institutions,* 3:469–70.

8. Nancy F. Cott, *Public Vows: A History of Marriage and the Nation* (Cambridge, Mass.: Harvard University Press, 2000), 43.

9. An Act regulating Divorces, § 1, provided that divorce could be obtained (1) in the case that either of the parties was already married at the time of the marriage; (2) for impotency or adultery; (3) when a wife abandoned a husband for a period of two or more years, or when she lived in adultery, or when she was convicted of a felony; (4) when a husband abandoned his wife for a period of two or more years, lived in adultery, or was convicted of a felony; (5) when a husband's treatment of his wife was "extremely barbarous and inhuman"; or, (6) "for any other cause, and in any other case where the court, in their discretion, shall consider it reasonable and proper that a divorce should be granted." Act of January 17, 1831, ch. 31, 1831 Revised Laws of Indiana 213 (An Act regulating Divorces).

10. Act of February 17, 1838, ch. 31, 1838 Revised Statutes of the State of Indiana 242 (An Act regulating Divorces); see also Cott, *Public Vows,* 50.

11. Norma Basch, *Framing American Divorce: From the Revolutionary Generation to the Victorians* (Berkeley: University of California Press, 1999), 214n4.

12. Cited in Charles Kettleborough, ed., *Constitution Making in Indiana: A Source Book of Constitutional Documents with Historical Introduction and Critical Notes* (Indianapolis: Indiana Historical Commission, 1916), 1:167–68.

13. Cited in Roderick Phillips, *Putting Asunder: A History of Divorce in Western Society* (Cambridge: Cambridge University Press, 1988), 456.

14. In 1824, legislators adopted an "omnibus" clause that permitted a divorce "in all cases where the court in its discretion" deemed it "just and reasonable." Howard, *History of Matrimonial Institutions*, 3:115. For this wording, Howard cites Indiana Revised Laws (1824), 156, 157.

15. Act of January 17, 1831, ch. 31, 1831 Revised Laws of Indiana 213 (An Act regulating Divorces).

16. Ritter v. Ritter, 5 Blackf. 81, 89, 90 (1839).

17. See in general Peggy A. Rabkin, *Fathers to Daughters: The Legal Foundations of Female Emancipation* (Westport, Conn.: Greenwood, 1980); Norma Basch, *In the Eyes of the Law: Women, Marriage, and Property in Nineteenth-Century New York* (Ithaca, N.Y.: Cornell University Press, 1982).

18. *Report of the Debates and Proceedings of the Convention for the Revision of the Constitution of the State of Indiana* (Indianapolis: A. H. Brown, 1850). An 1852 act provided that a married woman's lands could not be held liable for her husband's debts and that the profits from such lands "shall be her separate property, as fully as if she was [*sic*] unmarried." However, the same law prohibited her from encumbering or

conveying the title to the land unless her husband joined in the deed. Act of May 31, 1852, ch. 52, § 5, 1852 Revised Statutes of the State of Indiana 321 (An Act touching the marriage relation and liabilities incident thereto).

19. In 1879, Indiana wives were granted the legal right to carry out business ventures and perform labor and services in their own names. Profits from such activities were considered married women's sole and separate property. Act of March 25, 1879, ch. 67, § 2, 1879 Laws of the State of Indiana 160 (An Act concerning married women). Additionally, in 1881, married women's legal disability to enter into contracts was removed (with the exception noted in the preceding footnote). Act of April 16, 1881, ch. 60, § 1, 1881 Laws of the State of Indiana 527, 527–28.

20. See generally Grossberg, *Governing the Hearth,* 23–43.

21. Berkshire v. Caley, 157 Ind. 1, 8, 60 N.E. 696, 699 (1901); and for general overviews of custody law change in the era, see Grossberg, *Governing the Hearth,* ch. 7; Mary Ann Mason, "From Fathers' Rights to Mothers' Love: The Transformation of Child Custody Law in the First Century of the New Republic, 1790–1890," ch. 2 in *From Father's Property to Children's Rights: The History of Child Custody in the United States* (New York: Columbia University Press, 1994).

22. See Jamil Zainaldin, "The Emergence of a Modern American Family Law: Child Custody, Adoption, and the Courts, 1776–1851," *Northwestern University Law Review* 73 (March–April 1979): 1038; Grossberg, *Governing the Hearth,* 268–80; E. Wayne Carp, *Family Matters: Secrecy and Disclosure in the History of Adoption* (Cambridge, Mass.: Harvard University Press, 1998), 1–35.

23. Dunn v. Means, 48 Ind. App. 383, 387, 95 N.E. 1015, 1016 (1911); see also Cooley v. Powers, 63 Ind. App. 59, 113 N.E. 382 (1916).

24. See James Willard Hurst, *Law and Social Order in the United States* (Ithaca, N.Y.: Cornell University Press, 1977), ch. 5.

25. James H. Madison, *The Indiana Way: A State History* (Bloomington: Indiana University Press, 1986), 33–34, 49, 107.

26. Act of January 28, 1818, ch. 5, § 59, 1818 Laws of the State of Indiana 94 (An Act to reduce into one act, all the acts and parts of acts relative to Crime and Punishment).

27. For example, on January 20, 1842, the General Assembly approved An Act to prohibit the amalgamation of whites and blacks, ch. 130, 1842 General Laws of the State of Indiana 142. Section one of this act stated: "*Be it enacted by the General Assembly of the State of Indiana,* That hereafter no negro man, mulatto, or any man having one-eighth of negro blood shall be permitted to marry any white woman of this State, nor shall any white man be permitted to marry any black woman, mulatto, or any woman having one-eighth part or more of negro blood."

28. Cott, *Public Vows,* 43.

29. State v. Gibson, 36 Ind. 389, 403 (1871).

30. Ibid., 403, 404.

31. Grossberg, *Governing the Hearth,* 138–40.

32. See generally Richard Wires, *The Divorce Issue and Reform in Nineteenth-Century Indiana* (Muncie, Ind.: Ball State University Press, 1976).

33. Cited in Basch, *Framing American Divorce,* 60; see also Hartog, *Man and Wife,* 264–65.

34. Val Nolan Jr., "Indiana: Birthplace of Migratory Divorce," *Indiana Law Journal* 26 (Fall 1950): 515, 517–20.

35. McQuigg v. McQuigg, 13 Ind. 257, 258 (1859).

36. The information on the Greeley-Owen exchange is drawn from Phillips, *Putting Asunder,* 457–58.

37. Cited in Cott, *Public Vows,* 51–52.

38. By 1859, the legislature had mandated that a party seeking an Indiana divorce be a bona fide resident of Indiana for one year before filing a divorce petition and a resident of the county in which it was filed at the time of the filing. The petitioner had to prove his or her residency status to the satisfaction of the court. Act of March 4, 1859, ch. 60, § 1, 1859 Laws of the State of Indiana 108. By 1873, the residency requirement had been raised to two years, and the petitioner was required to have resided in the county where the petition was filed for at least six months prior to the filing of the divorce petition. Act of March 10, 1873, ch. 43, § 7, 1873 Laws of the State of Indiana 107, 109. Additionally, the same 1873 revision to Indiana's divorce laws eliminated the contested omnibus clause and declared that divorce could be obtained for only the seven following reasons: 1) adultery; 2) impotency; 3) abandonment for a period of two years; 4) cruel and inhuman treatment of either spouse by the other; 5) habitual drunkenness of either spouse; 6) a husband's failure to make reasonable provisions for his family for a period of two years; and, finally, 7) the conviction of either party of an "infamous crime." Ibid., § 8, 109.

39. Jenness v. Jenness, 24 Ind. 355, 360, 361 (1865).

40. For a fuller development of this point, see Michael Grossberg, "Balancing Acts: Crisis, Change, and Continuity in American Family Law, 1890–1990," *Indiana Law Review* 28, no. 2 (1995): 273–308.

41. In 1877, Indiana's legislature declared that, in order to marry, females must have reached sixteen years of age and males must have reached eighteen years of age. Additionally, the parties could not be more closely related than second cousins. Act of March 5, 1877, ch. 54, 1877 Laws of the State of Indiana 94 (An Act to amend section first of an act entitled "An act declaritory [*sic*] of the law regulating marriages, and enforcing the provisions thereof by proper penalties, approved March 5th, 1852"). By 1905, the state had instituted a licensing provision that required parties to secure a marriage license, and the State Board of Health was designated the central administrative agency to govern marriage licenses. Parties applying for a license had to provide the following information: "the full Christian name and surnames, residence, color, occupation and birthplace of their parents, including the maiden name of the mother, together with such other facts as may be necessary to determine whether any legal impediment to the proposed marriage exists." Act of March 6, 1905, ch. 126, 1905 Laws of the State of Indiana 215, 215–17 (An Act regulating the issuance of licenses to marry).

42. As early as 1852, Indiana prohibited anyone deemed insane or idiotic from marrying. Act of March 5, 1852, ch. 67, § 2, 1852 Revised Statutes of the State of Indiana 361 (An Act declaratory of the law regulating Marriages, and enforcing the provisions thereof by proper penalties). See also Phillips, *Putting Asunder,* 509; and see generally Matthew J. Lindsay, "Reproducing a Fit Citizenry: Dependency, Eugenics,

and the Law of Marriage in the United States, 1860–1920," *Law and Social Inquiry* 23 (Summer 1998): 541, 572.

43. Alexandra Minna Stern, "Better Babies Contests at the Indiana State Fair: Child Health, Scientific Motherhood, and Eugenics in the Midwest, 1920–35," in *Formative Years: Children's Health in the United States, 1880–2000,* ed. Alexandra Minna Stern and Howard Markel (Ann Arbor: University of Michigan Press, 2002), 121–52, nn 32 and 33.

44. Buck v. Bell, 274 U.S. 200, 207 (1927). Carrie Buck was not, in point of fact, an imbecile.

45. Van Walters v. Bd. of Children's Guardians of Marion County, 132 Ind. 567, 569, 32 N.E. 568, 569 (1892). See also Frank Sullivan Jr., "Indiana as a Forerunner in the Juvenile Court Movement," *Indiana Law Review* 30, no. 1 (1997): 279, 280–81.

46. By 1885, children younger than twelve years of age were prohibited from being employed by any manufacturer of metals, machinery, iron, steel, or tobacco. Furthermore, children under twelve years of age could not work longer than eight hours per day. Act of April 13, 1885, ch. 88, § 2, 1885 Laws of the State of Indiana 219. The Indiana General Assembly increased the age limitation to fourteen years of age in 1897. Act of March 2, 1897, ch. 65, § 2, 1897 Laws of the State of Indiana 101. Even more detailed labor regulations applied to girls under age sixteen. They were prohibited from working between the hours of 10:00 PM and 6:00 AM, and, if they were employed in bakeries, mercantile establishments, laundry facilities, printing offices, or renovating works, they could not work more than sixty hours per week or ten hours per day. Act of March 2, 1899, ch. 142, 1899 Laws of the State of Indiana 231–40.

47. See, for example, Hugh D. Hindman, *Child Labor: An American History* (Armonk, N.Y.: M. E. Sharpe, 2002), 144–46.

48. Act of March 8, 1897, ch. 165, Laws of the State of Indiana (An Act concerning the education of children). The General Assembly raised the age for compulsory school attendance to age sixteen in 1913. Act of March 14, 1913, ch. 213, Laws of the State of Indiana (An Act concerning the school attendance of children); James H. Madison, *Indiana through Tradition and Change: A History of the Hoosier State and Its People, 1920–1945* (Indianapolis: Indiana Historical Society, 1982), 180–81.

49. State v. Bailey, 157 Ind. 324, 61 N.E. 730 (1901).

50. Sullivan, "Indiana as Forerunner," 286.

51. Ibid., 292, and see generally 287–97.

52. For a general discussion of these issues, see Michael Grossberg, "A Protected Childhood: The Emergence of Child Protection in America," in *American Public Life and the Historical Imagination,* ed. Wendy Gamber, Michael Grossberg, and Hendrik Hartog (South Bend, Ind.: University of Notre Dame Press), 213–39.

53. Act of March 9, 1889, ch. 11, 1889 Laws of the State of Indiana 185–88 (An Act relating to the care, custody, and binding out of children, and providing punishment for persons who cruelly treat or neglect them). Section 8 of the act provided that "any duly organized or incorporated humane society, having for one of its objects the protection of children from cruelty, may offer agents or officers employed by them to the proper authorities of any city for the purpose of being

commissioned to act as police officers through the limits of said city, for the purpose of arresting all offenders against this Act." In the same year, a Board of Children's Guardians was established for the protection of abused and neglected children. The board consisted of six members, three of whom were required to be women. Act of March 9, 1889, ch. 11, 1889 Laws of the State of Indiana 188–90 (act establishing the Board of Children's Guardians in townships with populations greater than 75,000 residents); see also Grace Abbott, *The Child and the State* (Chicago: University of Chicago Press, 1938), 8.

54. See Robert S. Lynd and Helen Merrell Lynd, *Middletown: A Study in Contemporary American Culture* (New York: Harcourt, Brace, 1929), 434.

55. Madison, *Indiana through Tradition and Change,* 171.

56. Cited in Stern, "Better Babies Contests at the Indiana State Fair," 128–29.

57. Ibid., 139.

58. Madison, *Indiana through Tradition and Change,* 321–24.

59. See, for example, Lynd, "The Houses in Which Middletown Lives," "Marriage," "Child Rearing," and "Food, Clothing, and Housework," ch. 9–12 in *Middletown,* 93–181; and see also Madison, *Indiana through Tradition and Change,* 146.

60. For a fuller discussion of these issues, see Michael Grossberg, "How to Give the Present a Past? Family Law in the United States, 1950–2000," in *Cross Currents, Family Law and Policy in the United States and England,* ed. Sanford N. Katz, John Eekelaar, and Mavis Maclean (Oxford: Oxford University Press, 2000), 1–29.

61. "Difference of Color" was eliminated as a factor contributing to a void marriage in the 1965 revision of Indiana's marriage statute. Act of February 20, 1965, ch. 15, Laws of the State of Indiana 24.

62. Indiana's first sterilization legislation was contained in its criminal procedure code. A 1907 act required all state institutions "entrusted with the care of confined criminals, idiots, rapists and imbeciles" to appoint two skilled surgeons to the institution's staff. These surgeons, in conjunction with the institution's board of managers, were given the responsibility of determining whether there was "a probability of improvement of the mental condition of the inmate," and, if there was no such probability, the surgeons were authorized to sterilize the inmate. 1907 Ind. Acts 377–78. Sexual sterilization of prisoners was ruled unconstitutional in 1921. Willams v. Smith, 190 Ind. 526, 131 N.E. 2 (1921).

In 1927, the state broadened the scope of its eugenic movement to include the insane, the feeble minded, and epileptics. Superintendents of hospitals or other state institutions were given the authority to sterilize patients in their care if such sterilization would be "for the best interests of the patient and of society." Act of March 11, 1927, ch. 241, 1927 Laws of the State of Indiana 713 (An Act to provide for the sexual sterilization of inmates of state institutions in certain cases).

Throughout the 1930s, the legislature refined its sterilization policies. Beginning in 1931, the determination of whether sterilization was warranted became a required feature of any commitment hearing. The court was required to decide the issue of the commitment as well as the issue of whether the welfare of society and the patient required sterilization. Act of March 3, 1931, ch. 50, 1931 Laws of the State of Indiana 116 (An Act providing for the sexual sterilization of feeble minded persons in certain cases, prescribing the power of the courts and defining the duties of medical examiners and the superintendent of institutions for the feeble minded in relation thereto).

By 1937, patients and inmates were given the right to appeal the sterilization decision (through their guardians) to the circuit court. Act of March 11, 1937, ch. 244, 1937 Laws of the State of Indiana 1164 (act amending the 1927 act for sexual sterilization of inmates of state institutions).

These laws remained active until their repeal in 1974. 1974 Ind. Acts 262; see also IC §§ 16-13-13-1 through 16-13-16-1 (Michie 1983). All statutes relating to Sterilization of Patients Acts of 1927 (Act of March 11, 1927, ch. 241, 1927 Laws of the State of Indiana 713 [An Act to provide for the sexual sterilization of inmates of state institutions in certain cases]), 1931 (Act of March 3, 1931, ch. 50, 1931 Laws of the State of Indiana 116 [An Act providing for the sexual sterilization of feeble minded persons in certain cases, prescribing the power of the courts and defining the duties of medical examiners and the superintendent of institutions for the feeble minded in relation thereto]), 1935 (Act of March 13, 1935, ch. 312, 1935 Laws of the State of Indiana 1502), as well as 1937's § 22-1603(a) (Sterilization—Appeal to Court) (Act of March 11, 1937, ch. 244, 1937 Laws of the State of Indiana 1164 [act amending the 1927 act for sexual sterilization of inmates of state institutions]) were repealed by 1974 Ind. Acts 262.

63. Act of March 11, 1935, ch. 208, 1935 Laws of the State of Indiana 1009 (An Act to promote public morals . . .).

64. Pennington v. Stewart, 212 Ind. 553, 559, 10 N.E.2d 619, 622 (1937).

65. Argiroff v. Argiroff, 215 Ind. 297, 19 N.E.2d 560 (1939). See also Langdon v. Langdon, 204 Ind. 321, 183 N.E. 400 (1932).

66. Estate of Dittman v. Biesenbach, 124 Ind. App. 198, 115 N.E.2d 125 (1953).

67. Anderson v. Anderson, 235 Ind. 113, 131 N.E.2d 301 (1956).

68. Marla K. Clark, "Marriage," *West's Indiana Law Encyclopedia,* vol. 19 (Eagan, Minn.: West, 2003), 223–61; and see In re Sutherland's Estate, 246 Ind. 234, 204 N.E.2d 520 (1965); Reger v. Reger, 242 Ind. 302, 177 N.E.2d 901 (1961); Anderson v. Anderson, 235 Ind. 113, 131 N.E.2d 301 (1956); Bolkovac v. State, 229 Ind. 294, 98 N.E.2d 250 (1951).

69. For historical analyses of these issues see Basch, *Framing American Divorce;* Phillips, *Putting Asunder;* Herbert Jacob, *Silent Revolution: The Transformation of Divorce Law in the United States* (Chicago: University of Chicago Press, 1988); and J. Herbie DiFonzo, *Beneath the Fault Line: The Popular and Legal Culture of Divorce in Twentieth-Century America* (Charlottesville: University of Virginia Press, 1997).

70. The Domestic Relations Counseling Bureau was established on February 17, 1972, by P.L. 202, 1972 Ind. Acts 955, which stated that "such bureau shall provide counseling service to parties to divorce, separation, or annulment actions filed in said courts and referred to it by the various judges and with the intent to assist in a reconciliation of the parties, in the care and treatment of children, if any, and in possible solution of any marriage problems, all in promotion of the general welfare. The bureau may also receive cases referred to it by attorneys of law, the ministry, or other agencies before a divorce action is filed, and may counsel other married couples who seek its services of their own volition." Ibid., 956.

71. In re Gault, 387 U.S. 1 (1967); In re Winship, 397 U.S. 358 (1970); McKeiver v. Pennsylvania, 403 U.S. 528 (1971); Act of March 10, 1978, 1978 Ind. Acts 1196 (codified as amended in scattered sections of the Indiana Code); and see Sullivan, "Indiana as Forerunner," 301–3.

72. See generally Eva R. Rubin, *The Supreme Court and the American Family: Ideology and Issues* (Westport, Conn.: Greenwood, 1986), 28–38; Robert L. Stenger, "Expanding Constitutional Rights of Illegitimate Children, 1968–1980," *Journal of Family Law* 19, no. 3 (1980–81): 407, 408–9.

73. S. M. V. v. Littlepage, 443 N.E.2d 103 (Ind. App. 1982).

74. Uniform Marriage and Divorce Act, § 402, 9A U.L.A. 561 (1987), 9A U.L.A. 287 (1994).

75. *West's Indiana Law Encyclopedia,* vol. 10A, § 201 (St. Paul, Minn.: West, 1983), 398; and for a general discussion of changes in the era, see Mason, *From Father's Property to Children's Rights,* 121–85.

76. Maloblocki v. Maloblocki, 646 N.E.2d 358 (Ind. App. 1995).

77. In re Marriage of Myers, 180 Ind. App. 284, 387 N.E.2d 1360 (1979).

78. The provisions of joint legal custody are governed by Indiana Code §§ 31-17-2-13 through 31-17-2-15. The court is permitted to award joint legal custody if it finds that such custody would be in the best interests of the child. Ind. Code. Ann. § 31-17-2-3 (Michie 1999). In deciding whether to award joint legal custody, the court must first consider whether the persons awarded joint custody would agree to such an award. Additionally, the court must consider other factors, including 1) the fitness and suitability of the parties awarded joint custody; 2) whether the parties will be willing and able to communicate and cooperate; 3) the wishes of the child (more consideration is given to this factor if the child is fourteen years of age or older); 4) whether the child has a "close and beneficial relationship" with the parties awarded joint custody; 5) whether the parties awarded joint custody live near each other and will continue to do so; and, finally, 6) the "the nature of the physical and emotional environment in the home" of each of the parties. Ind. Code Ann. § 31-17-2-15 (Michie 1999). However, an award of joint legal custody does not require an equal division of physical custody of the child. Ind. Code Ann. § 31-17-2-14 (Michie 1999). And for judicial acceptance of joint custody see *Eyler v. Eyler,* 492 N.E.2d 1071 (Ind. 1986).

79. Theodore Caplow et al., *Middletown Families: Fifty Years of Change and Continuity* (Minneapolis: University of Minnesota Press, 1982), 49.

80. Baehr v. Lewin, 74 Haw. 645, 852 P.2d 44 (1993); and Baehr v. Miike, 23 Fam. L. Rep. (BNA) 2001 (December 10, 1996).

81. The Defense of Marriage Act, Public Law 104-199, was enacted on September 21, 1996, "to define and protect the institution of marriage." Defense of Marriage Act, 28 U.S.C. § 1738C (2000). Cott, *Public Vows,* 218, and see generally 212–21; and Mark Strasser, *Legally Wed: Same-Sex Marriage and the Constitution* (Ithaca, N.Y.: Cornell University Press, 1997).

82. An Act to Amend the Indiana Code concerning family law, P.L. 198-1997, 1997 Ind. Acts 2879; Indiana Code 31-11-1-1 provides: Sec. 1. (a) Only a female may marry a male. Only a male may marry a female. (b) A marriage between persons of the

same gender is void in Indiana even if the marriage is lawful in the place where it is solemnized. Ind. Code. Ann. § 31-11-1-1 (Michie 1999).

83. D. H. v. J. H., 418 N.E.2d 286 (Ind. App. 1981); and see Mason, *From Father's Property to Children's Rights,* 127–28.

84. Pryor v. Pryor, 714 N.E.2d 743 (Ind. App. 1999); Marlow v. Marlow, 702 N.E.2d 733 (Ind. App. 1998); and, for a general overview, see Mason, *From Father's Property to Children's Rights,* 127–28.

85. It is difficult to document the exact range of American family variations at any one particular time. The most exhaustive example is Chester G. Vernier's multi-volume study published in the mid-1930s: *American Family Laws: A Comparative Study of the Family Law of the Forty-eight American States, Alaska, the District of Columbia and Hawaii (to Jan. 1, 1931)* (Stanford, Calif.: Stanford University Press, 1931–38), 5 vols.

FIVE

Sheila Suess Kennedy

THE POOR YOU HAVE ALWAYS WITH YOU

The Problem of the "Sturdy Beggar"

The philosopher George Santayana warned that those who do not know their own history are doomed to repeat it. That admonition is especially pertinent to discussions of social welfare in Indiana, where assistance programs reflect historic attitudes about poverty and where service delivery is largely a product of the state's political culture. In Indiana, as elsewhere, supporters of social welfare programs and critics of those programs are still arguing about policies dating to 1349, when England enacted the Statute of Laborers, prohibiting alms, or charity, for those who had the ability to work—that is, to "sturdy beggars."[1] This first attempt to deal with what later would be called welfare was not about providing assistance; it was about forcing people to work.

Not until 1601, in the reign of Elizabeth I, would a tax be levied to provide material assistance to the poor. The Elizabethan Poor Law established three categories of needy people: children without parents (or at least without parents who could care for them adequately); the able-bodied; and the incapacitated, helpless, or "worthy" poor. Vagrants, or able-bodied persons who refused to work, could be "committed to a house of correction, whipped, branded, put in pillories and stoned, or even put to death."[2] Help was limited to the deserving, or "worthy," poor.

The Elizabethan Poor Law's distinction between the "deserving" and "undeserving" poor was carried to the colonies and reproduced in the laws of the various states, including Indiana. It was the model that settlers brought to the New World; it was the approach adopted by the original thirteen colonies; and, as people moved west, it was the approach incorporated in the Ordinance of 1787, which prescribed rules for governing the Northwest Territory.[3] To a significant extent, the distinction between the deserving and undeserving poor, the categorizing of people needing assistance, and the emphasis on work have remained the primary lens through which both federal and state policymakers view social welfare and poverty issues.

The belief that poverty is evidence of divine disapproval—and that virtue is rewarded by material success—was held by a number of the early Protestants who settled the colonies, and that belief has continued to influence American law and culture. By the early 1900s, moral opprobrium directed at the poor had found an ally in science, and poverty issues were caught up in the national debate between social Darwinists like William Graham Sumner and their critics—notably, William Jennings Bryan.[4] In language reminiscent of earlier admonitions against rewarding "sturdy beggars," Sumner wrote:

> But the weak who constantly arouse the pity of humanitarians and philanthropists are the shiftless, the imprudent, the negligent, the impractical, and the inefficient, or they are the idle, the intemperate, the extravagant, and the vicious. Now the troubles of these persons are constantly forced upon public attention, as if they and their interests deserved especial consideration, and a great portion of all organized and unorganized effort for the common welfare consists in attempts to relieve these classes of people.[5]

It was not until the Great Depression that blaming the poor for their own poverty became a minority position and that American lawmakers widely acknowledged the need for some sort of social safety net. It would be a mistake, however, to assume that the dislocations of the 1930s or the passage of New Deal legislation changed Americans' deeply rooted beliefs about their own history or self-reliance. As social historian Stephanie Coontz has written, "Most Americans agree that prior to federal 'interference' in the 1930s, the self-reliant family was the standard social unit of our society. Dependencies used to be cared for within the 'natural family economy' and even today the healthiest families 'stand on their own two feet.'"[6]

Coontz and others have demonstrated that this widely held belief in self-sufficiency is inconsistent with the reality of the American experience. Pioneer families owed their existence to massive federal land grants and state economic investment in new lands. In the early twentieth century, western populations depended on government construction of dams and federally subsidized irrigation projects. During the Depression, electrification projects and other government subsidies were critical to the survival of the family farm. In the 1950s, Coontz notes, suburban families were "more dependent on government handouts than any so-called 'underclass' in recent U.S. history," thanks to the GI Bill and the National Defense Education Act, which subsidized the educations of a whole generation;[7] the Federal Housing Authority and the Veterans Administration, which allowed Americans to purchase homes with artificially low down payments and subsidized interest rates; and billions of dollars of government-financed inventions, production processes, and research, which enabled businesses to flourish.

By the 1970s, Social Security and industry pensions had virtually wiped out the historic tendency for the elderly to be the poorest sector of the population. Even between 1965 and 1971, during the height of Great Society antipoverty initiatives, 75 percent of American social welfare dollars went to those who were not poor.[8] Nevertheless, despite the lessons of the Depression and the documented, pervasive reliance of middle- and upper-income families on a wide variety of government assistance programs, acceptance of poor relief and welfare continues to be viewed by many Americans, including Hoosiers, as evidence of a moral or character deficit. That viewpoint is woven into the fabric of Indiana's law.

The State Welfare System

Historically, Indiana's approach to social welfare has mirrored the policies of the nation as a whole. This correspondence should not surprise anyone: the publication of *Middletown* by Robert and Helen Lynd in 1929 put Muncie, Indiana, on the map as the typical American community, and other studies have used Indianapolis as a similar example of the quintessential American city.[9] Furthermore, since the 1930s, welfare policies in all the states have been largely responsive to federal mandates. Certain elements of Indiana's welfare system, however, can best be understood in the context of the state's particular legal and political culture.

Indiana's constitution, unlike the constitutions of many other states, vests legal authority primarily in state-level institutions. There are no city charters, and home rule continues to elude municipal and county officials despite numerous efforts to legislate greater local autonomy. Governmental subdivisions have only such authority as has been specifically granted by the state, and, not surprisingly, they zealously guard what power they do have.

Indiana traditionally has had a vibrant two-party system. Although the state has been predictably Republican in presidential contests for at least the last thirty years, Democrats are well represented in Indiana's congressional delegation and hold a majority of city halls. The legislature is closely divided; in 2004, for example, Republicans controlled the Senate, and Democrats the House, confirming a trend that began in the late twentieth century. Local politics, however, tell a different story; nearly all local jurisdictions are controlled by one party. Because party affiliation in Indiana originally was rooted in opposing ethnic or religious cultures, the identity of the dominant party in any town or county is often a function of the ethnicity of those who originally settled there.

Although America as a whole is religiously diverse (albeit overwhelmingly Christian), many, if not most, regions of the country have been shaped by a majority religious culture. Massachusetts reflects its Catholic heritage, North Carolina's culture is recognizably Baptist, Utah's is predominantly Mormon, and so on. In Indiana, however, very few, if any, political subdivisions have a dominant religious culture. That religious diversity—and the corresponding need to bridge divisions growing out of competing worldviews—has contributed to the state's political culture in a number of ways, not least by fostering what George Geib, a noted Indiana political historian, has called a "back stairs" or "let's make a deal" political climate, in which negotiation and accommodation are preferred over confrontation.[10]

Because state-level politics historically have been competitive, in the early days of the state, so-called floating voters were prized, and their votes were bought with patronage. Geib argues that the first "deserving poor" in Indiana were "floating voters" who would move to a one-party city or town, pledge support to its dominant party, and be rewarded with employment. "Politics in Indiana is rarely about issues," Geib notes. "It is about patronage. Failure to understand the importance of patronage is failure to understand Indiana's political history."[11] The importance of patronage in Indiana history explains many things, including the persistence of the township trustee system of poor relief.

The legal organization of social welfare came hard on the heels of the passage of the Ordinance of 1787, which set up governmental structures for the Northwest Territory, including the areas that became Indiana. In 1790, the territorial legislature authorized the organization of counties and their division into townships and provided for "overseers of the poor."[12] The overseers were to investigate cases of need and report back to justices of the peace, who had the power to grant aid. A 1795 law established "outdoor relief" in the Northwest Territory. (Indoor and outdoor relief were terms carried over from the Elizabethan Poor Law. Outdoor relief meant that assistance was provided to the poor in their normal place of residence. Indoor relief meant the workhouse or the asylum.)[13] These laws provided for the appointment of two agents, or overseers, in each township and empowered them to levy taxes to establish workhouses for poor people who were able to work. Children whose parents were dead or otherwise unable to care for them could be bound out by the agents as apprentices. In 1799, the law was amended to allow the agents to take bids and similarly "farm out" to successful bidders those adults who were unable to support themselves.[14] In 1852, township trustees were made responsible for poor relief.

Poor relief was part of the criminal justice system, a circumstance that continued until 1936. The very first institutions established in Indiana were county jails and county poor asylums; the jails consisted of two apartments, one for debtors and another for lawbreakers. The first county poor asylum opened in 1824; twenty-five years later, every county had one. The language of the Indiana constitutions of 1816 and 1851 suggests that these facilities were intended to be homes for the aged and infirm, but the reality was quite different. "The poor asylum was, in reality, an unlikely combination of mental institution, nursing home, hospital, agricultural enterprise, retirement village, orphanage, and refuge for the blind, deaf, retarded or physically handicapped—or any combination of these."[15] The only reference to the sick in the poor law of 1795 was in an instruction to the overseer for handling cases in which the poor residing in one jurisdiction would "sicken or die" in another. Not until 1838 were overseers required to provide medical aid for poor people who needed it.[16]

In the years leading up to the Civil War, a number of private citizens and voluntary associations expressed concern about conditions in county poor asylums and worked to provide specialized institutions for the mentally ill and for blind or deaf children. In 1844, Indiana opened the Asylum for the Education of the Deaf and Dumb (now the Indiana School for the

Deaf) and, three years later, the Indiana Institute for the Education of the Blind (now the Indiana School for the Blind). Private orphans' homes were established in an effort to keep children out of poor asylums, where they got little education and were surrounded by adults who were likely to be either sick or criminal. Partly in response to these voluntary efforts, the legislature authorized county commissioners to establish county orphanages and to employ a matron to care for the children. County homes soon became important centers of patronage for the commissioners, who hired their staffs and chose the vendors to furnish their supplies. Other specialized institutions were established in due course. In 1845, the legislature authorized construction of the first of several facilities for the mentally ill, the Indiana Lunatic Asylum. Gradually, institutions intended for the poor or disabled were separated from those meant to serve the needs of criminal justice.

In the 1880s, a national reform movement emerged to address issues of social welfare, spurred in part by the graphic depictions of poverty in the novels of Charles Dickens and in part by a growing recognition that the systems in place were "expensive, inadequate and unsatisfactory."[17] In Indiana, patronage abuses were widespread and ranged from poor management to outright fraud. Scandals were frequent. "State employees were more often than not patronage employees who could be, and often were, replaced whenever one political party defeated the other. Superintendencies of the state hospitals, prisons and reformatories were particular political plums."[18]

In 1889, pressured by reformers, the legislature established a Board of State Charities to investigate the entire system of public charitable and penal institutions and make annual reports and recommendations for improvement. Over the ensuing decades, the state board was given additional duties, and county boards were established; however, none of them was given meaningful authority. They were advisory only, and depended upon appeals to lawmakers and to the public conscience for their effectiveness.[19]

Legal responses to the scandals of the late 1800s also affected township trustees. Prior to 1897, township assistance had been funded by county budgets. In 1895, when trustees were first required to report on their activities, more than 70,000 people out of a total state population of less than 2.2 million were receiving poor relief.[20] Disclosure of the numbers caused a sensation. "In 1897, because of allegedly irresponsible expenditures, townships were required to pay for all assistance which they authorized. Local financing was thus adopted to encourage fiscal responsibility. The 1897 Acts also provided for more detailed reporting and accounting procedures."[21] The change, it was argued, would act as a check on the trustees' activities and provide an "incentive for reducing costs, and a means of discouraging pauperism in Indiana."[22] Two years later, a second law required the trustees to cooperate with private charities and to provide relief "without encouraging economic dependency."[23]

For the next several years, Indiana's patchwork, reactive approach to social welfare continued. The government established state and county hospitals and provided for state supervision of the care provided to dependent and neglected children. Children were also the intended beneficiaries of a number of so-called protective laws that included mandatory school attendance, prohibitions against importation of dependent children, child labor laws, and penalties for parents who neglected their children. In 1919, a Mother's Aid law authorized financial assistance to needy mothers in order to prevent the breakup of families for economic reasons.[24]

The Great Depression brought needs of an entirely different magnitude. Poor relief always had been considered a state and local responsibility, and President Herbert Hoover did not believe that the federal government should get involved, no matter how dire the circumstances. Instead, he urged voluntary agencies to fill the needs of the nation's new poor—needs they were manifestly unable to meet. When Franklin Roosevelt was inaugurated in 1933, he was faced with an unprecedented level of destitution. Roosevelt's response was to implement a number of national public works programs: the Civilian Conservation Corps, the Public Works Administration, the National Youth Administration, and the Works Progress Administration (later the Works Projects Administration) provided work and dignity to millions. By keeping the wages they paid lower than those paid by the private sector, the programs encouraged participants to take private employment once it became available.

In addition, funds for poor relief were provided to the states through the Emergency Relief and Reconstruction Act of 1932[25] and the Federal Emergency Relief Act of 1933.[26] The effect of such legislation was to transfer responsibility for a large number of poor citizens from township and county units of government to state and federal government agencies. The Federal Emergency Relief Administration, created by the act of the same name, was the first national relief agency. Although its main programs were emergency work efforts, it also directed cash payments to needy individuals who passed a means test.

At the beginning of the Depression, Indiana's only resources for meeting the needs of the unemployed were the township trustees and private philanthropy. In 1933, the Indiana legislature created a Governor's Commission on Unemployment Relief; the commission eventually assumed responsibility for determining which counties were entitled to federal aid and for ensuring compliance with the federal rules that came with the money.[27] That same year, as part of a reorganization of Indiana government, the Board of State Charities became part of the executive branch, under Governor Paul McNutt, and was renamed the State Department of Public Welfare.[28]

In his 1935 State of the Union message, President Roosevelt announced his intent to propose legislation that would provide unemployment insurance, old-age insurance, and benefits for children, mothers, and the handicapped and that would address "other aspects of dependency."[29] Roosevelt's proposals were patterned after social insurance measures that had been in place in much of Europe since the early 1900s. Congress responded by passing the Social Security Act of 1935.[30] Social welfare funding became a major item in the federal budget and ushered in an increasingly complex relationship between the federal government and the states in the funding and operating of the social safety net.

The Social Security Act conditioned eligibility for funds on state financial and operational participation and on the designation of a single state agency to administer the program. The Welfare Act of 1936,[31] referenced above, brought Indiana into compliance: it replaced the Board of State Charities with the State Department of Public Welfare, created county-level welfare agencies, and abolished a variety of existing agencies and pension systems.[32] The passage of the Welfare Act established the framework within which the state operates to this day: welfare programs are supervised by the state but administered by the counties. Politically, such a system makes enormous sense in a state like Indiana, where control of state-level patronage can change with the next election but local political control and patronage are relatively stable. Such considerations, along with Indiana's general suspicion of state control, outweighed arguments for a more centralized welfare system; even after the state assumed much more direct control of county welfare offices, those same considerations protected—and continue to protect—the original township trustee system.

From 1936 until the welfare reform efforts of the 1990s, the State Department of Public Welfare administered state and federal legislative initiatives and responded to the shifting priorities they represented. State participation in Medicaid, which Congress enacted in 1965, required significant financial and administrative resources. (Indiana, characteristically, was among the last states to participate in the program). Periodically, the department reorganized, regrouped, and added or subtracted program responsibilities. Probably the most significant reorganization occurred in 1991, during the Bayh administration, when programs that had been scattered throughout state government were consolidated with the State Department of Public Welfare into a massive new agency, named the Family and Social Services Administration (FSSA).

The township trustee system has an even longer pedigree. "Since 1897, with the emergence of the role of the township trustee as chief administrator," Louis Rosenberg noted in 1973, "township level financing and general assistance have not been significantly changed."[33] The statement was still true in the first years of the twenty-first century, despite the systemic defects that Rosenberg and many others have identified.

Township trustees administer what is sometimes called general assistance. Unlike most federal and state welfare programs, general assistance is not categorical, that is, it does not require that a recipient fall within a specified category of person entitled to aid. Trustees have discretion to provide virtually any goods or services in emergencies and considerable discretion in other situations. Trustees can—and frequently do—hire family members for staff positions, pay rent for offices located in their own homes, and reward political allies by listing them as preferred vendors. (Trustees do not give cash assistance; instead, they issue vouchers for goods and services. Those vouchers are redeemed by "approved" vendors.) The trustee has final authority over the township assistance program, subject only to supervision by an elected township advisory board and the State Board of Accounts. The jurisdiction of the State Board of Accounts is limited to assuring that monies are not stolen or misappropriated; it has no authority to review the manner in which aid is dispensed, the adequacy of that aid, or the consistency of different townships' operations.[34]

General assistance remained important in Indiana even after the introduction of federal categorical programs, because the state and federal social safety nets left so many gaps. Under the Aid to Families with Dependent Children (AFDC, previously called Aid to Dependent Children) program, families with children whose parents were both in the home and not disabled were generally ineligible for assistance. A single man who was neither aged nor disabled was not eligible. Poor families without children were ineligible. Those who were temporarily needy or waiting for approval to participate in a welfare program fell outside the safety net.[35] Welfare reform has done little to change that situation or to fill those gaps.

Even people receiving welfare often did not receive an amount sufficient to live on. A report issued in 1972 by the Community Services Council of Metropolitan Indianapolis calculated that an Old Age Assistance recipient without other income would be able to cover only 43 percent of basic needs with the maximum allowable benefit.[36] Payments under other programs were similarly inadequate. Although Indiana always has been home to a robust nonprofit sector, private charity alone has never been sufficient. In 1967, private agencies in Marion County provided approximately 5 percent of the total amount of general and emergency relief distributed in the county.[37] The situation today is not appreciably different, and the need for general assistance has not abated.

Because of the inadequacy of benefits and the inability of private charity to fill the gaps, township general assistance has often meant the difference between eating and going hungry. Unfortunately, the system is wasteful and incredibly inefficient. It has resisted efforts at reform, however, largely because it continues to serve as an important source of patronage for local political parties and for the trustees, who wield considerable—if largely unrecognized—political power in the state.

The defects identified by Louis Rosenberg in 1973 still characterize the system thirty years later. Those defects are both administrative and constitutional.

- Because the law provides that every township have its own trustee and poor relief system, there are no economies of scale. Each of Indiana's 92 counties and 1,008 townships supports an office with administrative staff and overhead, even in small or thinly populated townships where overhead costs easily exceed the relatively minimal sums spent for actual poor relief. A 1972 Indiana Welfare Task Force study found that county-level welfare offices administered relief at a cost substantially lower than that incurred by township trustees.[38]
- Furthermore, the trustee system prevents resources from being allocated in accordance with need. Indiana's poor are not distributed evenly through the state; they are concentrated in a few urban centers, notably Center Township in Marion County and Calumet Township in Lake County. Those townships periodically face fiscal crises; in

the past, Marion County has had to issue bonds to cover poor relief costs that exceeded available revenues.

- Trustee poor relief must be funded from township tax revenues. The tax bases of the townships—the smallest unit of Indiana government—vary as widely as the population of poor residents, leading to significant discrepancies in township abilities to fund poor relief. This raises serious questions about uniformity and equal treatment. Studies of the system have found substantial disparities in benefits.[39]
- The ability of township trustees to exercise discretion is both a strength and a weakness. Discretion allows help that is tailored to real need, but the absence of standards also invites abuse. Determination of eligibility, the amount and duration of assistance, and the selection of vendors authorized to accept the vouchers issued for goods and services are all decisions made by the trustee, and checks on the exercise of that discretion are minimal in all but the most populous townships.
- There are serious questions of due process—or absence of due process—raised by township assistance laws and practices. The general lack of standards, particularly when coupled with the inadequate notice and hearing provisions that have characterized the highly informal township assistance process, invite due process violations. This is especially troubling because applicants for township poor relief are unlikely to have the resources to recognize the violations, much less to litigate them. Trustees are seldom held constitutionally accountable by those they are supposed to serve.

There have been periodic efforts to consolidate, reform, or even eliminate township poor relief, but constituencies for such changes have been small. The trustees are well organized and politically influential, and poor relief is their major remaining responsibility. The system may be costly, inefficient, and frequently unfair, but significant legislative change appears unlikely. Those changes that have occurred usually have been prompted by litigation, and mostly in the federal courts and stemming from cases originating elsewhere, such as *Goldberg v. Kelly,* in which the U.S. Supreme

Court addressed due process issues in the context of welfare benefits.[40] As Rosenberg noted, Indiana courts have been highly deferential to legislative delegations of discretion to the trustees, and, in any event, challenges have not been numerous.[41]

Contemporary Welfare Reform

In 1996, Congress and the Clinton administration agreed upon a massive reformation of the way in which the government provides assistance to poor Americans. The Personal Responsibility and Work Opportunity Reconciliation Act of 1996 (PRWORA), a response to years of criticism of the welfare system, was intended to "change welfare as we know it" by emphasizing work and the temporary nature of assistance.[42] PRWORA replaced AFDC, a part of the Social Security Act that had been the primary income assistance program in Indiana for sixty years.

Whatever the merits of PRWORA or the deficiencies in the system that preceded it, the legislation reflected long-standing and increasingly vocal public beliefs about self-reliance, poverty, and the proper role of government. Social critics noted that the broad constituency for self-reliance focused its criticisms of government involvement almost exclusively upon the relatively minor portion of social welfare spending that was directed to the poor. Other programs, such as Social Security and Medicare for older Americans, Pell Grants for students, Veterans Administration mortgages for veterans, and tax incentives for business, did not carry a similar stigma.

Much of the rhetoric, popular and political, was grounded in familiar historical debates about the nature of poverty and distinctions between the deserving and undeserving poor. Although the "sturdy beggar" was not explicitly invoked, policymakers spent considerable energy trying to fashion programs that would require recipients to work. Job training was made a priority, and other changes supported the "work-first" emphasis: time limits on assistance replaced categorical entitlements, and family caps precluded higher payments to families having additional children while receiving welfare.

On this issue, Indiana acted in advance of most states. In June 1994, the state requested that the federal government grant waivers of some of the federal requirements that restricted its administration of AFDC. The state asked for permission to conduct a new program as an experiment; most AFDC recipients (called the treatment group) would be subject to the new rules, but a smaller number (the control group) would remain governed by the prior AFDC regulations. The two groups would be compared in order to determine the effectiveness of the new program. Having two groups made evaluation easier, but the plan prompted a lawsuit alleging that the differential treatment violated equal protection guarantees. That suit, *N. B. v. Sybinski,* was unsuccessful.[43]

In December, a first set of waivers was granted, and changes were phased in. In anticipation of federal approval of a second set, the Indiana legislature passed a number of additional program restrictions in 1995; the federal government, however, did not grant all of the second set of waivers requested, leaving the state with a number of statutes that violated federal law.[44] Many of the changes made by the waivers anticipated portions of PRWORA, especially the work-first emphasis.

AFDC was a highly regulated matching funds program. Under PRWORA, the state receives a block grant with relatively few restrictions, to be used to provide Temporary Assistance to Needy Families (TANF). Like its predecessor, the program is administered by the most recent incarnation of the state welfare department—the Family and Social Services Administration—through county offices which provide services largely through contracts negotiated with for-profit and not-for-profit intermediaries. Since the passage of PRWORA and the subsequent lapse of Indiana's waivers, the FSSA has embraced the new approach.

Indiana also has been a national leader in the implementation of section 104 of PRWORA, known popularly as Charitable Choice. Recognizing that most social services are provided by government contractors and responding to concerns that faith-based organizations had encountered barriers to participation, Congress included a specific requirement in section 104 that states contract with faith-based social service providers on the same basis as with other nonprofits. The bill specified that pervasively sectarian organizations were not to be discriminated against, that they should be allowed to maintain hiring policies based upon their religious dictates, and that they could not be required to remove religious iconography from areas where services were delivered.[45]

President George W. Bush made Charitable Choice the centerpiece of his administration's Faith-Based Initiative, and the approach has triggered an increasingly acrimonious public debate. Because no new funds were appropriated for the social services involved and because significant numbers of religious nonprofits historically have contracted with government agencies, some scholars have suggested that the new initiative is less about adding religious contractors than about preferring some religious approaches over others. Religious providers who traditionally have partnered with the government—Catholic Charities, Lutheran Social Services, Jewish Welfare, and the like—have tended to view poverty as a social justice issue. Their services are faith-based only in the sense that they are predicated on a religious duty to feed the hungry and clothe the naked while working to change the social factors believed to cause poverty; there is little explicit religious content to their service delivery. To its critics, Charitable Choice appears to target religious providers who consider poverty evidence of personal moral failure or poor values and whose services focus upon transformation of individual recipients.[46]

The Charitable Choice initiative also assumed the existence of significant untapped resources, the hypothesized armies of compassion, or volunteers that could be enlisted to help the government fight poverty. In fiscally and legally conservative Indiana, the promise of partners who would help carry the load was particularly attractive. Beginning in 2001, the FSSA employed a private consulting firm, Crowe Chizek, at $250,000 a year, to reach out to untapped resources among religious congregations and nonprofits.[47] Workshops were held around the state, and faith-based organizations were encouraged to bid for contracts to deliver social programs, especially job training and placement. Despite those efforts, participation by new religious contractors has been minimal, perhaps inhibited by cutbacks in funding necessitated by the state's severe fiscal crisis during the first decade of the twenty-first century.

In September 2003, after five years of welfare reform, an evaluation report commissioned by the FSSA identified the goals of Indiana's welfare program: to increase client employment and to decrease reliance on welfare; to make work more financially rewarding than public assistance; and to encourage responsible parenting. Despite "consistency over time in goals and approach," the report noted substantial fluctuation in both the welfare case load and the state's economy over the period of the study. Like most states, Indiana had seen a significant decline in its case load immediately following passage of PRWORA. A very substantial part of the decline, however, was the result of robust economic growth and attendant job availability. Virtually anyone who wanted to work could find a job. The situation changed in mid-2000. The economy entered a recession, the state faced budget shortfalls, unemployment climbed, and welfare rolls grew once again.[48]

The evaluation reported a mixture of successes and failures:

> [T]he program has had real effects on participants, increasing employment and decreasing their use of welfare. The size of these effects is generally in the middle range of impacts found for welfare reform programs in other states. Indiana's program also has been cost effective, with the savings in welfare payments outweighing the costs of providing additional child care and employment services. *The observed impacts, however, have not on average resulted in increased income for families. By that measure, therefore, the program has not made families better off financially.* (emphasis added)[49]

Indiana's legal and political systems continue to reflect the state's historic priorities: keeping taxes low and protecting political patronage and the status quo. Indiana's poor citizens generally do not vote, they do not organize, and they do not make political contributions; accordingly, they rarely are high on the political agenda. The lack of legislative attention to welfare programs and poverty issues, however, does not mean that welfare in Indiana is working.

The state's administration of poor relief and welfare programs continues to be plagued by scandals and allegations of mismanagement. Throughout 2002 and 2003, a barrage of news stories alleged improprieties and patronage abuses at the FSSA, and several criminal investigations were launched. The sheer size of the agency poses problems for program managers and frustrates attempts to ensure compliance with federal rules.

Over the past twenty years, there has been a steady increase in the number of lawsuits brought to protect the rights of the needy. A very partial list of those suits is illustrative of the problems:

- *Dixon v. Davis*[50] and *Stone v. Hamilton*[51] were challenges to Indiana's administration of the food stamp program. In *Dixon,* the federal district court ordered the state to correct improper denials of food stamps and, in *Stone,* held that the state had violated federal due process guarantees by demanding that food stamp recipients reimburse overpayments that had been caused by agency error.[52]
- There have been a large number of cases involving Medicaid. Most—notably *Bailey v. Sullivan,*[53] *Taylor v.*

Sullivan,[54] *Thie v. Davis,*[55] *Jones v. Davis,*[56] *Elliot v. Humphries,*[57] *Humphreys v. Day*[58] and *Minniear v. Davis*[59]—have involved assertions that Indiana was not following federal law. Another case, *Collins ex rel. Collins v. Hamilton,*[60] successfully challenged Indiana's practice of denying funding for medically necessary inpatient psychiatric services for Medicaid-eligible children.[61] As a result of that policy, parents and guardians of such children faced a Hobson's choice—they could have their children made wards of the state in a CHINS proceeding (which effectively declares the parent unfit and deems the child "in need of services"), in which case the county of residence would be required to pay for the hospitalization, or they could keep custody of their children and forgo needed treatment.

- A long line of cases has involved the state's administration of AFDC and TANF in addition to trustee-administered poor relief, while still others have challenged provisions of Indiana landlord-tenant or creditor-debtor laws, which generally have favored the landlord and the creditor. Results of these challenges have been mixed.

Indiana has been consistently reluctant to spend money on programs benefiting the poor. Fiscal concerns repeatedly have trumped humanitarian ones. Over and over, it has been necessary to force public officials to provide even those benefits that federal law requires—indeed, virtually all of these cases have been brought on grounds of alleged state noncompliance with federal law. In this, Indiana is not markedly different from most other Midwest states. With the notable exception of Wisconsin, none of Indiana's neighbors have pioneered comprehensive welfare programs or made it a priority to address the needs of the poor.

Lost in the welter of litigation and concerns about local control and property tax levels is recognition of the mismatch between existing welfare systems and the needs of poor people. In 2001, the Center on Budget and Policy Priorities issued a report entitled *Poverty Despite Work,* focusing upon the nation's substantial and growing number of working parents unable to reach economic self-sufficiency. In 1999, Indiana reported 66,000 such families, and a child poverty rate of 11.7 percent—lower than the national average, but well above the state's overall poverty rate of 9.9 percent for that year. The number of Indiana families receiving TANF, which had declined by 52 percent during the period of rapid economic growth between 1993 and 2000, rose 38 percent between 2000 and 2002, to 48,000 families. Approximately 32,000 Indiana children lacked health insurance in 1999, and child care was unaffordable for many.[62]

In 2003, Charles Warren wrote "Prospects for Indiana Families," using data from the 2000 census to paint a similar picture. In 2000, there were 6,080,485 Hoosiers, 5.9 million of whom lived in 2.3 million households. The African American population of the state had increased by 18 percent since 1990, and the Latino population had more than doubled. The state had 556,000 married couples with children, 160,000 single mothers, and 51,400 single fathers. Median household income was just over $41,000 annually. This last figure was the lowest among the Great Lakes states and thirtieth among all of the states, and—more worrisome—had declined by 4.8 percent since 1998. The numbers were a bit better when median family income was measured; at $50,261, Indiana ranked twenty-first nationally, and fifth among the six Great Lakes states. The report found that wages in Indiana were continuing to decline as the state's economy shifted from manufacturing to service jobs, that job growth was concentrated in lower-wage industries, and that the wage gap between men and women was among the largest in the nation.[63]

Indiana's poor are disproportionately urban and, as noted previously, not well served by a costly, anachronistic township trustee system spread throughout 1,008 offices. The state welfare apparatus consists of a hodgepodge of programs, divisions, and regulations that are difficult even for lawyers to understand. Programs and administration vary from county to county. Many needy individuals do not know what their rights are, what help is available, or where to go to find out. Benefit levels are frequently too low to cover living expenses, especially for the disabled or mentally ill, who often do not have the option of employment. For the "sturdy" poor who can work, lack of access to adequate child care and transportation are often insurmountable obstacles.

Poverty levels cannot be considered in a void; they are, to a considerable extent, a function of economic development. Economic development, in turn, requires a public school system capable of producing an educated workforce and a civic culture—a quality of life—that is attractive to businesses and those they employ. Included in quality of life are public amenities of all kinds: public transportation, museums and libraries, vibrant arts communities, public parks, and universities. Indiana historically has been unwilling to invest in most such amenities, believing that the best way to attract business and create jobs is to keep taxes low. Many of the legal and policy changes that would be most meaningful to the poor—reliable public transportation, good schools with all-day kindergarten and free textbooks, affordable health care—would arguably drive economic development as well, but thus far that argument has not been persuasive to Indiana lawmakers.

The interrelatedness of these issues can be daunting, and the policy prescriptions are contested. But a start might be made by revamping the current township trustee system and making better use of the dollars now being spent on township poor relief administration. Indiana's ability to do so will depend upon the willingness of lawmakers to put the needs of the state's most vulnerable citizens ahead of local patronage considerations. If history is any guide, that willingness may be a long time coming.

Notes

The author wishes to thank Jacqueline Bowie Suess, Fran Quigley, George Geib, and Mark St. John for their invaluable assistance with research for this chapter.

1. Statute of Laborers, 23 Edw. 3, c. 1 (1349); Joel F. Handler and Yeheskel Hasenfeld, *We the Poor People: Work, Poverty, and Welfare* (New Haven, Conn.: Yale University Press, 1997), 21.

2. Poor Law, 43 Eliz., c. 2 (1601); Indiana Department of Public Welfare, *The Evolution of Indiana's Public Welfare System* (Indianapolis: Indiana Department of Public Welfare, 1985), 1.

3. Northwest Ordinance of 1787, *Journals of the Continental Congress, 1774–1789,* ed. Worthington Chauncey Ford, vol. 32 (Washington, D.C.: Government Printing Office, 1936), 334–43.

4. Andrew D. Walsh, *Religion, Economics, and Public Policy: Ironies, Tragedies, and Absurdities of the Contemporary Culture Wars* (Westport, Conn.: Praeger, 2000).

5. William Graham Sumner, "The Forgotten Man," in *Social Darwinism: Selected Essays of William Graham Sumner,* ed. William E. Leuchtenburg and Bernard Wishy (Englewood Cliffs, N.J.: Prentice Hall, 1963), 118.

6. Stephanie Coontz, *The Way We Never Were: American Families and the Nostalgia Trap* (New York: Basic Books, 1992), 69.

7. Ibid., 76.

8. Ibid., 80.

9. David J. Bodenhamer and Robert G. Barrows, eds., *Encyclopedia of Indianapolis* (Bloomington: Indiana University Press, 1994), 1–2.

10. George Geib, interview by author, September 29, 2003.

11. Ibid.

12. Indiana Dept. of Public Welfare, *Evolution,* 2.

13. Ibid.

14. Ibid., 2–3.

15. Ibid., 3.

16. Ibid., 4.

17. Ibid., 5–6.

18. Ibid., 6.

19. Ibid., 6–7.

20. Ibid., 8.

21. Louis Rosenberg, "Overseeing the Poor," *Indiana Law Review* 6, no. 3 (1973): 385.

22. Indiana Dept. of Public Welfare, *Evolution,* 8.

23. Ibid.

24. Ibid., 10.

25. 47 Stat. 713 (1932).

26. 48 Stat. 351 (1933).

27. Indiana Dept. of Public Welfare, *Evolution,* 12.

28. Ibid.

29. Ibid., 13.

30. 49 Stat. 620 (1935).

31. Welfare Act of 1936 (1936 Ind. Acts 12–80, as amended by 1986 Ind. Acts 403–72).

32. Indiana Dept. of Public Welfare, *Evolution,* 14.

33. Rosenberg, "Overseeing the Poor," 387.

34. Ibid., 391–93.

35. Ibid., 394–95.

36. Ibid., 395n54.

37. Ibid., 396n58.

38. Ibid., 400.

39. Ibid., 403.

40. Goldberg v. Kelly, 397 U.S. 254 (1970).

41. Rosenberg, "Overseeing the Poor," 396.

42. 110 Stat. 2105 (1996).

43. N. B. v. Sybinski, 724 N.E. 1103 (Ind. Ct. App. 2000).

44. Jacqueline Bowie Suess, *Welfare Reform in Indiana: A Practitioner's Desk Book* (Indianapolis: Indiana Civil Liberties Union, 1998), 3–4.

45. 110 Stat. 2105 (1996), § 104; Sheila Suess Kennedy and Wolfgang Bielfield, *Charitable Choice: First Results from the Three States* (Indianapolis: Center for Urban Policy and the Environment, 2003), 1.

46. Sheila Suess Kennedy and Wolfgang Bielfield, "Government Shekels without Government Shackles? The Administrative Challenges of Charitable Choice," *Public Administration Review* 62, no. 1 (2002): 4–11; Sheila Suess Kennedy, "Tilting the Level Playing Field: Public Administration Meets Legal Theory," *Brooklyn Journal of Law and Policy* 11, no. 2 (2003): 495–523.

47. Kennedy and Bielfield, *Charitable Choice,* 45.

48. Erik Beecroft, et al., *The Indiana Welfare Reform Evaluation: Five-Year Impacts, Implementation, Costs and Benefits, Report to the Indiana Family and Social Services Administration* (Cambridge, Mass.: Abt Associates, 2003), vi.

49. Ibid., vi–vii.

50. Dixon v. Davis, IP 98-1597-C (S.D. Ind. 1999).

51. Stone v. Hamilton, 308 F.3d 751 (7th Cir. 2002).

52. Ibid., 757–58.

53. Bailey v. Sullivan, IP 94-89-C (S.D. Ind. 1995).

54. Taylor v. Sullivan, IP 93-1728-C (S.D. Ind. 1996).

55. Thie v. Davis, 688 N.E.2d 182 (Ind. Ct. App. 1997).

56. Jones v. Davis, IP 97-1764-C (S.D. Ind. 1998).

57. Elliot v. Humphries, IP 00-1346-C (S.D. Ind. 2000).

58. Humphreys v. Day, 735 N.E.2d 837 (Ind. Ct. App. 2000).

59. Minniear v. Davis, IP 97-1502-C (S.D. Ind. 1998).

60. Collins ex rel. Collins v. Hamilton, 231 F. Supp. 2d 840 (S.D. Ind. 2002) (appeal pending).

61. Collins, 231 F. Supp. 2d at 849.

62. Center on Budget and Policy Priorities, *Poverty Despite Work in Indiana: Executive Summary* (Washington, D.C.: Center on Budget and Policy Priorities, 2001), i, ii.

63. A household consists of individuals living at the same domicile, whether or not related; a family consists of individuals related by blood, adoption, or marriage. Charles Warren, "Prospects for Indiana Families" (presentation at the Indiana Family Impact Seminar, Indianapolis, January 8, 2003).

PART III

Law and Crime

SIX

Susan K. Carpenter

"CONSPICUOUSLY ENLIGHTENED POLICY"

Criminal Justice in Indiana

It is easy to lose sight of the critical importance of state constitutions in the protection of fundamental rights. Although the federal Bill of Rights enshrined many protections against abuse of governmental power, initially it applied only to the national government, not to the states.[1] Not until the second half of the twentieth century did the U.S. Supreme Court hold that most of the requirements of the Bill of Rights applied to the states as well. The states were thus the repositories and protectors of fundamental rights long before the national government assumed that role. Each state constitution not only reflected local concerns but also embodied the revolutionary philosophy common to the U.S. Constitution and its Bill of Rights: restraint of governmental power. As one scholar notes, "Tyranny was, above all, an abuse of criminal justice: arbitrary cruelty, kangaroo courts, the use of massive power to crush dissent or terrify it into silence. The nightmare image was King George III, a despot sitting on a faraway throne, and the pathologies of English criminal justice."[2] The goal of a bill of rights was to protect citizens from the overweening power of government, a power most often expressed through the criminal process.

Indiana's first charter, the constitution of 1816, mirrored the form and language of the existing federal and state constitutions. It was far more detailed in its criminal justice provisions than was its immediate predecessor document, the Northwest Ordinance of 1787. This earlier law had provided scant protection to settlers, when compared to the rights extended to citizens of the newly independent states. Article II of the ordinance listed the rights of the accused: habeas corpus, trial by jury, the use of common-law procedures in trials, bail except in capital offenses, moderate fines, a prohibition against cruel or unusual punishments, and a bar to deprivation of liberty "but by the judgment of [one's] peers, or the law of the land."[3] The 1816 document expanded these protections significantly in its first article. Among the newly listed guarantees were searches only for reasonable cause and under warrant (the words tracked precisely those of the Fourth Amendment to the U.S. Constitution) and rights to counsel, speedy trial in open court, proportionate punishment, freedom from double jeopardy, and most of the other rights that by then had become part of the standard American lexicon.[4]

Thirty-five years later, political leaders responded to Governor James Whitcomb's call for a constitutional convention to draft a new document more in line with the democratic ethos then embraced by Hoosiers. Indiana's citizenry in 1851 approved the convention's remarkably enlightened and progressive document and thereafter honored its provisions in practice. The new constitution included a bill of rights in thirty-seven sections, fourteen explicitly involving criminal justice. Although some reflected guarantees similar to those in the Bill of Rights to the U.S. Constitution, a surprising number either were more detailed than their federal counterparts or had no federal parallel. As Indiana Supreme Court chief justice Randall T. Shepard has remarked, "Indiana was an early and noteworthy participant in using its bill of rights to defend personal liberty."[5] A salient example is the right to counsel in a criminal case.

The Sixth Amendment to the U.S. Constitution affirms that an accused citizen has a right to the assistance of counsel. Unless that citizen could afford to retain counsel, however, the Sixth Amendment guaranteed nothing until 1932, when, in *Powell v. Alabama,* the U.S. Supreme Court held that representation by counsel constituted a fundamental due process right in capital cases.[6]

In contrast, the guarantee of the right to counsel has been more than a theoretical entitlement in Indiana virtually since the ratification of the 1851 constitution. As early as 1854, in *Webb v. Baird,* the Indiana Supreme Court held that a destitute citizen charged with burglary had a right to representation by counsel at public expense: "It is not to be thought of, in a civilized community, for a moment, that any citizen put in jeopardy of life or liberty, should be debarred of counsel because he was too poor to employ such aid. No court could be respected, or respect itself, to sit and hear such a trial."[7] This decision antedated by more than a century the U.S. Supreme Court decision guaranteeing counsel in all felony cases, *Gideon v. Wainwright.*[8] The right to counsel in critical pretrial proceedings in Indiana dates from 1920.[9] Article I, section 13, of the 1851 constitution has been interpreted to assure the assistance of counsel in misdemeanor cases since 1951—a right not yet recognized as a matter of federal constitutional law.[10] Not until the 1950s and 1960s did the Warren Court hold that the Fourteenth Amendment's due process clause incorporated most of the substantive guarantees of the Bill of Rights, making them applicable to the states.

The political and philosophical climate in the mid-nineteenth century provided the inspiration for the new constitutional guarantees. The revolutionary and early national fear of tyranny exercised through criminal process persisted, but new ideas and influences pervaded the debates at the 1850 constitutional convention. Egalitarianism (albeit for white males only), individualism, and optimism about human progress created the foundations for a new approach to social control. Enlightenment-era penal theories, the religious revival known as the Second Great Awakening, and the Jacksonian emphasis on equality all influenced the elected delegates to the convention. Sovereign authority, including any power to punish, had to be limited; crimes had to be clearly defined and the process of allocating punishment controlled; and the innate rights of the citizen had to be respected. Although the state itself was a creation of the democratic majority, it still required careful management and limitation.

The new American system embodied in both Indiana constitutions distinguished itself from other forms of government, however advanced, in its emphasis on liberty and, increasingly, equality. "At the very least, liberty implied that no white man would be subject to the arbitrary rule of another and that the community of white men might rule themselves by means of majority rule."[11]

As free, self-governing citizens, these voters believed that outmoded, tyrannical laws and punishments not only were inappropriate in their new society but actually contributed to social disorder. New criminal codes therefore were to be established to secure the new relationship between authority and citizen. The 1816 Indiana constitution reflected this stance by mandating that the legislature enact a penal code "founded in the principles of reformation, and not of vindictive Justice."[12] This lofty goal, like other progressive objectives in education and social welfare, was not accomplished in the first decades of statehood, but delegates to the 1850 constitutional convention reaffirmed the goal as a fundamental principle.[13]

The convention considered criminal justice issues at length. One such issue, whether the grand jury system should continue, resulted in a compromise permitting the legislative branch to "modify, or abolish" the grand jury.[14] In the great wave of antebellum constitutional reform, only two other midwestern states, Michigan and Ohio, debated such an option, but Indiana was the only state to include a clause in its constitution permitting the legislature to take such action. The reason was stated simply: the grand jury met in secret and was ex parte in its actions, thus violating democratic principles of openness and equality.[15]

Another question before the delegates, whether the governor's power to pardon should be severely limited, produced a provision permitting reprieves, commutations, and pardons "subject to such regulations as may be provided by law" and, should the legislature so decide, only with the "advice and consent" of a council except in cases "left to his sole power by law."[16] The convention also debated whether capital punishment should be abolished and amended the bail section in the article I guarantees of rights, substituting "murder and treason" for "capital offenses" because the "Legislature might, at some future day, abolish the punishment of death. They might say that no man shall forfeit his life for any offense."[17]

The constitution of 1851 reflected its drafters' beliefs in egalitarianism, libertarian individualism, simple fairness, and human perfectibility. Its aim was the continuing reform of government, as Phineas M. Kent, delegate from Floyd County, asserted during the grand jury debate: "We, sir, are a progressive people; this is a progressive nation, and this too is an age of great and rapid advancement in all those reforms of government, which have made this the greatest among the nations of the earth."[18] The result was a number of changes in criminal justice, including provisions requiring special facilities for juveniles and proportionality of punishment and reformative justice, guaranteeing the right to jury trial in all cases, stipulating the jury as the arbiter of both law and fact, and mandating face-to-face confrontation with witnesses and representation by counsel.

Since 1851, state leaders, reformers, and the courts have undertaken even more progressive measures, amending the constitution to permit appellate review and revision of sentences and interpreting constitutional provisions, for example, to establish separate penal facilities for women. Other advances include an assurance of meaningful appellate review by providing counsel and a transcript to the indigent and the exclusion of illegally obtained evidence from criminal trials. Fundamental decency and the requirements of a civilized society have been cited frequently in support of these reforms.

It is unnecessary to examine all changes in criminal justice to understand the role of law in this most fundamental area of Indiana society, but even a cursory review suggests three central themes. In each era of the state's history, Hoosiers have sought to limit the government's power to punish; they have insisted that the law of crime and punishment be clear and regular in its administration; and they have insisted equally on basic respect for individual rights and for citizen participation in the criminal process. The following sections examine these themes.

Limitations on the Sovereign's Right to Punish

Indiana's 1851 constitution distinguishes itself in particular in regard to punishment. It is one of twenty state charters that bar cruel and unusual punishments and one of nine that mandate proportionality of punishment (three of these nine have no other restrictions on penal sanctions).[19] Indiana's constitution is one of three that require a "penal code . . . founded on the principles of reformation and not of vindictive justice."[20] Only Oregon and Alaska have demonstrated a similar commitment to these principles.

Brutal physical punishments associated with despotic government fell from favor in antebellum America. Opponents of corporal punishment called for its abolition and denounced it as a violation of the rights and civil liberties of its victims, "reflect[ing] a fundamental shift in attitudes towards institutional patterns of authority."[21] New political and personal relationships, various reform groups argued, mandated that "discipline in their respective institutions should reflect the democratic principles of the nation."[22] A citizen should not be punished as a subject would be. In 1820, for example, Indiana citizens were "shocked by the shameful spectacle of a fellow citizen tied to a sign post and flogged like a dog"[23] after a local court had ordered whipping as a punishment. Upon completion of the first Indiana prison in the 1820s, the legislature abolished whipping and substituted "equivalent terms of confinement for all offenses previously liable for punishment by stripes."[24]

This change in the nature of punishment, from whippings in the town square to institutional confinement, expressed a radical shift in how criminal behavior was explained and viewed. In a society in which all were equal, crimes were an offense by a member of a democratic society against his equals rather than affront to a hierarchical authority, such as the king or the Puritans' God. If crime was not sin or *lèse-majesté,* it required a different explanation and a new response. Physical punishment "merely repressed"[25] but did nothing to reform. Physical punishments not only were ineffective, but they missed the mark by not reaching the root causes of crime. Nineteenth-century theorists perceived human nature as malleable and rational, and "antebellum reformers declared that deviant behavior reflected bad environmental influences, not innate human depravity."[26] This new view of human nature reflected religious influences, particularly that of the Second Great Awakening, which "enhanced popular belief in the perfectibility of human beings."[27] If deviance was not innate, reform was both possible and necessary.

The penitentiary altered the deviant's environment and gave wayward individuals a chance to reform by removing them from temptation and by making them perform useful labor. Although noble aims inspired the creation of the penitentiary, the system that resulted never accomplished many of these lofty goals. Funding generally was inadequate, and prison labor in Indiana, as elsewhere, often was used to enrich the private contractors who ran the penal institutions. In practice, the private contractors were not enlightened masters. The state resumed control of the prison in the mid-1850s but continued for some time to contract labor.[28]

Certainly, the delegates to the 1851 convention were not naïve about the character of the Jeffersonville State Prison. The inclusion of juveniles in the general prison population proved especially troublesome to reformers. At the convention's request, the prison warden provided information on inmates admitted from September 1822 to November 1850. Of 1,131 convicts, 157 (or more than one-eighth of the total) were less than twenty-one years of age, some as young as eleven years old. Neither "the prevention of crime and the reformation of the offender," James R. M. Bryant, of Warren County, argued, could possibly be advanced by sending Indiana's children, perhaps already victimized by "dissolute parents and neglected education," to "this school of vice and infamy." The other delegates agreed, and the final document required the General Assembly to establish appropriate institutions for the restraint and reformation of juvenile offenders.[29]

Juvenile facilities did not, however, spring up overnight: then, as now, fiscal realities impeded change—there was no funding for separate juvenile facilities until 1867. As David Bodenhamer notes, "The reform impulse so evident in the constitutional convention was unable to overcome the fiscal conservatism of Indiana legislatures."[30] Nevertheless, in 1903, Indiana distinguished itself as the second state in the union to establish a juvenile court system. This scheme, modeled on that of Illinois (1899), incorporated a parental care and treatment philosophy and required probation officers to investigate children's backgrounds and provide more individualized treatment and supervision.[31]

Reformers also expressed concern about the proper correction of women who ran afoul of the law and, in 1873, built "the first penal institution for women that was not an appendage of something built for men."[32] The Female Prison and Reformatory Institution for Girls and Women resulted from the efforts of Charles and Rhoda Coffin, a Quaker couple from Richmond, Indiana.[33] In Indiana, as in Pennsylvania and elsewhere, Quakers were leaders in a wide array of reform movements, including prison reform. Quaker religious beliefs emphasized egalitarianism and held that "individuals could strive toward perfection through self-discipline."[34] Opposed to severe castigation, "Quakers clearly relied on their religious precepts to form their ideas about reclaiming offenders through friendly persuasion and solitary meditation."[35]

The Coffins investigated the treatment of women in the state penitentiary and described it as a "vast bawdy house" in which female inmates were "forced to minister to the lust of the officers, or if they refuse, submit to the infliction of the lash until they do."[36] The governor and legislature confirmed these accusations, and a separate women's facility, which also segregated juveniles from adults, came into existence in 1873 in Indianapolis.[37] The law establishing the prison imposed the novel requirement that all officers as well as the superintendent be female (although the superintendent's husband could act as steward); the institution's first superintendent, the Quaker Sarah Smith, was the first woman to be in charge of a completely separate women's prison.[38] In 1877, the law mandated an all-female board of managers, and Rhoda Coffin became the board president. The prisoners served determinate, rather than indeterminate, sentences and thus it was not a "reformatory" in the late-nineteenth-century sense. Discipline was mild, however. Inmates "lived in an atmosphere of tablecloths and china designed to copy, as much as possible" the domesticity the staff strove to inculcate.[39] By the turn of the century, other states had also established separate women's correctional facilities.

This pioneering institution heralded a new wave of late-nineteenth-century penal reform. Theories explaining criminal deviance on psychological and physiological as well as environmental grounds emerged.

Challenges to older theories questioned the efficacy of rehabilitation through silence, confinement, and useful labor, primarily because overcrowded prisons vitiated any efforts to achieve solitary contemplation. Also, organized labor objected to prison labor as unfair competition; indeed, in 1866, Illinois amended its constitution to ban contracted convict labor.[40] In response, there were efforts to distinguish between the incorrigible and the salvageable. Good-time laws rewarding compliant behavior existed in twenty-three states by 1869 and were combined with indeterminate sentences and habitual offender statutes as well as parole supervision.[41]

The progressive philosophy—which flowered around the turn of the century and prevailed until the 1970s, when determinate sentences returned to favor—represented a radical change in the way in which the state's authority was viewed:

> The most distinguishing characteristic of Progressivism was its fundamental trust in the power of the state to do good. . . . In criminal justice, the issue was not how to protect the offender from the arbitrariness of the state, but how to bring the state more effectively to the aid of the offender. . . . Thus, a policy that called for the state's exercise of discretionary authority in finely tuned responses was, at its core, Progressive.[42]

Whether the cause of deviance was environmental influences or psychological difficulties, each case was different. One offender might require probation in the community, another incarceration.[43]

Indeterminate sentencing transferred discretion from judges, who theretofore had imposed fixed terms, to prison boards. Sentences were not completely indeterminate; instead, the statute established a range, and the prison board evaluated the prisoner's comportment and determined when he had demonstrated his reformation and eligibility for release. "The indeterminate sentence pointed in two directions: leniency and rehabilitation for the savable; eternal damnation for the rest," whereas habitual criminal laws focused on incorrigible offenders.[44] Well-behaved prisoners earned good-time credit, reducing their maximum period of incarceration, subject to revocation for misbehavior. The indeterminate sentence allowed a board to decide when an inmate had demonstrated behavior warranting release on parole. Parole was conditional release and could be terminated—and the parolee returned to the correctional facility—at the prison board's discretion.[45]

Indeterminate sentencing applied originally to first offenders but soon was available to all offenders whose sentences contemplated a probability of release. Advocates represented this innovation as wholesome: it separated the wheat from the chaff and created incentives as well as hope, the Indiana Supreme Court observed in 1898. The court specifically found that the new sentencing scheme did not violate the constitutional separation of powers by conferring judicial authority on the executive branch board of prison managers; it also did not, the justices ruled, impose cruel, unusual, or disproportionate punishment, nor was it vindictive, any of which would have been unconstitutional. In fact, the court mused, determinate sentences were crueler, depriving the convict of hope and the incentive to reform.[46]

Alongside this current of optimism ran a darker stream—life sentences for repeat offenders who apparently were not amenable to reformation. Scientific explanations of deviance, from phrenology to genetic predisposition, had captured public attention, and deep concern existed about the reproduction of criminal behavior. In response, Indiana passed the first law (1907) that made sterilization official policy. The law, solemnly reciting that "heredity plays a most important part in the transmission of crime, idiocy, and imbecility," simply may have ratified existing practice: by one report, three hundred inmates already had undergone forced vasectomies at the Jeffersonville prison.[47] Within a generation, about half the states had some sort of eugenics statute.[48] In 1927, the U.S. Supreme Court embraced eugenics in *Buck v. Bell,* in which Oliver Wendell Holmes Jr. wrote the infamous phrase "Three generations of imbeciles are enough" in upholding the constitutionality of a Virginia forced sterilization law.[49] In 1921, well before *Buck v. Bell,* the Indiana Supreme Court held the Indiana sterilization statute unconstitutional, finding that it violated the due process clause of the Fourteenth Amendment to the U.S. Constitution by denying the prisoner an opportunity to cross-examine witnesses and to produce experts to controvert his alleged membership in the class of "confirmed criminals, idiots, rapists, and imbeciles."[50]

In March 1927, shortly before *Buck v. Bell* was decided, the Indiana legislature enacted a new sterilization law that incorporated due process protections, including a thirty-day notice to the inmate and his parents, legal guardians, next of kin or guardian ad litem; an evidentiary hearing before the board of the penal institution; and an appeal of right to the circuit court and, if necessary, to the Indiana Supreme Court.[51]

By the late twentieth century, belief in the capacity of government to do good, particularly in reforming criminals, had been seriously undermined. California abolished indeterminate sentences in the 1970s, and Indiana did so in 1977.[52] The state sought to create a "rational and modern" system and relied on the Model Penal Code promulgated by the American Law Institute in 1962 to reconcile differences among the state and federal criminal laws, as well as on revisions to the criminal code in other states and countries.[53] Courts imposed fixed, determinate terms within a statutory range of years. Good-time credit remained available, and sentences could be reduced by participation in educational and rehabilitative programs.[54]

Restorative justice remains a compelling principle in Indiana criminal law. The state amended its constitution in 1970 to permit review and revision of sentences (discussed below) and amended it again in 1996 to acknowledge the rights of victims in the criminal process.[55] Community corrections programs begun in three counties in 1981 had spread to sixty-two counties by 2001, providing preventive interventions as well as services to adult and juvenile offenders and to victims. Programs available to offenders diverted from state correctional facilities include house arrest/home detention, in some cases with electronic monitoring; residential facilities; work release; community work service and restitution; day reporting; and a variety of victim-offender reconciliation or mediation programs.[56] Restorative justice is an important component in many local criminal justice programs. The Center for Community Justice in Elkhart, Indiana, for example, provides mediation and reconciliation services as well as restitution to victims and the community in adult and juvenile cases, helping to reform and reintegrate offenders and to heal communities.[57]

The proportionality requirement of the state bill of rights, reflecting eighteenth-century Enlightenment penal philosophy, has played an important role in Indiana jurisprudence. Although the Eighth Amendment to the federal Constitution bans cruel and unusual punishment, only nine state constitutions, as noted earlier, mandate proportionality in sentencing.[58] Significantly, the Indiana Supreme Court has viewed the requirement as "a limitation on the acts of the legislature" and not as a basis for an appellate court to "set aside a conviction and sentence, within the statute, merely because on the record it may seem severe."[59] As a limitation on legislative action, it was the basis for overturning a statute specifying a term of ten to twenty-five years for robbery when the penalty for armed robbery had been established as ten to twenty years; the legislature could not constitutionally "provide a punishment for a lesser included offense which is greater in years on the face of the statute than the greater offense."[60] The Indiana Supreme Court reached the same conclusion in the case of a defendant sentenced to six years for distributing fake marijuana (a noncontrolled substance represented to be a controlled substance), a term "twice as long as the maximum penalty he would have faced" had he dealt real marijuana.[61] And, in a case involving habitual offender enhancement, the court found that the enhancement penalty must be proportional with regard to the nature and gravity of both the present felony and the predicate felonies supporting the habitual enhancement. The court reduced a thirty-five year sentence to five years, noting that the present felony was "ultimately based upon a conviction for conduct that the legislature has classified as a misdemeanor" and that none of the convictions involved injury to person or property, making the original sentence entirely disproportionate.[62]

In 1970, voters ratified new language in article VII. They amended section 4 to provide the supreme court with the power to "review and revise" sentences. A new section 6 replaced outmoded language to permit review and revision of sentences by the court of appeals pursuant to supreme court rules and to guarantee in criminal cases "an absolute right to one appeal."[63] This proposal, as Judge Charles S. White of the court of appeals noted, had to be intended to change the practice and "not merely for the purpose of constitutionalizing the existing exceedingly limited review and revision practice. This is underscored by the Commission comments in reference to 'the efficacious use to which that power has been put by the Court of Criminal Appeals in England.'"[64] Indiana again chose to emulate progressive law, and in 1978 the supreme court established rules for appellate review of sentences.[65]

Relying on these rules and on constitutional authority, the supreme court and court of appeals have created a substantial body of law outlining appropriate considerations for the imposition of sentences by trial courts and have not hesitated to revise sentences determined to be disproportionate or vindictive.[66] The courts have not been constrained by the limitations of sections 16 and 18. Instead, sentence review and revision have been guided by the language of the supreme court's rules and have involved substantial reevaluation of the trial court's use of its discretion in sentencing, such as reducing sentences without finding abuse of that discretion;[67] finding that the defendant received the maximum sentence but was not within the class of offenders for whom the maximum possible sentence was appropriate;[68] finding mitigation in deep mental disturbance obviously related to the crime even though the trial court found no such mitigation;[69] or finding that the trial court gave insufficient weight to a mitigating circumstance.[70] As a consequence, Indiana case law creates guidelines and standards for the exercise of sentencing discretion and promotes more uniform, fairer sentencing without imposing elaborate grids or points systems that may increase uniformity at the expense of individualized consideration of each offender and offense. The trial court is required to give a comprehensive explanation of any departure from the presumptive, or standard, sentence.

The state constitution's mandate that the penal code be founded on the principle of reformation and not on vindictive justice has not been found to prohibit capital punishment,[71] despite eloquent arguments that it should,[72] a result consistent with the 1850–51 constitutional convention's failure to abolish executions. State courts have viewed cruel and unusual punishment, proportionality, and reformation versus vindictiveness primarily as constraints on the entire penal code, not on particular punishments, especially those with a long historical pedigree. Nevertheless, these sections, in conjunction with the 1970 amendments, provide a state constitutional foundation for appellate sentencing review and a solid basis for constraint of legislative imposition of apparently irrational punishments.

Clarity and Regularity of Process

The drafters of the Indiana constitution of 1851 believed that criminal justice in a democratic society required clear, accessible laws written in plain language that every citizen—not just elites and attorneys—could understand. Common-law crimes, that is, nonstatutory crimes, were repudiated on the theory that, as one legal scholar has noted, "judges had too much power, if they could invent new crimes, or extend old ones by analogy."[73] The constitution also baldly laid down the rule that "[c]rimes and misdemeanors shall be defined, and punishment therefor fixed, by statutes of this State, and not otherwise."[74] The law, in addition to being codified, must be comprehensible to those it binds: "[I]t is of the highest importance," one convention delegate argued, "that it be placed in such a form that its general principles, at least, may be accessible to and known by all. It should be reduced to determinate propositions and settled and fixed, so that the administration of it may be uniform in all the courts throughout the State."[75] To that end, a number of delegates insisted that Latin and terms of art not generally in use should be eschewed: Alexander C. Stevenson, a delegate from Putnam County, even moved to strike the word "peers" in the guarantee of trial by jury because the term was not found in the 1816 constitution or in any other state constitution and was not clear in its meaning; if it meant "political equals," it added nothing to a constitution already providing that all men are born free and equal—and "peers" was duly stricken.[76] "Habeas corpus" nearly suffered the same fate.

The convention delegates were deeply serious in their search for a system that would ensure fairness in process and outcome as well as hope of rehabilitation. The usefulness of any criminal justice system, the delegates noted, was "mainly in proportion as it is open, and mild, and merciful."[77] Thomas W. Gibson, of Clark County, argued, "Man's nature has been and can be changed by circumstances."[78] This meant that the state must operate by the maxim, distilled from English law, that it was better that the guilty should escape punishment than that the innocent be wrongly punished. As John Petit, of Tippecanoe County, observed,

> It is more desirable for the State, that she should save from punishment those who are not guilty, than that she should actually punish to the fullest extent every guilty man. . . . This . . . maxim of the law . . . has long been very generally approved by civilized man.[79]

The delegates understood that the law could not substitute for the institutions of society—family, schools, churches, and community—in forming character and that, in comparison with them, law was, as John B. Niles, of La Porte County, suggested, only a "palliative."[80] They also understood that the purpose of a constitution was to embody eternal principles that even a majority could not abrogate:

> Other gentlemen seem to think that Constitutions are to embody whatever suits the will of the majority; but . . . a Constitution is made for the benefit of the minority—to protect the rights of the minority against the aggressions and the power of a triumphant majority. Of what use and validity is a Constitution unless the object be to protect the weak? The object of a Constitution should be to guarantee important rights.[81]

Indiana distinguished itself not only in establishing the right to counsel and a progressive approach to punishment but also in assuring the availability and fairness of review in criminal cases. It is notable that "more than one-third of the 154 delegates who served at the convention were trained in the law."[82] Three of these delegates later became members of the Indiana Supreme Court.[83] One, Alvin P. Hovey (who also served as governor from 1889 to 1891), wrote the decision in *Falkenburgh v. Jones,* the landmark case establishing the right of a criminal defendant to obtain a transcript of his trial at public expense, just three years after the ratification of the new constitution.

Falkenburgh had been tried for grand larceny. Because of his indigence, the trial court assigned him counsel at public expense. Following his conviction, he sought an appeal but was unable to pay the fees demanded by the court clerk to produce the transcript of the trial proceedings. The Supreme Court of Indiana made short work of the clerk's claim that he was entitled to be paid before producing the trial record. Certainly that would have been true, had Falkenburgh the means to pay; but Indiana statutes provided that, once the trial court determined the individual was without means to defend himself and granted his application for counsel, "all other officers requisite for the defence . . . shall do their duty therein without taking any fee or reward from such person." This was "merely declaratory of the common law." Indiana law was quite different from that of Great Britain, however, in that no authority constitutionally could require performance of services without compensation, as stated in article I, section 21, of the state's constitution. Because Indiana's statutes provided that the clerk should receive annual compensation for any extra services, the county would reimburse the clerk for such services, albeit after and not before the pauper had received his record for appeal. Judge Hovey's opinion relied on the state bill of rights guarantee that "[j]ustice shall be administered freely, and without purchase; completely, and without denial; speedily, and without delay":

> [W]e have felt constrained to give a liberal construction to our statutes in favor of the pauper, for we can scarcely conceive of a system of laws so inhuman and cruel that would consign the destitute and friendless to conviction and infamy, without affording full and ample means for investigation. Such a system would, in many cases, make poverty equivalent to crime; for without the means of procuring writs, witnesses and records, the innocent might, and frequently would be convicted; and that part of our constitution which provides that "justice shall be administered freely and

> without purchase, completely and without denial," would be an empty boast, and worse than mockery to the poor.[84]

In the following year, the court, per curiam, held that a statute prohibiting testimony by an Indian or anyone with "one-eighth or more negro blood" in any case in which a white person was a party did not apply to testimony by an African American witness called by the African American defendant in a criminal prosecution involving a white victim. "We do not think the state was contemplated as a person of any particular color by the statute."[85] Simple fairness prohibited the exclusion of testimony essential to the defense of the accused.

The fundamental right of a criminal defendant to appeal a conviction appears to have been assumed in *Falkenburgh v. Jones* in 1854. Almost a century later, the Indiana Supreme Court extended the right to include assistance of counsel on appeal. In 1941, in *State ex rel. White v. Hilgemann,* the court found that the "right of a defendant in a criminal case to have counsel to perfect and prosecute an appeal to this court seems not to have been expressly decided."[86] The justices noted that the court had held in 1940 that "the Constitution of Indiana guarantees an absolute right to a review by this court" and that, although this right could be regulated, it could not be curtailed or denied by statute.[87] Because the right to appellate review is guaranteed, all the process appurtenant to that appeal also is guaranteed: "The right to a review is but a hollow grant to one who cannot provide himself, and is not provided, with counsel, learned and skilled in the law; and therefore withholding counsel as a practical matter withholds the right to review, and hence to corrective judicial process, and hence to due process of law."[88] In its comments to the proposed amendment of article VII, section 6, the Judicial Study Commission in 1966 emphasized that appellate jurisdiction should be established by court rule, "but . . . not infringe the traditional right to one appeal."[89]

In some cases, the law does not provide for a direct appeal—for example, when the defendant pleads guilty. Miscarriages of justice can occur in guilty plea cases, however, and Indiana was among the first states to develop a procedure for relief in this situation. A landmark nineteenth-century decision of the Indiana Supreme Court, *Sanders v. State* (1883), first exposed the possibilities of using coram nobis as a procedure for vindicating basic rights of convicted persons and led to widespread adoption of coram nobis in other states as postconviction remedy.[90] In *Sanders,* the defendant's guilty plea was extorted by fear of mob violence.

Normally, the appellate court reviews the record of the proceedings in the trial court, generally including a full transcript of the witness testimony and evidence presented (hence its critical importance, as recognized in *Falkenburgh*). In some cases, however, the record may not reflect events critical to the result of the case, such as the mob actions that had coerced Sanders's admission. Coram nobis proceedings allowed creation of a full record to permit the appellate court to rectify errors that otherwise would not be reviewable because the errors were not part of, or not refuted in, the transcript of the in-court proceedings. Because "appeals in early common law did not lie as a matter of right and were limited exclusively to errors of law . . . an error in fact unknown at the time of trial, which would have brought about a different result, was without remedy." The writ of coram nobis, therefore, was "employed to vacate a judgment of conviction predicated on an error in fact unknown to the court" and not appearing in the record.[91] Such errors include the coercive influences and atmosphere outside the court, as in *Sanders,* as well as other types of evidence that are not apparent in the record—for example, newly discovered evidence or witnesses who were available but were not called through the defense attorney's negligence. The Indiana Supreme Court decision in *Sanders* constitutes another cornerstone in the state's remarkable criminal justice edifice, establishing procedures for collateral challenges to a criminal conviction nearly seventy years before the U.S. Supreme Court held that such were required under due process.[92]

In 1945, the General Assembly passed the Public Defender Act, establishing a state-funded office to assist indigent prisoners in postconviction proceedings.[93] The act responded to a growing number of challenges brought by pro se petitioners and to a Seventh Circuit opinion finding the available Indiana procedure for such challenges insufficient. Chief Justice James Emmert noted in an opinion concerning the statute that many prisoners filed petitions for writs of habeas corpus and coram nobis in the trial courts as well as writs of mandate in the Indiana Supreme Court; because these inmates were not entitled to counsel, their efforts at self-representation created a real burden on these courts.[94] In 1944, the Seventh Circuit held in *Potter v. Dowd* that habeas corpus in Indiana was not an adequate and available state remedy that had to be exhausted before seeking federal review of a conviction and sentence and the same held true for coram nobis for paupers who could not afford counsel or the production of a trial record; the petitioner in that case received federal review of his conviction.[95] The Public Defender Act was passed "to provide counsel in behalf of pauper prisoners, avoid the objections noted in the *Potter* case, and to try these cases in the state courts rather than force them into the Federal District Courts."[96]

The U.S. Supreme Court, in *Lane v. Brown,* a 1963 case challenging the implementation of this Public Defender Act, noted that "Indiana seems to have long pursued a conspicuously enlightened policy in the quest for equal justice to the destitute," although not without occasional difficulties.[97] Brown had been convicted of murder and sentenced to death; the conviction and sentence were affirmed on direct appeal. Brown filed a petition for coram nobis in the state trial court and was represented by the state public defender at the hearing on the coram nobis petition. Brown subsequently requested representation by the state public defender on appeal of the denial of that petition, but the state public defender refused on the ground that the appeal would not be successful. The Supreme Court of Indiana refused to order appointment of other counsel or the production of a transcript of the coram nobis proceeding to be used on appeal. Brown then proceeded into federal court, asserting the denial of his Fourteenth Amendment right to equal protection, because any defendant who could afford to purchase a transcript would have had a right to appeal in such circumstances. The Indiana Supreme Court had found that only the public defender could procure a transcript and that an indigent could not procure such a transcript at public expense in order to appeal pro se: "The upshot is that a person with sufficient funds can appeal as of right to the Supreme Court of Indiana from the denial of a writ of error *coram nobis,* but an indigent can, at the will of the Public Defender, be entirely cut off from any appeal at all."[98] Because it was settled law that a state had to make appellate transcripts available to indigent criminal defendants if such transcripts could be purchased by defendants with means, whether on direct appeal or in state postconviction actions,[99] the U.S. Supreme Court found that Brown had to be provided a transcript at public expense for his coram nobis appeal regardless of the public defender's opinion of its merits,[100] noting that "[w]e have no doubt that Indiana, with its historic concern for equal justice under law, will find no practical difficulty in correcting the constitutional deficiency which this case exposes."[101] Indiana today continues to provide counsel for all indigents incarcerated in correctional facilities in challenges to current convictions and sentences, in both capital and noncapital cases, under Rule 1 of the Indiana Rules of Post-Conviction Remedies, originally adopted in 1969 as a rule of the Indiana Supreme Court.

Consonant with its tradition of affording counsel and other assistance to persons accused of crime, Indiana law provides for special protections for defendants in capital cases. In 1989, the Indiana General Assembly established state funding to reimburse counties for 50 percent of the costs of the defense of a capital case at trial and on appeal (a cost previously borne entirely by the county) if the case was tried in compliance with guidelines promulgated by the Indiana Public Defender Commission created by the same statute.[102] The commission's first set of guidelines went into effect September 1, 1990. The second set, in large part adopted by the Indiana Supreme Court, became Rule 24 of the Indiana Rules of Criminal Procedure, effective January 1, 1992 (since amended).

Indiana was the second state in the nation to promulgate such standards. The Indiana rule requires two attorneys with specified training and experience, objective limits on work load while the capital case is pending, and hourly compensation for all time and services that the trial court finds reasonable and necessary to the defense.[103] The rule specifically mandates that counsel "shall be provided with adequate funds for investigative, expert, and other services necessary to prepare and present an adequate defense at every stage of the proceeding, including the sentencing phase."[104] As commission chair Norman Lefstein, former dean of the Indiana University School of Law–Indianapolis, noted,

> The overriding goal of Rule 24 was to assure that defendants in capital cases would receive "quality representation in accordance with constitutional and professional standards," as stated in the rule. Although it is impossible to assess whether that has actually occurred, there is evidence that the Rule has made a difference in the performance of defense counsel and that it has influenced prosecutors in deciding whether to seek the death penalty.[105]

Failure to comply with the standards set by Rule 24 has been a factor in the reversal of at least one capital case.[106]

The success of these standards and of the reimbursement process in capital cases prompted further state-funded incentives for improved criminal defense services in noncapital cases. The state now provides 40 percent reimbursement in felony cases to counties meeting program standards established by the Public Defender Commission.[107] The state also funds the Indiana Public Defender Council, statutorily created in 1977 to provide training and support services to pauper counsel in all criminal cases statewide. The council publishes comprehensive manuals and research aids and assists in individual cases, with a substantial resource commitment to capital cases.[108]

Once again, Indiana balanced toughness with fairness: after adopting determinate sentences and a new death penalty statute in 1977, the legislature also created resources for public defenders in the Public Defender Council. As the supreme court reviewed capital sentences imposed under the 1977 death penalty law, the court saw the need for standards, support services, and adequate compensation for attorneys. The supreme court's Criminal Rule 24 and funding for defense services supplied by the legislature have made Indiana a model for capital litigation.

Respect for Every Citizen's Rights and Citizen Participation

As noted earlier, numerous Indiana cases protected citizen rights at the state level before federal due process requirements were found to be applicable. In *Callender v. State,* nearly forty years before the federal landmark case, *Mapp v. Ohio* (1961), Indiana adopted an exclusionary rule for illegally seized evidence, barring its admission.

The superior court of Elkhart County had convicted Edward Callender of unlawfully keeping intoxicating liquor with intent to sell, barter, exchange, give away, furnish, or otherwise dispose of it. The sole evidence against him derived from a search pursuant to a search warrant, apparently relying on the Prohibition Law of 1917 (Ind. Acts 1917, ch. 4). The Indiana Supreme Court observed that the warrant was not issued in conformity with state or federal law, having been signed by the chief of police, not a judge, and no affidavit in support of the warrant request having been presented to any judicial officer authorized to issue a warrant. The court cited U.S. Supreme Court precedent for the exclusion of evidence in federal court when seized without a valid warrant and further noted that the Prohibition Law of 1917 did not authorize searches and seizures in order to obtain evidence for a criminal prosecution, as opposed to seizing intoxicating liquors that were contraband. Citing article I, section 11, of the state constitution, prohibiting unreasonable search or seizure, and article I, section 14, prohibiting compelled self-incrimination, the Indiana Supreme Court held that evidence discovered pursuant to an invalid warrant could not be admitted against the defendant at trial. Because no legally admissible evidence supported the verdict, the justices reversed Callender's conviction.[109] The tradition continues; searches sustainable under the Fourth

Amendment may be improper under section 11. For example, in a 2002 case involving a warrantless search of defendant's car, "Article 1, Section 11 must be liberally construed," the state court ruled, "to protect Hoosiers from unreasonable police activity in private areas of their lives."[110]

Other provisions of the state bill of rights remain vital in Indiana jurisprudence. In *Malinski v. State,* the Indiana Supreme Court determined that the state bill of rights continues to provide greater rights for Hoosiers than does the federal Constitution: "In light of Indiana's history of an expansive state right to counsel, we agree with Malinski that an incarcerated suspect has a right under section 13 to be informed that an attorney hired by his family is present at the station and wishes to speak to him."[111] In addition, this section's guarantee of the right "to meet with the witnesses face to face" requires "face to face confrontation, while the federal clause mandates only a general right to be confronted with the witnesses."[112]

Article I, section 15, has no federal analogue in its mandate that "no person arrested, or confined in jail, shall be treated with unnecessary rigor." This section is cited in a 1931 decision upholding the convictions of two police officers for assault and battery on a prisoner in their custody in an attempt to procure a confession.[113] In conjunction with section 14's privilege against compulsory self-incrimination, section 15 provides the basis for suppression of physically coerced or otherwise improperly induced confessions, as the Indiana Supreme Court noted in 1938: "The state does not expect, it expressly forbids and condemns, such methods. It is better that some criminals escape punishment than that the officers of the law turn lawless in their zeal to procure evidence."[114]

The presumption in section 17 of the Indiana constitution that all offenses, except murder and treason, are bailable by sufficient sureties is a unique protection to state citizens, and section 16's prohibition against excessive bail also is found in the Eighth Amendment to the federal Constitution. Indiana law holds that the right to bail in a murder case "when the proof is not evident or the presumption strong is a fundamental right guaranteed by our Constitution."[115] As such, denial of bail can be appealed,[116] as can setting of unreasonably high bail.[117]

A particular point of pride for the 1850 convention delegates, emphasized in their address to the electors of the state on February 8, 1851, was the new constitutional guarantee of the right to trial by jury in all cases, criminal and civil. The 1816 constitution, by contrast, had denied the right to trial by jury in petit misdemeanors and civil cases if the amount in controversy did not exceed $20.[118] The new 1851 constitution's right to jury trial in misdemeanor cases is not provided by the Sixth Amendment.[119]

The constitution of 1851 contained unique language stipulating that in "all criminal cases whatever, the jury shall have the right to determine the law and the facts."[120] This language survives in only two other state constitutions, Georgia's and Maryland's, and has been a subject of much contention.[121] The language can be traced to the 1735 seditious libel trial of John Peter Zenger for his printing of articles attacking the royal governor. Zenger was represented by Alexander Hamilton, who secured an acquittal by his argument—contrary to the instructions of the court—that truth was a defense to libel and that the jury had the right to decide the law and not the facts only.[122]

Despite its historical antecedents, this section has been variously interpreted. The 1816 constitution provided in article I, section 10, that truth was a defense to libel and that the jury determined the law and facts in such cases "under the direction of the court, as in other cases." Article I, section 19 of the 1851 charter embodied a new guarantee, one not limited to libel cases. In two cases decided in 1858, *Williams v. State* and *Daily v. State,*[123] the Indiana Supreme Court held the language meant what it said: the jury under the Indiana constitution decided the law for itself, and the trial court could not impair or limit that right by instruction.[124] These rulings conformed to the prevailing American philosophy concerning trial by jury. In the colonies and, to an even greater extent, in the newly formed states, the law reflected "an emerging conception of the jury as a democratic instrument."[125] The law and its implementation must embody local values, as David Bodenhamer has noted: "This expansive conception of the jury's role restrained judicial authority by removing from the judge the right to decide which precedent applied to the issue at hand. Simultaneously, it permitted local juries to reject by means of an acquittal whatever parts of the law were inconsistent with the community's views of justice and morality."[126]

Just such an emphasis on local values and local control pervaded the 1850 convention debates. James Rariden, of Wayne County, argued that it was nearly impossible to convict on charges of selling spirituous liquors, pointing out that the law failed when it prohibited what the citizenry did not condemn: "The laws of trade, when quickened by popular taste and passion, are no more to be restricted by an enactment of the Legislature than is the law of gravitation to be suspended by a Governor's proclamation."[127]

Perhaps this view of the jury's power is more appropriate in a lightly populated frontier than in a complex urban society, as Bodenhamer suggests.[128] Because "the practice of permitting the jury to determine the law developed in part because judges were not professionally trained" and thus "no more likely to know the law than the jury,"[129] the concept may have become outmoded. Increased professionalization of attorneys and judges, codification of laws, and publication of appellate opinions—growing legal specialization and complexity, in short—appear to have undermined both confidence in and perceived need for reliance on jurors' total discretion in determining the law. This result appeared earlier in other states than in Indiana. Elsewhere, by the mid-nineteenth century, "fears of majoritarian tyranny, a desire to ensure uniform justice, and a recognition that an unlimited jury boded ill for judicial power combined to produce a new maxim: the judge decides in matters of law; the jury in matters of fact."[130]

Some of the reforms vital to the framers of the 1851 constitution—popular, democratic election of judges, in this instance—over time likely lessened the need for section 19. Locally elected judges provided for community-based justice even if jurors lacked untrammeled authority to decide the law.[131] As early as 1885, the Indiana Supreme Court stated that section 19 "evidently means that the jury have the right to determine all questions of law applicable to such matters . . . but can not be rightfully construed to mean that the jury are the sole judges of the law in every respect in a criminal cause."[132]

By the 1920s and 1930s, the Indiana Supreme Court held that section 19 did not apply to "questions concerning the admissibility of evidence; that the jury's law determining function did not include a right to make law; that the jury was bound to give supreme court decisions highest respect; the constitutional provision did not mean the jury had the right to fix punishment for crimes; and that the law the jury had the right to determine was existing law as found in the statutes of the State."[133]

Every generation finds its own particular virtues or vices in section 19. Any jury has the power to nullify a law by acquitting an obviously guilty defendant. Its power to convict the innocent is also a fact, but trial and appellate courts have the power and duty to rectify such a result, whereas a jury verdict of acquittal, under our state and federal constitutions, bars any further prosecution. The most recent exegesis of section 19 came in 2003 when the Indiana Supreme Court unanimously held that the right to determine the law does not encompass the right to disregard the law and that "although there may be some value in instructing Indiana jurors that they have a right to 'refuse to enforce the law's harshness when justice so requires,' the source of that right cannot be found in article I, section 19 of the Indiana Constitution."[134]

During the 1850 convention, John B. Howe, of LaGrange County, suggested that "if we would retain our liberties," the state's maxim should be "politically conservative, and socially progressive."[135] After a century and a half, the maxim remains an appropriate guide to the role of Indiana law in matters of crime, punishment, and rights of defendants. With rather minor changes, the 1851 constitution has provided a sound basis for our criminal justice system, protecting fundamental values of liberty and equality while accommodating significant changes. Indiana began its statehood in the wave of a political revolution that embraced Enlightenment thought with regard to penal sanctions, fair process, and protection of individual rights, and it has maintained this heritage of progressive innovations in its philosophy of criminal justice.

The values expressed in the 1851 constitution have been realized in practice to a remarkable degree, often well in advance of their recognition and implementation by the nation as a whole. In the guarantee of the right to counsel for the indigent in a felony or misdemeanor, on appeal or in post-conviction proceedings, in the treatment of juveniles and women, in appellate review and revision of sentences, in exclusion of illegally obtained evidence, and in other significant areas, Hoosiers can take justifiable pride in a constitution, laws, and court decisions that have served to make real the promise of the 1851 charter that Indiana's "penal code shall be founded on the principles of reformation, and not of vindictive justice."

Notes

1. Lawrence M. Friedman, *Crime and Punishment in American History* (New York: Basic Books, 1993), 72, citing Barron v. Baltimore, 32 U.S. (7 Pet.) 243 (1833).
2. Friedman, *Crime and Punishment in American History*, 72.
3. Northwest Ordinance of 1787, art. II, *Journals of the Continental Congress, 1774–1789*, ed. Worthington Chauncey Ford, vol. 32 (Washington, D.C.: Government Printing Office, 1936), 334–43.
4. Ind. const. of 1816, art. I, §§ 8, 10–16, 18.
5. Randall T. Shepard, "Second Wind for the Indiana Bill of Rights," *Indiana Law Review* 22, no. 2 (1989): 575–86, 576.
6. Powell v. Alabama, 287 U.S. 45 (1932).
7. Webb v. Baird, 6 Ind. 13, 18 (1854).
8. Gideon v. Wainwright, 372 U.S. 335 (1963).

9. Batchelor v. State, 189 Ind. 69, 125 N.E. 773 (1920).

10. Bolkovac v. State, 229 Ind. 294, 98 N.E.2d 250 (1951).

11. Harry L. Watson, *Liberty and Power: The Politics of Jacksonian America* (New York: Noonday Press, 1990), 43.

12. Ind. const. of 1816, art. IX, § 4.

13. James H. Madison, *The Indiana Way: A State History* (Bloomington: Indiana University Press, 1986), 53.

14. Ind. const. of 1851, art. VII, § 17.

15. Richard D. Younger, *The People's Panel: The Grand Jury in the United States, 1634–1941* (Providence, R.I.: Brown University Press, 1963), 57–84. For more on the grand jury debate in Indiana, see David J. Bodenhamer, "Criminal Justice and Democratic Theory in Antebellum America: The Grand Jury Debate in Indiana," *Journal of the Early Republic* 5 (Winter 1985): 57–84.

16. Ind. const. of 1851, art. V, § 17.

17. *Report of the Debates and Proceedings of the Convention for the Revision of the Constitution of the State of Indiana 1850* (Indianapolis: 1850; repr., Indianapolis: Indiana Historical Bureau, 1935), 2:1381.

18. Ibid., 2:1872.

19. Barry Latzer, *State Constitutions and Criminal Justice* (Westport, Conn.: Greenwood, 1991), 205–6.

20. Indiana const. of 1851, art. I, § 18.

21. Myra C. Glenn, *Campaigns against Corporal Punishment: Prisoners, Sailors, Women, and Children in Antebellum America* (Albany: State University of New York Press, 1984), 55.

22. Ibid.

23. David J. Bodenhamer, *The Pursuit of Justice: Crime and Law in Antebellum Indiana* (New York: Garland, 1986), 13n28, 159, citing the *Indiana Centinel,* May 6, 1820.

24. Bodenhamer, *Pursuit of Justice,* 14, citing 1822 Ind. Acts 23, 40–41n30, 159.

25. Glenn, *Campaigns against Corporal Punishment,* 41.

26. Ibid., 50.

27. Watson, *Liberty and Power,* 56.

28. Bodenhamer, *Pursuit of Justice,* 16.

29. Delegate James R. M. Bryant, *Report of the Debates,* 2:1903.

30. Bodenhamer, *Pursuit of Justice,* 17–18.

31. Frank Sullivan Jr., "Indiana as a Forerunner in the Juvenile Court Movement," *Indiana Law Review* 30, no. 1 (1997): 279–303, 280, 286.

32. Friedman, *Crime and Punishment in American History,* 233.

33. Mark Colvin, *Penitentiaries, Reformatories, and Chain Gangs: Social Theory and the History of Punishment in Nineteenth-Century America* (New York: St. Martin's, 1997), 162.

34. Ibid., 45–46.

35. Ibid., 46.

36. Ibid., 162, citing Estelle B. Freedman, *Their Sisters' Keepers: Women's Prison Reform in America, 1830–1930* (Ann Arbor: University of Michigan Press, 1981), 60.

37. Colvin, *Penitentiaries, Reformatories, and Chain Gangs,* 162.

38. Ibid., 163.
39. Ibid.
40. Friedman, *Crime and Punishment in American History,* 158.
41. Ibid., 159.
42. David J. Rothman, *Conscience and Convenience: The Asylum and Its Alternatives in Progressive America,* rev. ed. (New York: Aldine de Gruyter, 2002), 60.
43. Ibid., 5.
44. Friedman, *Crime and Punishment in American History,* 161.
45. Ibid., 162.
46. Miller v. State, 149 Ind. 607, 49 N.E. 894 (1898).

> The appellant was convicted of burglary, and the punishment prescribed therefor by the Criminal Code of 1881 was imprisonment in the state prison for any determinate period, at the discretion of the jury, of not less than 2 years and not more than 14 years. Burns' Rev. St. 1894, § 2002 (Rev. St. 1881, § 1929; Horner's Rev. St. 1897, § 1929). Under that statute, if the evidence had shown that appellant was guilty of breaking into an old outhouse, with intent to commit a felony, though he found nothing therein on which to commit the felony, and though the outhouse was practically worthless, yet the jury, in their uncontrollable and unbridled discretion, could send him to the state prison for 14 years, and he would be without remedy. Certainly, that is more cruel punishment than that provided by the reformatory act. Under the law prior to that act, when the ponderous iron doors of the prison close on the convict, it not only shuts him in, and shuts out the bright angel of liberty, but it also shuts out of the convict's heart all hope, which is the anchor of the soul, because in the absence of such legislation he is utterly powerless by any amount of good conduct or penitence to assuage or mitigate the severity of his punishment. Is it at all strange that, with liberty and hope gone, the convict's heart should break, or that he should, in his helpless condition, settle down to the belief that society was his bitter-hating enemy; and thus brooding over the subject through the long years of his prison toil without recompense, and tears all in vain, is it all strange that he should, at the expiration of his term, come out of prison the bitter-hating enemy of society? Clearly not. It was to remedy this manifest evil to society and to the criminal classes themselves that the legislation in question was enacted. So that, when the convict is brought within the prison walls, if his crime be not treason or murder in the first or second degree, the hope of liberty is not shut out of his heart, the anchor of his soul is not taken away, but society whispers in his ear the brotherly message, through the statute in question, that "the restoration of your liberty is largely in your own hands." "Your own good conduct and reformation may restore you to liberty and to society as a useful citizen, even before you have served the minimum or shortest time fixed in the Criminal Code for the punishment of your crime, namely, in one year

> after your imprisonment begins," because the minimum term of imprisonment prescribed by the Criminal Code for a large majority of the felonies falling within the reformatory act is two years, and some three years. 149 Ind. 614–15, 49 N.E. 896.

47. Friedman, *Crime and Punishment in American History,* 335–36n49, citing Mark H. Haller, *Eugenics: Hereditarian Attitudes in American Thought* (New Brunswick, N.J.: Rutgers University Press, 1963), 49, 136. Other sources claim "at least 465 men." See Scott Christianson, *With Liberty for Some: Five Hundred Years of Imprisonment in America* (Boston: Northeastern University Press, 1998), 195n156, citing Arthur E. Fink, *Causes of Crime: Biological Theories in the United States, 1800–1915* (Philadelphia: University of Pennsylvania Press, 1938), 194–97.

48. Friedman, *Crime and Punishment in American History,* 336.

49. Buck v. Bell, 274 U.S. 200, 207 (1927).

50. Williams v. Smith, 190 Ind. 526, 527–28, 131 N.E.2 2 (1921).

51. J. H. Landman, *Human Sterilization: The History of the Sexual Sterilization Movement* (New York: Macmillan, 1932), 54–56.

52. Friedman, *Crime and Punishment in American History,* 306.

53. Indiana Criminal Law Study Commission, Indiana Penal Code Proposed Final Draft (Indianapolis: n.p., 1974).

54. Ind. Acts 1976, P.L. 148, § 8, as amended by Ind. Acts 1977, P.L. 340, § 134, codified at IC § 35-50-6-3; Ind. Acts 1993, P.L. 243-1993, § 2, codified at IC § 35-50-6-3.3.

55. Ind. const. of 1851, art. I, § 13(b) (as amended, 1996).

56. Indiana Department of Correction, "Community Corrections," http://in.gov/indcorrection/community.htm.

57. Center for Community Justice, Annual Report (Elkhart, Ind.: n.p., 2002).

58. Interpreted to prohibit punishments "such as that inflicted at the whipping post, in the pillory, burning at the stake, breaking on the wheel, etc." and not to prohibit imprisonment for any term of years or the death penalty. Hobbs v. State, 133 Ind. 404, 32 N.E. 1019, 1021 (1893).

59. Blue v. State, 224 Ind. 394, 400–401, 67 N.E.2d 377, 379 (1946).

60. Dembowski v. State, 251 Ind. 250, 253, 240 N.E.2d 815, 817 (1968).

61. Conner v. State, 626 N.E.2d 803, 805–6 (Ind. 1993).

62. Clark v. State, 561 N.E.2d 759, 766 (Ind. 1990).

63. Ind. const. of 1851, art. VII, § 6.

64. Gray v. State, 159 Ind. App. 200, 208, 305 N.E.2d 886, 890–91 (1974).

65. This authority later was amended and incorporated into the Indiana Rules of Appellate Procedure: "The Court may revise a sentence authorized by statute if, after due consideration of the trial court's decision, the Court finds that the sentence is inappropriate in light of the nature of the offense and the character of the offender." Ind. R. App. P. 7(B).

66. "[T]he addition of twenty-four additional years evidences a vindictiveness proscribed by Art. I, § 18 of our State Constitution." Fointno v. State, 487 N.E.2d 140, 149 (Ind. 1986).

67. Beatty v. State, 567 N.E.2d 1134, 1138 (Ind. 1991).

68. Buchanan v. State, 767 N.E.2d 967, 974 (Ind. 2002).

69. Barany v. State, 658 N.E.2d 60, 67 (Ind. 1995).

70. Brewer v. State, 646 N.E.2d 1382, 1385 (Ind. 1995).

71. Driskill v. State, 7 Ind. 338, 343 (1855); Dillon v. State, 454 N.E.2d 845, 852 (Ind. 1983), *cert. denied,* 465 U.S. 1109 (1984).

72. For example, see the concurring and dissenting opinion of Justice DeBruler and dissenting opinion of Justice Prentice in *Adams v. State,* 259 Ind. 64, 74–101, 271 N.E.2d 425, 431–45 (1971).

73. Friedman, *Crime and Punishment in American History,* 65.

74. Ibid., 65n9; former 1 Ind. Rev. Stat. 1852, ch. 61, § 2, currently codified at IC § 1-1-2-2, as amended by Ind. Acts 1978, P.L. 2, § 101 (which deleted "and misdemeanors" after crimes).

75. Delegate Walter March, *Report of the Debates,* 2:1761.

76. Ibid., 2:1378.

77. Ibid., 1:186.

78. Ibid., 1:163.

79. Ibid., 1:146.

80. Ibid., 1:185.

81. Ibid., 1:576.

82. Brent E. Dickson, Thomas A. John, and Katherine A. Wyman, "Lawyers and Judges as Framers of Indiana's 1851 Constitution," *Indiana Law Review* 30, no. 1 (1997): 397–408, 397.

83. Ibid., 403.

84. Falkenburgh v. Jones, 5 Ind. 296, 297 and 299 (1854).

85. Woodward v. State, 6 Ind. 492 (1855).

86. State ex rel. White v. Hilgemann, 218 Ind. 572, 34 N.E.2d 129, 130 (1941).

87. Ibid., relying upon Warren v. Indiana Tele. Co., 217 Ind. 93, 26 N.E.2d 399 (1940).

88. Ibid.

89. Judicial Study Commission, Report (Indianapolis: n.p., [1966]), 141. (commission members include Dr. Herman B. Wells, Sen. F. Wesley Bowers, Rep. Robert V. Bridwell, Rep. Robert D. Anderson, Rep. John W. Donaldson, C. Ben Dutton, Sen. William W. Erwin, William M. Evans, Carl M. Gray, Sen. A. Morris Hall, Gilmore S. Haynie, Rep. David F. Metzger, and Sen. Leonard Opperman).

90. Sanders v. State, 85 Ind. 318 (1883); Donald E. Wilkes, *Federal and State Postconviction Remedies and Relief,* 2d ed. (Norcross, Ga.: Harrison Company, 1987; supp. 1990), 258. Citations omitted.

91. Eli Frank, *Coram Nobis* (Albany, N.Y.: Newkirk Associates, 1953), 1.

92. Shepard, "Second Wind for the Indiana Bill of Rights," 578; the case establishing the federal right was Young v. Ragen, 337 U.S. 235 (1949).

93. Ind. Acts 1945, ch. 38 §§ 1–5 (current version enacted by Ind. Acts 2004, P.L. 98-2004, § 19, codified at IC §§ 33-40-1-1 through 33-40-1-6).

94. State ex rel. Lake v. Bain, 225 Ind. 505, 514–15, 76 N.E.2d 679, 683 (1948).

95. Potter v. Dowd, 146 F.2d 244, 247–50 (7th Cir. 1944).

96. State ex rel. Lake v. Bain, 76 N.E.2d at 684.

97. Lane v. Brown, 372 U.S. 477, 478 (1963) (indigent's access to an appeal of the denial of a collateral attack on his conviction cannot be determined by state public defender; transcript must be provided at public expense to indigent when state public defender will not provide representation).

98. Ibid., 477–82.

99. Griffin v. Illinois, 351 U.S.12 (1956) (if state appellate system provides trial transcripts to those who can purchase them on direct appeal, constitution requires adequate and effective appellate review for indigent); Smith v. Bennett, 365 U.S. 708 (1961) (*Griffin* principle applies to state postconviction proceedings).

100. In *Eskridge v. Washington Prison Board,* 357 U.S. 214 (1958), the court found that a trial judge could not deny an individual a free trial transcript based on the trial judge's conclusion that the trial had been fair and impartial.

101. Lane v. Brown, 372 U.S. at 485.

102. Ind. Acts 1989, P.L. 284-1989.

103. Ind. Crim. Rule 24 (C)(1) (amended Dec. 22, 2000, effective Jan. 1, 2001). Attorneys fees originally were $70 an hour, later increased to more than $90, subject to adjustment by the State Court Administrator's Office.

104. Norman Lefstein, "Reform of Defense Representation in Capital Cases: The Indiana Experience and Its Implications for the Nation," *Indiana Law Review* 29, no. 3 (1996): 495–533.

105. Ibid., 505.

106. Prowell v. State, 741 N.E.2d 704 (Ind. 2001).

107. Ind. Acts 2004, P.L. 98-2004, § 19(b), codified at IC § 33-40-6-4. As the number of counties participating in this program has grown, funding has become problematic in light of the recent fiscal crisis. Nevertheless, Indiana continues to invest in competent counsel and to innovate in providing criminal defense services for the indigent.

108. Ind. Acts 2004, P.L. 98-2004, § 19, codified at § 33-40-4.

109. Callender v. State, 193 Ind. 91, 91–99,138 N.E. 817, 817–19 (1923).

110. State v. Gerschoffer, 763 N.E.2d 960, 965 (Ind. 2002). Also see Brown v. State, 653 N.E.2d 77 (Ind. 1995).

111. Malinski v. State, 794 N.E.2d 1071, 1079 (Ind. 2003). Federal law requires advisement of the rights to remain silent and to consult counsel but does not require that the defendant be informed that an attorney is present and asking to see the defendant.

112. Miller v. State, 517 N.E.2d 64, 71 (Ind. 1987).

113. Bonahoon v. State, 203 Ind. 51, 178 N.E. 570 (1931).

114. Kokenes v. State, 213 Ind. 476, 492, 13 N.E.2d 524, 531 (1938).

115. Bozovichar v. State, 230 Ind. 358, 363, 103 N.E.2d 680, 682 (1952).

116. Ibid.

117. Hobbs v. Lindsay, 240 Ind. 74, 162 N.E.2d 85 (1959).

118. Charles Kettleborough, *Constitution Making in Indiana: A Source Book of Constitutional Documents with Historical Introduction and Critical Notes* (Indianapolis: Indiana Historical Commission, 1916; repr., Indianapolis: Indiana Historical Bureau, 1971), 1:404–5.

119. Shepard, "Second Wind for Indiana Bill of Rights," 579, citing State ex rel. Rose v. Hoffman, 227 Ind. 256, 85 N.E.2d 486 (1949).

120. Ind. const. of 1851, art. I, § 19.

121. Shepard, "Second Wind for Indiana Bill of Rights," 582n42.

122. Robert D. Rucker, "The Right to Ignore the Law: Constitutional Entitlement versus Judicial Interpretation," *Valparaiso University Law Review* 33 (Spring 1999): 449–83, 452.

123. Williams v. State, 10 Ind. 503 (1858); Daily v. State, 10 Ind. 536 (1858).

124. Rucker, "Right to Ignore the Law," 462–63.

125. David J. Bodenhamer, *Fair Trial: Rights of the Accused in American History* (New York: Oxford University Press, 1992), 32.

126. Ibid., 33.

127. *Report of the Debates,* 1:190.

128. Bodenhamer, *Pursuit of Justice,* 84–86.

129. Rucker, "Right to Ignore the Law," 472.

130. Bodenhamer, *Fair Trial,* 61.

131. Ibid., 61–62.

132. Anderson v. State, 104 Ind. 467, 477 (1885); cited in Rucker, "Right to Ignore the Law," n94.

133. Rucker, "Right to Ignore the Law," 465.

134. Holden v. State, 788 N.E.2d 1253, 1255 (Ind. 2003).

135. *Report of the Debates,* 2:1938.

SEVEN

Margret G. Robb and Nancy Gettinger

JUVENILE LAW

The Quest to Redeem Youthful Offenders

Indiana has embraced the value of children and their place in society. But where does Indiana fit in regard to the evolution of juvenile justice in the United States? At times, Indiana has been at the forefront of the juvenile justice movement and innovative in its approach to the problems of children and families. The Indiana Parenting Time Guidelines, for example, represent a unique approach to visitation for children of divorce. At other times, Indiana merely has responded to directives from the federal government, reacted to lawsuits, or followed national trends. There have been times when Indiana courts have been agents of change, and there have been other times when the legislative or executive branch has taken the lead. But at all times, Indiana has upheld the value of its children.

Indiana's historical approach to looking after children, particularly those within the justice system, has recognized and responded to several basic premises:

1. Children are not miniature adults and need to be dealt with in accordance with their age, development, and special needs.
2. Children need protection, and any response to troubled youth has to strike a balance between meeting the needs of society at large and serving the best interests of children.

3. Children need consistency and stability as well as the support of their families and community.
4. Children and their families have due process rights.
5. Courts dealing with troubled children and their families may have to expand their traditional judicial roles.

How Indiana has addressed each of these presumptions about children will be discussed in the following essay.

An Overview of the History of Juvenile Justice in the United States

To understand fully the evolution of Indiana's view of children within the legal system, it is important to understand the development of juvenile justice in the United States. The notion of childhood or adolescence as a separate and distinct developmental stage is a relatively new concept in this country, particularly within the criminal justice system. Although society has long recognized infancy as being somehow different or separate from adulthood, prior to the nineteenth century children over the age of about five years were considered mature, treated as miniature adults, and viewed as property. One author suggests that the root of this thinking dates back to biblical and medieval times, when "children were not seen as a distinct social group with unique needs and behaviors."[1] Eventually, under early English common law, children came to be viewed as incapable of forming the requisite *mens rea,* or state of mind, to commit a crime. Thus, the juvenile justice system evolved into a system that deals with and treats children differently.[2]

The United States inherited two concepts from England that are very significant in the development of its juvenile justice system. The first has to do with jurisdiction; the second is the doctrine of parens patriae.[3]

Jurisdiction is a court's ability to hear cases and a judge's power to make decisions in them. As stated, early English common law regarded children under the age of seven as unable to form the mens rea necessary to commit a crime and, therefore, as not chargeable with criminal conduct. Moreover, the law presumed that children between the ages of seven and fourteen were incapable of forming criminal intent. Thus, unless and until the court was able to determine that a child of that age understood right from wrong, it also lacked authority to hear and adjudicate a case alleging commission of a crime by that child.[4] This English idea that children whose conduct might otherwise constitute a crime are somehow different from adults who commit the same acts prompted this country's model of a separate juvenile court. The United States has developed separate juvenile courts or divisions of courts to adjudicate and dispose of cases when the offenders are under a certain age. For most criminal conduct, adult courts and juvenile courts have different jurisdictions based on the age of the defendant.[5]

English courts of equity or chancery evolved to adjudicate disputes that did not quite fit into or require the rigid procedures of the English law courts. When losses of liberty or property were not at issue, English judges exercised broad discretion in courts of equity to decide cases on conscience instead of a rigid set of rules and writs. Out of these courts of conscience grew the concept of parens patriae, which literally means "parent of the country."[6] Under this doctrine, the court could conduct relatively informal proceedings leading to a guardianship over a child to protect the child's interests and property. A court of equity could order the guardianship because the original intent of the doctrine was not to address the loss of liberty or property, but to provide protection or intervention in children's lives for the general good or welfare of the state.[7]

At about the same time the courts of equity developed in the early 1600s, England enacted its Poor Laws. The Poor Laws gave churches the authority to take control of vagrant, neglected, and wayward children. Most of these children were placed in workhouses or apprenticeships under the theory that they could be molded into or instructed on how to be good citizens. In a society in which the family was the foundation and the source of discipline, it was a logical extension of parens patriae to extend government control over children without families or children outside the boundaries of parental control.[8] When the government took control of the conduct of wayward youth, however, it still made no distinction between the punishment of an adult and the punishment of a child. There are recorded accounts as late as the nineteenth century of children put to death in England for minor crimes such as stealing.[9]

It is under parens patriae that the American juvenile justice system has thrived. The court becomes the parent; provides discipline, instruction, and protection when there is no able or willing parent; and protects society as a whole from errant children in the absence of a capable parent.

Separate Juvenile Correctional Facilities

In the American colonies, the family was the basic economic and social unit. Children were expected to work right along with adults under strict discipline. Early Puritan settlers believed that children had to be harnessed and strongly directed down the right and moral path. Families who gave up on particularly unruly or unmanageable children turned them over to the church. There was no need for a complicated legal process for children were, after all, property or chattel with which the family patriarch could do as he wished. When a family abrogated its property rights over a child in trouble, three things could happen: (1) the child might be turned over to a skilled craftsman to work as an assistant or apprentice; (2) he might be handed over to any responsible adult to be used in any way needed; or (3) he might be subjected to punishment such as flogging, whipping, beating, or branding by church officials—the same or equal punishment that an adult would receive for the same offense. The earliest known law in the American colonies relating to delinquent children, found in the General Laws and Liberties of the Massachusets [*sic*] Colony, passed in 1641, provided for the execution of children over sixteen years of age who "curse or smyte their natural father or mother."[10]

With the advent of the Industrial Revolution, factory life replaced family life. Children left home at an early age and entered the work force. Immigrants flocked to the United States seeking employment. The number of children living outside the control of the family increased, creating other social problems. States responded to the fear of a new and dangerous class of youth by creating so-called Houses of Refuge, the first one opening in New York City in 1825. For the first time, children, although still tried as adults for their crimes, were not sent to the same prisons as adults but rather to institutions where they were to be transformed into hard-working, productive members of the community.[11]

Houses of Refuge included both children accused of delinquency and children whose only "crime" was poverty and parental deprivation. In a famous 1839 case, the Pennsylvania Supreme Court reiterated that, under parens patriae, the state could do what it wanted with children. *Ex parte Crouse* involved a child who had been placed in the Philadelphia House of Refuge. Upon learning of the poor conditions in the house, her father sought a writ of habeas corpus. The court denied his claim, stating:

> The object of the charity is reformation, by training its inmates to industry; by imbuing their minds with principles of morality and religion; by furnishing them with means to earn a living; and, above all, by separating them from the corrupting influence of improper associates. To this end, may not the natural parents, when

> unequal to the task of education, or unworthy of it, be superseded by the *parens patriae,* or common guardian of the community? . . . The infant has been snatched from a course which must have ended in confirmed depravity; and, not only is the restraint of her person lawful, but it would be an act of extreme cruelty to release her from it.[12]

Besides the House of Refuge movement, around 1830 large cities began the practice of "placing-out." State-chartered agencies from cities like New York and Boston took poor children into custody and sent them via so-called orphan trains to the Midwest, where farmers would take in the children to work on farms. This rather unorthodox method of dealing with the social ill of poverty is now recognized as the beginning of the foster care system.[13]

Indiana's Early Treatment of Youthful Offenders

Although there were no prisons during Indiana's territorial period, each county had courthouses, jails, pillories, and whipping posts.[14] Beyond lengthy terms of incarceration, punishment for crimes featured the whipping post or the pillory. Murder and treason were punishable by death. Children and adults were subject to the same punishments.[15] However, in 1820, the General Assembly provided for a prison in Jeffersonville, Indiana: a two-story log cabin that included fifteen cells for men, women, and children.[16] In 1867, the Indiana legislature established the House of Refuge for Juvenile Offenders,[17] which became the Indiana Reform School for Boys in 1883 and the Indiana Boys' School in 1903. This installation is now known as the Plainfield Correctional Facility, one of ten juvenile correctional facilities in the state.

In 1867, a child between the ages of seven and eighteen years could be sent to the House of Refuge not only for delinquency but also for the *possibility* that he might become wayward. The judge of a circuit or criminal court could commit a child to the House of Refuge for his "future welfare and for the protection of society" if the judge found (1) that a child had, by "incorrigible or vicious conduct," rendered himself beyond the control of his parent or guardian; (2) that because of "moral depravity, or otherwise . . . the parents of a vagrant, incorrigible or vicious child were incapable of or unwilling to exercise the proper care and discipline"; or (3) that the child was "destitute of a suitable home and of adequate means of obtaining an honest living, or [was] in danger of being brought up to lead an idle and immoral life."[18] As in other states, the intent was to remove children from the adult penal system, but there was also an underlying concern about protecting children and society from the perceived ills of poverty and parental neglect.

Cases concerning children whose conduct rose to the level of a crime originated in the adult penal system, but might not necessarily remain there. Under certain circumstances, they might be referred to the juvenile system.[19] A grand jury hearing allegations about a child had the discretion to send the juvenile to the House of Refuge instead of issuing an indictment. Furthermore, after arraignment, the judge could, with the consent of the child, suspend the trial at any point and place the boy in the reform school. When a jury found a child guilty, it could commit the boy to the reform school instead of jail or prison.[20] On the other hand, a child in the juvenile system could be sent back to the adult facilities: the legislature determined in 1903 that if a child's conduct were so disruptive at the Indiana Boys' School as to be detrimental to the welfare of the institution, the child could be sent temporarily to the Indiana Reformatory.[21]

The Indiana House of Refuge and its subsequent incarnations sought to reeducate youth, lead them to a moral and disciplined life, and prepare them to support themselves. It furthered these objectives by physical labor, training, and discipline.[22] The superintendent, with the approval of his commissioners, had the discretion to "execute indentures of apprenticeship for children committed to the institution."[23]

The prevailing theory of juvenile reform at the time was that hard work could mold good character. The superintendent of the Indiana Reform School commented that "[i]t is really a shame that there are some who are yet to be convinced what a miracle of character is wrought when an officer takes forty, fifty or a hundred boys into the field to crack clods."[24]

Prevailing opinion also regarded delinquent youth as the product of poor environment and a genetic predisposition for bad behavior. One expert on penal theory of the time noted that "they are born to it . . . brought up for it. They must be saved."[25] The conventional wisdom in Indiana was that with the right training, such children could, in fact, be saved. Dr. Kenosha Session, superintendent of the Indiana School for Girls,[26] remarked at a 1904 meeting of the National Conference on the Education of Truant, Backward, Dependent and Delinquent Children (NCET)[27] that it is "our business in life to overcome our inheritance. I don't believe it is necessary for any one to succumb to his inheritance, whether it is mental, physical or moral defect. We have to learn how to teach these boys and girls to overcome the moral inheritances which interfere with their being good law-abiding citizens."[28] Corporal punishment was likewise part of the regimen. One researcher claims that "[f]loggings were common at the Indiana Boys' School until 1966."[29]

Indiana's Juvenile Correctional Facilities Today

The basic premise that troubled youth can be redeemed through education, training, and treatment remains the same today, but the means of achieving these objectives has been updated. Today, the Indiana Department of Correction (DOC) is much more in tune with the need for individualized plans of treatment.

Once the juvenile court makes an adjudication, it may order the DOC to assume custody of the child.[30] Initially, the youth goes through a two- to three-week evaluation process at an intake facility. The DOC uses a Juvenile Division Needs Assessment, an Initial Risk Assessment, and a Risk Re-Assessment for Community Supervision as tools to make decisions about the juvenile's commitment. The DOC relies on its Comprehensive Case Management System to structure a treatment protocol and determine the duration of the placement. The length of the placement corresponds to the time needed to successfully complete the treatment, unlike the more punitive model of determinate sentencing used in the adult penal system.[31]

Today, the DOC places youthful offenders in one of the ten juvenile facilities the agency operates. These facilities range from minimum security (staff secure) to maximum security (fencing with razor wire) and include a boot camp. Because of overcrowding, however, the DOC also contracts with some private providers. While in DOC custody, committed youth are provided educational, mental health, and vocational services to prepare them for their release. The department encourages families to participate and become involved in the treatment program. When children leave juvenile facilities, they are either released outright or paroled. DOC staff typically makes the release decisions and supervises the aftercare or parole. In three of Indiana's largest counties—Allen, Marion, and St. Joseph—juveniles receive specific reentry services through the Juvenile Transition Program. In this program, the DOC works with youth and their families from the time they enter the DOC until they are paroled, using the Comprehensive Case Management System and information from the family to plan treatment and rehabilitation and to meet the child's transition needs, including electronic monitoring, family preservation, education, and wraparound services.[32] Indiana invests in its youthful offenders with the hope that they will acquire the skills necessary to remain outside of the criminal justice system as adults.

Preadjudication Detention

Aside from the issues surrounding placement of juveniles after they have been adjudicated delinquent, Indiana also has had to face the question of how to detain children, if at all, prior to the court's determination of delinquency. Although Indiana courts have the option of detaining children arrested for crimes, pending trial, local jails have not proved to be a good option.

The federal government acknowledged the problem and enacted the Juvenile Justice and Delinquency Prevention Act in 1974.[33] The act consisted of four main mandates:

1. Deinstitutionalization of status offenders: Youth who are charged with status offenses may not be held in locked detention or correctional facilities.
2. Sight and sound separation of juvenile and adult offenders: Juveniles who are temporarily held in adult jails or lock-ups should not have sight or sound contact with adult inmates.
3. Removal of juveniles from adult jails and lockups: Accused delinquents may not be detained in adult jails or lockups for more than six hours.
4. Disproportionate minority confinement in the juvenile justice system: Overrepresentation of minority youth in locked juvenile facilities must be identified and addressed.

The act also provided grants to the states for developing alternatives to secure detention and created the Office of Juvenile Justice and Delinquency Prevention (OJJDP) to exercise oversight of states receiving funds under the act.

Although the act passed in 1974, and despite Indiana's prohibition on the preadjudication detention of juveniles,[34] by the late 1980s, Indiana remained out of compliance in many cases, prompting the OJJDP to demand a plan leading to compliance within three years. There were also several reported incidents of teen suicides as well as assaults and rapes on juveniles in county jails.[35] At the time, Indiana had more than seventy-five hundred violators and only nine separate preadjudication detention facilities.

At about the same time, several things happened that, arguably, prompted counties to remedy the problem of juveniles held in jails. First, a series of cases in federal courts raised a concern about liability. The cases clearly concluded that placing juveniles in adult jails violated the Fourteenth Amendment to the U.S. Constitution and raised the question whether a state's participation in the Juvenile Justice Delinquency Prevention Act created a private cause of action.[36] Second, the Indiana Supreme Court authorized the state public defender to seek funds to represent juveniles illegally detained in secure facilities.[37] And last, the DOC made money available to communities to build detention centers.

With a concerted effort, Indiana has been able to build facilities to meet the needs of youth detained pending trial without having to expose those youthful offenders to adult jails. By 1993, the state had fewer than one hundred violations of the Juvenile Justice Delinquency Prevention Act, and currently there are twenty-five juvenile detention centers in Indiana.

Juvenile Probation

In 1841, a Boston shoemaker by the name of John Augustus developed the precursor to juvenile probation. Augustus believed that youth were redeemable. He believed that, instead of punishment, youthful offenders needed rehabilitation that they were not getting while incarcerated. Using his own funds, he bailed out young men accused of crimes, provided them with temporary shelter and clothing, and helped them get jobs. Juvenile probation services are actually an extension of the early impetus to remove children from the adult criminal system in the first place. Juveniles are not adults. They are salvageable, but need special guidance to prepare them for responsible adulthood.

Around the turn of the century, probation became a state function.[38] The first Indiana Juvenile Court Act required the judge of the circuit court of cities with populations of more than fifty thousand to appoint at least one paid officer (compensated $3.00 per day for each day or part of a day the officer served). The judge had the discretion to appoint a second compensated officer "if in his opinion the circumstances require[d]."[39] Furthermore, the judge could "appoint other discreet persons of good moral character as are willing to serve without compensation" if the judge thought he needed even more probation officers.[40] The first juvenile court in Indiana, the Marion County Juvenile Court, reported that

> more than five hundred persons have enrolled themselves as such volunteer aids to the Court. Clergymen, businessmen, professional

> men, and women have come to the assistance as they were needed. Catholic priests, Jewish rabbis, ministers of about all other denominations, bankers, manufacturers, wholesale and retail merchants, lawyers, doctors and teachers, and indeed, men from all the better classes of our citizenship, aided by more than one hundred broad-minded, charitable women, constitute this army of volunteer officers.[41]

Today, all juvenile courts are required to "appoint a chief probation officer" and "may appoint other probation officers and an appropriate number of other employees to assist the probation department."[42]

The Evolution of a Separate Juvenile Court in the United States

Near the turn of the century, social reformers in the United States turned their attention to the treatment or mistreatment of children. Activists within the Progressive movement focused on the plight of American children and how they were victims of mistreatment by society's institutions. The Progressive reformers examined the treatment of children in the justice system and promoted the establishment of courts for juveniles separate and distinct from adult court.

In response to this movement, in 1899, the Illinois Juvenile Court Act created the first separate court to hear and determine the disposition of cases involving children between the ages of eight and seventeen. Creation of this court was largely the result of the efforts of a group of community activists who came to be known as "child-savers." These reformers were primarily civic-minded women, community leaders, and social workers influenced by maternal values and a belief in a child's natural innocence.[43] The reformers were concerned that children still were being treated as adults, not as children. They believed that, even if children were not sent to jail or prisons, they were nonetheless in punitive and prison-like environments in Houses of Refuge or reform schools when what they really needed was instruction and rehabilitation.

In 1892, the Women's Club asked the Chicago Bar Association to draft a bill to create the juvenile court. The principle behind the law was that, under the doctrine of parens patriae, the state became the guardian of the child after an adjudication of delinquency (i.e., the child had violated some state or city law or was deemed incorrigible or truant). The judge, like a parent, then could determine the child's specific needs, give the child sound advice, and offer the child a second chance via probation or, when necessary, sentence the child to a juvenile penal institution. The ultimate goal, however, was rehabilitation, not punishment, and the idea was that justice should be personalized to meet the child's individual circumstances.[44] The Chicago movement was very influential in framing juvenile court legislation in other states. By 1917, all but three states had juvenile courts, and, by 1923, there were six hundred independent juvenile courts in operation in the United States.[45]

Indiana established its own juvenile court system in 1903. Even prior to the passage of the Indiana Juvenile Court Act of 1903, however, one circuit court judge in Indianapolis had created a de facto juvenile court on his own.

Judge George W. Stubbs was serving on the Indianapolis police court in 1901 and, early in his tenure, saw an alarmingly high number of children appearing before him on criminal charges. He was distressed by the increase in crime among the young and even more worried about the practice of incarcerating children. Stubbs believed that children who could be treated, rehabilitated, and "saved" should not be stigmatized by serving time as a criminal. He also believed that children who were incarcerated with adults only learned more about crime and that they could be saved from a life of criminality if they could avoid jail or reform school. Judge Stubbs worked out an agreement with Mayor Charles Bookwalter and the chief of police, George A. Taffe: instead of detaining juveniles under the age of sixteen, officers took them home and directed the parents to appear in police court the following Friday with the offending youth. On that day, Judge Stubbs heard only cases involving youth, often holding hearings in chambers to protect the privacy of the families and the children. Although his informal system was better than bringing children into the adult criminal justice system, he remained dissatisfied with the lack of information he was able to gather regarding a child, the lack of appropriate means of punishment or discipline available to him, and the lack of monitoring in those cases in which the sentence was suspended.

When Judge Stubbs learned of the juvenile court in Chicago, he personally visited the court. While there, Judge Stubbs observed and gathered information. When he returned to Indiana, he initiated aggressive efforts to persuade the legislature to adopt a statutory scheme creating a juvenile court and specific juvenile court procedures.[46]

The Indiana Juvenile Court Act of 1903 created one of the first statutory juvenile courts in the nation.[47] The new law tracked closely the Illinois statute and adopted the parens patriae doctrine, giving the court authority to assume "care, custody and discipline of the child . . . as nearly as may be that which should be given by its parents."[48] Judge Stubbs, the first judge under this new statute, was an avid proponent of this paternalistic approach. "I have often observed that if I sat on a high platform behind a high desk . . . with the boy on the prison's bench some distance away, that my words had little effect on him; but if I could get close enough to him to put my hand on his head or shoulder, or my arm around him, in nearly every such case I could get his confidence."[49] The court had broad discretion from an extensive menu of options for disposing of cases according to what the court found to be in the child's best interests.[50]

The 1903 statute granted the juvenile court the jurisdiction to hear criminal cases of boys under sixteen and girls under seventeen. Such cases still could be filed in the adult criminal court, but, unless the charge was punishable by life imprisonment or death, the criminal court was required to notify the county probation officer,[51] allowing the officer the opportunity to investigate the circumstances giving rise to the charges as well as the "parentage and surroundings of the child."[52] The juvenile court also had jurisdiction to hear cases regarding dependent and neglected children.

Indiana juvenile courts had the power to protect children from notoriety and stigmatization by conducting trials in chambers. If the trial had to be held in the courtroom to accommodate a jury, the judge could exclude from the room individuals not necessary to the proceedings.[53] Children also were protected from incarceration with adults,[54] and only children alleged to have committed crimes could be detained in secure facilities. Boys and girls who came to the attention of the court because they had been "ill-treated or neglected" could not be committed to the Reform School for Boys or the Industrial School for Girls or to any state adult penal or reformatory institution.[55]

Finally, the statute adopted the medical model of treatment and rehabilitation of juveniles by permitting juvenile courts to place children in hospitals or institutions if they needed treatment or care.[56] Granting a court the discretion to facilitate treatment instead of meting out punishment was a departure from the typical role of a criminal court.

Children and Due Process: The Evolution of a Juvenile Code

These new juvenile courts featured substantial judicial discretion exercised through informal proceedings, on the theory that judges needed a great deal of latitude to gather information and assemble it in closed records without the encumbrance of strict rules of procedure and evidence. In a series of landmark cases, however, the U.S. Supreme Court eventually determined that children, like adults, have certain due process rights that may not be abridged. Thus, children now have the right against self-incrimination, the right to confront and cross-examine accusers, the right to counsel, the right of sworn testimony, and the right to appeal. They also have the right to proof beyond a reasonable doubt concerning criminal charges, but not the right to have the evidence heard by a jury.[57] The juvenile judge still has fairly broad discretion to adjudicate, and the juvenile system remains less than a fully adversarial, adult-style process. Today, if a child is to be removed from the juvenile court and tried as an adult, the child has a right to contest the transfer in a separate hearing.[58]

As noted earlier, Indiana began its special treatment of children in the correctional system as early as 1867 and enacted its first comprehensive juvenile law in 1903. The early juvenile court in Indiana examined more closely the root causes of delinquency and focused on the child instead of his alleged crime, a clear diversion from traditional criminal law. Although the 1903 juvenile act continued to provide alleged delinquents with the classic criminal due process rights to a speedy trial and bail,[59] it also granted the court wide discretion under the doctrine of parens patriae.[60] In 1945, the legislature made substantive changes to refine the juvenile court. It adopted a much more pure, or literal, policy of parens patriae, giving the court more latitude in treating children as a parent would instead of acting as the guardian of their individual constitutional rights. Indeed, the 1945 version of the code did not include a list of a juvenile's rights, although case law held that juveniles were entitled to notice and an opportunity to be heard.[61]

The 1945 Indiana Juvenile Court Act also required a preliminary inquiry into what kind of treatment, if any, the child needed. The act allowed waiver to adult court without a hearing.[62] It defined a delinquent child to include one who committed a crime or one of a laundry list of "status offenses," acts that would not be crimes if committed by an adult but had been deemed by the legislature wrongful conduct for a child, warranting the court's intervention.[63]

Between 1945 and 1967, Indiana's juvenile code, not unlike the juvenile system in most other states, existed as a rather unobserved, unchallenged entity. By the mid-1960s, however, the U.S. Supreme Court, apparently concerned that the juvenile courts were not living up to their well-intentioned goals, noted that "[t]here is evidence, in fact, that there may be grounds for concern that the child receives the worst of both worlds: that he gets neither the protections accorded to adults nor the solicitous care and regenerative treatment postulated for children."[64]

Then, in 1967, the Supreme Court's decision in *In re Gault* changed juvenile courts in Indiana and across the country.[65] The *Gault* decision held that, although juvenile courts do not have to become miniature criminal courts, they do have to provide certain procedural due process rights to children accused of delinquent conduct. The Indiana Court of Appeals and the Indiana Supreme Court looked to the *Gault* decision in interpreting Indiana Law.[66]

Responding to a shift in the paradigm, in 1967, the Indiana Judicial Conference appointed seventeen judges to a task force to study the impact of *Gault* and its progeny on the existing Indiana Juvenile Code. The committee's proposed changes to juvenile law failed in the 1969 General Assembly. The legislature formed a subcommittee of the Civil Code Study Commission to examine juvenile procedure. The subcommittee's proposed Juvenile Procedure Code likewise failed in both the 1971 and the 1972 sessions.

By 1975, the General Assembly had created the Juvenile Justice Division of the Indiana Judicial Study Commission to make recommendations for adapting the substantive law that covered both delinquent and dependent and neglected children. The recommendations were submitted to the 1978 General Assembly and to the Indiana Supreme Court.[67]

The division consisted of twenty-four members appointed on the basis of their training and expertise in juvenile justice. They represented a bipartisan group of correctional workers, educators, juvenile court judges, mental health workers, probation officers, prosecuting attorneys, state legislators, and welfare workers. In addition to these nineteen professionals, five at-large members of the general public provided invaluable assistance.[68]

Their deliberations produced a juvenile code, adopted by the legislature in 1978, that reflected the additional rights determined by the U.S. Supreme Court.[69] The new code also attempted to bring consistency to the treatment of juveniles living in large, urban counties and those in rural counties.[70] It established "beyond a reasonable doubt" as the standard of proof concerning delinquency and required the court to determine whether care, treatment, and rehabilitation were needed and were not likely to be received or accepted without the coercive intervention of the court.[71] It empowered the court to order parents to participate in that treatment under a parental participation order.[72] It also eliminated most of the eighteen rather vague status offenses.[73] The statute also offered a diversion option, allowing adjudication in the form of an informal adjustment.[74]

The 1978 code also recognized the need to protect the public. The new law attempted to strike a balance between the protection of society, the best interests of children, and the autonomy of the family. It fostered the "best interests of the child" standard and required the court to examine the "least restrictive alternative" for a child adjudicated a delinquent. The legislature moved away from a pure doctrine of parens patriae and closer to a more rigid due process protection of the rights of juvenile offenders. The law did not abandon the notion that children were to be treated differently in the criminal justice system but added recognition that they should not give up any constitutional rights afforded adults in the process.[75]

The 1978 legislation was the last substantive change to the Indiana Juvenile Code. It has been recodified[76] and updated to reflect changes in the federal law regarding abused and neglected children.[77] With the exception of changes in the law regarding waiver, the statutory scheme for juvenile justice in Indiana has remained fairly constant since the late 1970s.[78] Today's code reflects those values and attitudes toward children that have guided and continue to direct the courts' response to children who enter the juvenile justice system.[79] The code is not—nor is it intended to be—a stagnant document: it is always subject to revision and amendment.[80]

Protection of Children

In addition to early juvenile justice reforms, Progressive movement activists also turned their attention to the mistreatment of children in the workplace, the need for education for all children, and the expansion of women's rights.

Even before the reforms of the Progressive Era, Indiana had acknowledged that children have a special need to be cared for and protected from abuse and exploitation. As early as 1807, the Indiana territorial law provided for placement as "apprentices, all such poor children, whose parents are dead, or shall be . . . found unable to maintain them, males till the age of twenty-one and females till the age of 18."[81]

In 1865, Governor Oliver Morton established the Soldiers' and Seamen's Home for Civil War Veterans, in Knightstown. It became known two years later as the Soldiers' and Sailors' Orphanage, a place that focused on care for destitute children who needed education and maintenance.[82] For children with special needs, the Knightstown institution featured a wing called the Asylum for Feeble Minded Children. These programs later moved to the Eastern Hospital for the Insane and, finally, in 1890, to a permanent facility in Fort Wayne. Today it is known as the Fort Wayne Developmental Center and continues to serve developmentally disabled young adults in northern Indiana. In 1846, the legislature established the Indiana Asylum for the Education of the Deaf and Dumb, now the Indiana School for the Deaf.[83] Indiana established its Institute for the Education of the Blind in 1847 to provide residential or day school education to children who were blind or visually impaired. Both the Indiana School for the Deaf and the Indiana School for the Blind still operate, providing specialized education for hearing and visually impaired children. And, in 1889, the Indiana legislature enacted the Board of Children's Guardians Act, a statute creating a citizens' board in each county that was charged with "the care and supervision of neglected and dependent children less than fifteen years of age."[84]

In 1910, the juvenile court of Indianapolis reported to the governor that it had disposed of 5,141 cases since it had opened its doors in 1903 and that, of these, 807 had involved children who had been neglected or who were dependent.[85] "Some of these unfortunate waifs have been given to the Board of Guardians, some have been sent to the Indianapolis Orphans' Home, some to the Asylum for Friendless Colored Children, and some have been given to the Indiana Children's Home Society . . . [B]ut by far the larger number have been placed with relatives or friends or with other kind-hearted people."[86]

The line distinguishing delinquent children from those who were neglected was not a bright one in the early days of the Indiana juvenile court. In 1907, the law defined a neglected child as a "boy under the age of sixteen or any girl under the age of seventeen who has not proper parental care or guardianship; or who habitually begs or receives alms; or who is found living in any house of ill-fame, or with any vicious or disreputable persons; or who is employed in any saloon; or whose home by reason of neglect, cruelty or depravity on the part of its parent or parents, guardians or other person in whose care it may be, is an unfit place for such child; or whose environment is such as to warrant the state, in the interest of the child, in assuming its guardianship."[87]

A delinquent child, on the other hand, was defined as a child who

> shall violate any law of this state or any ordinance of a city; or who is incorrigible; or who knowingly associates with thieves or other vicious or immoral persons; or who is growing up in idleness or crime; or who knowingly visits or patronizes any policy shop or place where any gaming device is or shall be operated; or who patronizes, visits or enters any saloon or wine room where intoxicating liquors are sold; or who knowingly patronizes, visits or enters any public pool room or bucket shop; or who wanders

> about the streets of any city in the night time without being on any lawful business or occupation; or who wanders about in any railroad yards or upon railroad tracks; or who jumps upon any moving train or enters any car or engine without lawful authority; or who uses vile, obscene, vulgar, profane or indecent language; or who smokes cigarettes; or who loiters about any school building or school yard; or who is guilty of indecent or immoral conduct.[88]

Except for the commission of a crime, the statute did not clearly distinguish between delinquent and neglected children.

The 1978 code created the category of a child in need of services (CHINS), completely separate from the status offenders and the delinquents.[89] A CHINS is a child who comes to the attention of the court not because of delinquent conduct but because of allegations of abuse or neglect by his or her parent or guardian.[90] Although a juvenile court's CHINS adjudication does not involve any determination of commission of a crime, it nevertheless affords families due process and offers treatment, care, and rehabilitation. When the juvenile court intervenes in the lives of families unable or unwilling to provide a safe and secure environment for their children, it directs the creation of a case plan under which families can complete services with a goal of reunification. If the plan fails, the court may order an alternative permanent plan for the children. The court's responsibility to protect the safety and welfare of children always trumps its duty to safeguard the integrity of the family. The legislature perceived that children may need protection within a court proceeding and thus included a provision for a guardian ad litem or a court appointed special advocate (CASA) to safeguard and protect the best interests of the child during juvenile proceedings.[91]

Children as Part of a Family and a Community

Child Support

Children in the United States today are less likely to live with both parents than in the past. In 1970, 85 percent of children lived in two-parent homes, a figure that declined to 68 percent in 1997. In 1997, nearly 50 percent of all children living with only their mother were living in poverty.[92] In an effort to increase each child's accessibility to both parents, as well as both parents' accessibility to a child, Indiana adopted Child Support Rules and Guidelines and Parenting Time Guidelines applicable to families of divorce and families in which there has never been a marriage. All children, but perhaps particularly children in the juvenile justice system, need consistency and stability in their lives.

The federal government began to examine the need for child support enforcement as early as 1950, but it required enforcement of child support orders only for those cases in which state welfare agencies—that is, Medicaid and Aid to Families with Dependent Children—were providing public assistance.[93] The government was looking for a means to recoup rising federal welfare expenditures. With this exception, most states, including Indiana, regarded child support collection as a domestic matter that should be decided in the discretion of the state courts.

Over the next twenty-five years, federal law evolved to give states more authority in accessing information and more assistance in enforcement. Additional amendments to the Social Security Act creating key enforcement mechanisms and incentives for states to enforce and manage child support collection represented the most significant change.[94]

Inconsistent child support orders were a common problem. Many trial courts in Indiana and elsewhere had neither guidelines nor the time, resources, and expertise to develop a method of calculating a child support amount. If they did, the guidelines themselves varied from county to county, or even court to court. Thus, there was a lack of consistency among counties and even among judges within a single county.[95]

The federal government eventually required states to adopt consistent guidelines for child support orders. In response, the Judicial Reform Committee (now called the Judicial Administration Committee) of the Judicial Conference of Indiana began in June 1985 to research and formulate guidelines for use in Indiana courts.[96]

After a great effort to devise an equitable means of calculation, the committee ultimately chose to base the Indiana guidelines on the Income Shares Model, a method developed by the Child Support Project of the National Center for State Courts. The Income Shares Model presumes that a child should receive the same proportion of parental income that he or she would have received if the family had remained intact and, thus, includes both parents' incomes when calculating child support and factors in other children that a parent may have. Originally, the guidelines were just that, a tool to provide guidance for judges when making an award of child support, not a mandatory rule.

When Congress enacted the Family Support Act of 1988, however, making the use of guidelines by the states mandatory instead of discretionary, the committee revised the existing guidelines and submitted them to the Indiana Supreme Court for adoption by rule. The Indiana Child Support Guidelines became mandatory in all Indiana proceedings on or after October 1, 1989, in which child support is established or modified.[97]

The Family Support Act also requires that the guidelines be reviewed at least every four years. The Indiana guidelines were written in 1987, revised in 1988 and 1989, reviewed in 1993 and 1998, and most recently amended in 2003.[98] The review includes notice and the opportunity for input from the public and the practicing bar as well as the judiciary. It was during a public hearing held in preparation for the 1998 revisions that the concept of Parenting Time Guidelines was conceived.

Visitation

Although the stated topic of discussion for the public meeting in 1998 was the Indiana Child Support Guidelines, an overwhelming number of comments focused on inconsistency in the amount of time and the conditions under which noncustodial parents interacted with their children. The committee realized that the citizens of Indiana had concerns about access to their children and decided that, once the 1998 child support revisions were complete, it would investigate the issue of visitation.

The committee sought and received a grant to conduct a study.[99] The committee relied heavily on research done by Dr. Marguerite Rebesco, who had helped develop the visitation guidelines then being used by the courts in Lake County, Indiana. The result was the Indiana Parenting Time Guidelines, effective March 31, 2000, by Indiana Supreme Court rule. These are child-centered standards that represent a substantial diversion from the rigid "railroad schedule" traditionally used by courts when ordering visitation. The Parenting Time Guidelines take into account the child's developmental stages, and their greater flexibility empowers the family to make more decisions about the duration and frequency of the periods the child spends with each parent. The Parenting Time Guidelines create a presumptive arrangement for parental participation, but the court may deviate from the standards if there is an accompanying explanation why the departure it is necessary or appropriate.[100]

Court Experiments in Juvenile Justice

Access to two parents can provide stability and consistency to all children, but family involvement is especially important for children who find themselves in the juvenile justice system and need rehabilitation. Indiana juvenile judges have recognized that they alone cannot effectively address the issues of the troubled children who come before them. Thus, courts have learned to collaborate and cooperate with nonjudicial agencies to arrange appropriate services for the children and families who need them. When children are placed in residential treatment centers, they lose contact not only with their families but also with their communities, schools, neighborhoods, churches, and friends. There are several innovative projects under way in Indiana that specifically address the need for children to remain in their communities and for children and their families to work together. The following are but a few examples.

The Dawn Project

The Dawn Project is a state-level consortium of agencies, including those that provide education, child welfare, juvenile justice, and mental health and substance abuse services. Formed in 1997, the project fosters interagency cooperation and collaboration to better provide services to children with serious emotional and behavioral problems. The project was piloted in Marion County. It has documented results, such as decreases in length of stay in residential care, shorter length of stay for children who successfully complete residential programs, and a 50 percent reduction in the cost of residential care. The emphasis of the project is to reduce residential placements altogether when appropriate. It uses existing community resources to provide services and to assist family participation in community-based treatment teams, while at the same time keeping children in less restrictive placements without compromising their treatment or jeopardizing the safety of the community. The project seeks to treat children who come into the juvenile justice system and to prevent future delinquent conduct.[101] Indiana has enacted legislation that would provide statewide replication of the project.[102]

Lake County

In Lake County, Judge Mary Beth Bonaventura has recognized that (1) children who are placed outside their communities often do not receive the aftercare services so critical for their success; and (2) youth who return to their communities after time in a correctional facility often face the same socioeconomic factors and family issues that contributed to their delinquency in the first place. In cooperation with the Department of Correction, the Lake County Juvenile Court has developed a program of intensive case management for children who are released from the DOC. The DOC notifies the court thirty days before a projected release, and the court reassumes jurisdiction for purposes of providing services to and monitoring the progress of the child and his family. The court sets a hearing for the child and his parents during which the judge has a dialogue with the child about the child's readiness for discharge and the expectations for the child and family once the child returns to the community. After release from the DOC, the child appears for another hearing and is referred to one of three service providers for aftercare services.

The DOC has provided funds for local aftercare services because youth who participate in this unique program typically are placed in a DOC facility for a shorter duration. Judge Bonaventura has used the DOC's money for contracts with local social service agencies to work with the youth and their families in such areas as substance abuse, education, and family counseling. The court continues to monitor the progress that the family makes as the child reintegrates into the community.

Youth Opportunity Center, Inc.

Another Indiana community has responded to the need for placement of children in trouble by building its own facility. Private funds built the Youth Opportunity Center, Inc. (YOC), on seventy acres in Muncie, Indiana. The facility has twenty cottages and 123 beds and includes detention; emergency shelter care; diagnostic testing; and secure, semisecure, and open residential placement. Various grants and a per diem charged to the placing agency, court, or individual family for each child sustain its operation. The YOC's unique goal and mission is to provide "a caring, coordinated, and comprehensive continuum of behavioral health services for kids, families, and the juvenile justice system."[103] The YOC, in cooperation and collaboration with the Delaware County Juvenile Courts, the Office of Family and Children, the Probation Department, the Muncie Community School Corporation, and the Youth Service Bureau, treats the needs of children and families with a team approach, using treatment programs that rely on the skills and expertise of a variety of professionals. The families are involved both while the children are in residential treatment and while they receive aftercare assistance once the children return to their homes.

Family Court Project

Family court, another nontraditional approach to juvenile and family law, is a relatively recent movement in the American legal arena. The idea that families involved in multiple litigation would benefit from a unified family court took hold in the 1950s with the passage of the Standard Family Court Act, model legislation supported by a partnership of three organizations.[104] The act was a spark that ignited initiatives in several states, including Indiana, to examine the concept of a more coordinated method of dealing with families in litigation.[105]

Research indicates that troubled children and children in trouble may be involved in and affected by multiple and contemporaneous legal proceedings.[106] In 1997, Indiana Supreme Court chief justice Randall T. Shepard noted in his State of the Judiciary speech that children and families in Indiana might be well served by a more coordinated court system:

> The legal problems generated by tens of thousands of troubled families come to the courts in many ways—divorce, delinquency, children in need of services, domestic violence, to name a few. In counties of any size, it is possible that the same family may wind up in two or three different courtrooms depending on the legal label used for the cause that brought them to court. The solution to that problem is a family court. A family court is a place where you deal with the whole family in a single courtroom regardless of the legal label.

In 1999, the Indiana Supreme Court provided funds to launch pilot projects in three counties.[107] The project has since expanded and now includes Allen, Bartholomew, Boone, Brown, Crawford, Henry, Jackson, Johnson, Lake, LaPorte, Lawrence, Marion, Martin, Monroe, Montgomery, Orange, Owen, Pike, Porter, Putnam, St. Joseph, Tippecanoe, and Vigo counties.[108] These counties are engaged in innovative ways to better meet the needs of children and their families. "It is important to note that the Indiana Family Court Project is more than just case coordination and programming. It is a concept based on the significance of family in our culture and our legal system. It recognizes the unique stresses and safety issues in family litigation, the role of the family in affecting individual behavior, and the particularized need for timeliness and consistency in judicial rulings involving children."[109]

In Porter County, for example, all truant children are referred to the Family Court Division. Probation staff working with truant children previously had observed that prosecution and treatment in the court process did not seem to be working. According to the chief probation officer, Amy

Beier, and the Family Court Division supervisor, Alison Cox, it appeared that unless and until someone assessed and addressed the root cause of the truant behavior, the pattern of poor school attendance did not change, traditional juvenile court intervention notwithstanding.[110]

Currently, under the leadership of Judge Mary Harper, children who come to the attention of the prosecutor via reports of truancy are afforded the services available though the Community Service Access Center and intensive in-home case management, programs that are components of the Family Court Division. Porter County Family Court, in partnership with the Porter County Prosecutor's Office and Office of Family and Children, offers an alternative to adjudication for children with truant behavior. Those children become a part of Project Attend, which provides intensive casework and service referrals by special probation officers to monitor the children and their school attendance and, perhaps most significantly, to assess and meet the needs of the entire family.

One of the newest Family Court Project sites is Tippecanoe County. Judge Loretta Rush of Tippecanoe County Juvenile Court recognized early in her tenure on the bench that a significant number of children who come through her court both as CHINS and as delinquents are involved in drugs. Of course, the use of illegal drugs is a crime, but an infant born with a trace of an illegal substance in his or her system also meets the statutory definition of a CHINS.[111] Judge Rush soon concluded that, when children use drugs, it is a family issue, not just a behavior problem of the child. She has implemented a family drug court to provide treatment and oversight for both the children identified as drug users and their families. Judge Rush has noted that providing treatment for the child in a vacuum has no long-lasting effect. When children remain in the environment where the drug usage started, the entire family has to become involved in the treatment.[112] The Coalition for a Safe and Drug-Free Tippecanoe County, a collaborative effort involving thirty agencies, including the court, has recently received a grant to launch a campaign to promote prevention of drug use.

In many respects, Indiana has been and remains at the forefront of juvenile justice in this country. Early on, an insightful judge recognized that children are not adults and must be handled differently and separately from adults in the criminal justice arena. Indiana was one of the first states to establish a juvenile court. Today, thoughtful, innovative, and insightful judges are recognizing that children cannot be treated in isolation and are including families in rehabilitation and prevention of juvenile delinquency. Probably most significantly, judges are embracing collaborative efforts and engaging the community in meeting the needs of children and families in trouble.

Notes

A grateful thanks goes to Tina M. Cooper, senior law clerk to the Honorable Margret G. Robb of the Indiana Court of Appeals, without whose assistance this chapter would have been extraordinarily difficult.

1. Mary J. Clement, *The Juvenile Justice System: Law and Process,* 2d ed. (Woburn, Mass.: Butterworth-Heinemann, 2002), 5.

2. Ibid.

3. Ibid.

4. However, if the child were, in fact, determined competent to commit the crime, then he or she was treated no differently than an adult, was tried in the same court as an adult, and was subject to the same punishment that an adult might receive if convicted for the same criminal act.

5. Jurisdictional age limits vary among the states. Under individual state laws, certain factors other than age may be used to determine whether a juvenile is transferred to adult criminal court. Such waivers are exceptional, however; in most circumstances, the premise is that, if a child is under a certain age, he or she is outside the jurisdiction of the adult criminal court.

6. Under English common law, the sovereign was considered the "general guardian of all infants, lunatics, and idiots." Fontain v. Ravenel, 58 U.S. (17 How.) 369, 391–93 (1854). After the development of the courts of equity or chancery in the early 1600s, however, the sovereign's power was delegated to the courts.

7. Clement, *Juvenile Justice System,* 5. See also Dave Schichor, "Historical and Current Trends in American Juvenile Justice," *Juvenile and Family Court Journal* 34 (August 1983): 61–75.

8. Clement, *Juvenile Justice System,* 7.

9. Wiley B. Sanders, ed., *Juvenile Offenses for a Thousand Years: Selected Readings from Anglo-Saxon Times to 1900* (Chapel Hill: University of North Carolina Press, 1970).

10. Ibid., 317–18.

11. Apparently, there was not much reformation of youth in such institutions. "Although the idea of teaching children values of thrift, honesty, and individual responsibility was meritorious, reform institutions were huge, structurally modeled after adult institutions that permitted no individual treatment or educational facilities." Clement, *Juvenile Justice System,* 11.

12. Ex parte Crouse, 4 Whart. 9 (1839).

13. Clement, *Juvenile Justice System,* 23. See also Children's Aid Society, "The Orphan Train Movement," http://www.childrensaidsociety.org/about/train. Orphan

trains stopped in more than forty-five states. Indiana welcomed the largest number of children.

14. *Laws Passed in the Territory of the United States Northwest at the River Ohio from 1791 July to December, 1792* (Philadelphia: Printers of the Laws of the United States, 1794), 27–29.

15. Ibid., 29.

16. 1821 Laws of the State of Indiana, ch. 9, § 6.

17. As early as 1851, the warden of the Indiana state prison reported to the delegates of the Constitutional Convention of 1850–51 that one-eighth of all prisoners had been juveniles. As a result, the General Assembly was required to provide a House of Refuge for Indiana juveniles. David Bodenhamer, *The Pursuit of Justice: Crime and Law in Antebellum Indiana* (New York: Garland, 1986), 16–17.

18. 1867 Ind. Acts ch. 62, § 10.

19. This is in contrast to our current system, wherein juveniles originate in the juvenile system and only under certain circumstances end up in the adult system.

20. 1867 Ind. Acts ch. 62, § 11–12.

21. 1903 Ind. Acts ch. 237, § 3.

22. The superintendent was charged with the duty to "govern them in accordance with such rules and regulations as the Board of Commissioners may prescribe, and shall employ such methods of discipline as will, as far as possible, reform their characters, preserve their health, promote regular improvement in their studies, trades and employments, and secure to them fixed habits of industry, morality and religion." 1867 Ind. Acts ch. 62, § 7.

23. 1867 Ind. Acts ch. 62, § 18.

24. Robert M. Mennel, *Thorns and Thistles: Juvenile Delinquents in the United States, 1825–1940* (Hanover, N.H.: University Press of New England, 1973), 105.

25. Anthony M. Platt, *The Child Savers: The Invention of Juvenile Delinquency* (Chicago: University of Chicago Press, 1969), 45, quoting Enoch C. Wines, *The State of Prisons and Child-Saving Institutions in the Civilized World* (Cambridge, Mass.: Harvard University Press, 1889), 132.

26. The Indiana Girls' School evolved from what formerly had been called the Indiana Reformatory Institution for Women and Girls. In 1899, the legislature created the Indiana Industrial School for Girls, and, in 1907, the name was changed to the Indiana Girls' School. It is still in existence and operation today and is known as the Indianapolis Correctional Facility.

27. With the advent of professionalism within corrections across the United States, NCET was formed in 1904 to help reform school officers define and defend their functions.

28. Mennel, *Thorns and Thistles,* 100–101.

29. Howard James, *Children in Trouble: A National Scandal* (New York: David McKay, 1969), 105.

30. IC § 31-37-19-1.

31. Except under certain circumstances, the juvenile court does not "sentence" for determinate periods of time. See IC § 31-37-19-9 (if the child committed certain heinous crimes, the court may order wardship to the DOC "for a fixed period that

is not longer than the date the child becomes eighteen (18) years of age," and the DOC may not reduce the period ordered.) See also IC § 31-37-19-10 (if the child is convicted of certain felonies and has two prior delinquency adjudications, the court may sentence the child to an authorized facility for not more than two years, and the DOC may not reduce the period ordered).

32. Randy Koester, interview by author Nancy Gettinger, September 12, 2003; National Center for Juvenile Justice, "State Juvenile Justice Profiles: Indiana," http://www.ncjj.org/stateprofiles/profiles/IN04.asp?state=IN04.asp&topic=Profile.

33. Juvenile Justice and Delinquency Prevention Act, 42 U.S.C. 5601. The act originally was sponsored by Sen. Birch Bayh from Indiana. The act has been reauthorized several times, most recently in 2002.

34. As early as the 1945 version of the Indiana Juvenile Code, detention of a child in a prison, jail, or lockup within sight and sound of adult offenders was prohibited. See 1945 Ind. Acts ch. 356, § 22 (codified at IC § 31-37-7-1).

35. On August 1, 1986, a fifteen-year-old committed suicide in the Howard County Jail; on July 18, 1988, a seventeen-year-old committed suicide in the Knox County Jail; and on February 4, 1989, a juvenile killed himself in a Seymour lockup. Jeffrey Bercovitz, "Juveniles in Indiana's Jails," *Res Gestae*, August 1989.

36. D. B. v. Tewksbury, 545 F. Supp. 896, 905 (D. Or. 1982) (pretrial punishment in jail violates the Fourteenth Amendment); Doe v. McFaul, 599 F. Supp 1421, 1430–31 (N.D. Ohio 1984) (violation of the Eighth and Fourteenth Amendments and the act, but no right to a cause of action under the act); but see Hendrickson v. Griggs, 672 F. Supp 1126, 1144 (N.D. Iowa 1987) (act gives juveniles a remedy to "prevent deprivation of congressionally created rights").

37. No lawsuits were filed by the state public defender, but authority to investigate these cases gave the office the opportunity to educate and to provide state court judges and counties with information about the federal law. Laurie Elliott, legal counsel and training specialist, Children's Law Center of Indiana, Inc., interview by author Nancy Gettinger, July 22, 2003. Indiana has twenty-three secure juvenile detention facilities where children may be detained while they are awaiting adjudication. Juveniles who are postadjudication also may be detained in these facilities while awaiting permanent placement following disposition, or youth may be detained as a sanction for probation violation.

38. Indiana's Juvenile Court Act of 1903 provided for probation officers to be appointed by the juvenile court judge and compensated three dollars a day for those days that they actually were on duty. 1903 Ind. Acts ch. 237, § 2. However, the juvenile court actually was assisted by as many as five hundred volunteer probation officers, including clergy, bankers, manufacturers, wholesalers, lawyers, doctors, and teachers. See Marion Superior Court Juvenile Division, *Celebrating 100 years! 1903–2003* [pamphlet] (Indianapolis: Marion Superior Court [2003]).

39. 1903 Ind. Acts ch. 237, § 2.

40. Ibid.

41. Juvenile Court of Marion County, 1903–1905 Report 7. Copy available at the Indiana State Library.

42. IC § 31-31-5-1.

43. Platt, *Child Savers,* 10.

44. Clement, *Juvenile Justice System,* 18–19. See also Platt, *Child Savers,* 10 (reformers adopted the "medical model" and the rehabilitative ideal with regard to the correction of children).

45. Platt, *Child Savers,* 9.

46. See generally ibid., 284–87.

47. The Illinois Juvenile Court Act, 1899 Ill. Laws 131, was approved on April 21, 1899, and the Colorado Juvenile Court Act, 1903 Colo. Sess. Laws 178, was approved on March 7, 1903.

48. 1903 Ind. Acts ch. 237, § 10.

49. Mennel, *Thorns and Thistles,* 133, citing the U.S. Congress, *Children's Courts in the United States,* 58th Cong., 2d sess., 1904, H. Doc. 701, in which Judge Stubbs is quoted.

50. 1903 Ind. Acts ch. 237, § 3.

51. Ibid.

52. 1903 Ind. Acts ch. 237, § 2. The requirement of a preliminary inquiry by an intake officer still exists today. See IC §§ 31-34-8 et seq. Probation officers had other duties as well under the new law. If, upon completion of the investigation, the probation officer believed the child was guilty, the case was certified to juvenile court. The probation officer attended the trial to represent the interests of the child and was responsible for monitoring the progress of the child after adjudication.

53. 1903 Ind. Acts ch. 237, § 4.

54. Ibid., § 3.

55. Ibid.

56. Ibid.

57. In re Gault, 387 U.S. 1 (1967) (right to counsel, notice of charges, full due process hearing on this issue); In re Winship, 397 U.S. 358 (1970) (right to proof beyond a reasonable doubt). See also Breed v. Jones, 421 U.S. 519 (1975) (right to be free from double jeopardy). But see McKiever v. Pennsylvania, 403 U.S. 528 (1971) (no right to jury trial). In response to these decisions, the legislature amended the Indiana Juvenile Code to include a separate section for a procedure that clearly delineates those rights. That section of the juvenile code will be discussed in detail in the text.

58. IC §§ 31-30-3 et seq.

59. 1903 Ind. Acts ch. 237, § 3.

60. The act specifically provided that it "shall be liberally construed, to the end that its purpose may be carried out, to wit: That the care, custody and discipline of the child may approximate as nearly as may be that which should be given by its parents, and in all cases where it can properly be done, the child is to be placed in an approved family home and become a member of the family, by legal adoption or otherwise." 1903 Ind. Acts ch. 237, § 10.

61. Ford v. State, 122 Ind. App. 315, 317, 104 N.E.2d 406, 407 (1952) (failure to give notice required by statute renders judgment void). See also Harris v. Souder, 233 Ind. 287, 291, 119 N.E.2d 8, 10 (1954) (agreeing with *Ford*).

62. 1945 Ind. Acts ch. 356, § 14.

63. 1945 Ind. Acts ch. 356, § 4. Among the lengthy list of "offenses" were "[a]ssociates with immoral or vicious persons," "[u]ses vile, obscene, vulgar or indecent language," "[d]eports himself so as to wilfully injure or endanger the morals or health of himself or others," and "[i]s found begging, receiving or gathering alms."

64. Kent v. U.S., 383 U.S. 541, 556 (1966).

65. In re Gault, 387 U.S. 1 (1967).

66. Bible v. State, 253 Ind. 373, 254 N.E.2d 319 (1970) (juveniles not entitled to jury trial, but acknowledging and agreeing with *Gault* holding). See also Lewis v. State, 259 Ind. 431, 435, 288 N.E.2d 138, 142 (1972) (right to counsel); Warner v. State, 254 Ind. 209, 217, 258 N.E.2d 860, 863–64 (1970) (reasonable doubt standard); Pigg v. State, 253 Ind. 329, 331, 253 N.E.2d 266, 267 (1969) (right to testify on own behalf).

67. Ind. Acts 1975, P.L. 2.

68. Juvenile Justice Division of the Judicial Study Commission, foreword to the Proposed Amendments to the Indiana Juvenile Code (n.p., 1978).

69. See Breed v. Jones, 421 U.S. 519 (1975); McKiever v. Pennsylvania, 403 U.S. 528 (1971); and In re Winship, 397 U.S. 358 (1970), *supra* n57.

70. Juvenile Justice Division of the Indiana Judicial Study Commission to the Judicial Study Commission, letter of transmittal of the proposed Indiana Juvenile Code, October 6, 1977.

71. Former IC § 31-6-4-1 (1978), now IC §§ 31-37-14-1 (burden of proof) and 31-37-2-1 (court intervention required).

72. Former IC § 31-6-4-17 (1978), now IC § 31-37-19-24. This particular provision in the code is especially noteworthy. The parental participation order reflects the philosophy of the Indiana legal community that juveniles cannot be treated in a vacuum. Indeed, under this view, the entire family needs to be involved in and, if need be, ordered into the treatment, care, and rehabilitation of the child.

73. Former IC § 31-6-4-1 (1978), now IC §§ 31-27-2 et seq. There are now only five status offenses: leaving home without reasonable cause and without permission, violating the compulsory school attendance law, habitually disobeying reasonable and lawful commands of a parent or guardian, committing a curfew violation, and violating laws regarding minors and alcohol.

74. Former IC § 34-6-4-12 (1978), now IC §§ 31-37-20 et seq.

75. See former IC § 31-6-1-1 (1978). The purpose of the 1978 code included the need to protect the public; to guarantee due process and protect the legal rights of parents and children; to get children and their families the care, treatment, and rehabilitation that they need; to offer alternatives to adjudication by providing for diversionary programs when appropriate; and to help parents fulfill their obligations, removing children from their homes only when it is in their best interests.

76. IC §§ 31-10-1-1 et seq.

77. Most of the significant changes to the juvenile code were enacted in 1998 in response to the Adoption and Safe Families Act (ASFA) passed by Congress in 1997. ASFA requires states to seek more timely permanent placements for children in order to continue to receive reimbursement for foster care placements. The safety and welfare of children is paramount, but local welfare agencies and juvenile courts

are required to expedite cases in which children are removed from the home, make reasonable efforts to reunify the family, and provide services for rehabilitation, but to begin the termination of parental rights proceedings in those cases where the efforts fail and children have been out of the home for more than fifteen months. AFSA, 42 U.S.C. 629.

78. IC §§ 31-32-5-1 et seq.

79. The current statute expands the previous purpose section and emphasizes the need for services and treatment as opposed to punishment and detention for children. IC § 31-10-3-1. This section of the current code reflects the value that Indiana places on children and articulates its view that families are critical to the welfare and protection of children. It requires personal responsibility and fairness, yet recognizes the need to protect the community at large. This section of the code acknowledges that children can and should be treated and rehabilitated:

It is the policy of this state and the purpose of this title to:

> (1) recognize the importance of family and children in our society;
> (2) recognize the responsibility of the state to enhance the viability of children and family in our society;
> (3) acknowledge the responsibility each person owes to the other;
> (4) strengthen family life by assisting parents to fulfill their parental obligations;
> (5) ensure that children within the juvenile justice system are treated as persons in need of care, protection, treatment, and rehabilitation;
> (6) remove children from families only when it is in the child's best interests or in the best interests of public safety;
> (7) provide for adoption as a viable permanency plan for children who are adjudicated children in need of services;
> (8) provide a juvenile justice system that protects the public by enforcing the legal obligations that children have to society and society has to children;
> (9) use diversionary programs when appropriate;
> (10) provide a judicial procedure that:
> (A) ensures fair hearings;
> (B) recognizes and enforces the legal rights of children and their parents; and
> (C) recognizes and enforces the accountability of children and parents;
> (11) promote public safety and individual accountability by the imposition of appropriate sanctions; and
> (12) provide a continuum of services developed in a cooperative effort by local governments and the state.

80. It should be noted that the juvenile code remains under scrutiny and review. In April 2002, an executive order created the Commission on Juvenile Law. The mandate for the commission is to study the current juvenile code and to make recommendations to the legislature, the judiciary, and the governor regarding revi-

sions in the laws pertaining to juvenile delinquents and CHINS and in the laws governing their parents, guardians, and custodians. The commission is composed of lawmakers, judiciary, juvenile justice professionals (public and private), law enforcement, the state bar, parents, and citizens from around the state. In addition, one of the standing committees of the Indiana Judicial Center is the Juvenile Justice Improvement Committee, a group of juvenile judges who work to review and refine juvenile justice in Indiana.

81. Although the intent of the law may have been to take care of children in need, it resulted in the exploitation of children in mercantile factories and coal mines. In 1867, the legislature responded to this exploitation by limiting the number of hours children under the age of sixteen could work in the mills (1867 Ind. Acts ch. 126, § 1) and, in 1879, passed a prohibition against boys under the age fourteen working in the mines (1879 Ind. Acts ch. 10, § 21). By 1889, Indiana had a fairly comprehensive child labor law (1889 Ind. Acts ch. 201), and, in 1897, Indiana enacted compulsory education (1897 Ind. Acts ch. 165) and further limited the employment of children (1897 Ind. Acts ch. 65, §§ 1–3).

82. Once an orphanage for veterans' children, the Indiana Soldiers' and Sailors' Home now serves all Indiana youth in need.

83. The school became the sixth state school for the deaf in the nation and the first state school to provide free education for deaf children.

84. 1889 Ind. Acts ch. 125, § 2.

85. Report of the Juvenile Court of Marion County, April 17, 1903 to April 17, 1910, Indianapolis, Indiana.

86. Ibid.

87. 1907 Ind. Acts ch. 41, § 2.

88. 1905 Ind. Acts ch. 145, § 1. See also 1917 Ind. Acts ch. 111, § 1 (substantially the same as its precursor, but amending the definition to increase the age to eighteen for girls).

89. Former IC § 31-6-4-3 (1978). Even earlier than the statute that created a separate juvenile court and juvenile court procedures, Indiana, under the parens patriae doctrine, recognized the state's duty to protect maltreated children. The Board of Children's Guardians Act (1889 Ind. Acts ch. 125) authorized the circuit court to appoint in each county a six-member Board of Children's Guardians that could bring allegations of neglect to the circuit court and, if the court found the allegations true, it could give the board authority to place the child. There was not much due process involved. By creating the category of CHINS, the Indiana General Assembly guaranteed these children and their parents certain due process protections. See former IC §§ 31-6-4-8 (1978) (preliminary inquiry), 31-6-4-13 (1978) (initial hearing), and 31-6-4-14 (1978) (fact-finding hearing).

90. The statute, in addition to a list of acts or omissions on the part of a child's caretaker, also included a provision that if the child is a danger to himself or others, he may be a child in need of services. Former IC § 31-6-4-3(a)(3) (1978). Perhaps the line between a delinquent child and a child in need of services remains blurred.

91. 1945 Ind. Acts ch. 356, § 3, now IC §§ 31-9-2-28 (court-appointed special advocate) and 31-9-2-50 (guardian ad litem).

92. Juvenile Offenders and Victims: 1999 National Report. Howard N. Snyder, Melissa Sickmund (Washington, D.C.: U.S. Dept. of Justice, Office of Juvenile Justice and Delinquency Prevention, 1999).

93. 42 U.S.C. 602 (a)(11).

94. P.L. 93-647, Part D of Title IV of the Social Security Act, [§§ 451 et seq.], codified at 42 U.S.C. 651 et seq.

95. See commentary, Indiana Rules of Court, Child Support Rules and Guidelines, adopted effective October 1, 1989 (including amendments received through January 1, 2004) (latest version).

96. The committee relied on the expertise of Thomas J. Espenshade, author of *Investing in Children: New Estimates of Parental Expenditures* (Washington, D.C.: Urban Institute Press, 1984), in coming up with the Indiana Child Support Guidelines. The committee reviewed several models and chose the Income Shares Model for the guidelines. This model is based on the notion that children should receive the same proportion of parental income when living with a single parent as they would have received if the family were intact. The model apportions the cost of providing for children between the parents based on their means.

97. The Indiana Child Support Guidelines are still not absolutely rigid, in that they provide for a deviation from the guidelines upon a finding that the amount to be awarded under the guidelines would be unreasonable, unjust, or inappropriate.

98. The Indiana Child Support Guidelines as well as the Indiana Parenting Time Guidelines are now under the purview of the Domestic Relations Committee of the Indiana Judicial Committee instead of that of the Judicial Administration Committee. The Indiana Child Support Guidelines, including the 2003 amendments, can be found at Indiana Courts, "Indiana Child Support Rules and Guidelines," http://www.in.gov/judiciary/rules/child_support/child_support.doc.

99. The grant was from the Indiana Families and Fathers Initiative of the Indiana Family and Social Services Administration (FSSA). Since 1997, FSSA, through funding from the U.S. Department of Health and Human Services, has provided grants to further the goals of improving fathers' involvement in their children's lives, including visitation, payment of child support, establishing paternity, and improving coparenting relationships.

100. Indiana Courts, "Indiana Parenting Time Guidelines," http://www.in.gov/judiciary/rules/parenting.

101. Choices, "Indiana Dawn Project," http://www.choicesteam.org/program/alias/dawn+article=311+prog=31.

102. IC §§ 12-22-4-1 et seq.

103. Youth Opportunity Center, "Mission," http://www.yocinc.org/AboutUs/mission.php.

104. Those three national organizations were the National Parole and Probation Association (later the National Council on Crime and Delinquency), the National Council of Juvenile Judges (later the National Council of Juvenile and Family Court Judges), and the United States Children's Bureau.

105. It is generally acknowledged that the first family court in this country was established in Cincinnati, Ohio, in the early 1900s. Statewide family courts were

later developed in Hawaii and Rhode Island in the 1960s. In addition to the pilot projects in Indiana, family courts are currently in operation in California, Florida, Washington, and Oregon. *Indiana Family Court Projects: The First Four Years,* Frances G. Hill, Contract Consultant, Fall 2003, 1n. (*Family Court Report*)

106. As reported by Indiana's Family Court Pilot Projects that hear adversarial cases, the average number of cases per family in the projects ranges from 2.65 in Boone County to 5.92 in Montgomery County. The two smallest counties that have Family Court Pilot Projects, Putnam and Owen, were not included because their projects focus primarily on nonadversarial alternative dispute resolution. *Family Court Report,* 25.

107. Indiana's projects are unique in that, instead of imposing a single family court model on the project sites, the Indiana Supreme Court has given the counties who have received the grants the discretion and flexibility to design a model that fits the specific needs of each county. For a comprehensive report regarding the development of the family court concept in Indiana, see generally *Family Court Report.*

108. As of this writing, additional courts in Lake, Tippecanoe, Henry, Vigo, Bartholomew, Lawrence, Jackson, and Brown counties have applied for and are preliminarily approved to receive funding for the state fiscal year 2004–5.

109. *Family Court Report,* 7–8.

110. Amy Beier, chief probation officer, and Alison Cox, family court division supervisor, interview by author Nancy Gettinger, September 10, 2003.

111. IC § 31-34-1-10.

112. The Honorable Loretta Rush, Tippecanoe Juvenile Court judge, interview by author Nancy Gettinger, November 14, 2003.

PART IV

Rights

EIGHT

Virginia Dill McCarty

FROM PETTICOAT SLAVERY TO EQUALITY

Women's Rights in Indiana Law

One pot and a pan, a knife, spoon, and fork, a few dishes, one sheet and a quilt, a brooch or a locket may seem a pitiful accumulation of wealth by today's standards. But, to a Hoosier pioneer woman who had brought them with her on an arduous journey, they were precious beyond compare. They were the hallmarks of the civilization she had left behind. Yet, if she were a married woman, her possessions were at the mercy of her husband and his creditors. Her husband could deal with her personal property as he pleased, and his creditors could claim it for his debts. Such was the status of women under the law that prevailed at the time of Indiana statehood in 1816.

The story of women and Indiana law is a story of the struggles to reverse both English common law and Anglo-American customs regarding women's place in society. At times, the law was an instrument of reform. More often, it was an obstacle overcome only by shifts in popular attitudes and by subsequent political action. The barrier to change was high. Indiana law was starkly simple in its assumptions about the role of men and women, especially married women, as expressed in an 1896 opinion from the state supreme court:

> At common law a valid marriage made the husband and wife one person in law. The legal existence of the woman was suspended or merged in that of the husband. . . . The husband, by virtue of the marriage, was entitled to all the personal property . . . of his wife, which, when reduced to possession, [became] his absolute property, and was also entitled to the exclusive possession, use, and control of her real estate during their joint lives.[1]

The husband was entitled to any remuneration his wife earned from others and to any damages caused by injury to her. Neither spouse could sue the other for any physical or fiscal wrong.[2] A wife could not make a valid contract.[3]

These disabilities created what some women and men considered a form of legal slavery, although one by no means as limitless as African slavery. The justification was an old one, predating the American Revolution. Just as a nation required one ruler, English common law theory held, so too one person, the husband-father, must have authority over a family's affairs; women were not suited by nature for this role. A corollary principle was that all husbands, at all times, would do what was best for their wives and families. Neither proposition was any more true at that time than it is now. Many couples no doubt lived their lives amicably, but, in fact, domestic law permitted physical abuse and tyranny. When a husband absconded with his wife's property or physically abused her, she had no legal recourse.

Custom, as well as prohibitions in the law, kept early nineteenth-century women in the home and out of public affairs. Even in a revolutionary republic in which government rested on popular consent, women were not part of the body politic. No women could vote, except during one brief period in New Jersey.[4] No women held government office. No women were lawyers, and only a few were physicians. But the Revolution that had created a new theory of sovereignty also gave voice to rhetoric that inspired women. The sentiment that led to the words of the Declaration of Independence, "all men are created equal," inspired at least some women to believe that they, too, were created equal. Although Abigail Adams had to live in the patriarchal society of her day, she also abjured her husband John to "remember the ladies" when fashioning laws for the new nation and warned that women "will not hold ourselves bound by any Laws in which we have no voice, or Representation."[5]

There were three overlapping waves in the rebellion that came to be known as the women's movement. The first removed the common-law disabilities of married women. The second secured woman suffrage. The third campaigned, unsuccessfully, for an Equal Rights Amendment (ERA) to the U.S. Constitution. Each phase subjected its proponents to ridicule and derision for proposing radical and unnatural changes. Each battle was fought nationwide, and Indiana law dealt with each in succession. Women won each battle in Indiana, but the last was lost nationally.[6]

Although Indiana's constitution of 1816 did not mention women, the male-only General Assembly—and occasionally Hoosier courts—slowly began to whittle away at the legal restrictions on women. Even before statehood, legislators had favored the education of women. At the creation of Vincennes University in 1806, the trustees were urged to provide for the admission of women students as soon as possible.[7] Franklin College, in 1842, was the first private college in Indiana to admit women. Indiana University allowed women to take nondegree classes as early as 1837 and was the first major university in the country to admit them on an equal basis in 1867.[8]

In the 1830s, women in the North, including Indiana, publicly became involved in the movement to abolish slavery. Elizabeth Cady Stanton, of New York, and Lucretia Mott, of Philadelphia, attended the World's Antislavery Convention in 1840 in London, England, as delegates. All women were denied participation. In part as a result of this experience, they organized the first American women's rights convention, in Seneca Falls, New York, in 1848. Stanton proclaimed a women's declaration of rights patterned after the Declaration of Independence, part of which called for the recognition of property rights for women.[9] The Indiana legislature required no such prompting. A year earlier, it had passed a law removing from a husband's control any real property acquired by a woman before marriage and exempting its rents and profits from being counted against his debts. The statute also made a woman responsible for any debts she had incurred before marriage.[10] Although Indiana was not the first state to take this action—Mississippi had passed a similar law in 1837—the reason for its enactment had nothing to do with the desire to protect family assets in slaves, which had been the impetus behind the Mississippi law.

When Indiana held a constitutional convention in 1850, the delegates debated the radical proposals of Robert Dale Owen, of New Harmony.[11] He sought to write into the new constitution the protections of the 1847 statute concerning married women's real estate and to extend them to personal property. The debate was acrimonious, but his proposal passed by seven votes on November 27, 1850. A group of Indiana women who had organized around women's issues and openly advocated change placed a "card" of thanks to Owen in an Indianapolis newspaper. It was a political mistake. The next day, the convention reversed its approval of Owen's amendment.

In the end, no provision for married women made it into the Indiana constitution of 1851. Newspapers, the only media of the time, equated the drive for married women's property rights to the radical eastern states' "Bloomer" movement of which most Hoosiers disapproved. Clergymen proclaimed that giving married women property rights would destroy the sacred union that made women subservient to their husbands. However, Sarah T. Bolton, a prominent poet and the only woman for whom a bronze plaque hangs in the Indiana State House rotunda, joined other leading women in presenting Owen with an engraved silver pitcher at a gala affair in the Indiana House of Representatives chamber in 1851.[12]

That same year, the first Indiana Women's Rights Convention was held at Dublin. On October 15, the delegates advocated equal rights for women and African Americans as well as property rights for married women.[13] At the next year's meeting in Richmond, the Indiana Women's Rights Organization was created.[14]

When the General Assembly first met under the 1851 constitution, Owen again pushed his ideas about equal rights for women. This time he succeeded. The Married Women's Act reenacted, in substance, the 1847 act providing that a husband could not convey his wife's separately acquired land.[15] Then, in 1853, in a measure embodying Owen's goal, the General Assembly recognized a married woman's ownership and control of personal property acquired before marriage or by descent, devise, or gift.[16]

In *McCarty v. Mewhinney* (1856), the Indiana Supreme Court rather grudgingly acknowledged that some of the common law had been repealed. The court commented that the Married Women's Acts seemed designed "to destroy the community of interest between husband and wife."[17] Two years later, in *Reese v. Cochran,* the court disagreed with *McCarty's* statement of the act's purpose.[18] It declared that the legislature's aim was to protect a married woman and her children from her husband's debts, but the justices refused to extend the law beyond its literal wording to allow a wife to give away her personal property without her husband's consent.[19]

Encouraged by these improvements, women continued to fight for full property rights. On January 19, 1859, women for the first time appeared before the General Assembly to petition for property rights, suffrage, and temperance. Their petition was signed by one thousand men and women from Wayne County. Although the requests were logical and well-reasoned, the public generally greeted the petition with laughter and derision. People likened the petitioners to the talking dogs: the fact that they spoke in public was more consequential than what they said. One newspaper called it a "farce" and "disgraceful." Legislators ridiculed the women's requests and denied that they represented most Hoosier women.[20] Their appearance did not reap immediate results.

Following the Civil War, Indiana women secured the introduction of a woman suffrage amendment to the state constitution in December 4, 1865, but it failed to pass the General Assembly. This action placed Indiana women in the vanguard of the national movement: it was one year later that Susan B. Anthony and Elizabeth Cady Stanton formed the American Equal Rights Association, dedicated to suffrage for all.[21] In 1871, Indiana women reformers presented the Woman's State Suffrage Association's petitions for abolition of all of women's legal and political disabilities to a joint House and Senate session. After the resolution was amended to restrict suffrage to white women, the committee reported favorably on the measure, but the bill went nowhere.[22]

Indiana women were, no doubt, disappointed with the legislature's failure to act upon their petition, but their efforts and organization increased with each setback. As towns and cities grew and as servants became available for the well-to-do, women used this newly found free time to organize in the New Harmony tradition, at first for social and educational purposes, and then for charitable purposes. Suffragettes addressed the General Assembly again in 1873. From 1873 through 1877, various bills for women were introduced, but all failed.[23]

Nationally, women were attempting to use the new Civil War Amendments to gain civil rights for themselves. In *Bradwell v. State* (1872), the U.S. Supreme Court struck down one such effort by deciding that practicing law is not a privilege of U.S. citizenship that the states are required to honor.[24] In a concurring opinion that expressed a common view, Justice Joseph Bradley said that women, by the "natural and proper timidity and delicacy" of their natures, were unsuited to practice law, claiming it would violate the law of the creator.[25] In 1874, the U.S. Supreme Court, in a Missouri woman's suit, admitted that women were citizens but held that the U.S. Constitution did not provide a right to vote because voting was not a privilege of citizenship.[26]

In 1878, May Wright Sewall of Indianapolis and Zerelda Wallace,[27] of Crawfordsville, wife of antebellum Indiana governor David Wallace, organized the Indianapolis Equal Suffrage Society. Earlier, in 1873, women had organized the Indianapolis Women's Suffrage Society, evidently a predecessor organization. The women organized groups throughout the state, lobbied, petitioned, and held public meetings.

In 1879 and 1881, the women's perseverance paid off. The Indiana Supreme Court in 1879 advanced women's rights a small step by holding a married woman liable for a mechanic's lien on her separate land for improvements she had ordered. Although she still had no ability to contract, the court ruled that the lien was created by operation of law. A married woman ought to be allowed to improve her own separate property, the justices decided, in order fully to enjoy it.[28] More important, the General Assembly in 1879 and 1881 wiped out most common-law disabilities affecting married women.[29]

The 1881 act covered the same ground as the 1879 act, but for the first time abolished almost all a married woman's disability to make a contract.[30] A married woman could retain property that she bought with her own assets while married. Her earnings were her own. She could dispose of her personal property as she pleased, without her husband's consent, although she still could not do so with her real property. The legislature also incorporated court decisions holding a married woman responsible for her own debts. She could not deny that she was bound by her covenants in deeds. She was liable on her contracts to repair her own property. Her husband was relieved of responsibility for her business debts or for repairs or improvements to her real property, and he was responsible for her premarriage debts only to the extent of the personal property she contributed to him at or during the marriage.

Adding rights for married women sometimes led to an unintended consequence. A married woman whose husband was conveying his land was caught in a bind. The laws of descent gave her an intestate one-third interest in the property her husband owned during the marriage, even if he had conveyed it away, unless she also signed the deed. Understandably, grantees would not accept a deed of a husband's land without his wife's signature. Under the Married Women's Acts, however, the wife was responsible for her covenants in a deed. In a 1938 case, when a grantee received nothing from a deed because a husband's title failed, the grantor's wife alleged that she had received no consideration for signing the deed but had signed it merely to release her contingent interest. The Indiana Appellate Court ruled, sensibly, that she was not liable to the grantee.[31]

The drive for suffrage also took a first step in 1881. At that time, the House of Representatives was split evenly between Democrats and Republicans, and the Senate was controlled by the Republicans. Although the suffrage issue had not become partisan, more Republicans than Democrats supported the issue. The woman suffrage organizations in both Indiana and Indianapolis had become well organized. A proposed amendment to the Indiana constitution for woman suffrage sailed through in a special session. In that same session, a prohibition amendment to the Indiana constitution was passed.[32]

The Indiana constitution requires that a proposed amendment be passed by both houses in each of two consecutive General Assemblies before it may go before voters for ratification.[33] Understandably, suffragists threw themselves into the political campaign of 1882, trying to elect legislators who would vote in favor of the suffrage amendment in the next session. They organized local suffrage societies, wrote articles, traveled on lecture tours, sponsored meetings, and mailed postcards. Unfortunately, the women's amendment became intermingled with the prohibition amendment in the minds of the public. The liquor interests feared that a women's vote would mean a temperance vote. In 1883, their political allies, the Democrats, found a technicality to declare the 1881 vote on the suffrage amendment invalid, and the women's amendment did not pass the necessary second General Assembly.[34] The women did not give up. Woman suffrage amendments were presented in 1882; in each year from 1891 through 1899; in 1907; and once again in 1913.[35]

In 1897, women's hopes to establish voting rights under the Indiana constitution were dashed when the appeal of Helen M. Gougar for such rights was rebuffed by the Indiana Supreme Court.[36] The court's stance on suffrage did not guide its actions in all matters involving women's rights. Hoosier Antoinette Dakin Leach followed the lead of Myra Bradwell of Illinois when she applied to the Greene Circuit Court to admit her to practice law. When the judge refused, she appealed. In 1893, the Indiana Supreme Court broke with common-law precedent to admit her. The justices reasoned that times and women had changed and that if women wanted to pursue the law and became educated, there was no reason to deny them, even though the constitution and statutes referred only to men.[37] The decision essentially ratified what had occurred in local courts: women already were practicing law in Indiana. Elizabeth Jane Eaglesfield, the first woman lawyer known in Indiana, had been admitted to the bar in Vigo Circuit Court in September 1875.[38]

Organized opposition to suffrage did develop, as evidenced elsewhere by the rise of the National Organization Opposed to Women's Suffrage, founded in 1911 by a group of mostly wealthy women led by Mrs. Arthur Dodge and some Catholic clergy.[39] Equal rights advocates in Indiana countered by organizing the Woman's Franchise League in 1911, formed from two earlier suffrage groups. The Miami County chapter had a "flying squadron" founded by May Wright Sewall that toured that county in 1917, although they stopped short of chaining themselves to a fence, as other women did in Washington, D.C. Chapters of the General Federation of Women's Clubs, which had two million members nationwide, existed in almost every small town and city in Indiana, made up of mostly middle-class, respectable women.[40]

In 1917, the General Assembly finally passed legislation permitting Hoosier women to vote for municipal and school board officers. Although conventional wisdom held that the legislature had that power,[41] a citizen-taxpayer suit was filed immediately to prohibit the registration of women voters. When *Board of Commissioners v. Knight* reached the state supreme court, the justices chose to interpret the constitution strictly, enjoining the registration of women.[42]

Knight was the last gasp of the conservative movement in Indiana against the women's vote. By June 1918, Congress had passed and sent to the states for ratification the Nineteenth Amendment to the federal Constitution forbidding the states to deny the opportunity to vote on account of sex. On January 16, 1920, in a special session of the General Assembly, Indiana ratified the amendment. On August 10, 1920, it became the fundamental law of the land, almost seventy years after Hoosier women first had demanded the vote.[43]

The next year, an Equal Rights Amendment was introduced in Congress. Patterned after the Nineteenth Amendment, the proposed Twentieth Amendment stated that "[e]quality of rights under the law shall not be denied or abridged by the United States or by any state on account of sex." For fifty years, it went nowhere. The proposed amendment regained life only in the 1960s, a time of ferment in the women's movement. Spurred by Betty Friedan's *Feminine Mystique* (1963) and other feminist literature, independent "women's liberation" groups sprang up in cities and engaged in "consciousness raising" discussions concerning women's isolation and unproductiveness.[44] By 1967, the National Organization for Women (NOW) had formed to promote the ERA and other feminist goals.[45]

Three years earlier, Congress had passed Title VII of the Civil Rights Act of 1964.[46] After its passage, federal law protected women in private employment from sex discrimination. But the measure had little immediate effect, even though both the statute itself and a later decision by the U.S. Supreme Court served as a spur to state legislation on the subject. Indiana had adopted a civil rights law in 1961;[47] ten years later, it added a prohibition of sex discrimination.[48] This action came in the same year as the U.S. Supreme Court's ruling in *Reed v. Reed,* reversing a century of precedents, that sex discrimination violated the equal protection clause of the Fourteenth Amendment.[49]

Change in laws affecting women was not limited to the U.S. Supreme Court. In 1969, the Indiana Supreme Court declared that it would not follow outmoded common-law precedent preventing a wife from recovering damages for loss of her husband's consortium, whereas a husband could sue for loss of his wife's consortium. The rule had developed, the court said, when a wife was more of a servant than a companion. No longer was this the case. However, the court ruled that any damages due the wife belonged to her husband, who had the duty to support her from any recovery he received. To allow her recovery would give the couple a double recovery.[50]

In 1972, as the result of the determined efforts of U.S. senator Birch Bayh (D-Ind.), among others, Congress passed an Equal Rights Amendment to the U.S. Constitution and submitted it to the states for ratification. Lobbying for its passage was the bipartisan National Women's Political Caucus, an umbrella group formed in 1971 to pass the ERA, elect women to office, secure executive-level appointments for women in government and business, and allow women to choose an abortion. (An Indiana Caucus also organized the same year, founded by Mary Ann Butters, of Indianapolis, former reporter for the *Indianapolis Star* and later aide to then Indianapolis mayor Richard Lugar, a Republican, and by the author, a Democrat.) By the end of 1973, the Indiana State Teachers Association and the United Auto Workers, important unions in the state, had endorsed the ERA. In opposition were members of the National Committee to Stop ERA, begun by Phyllis Schlafly, a well-known Illinois Republican, who raised questions about the amendment's effect on women.

The ERA was introduced for ratification in the Indiana General Assembly in 1973. The League of Women Voters, after years of opposition, had endorsed the ERA. Judith Head, of Columbus, representing the league, Betty Newcomb, of Muncie, representing NOW, and the author, representing the Indiana Caucus, organized Hoosiers for the Equal Rights Amendment (HERA). Most established Hoosier women's groups joined. HERA grew into ERA Indiana, headed by Russell Lloyd, Republican mayor of Evansville, and by Harriet Inskeep, of Fort Wayne, a Democrat.

Most Democrats and a small group of Republicans in the General Assembly were steadfastly for the ERA through the years of battle. Representative Clifford Arnold (D-Michigan City) and William Latz (R-Fort Wayne) sponsored the resolution in the House. Senators Robert Garton (R-Columbus) and Phillip Hayes (D-Evansville) led the Senate effort. Then each of the major political parties took a position opposite to that which it had taken on the earlier Indiana suffrage amendment. Senate Republicans were almost all opposed, including President pro Tempore Phillip Gutman (Fort Wayne), Majority Leader Martin K. "Chip" Edwards (New Castle), and Senator Joan Gubbins (Indianapolis). Most Senate Democrats were in favor.

Legislative hearings produced what became the standard litany from proponents and opponents of the amendment. Supporters of ratification argued that women, more than half the U.S. population, were entitled to have their rights secured permanently in the Constitution. Opponents claimed that ratification would violate states rights, destroy the family, require women and men to use the same restrooms, cause women to be drafted and lose their husbands' financial support, and legalize abortion on demand. The Republican-controlled House passed the ERA joint resolution in 1973, but the measure lost in the Republican-controlled Senate. But the session was not an entire loss for advocates of equality of the sexes. Women lawyers reviewed existing Indiana law that referred to citizens by sex and delivered the list to the General Assembly. As a result, the legislature repealed the discriminatory provisions in Indiana statutes.

In 1975, Senator Gubbins sponsored a resolution to amend the ERA into the Indiana constitution. Its passage would have defeated the federal ERA. It passed the Senate, but died in the Democrat-controlled House. The pro-ERA coalition's attempt to elect favorable senators in 1976, bolstered by NOW members' door-to-door campaigning, succeeded in returning the Senate to Democratic control. Republicans controlled the House. The ERA resolution passed the House early in the 1977 session. On January 18, 1977, the Senate passed the ratification measure, 26 to 24, to the jubilation of a pro-ERA crowd that packed the Senate gallery. Indiana was the thirty-fifth—and last—state to ratify the ERA. No other state ratified, and the amendment failed nationally.[51]

Hoosier supporters of equality of the sexes soon turned their attention to other forms of discrimination against women. After department stores canceled credit cards for two Indiana Caucus women upon notice of their husbands' obituaries, the group lobbied successfully for an amendment to the Indiana civil rights law to forbid denial of credit on account of sex.[52]

They also tackled the Indiana inheritance tax law, which was sex-neutral on its face but handicapped women severely. Husbands usually died before their wives. Even if property had been held in joint names, the taxing authorities taxed all property that the survivor could not prove had belonged originally to the survivor alone.[53] This meant that a woman who had worked without salary on a farm or in a business with her husband was taxed on the full value of the asset. In 1979, property passing to a surviving spouse was freed from Indiana inheritance tax.[54] The federal government later followed the Hoosiers' lead and exempted surviving spouses of decedents who died after December 31, 1981, from federal estate tax.[55]

Women's rights became entangled in an antipornography campaign in 1984 in a case from Indianapolis that ultimately reached the U.S. Supreme Court. In July, Beulah Coughenour, a Republican member of the Indianapolis and Marion County City-County Council, won passage of an ordinance that defined pornography as the sexually explicit subordination of women and thus as a discriminatory practice subject to regulation by the Indianapolis Human Relations Commission. Modeled on a similar measure introduced but not implemented in Minneapolis—and spurred by proposals from national feminist leaders Catherine MacKinnon and Andrea Dworkin—the ordinance brought together two groups, radical feminists and the religious right, in a marriage of convenience.[56] Local civil rights organizations opposed the ordinance, which upon passage was immediately subject to a legal challenge brought by a large number of national organizations, including the American Booksellers Association, the Association for American Publishers, and the Council for Periodical Distributors. In *American Booksellers Ass'n v. Hudnut,* U.S. District Court judge Sarah Evans Barker, a Republican appointee and the first woman federal judge from Indiana, permanently enjoined the ordinance as unconstitutionally vague. The court expressly rejected the contention that sexually explicit works constituted subordination of women and thus should be considered conduct instead of speech.[57] In 1986, the U.S. Supreme Court, without comment, unanimously affirmed the decision.

A breakthrough for women in Indiana courts followed the adoption by the board of trustees of the Indiana State Teachers' Retirement Fund of a schedule that paid retired male teachers $15.00 a month more than female retirees, although both made the same contributions. The state supreme court held this action unconstitutional under the Fourteenth Amendment to the U.S. Constitution and article I, section 23 of the Indiana constitution. Justice Roger DeBruler authored the opinion, holding that the provision did not foster the object of the statute—to encourage teaching as a career.[58] Fifteen years later, the Indiana Court of Appeals extended constitutional protection to homeless women and their children after the trustee of Center Township of Marion County had found shelter for homeless men but not for homeless women and families.[59]

The common law of husband and wife continued to raise practical issues. A husband was liable for his wife's debts only if they were for "necessaries." In *Memorial Hospital v. Hahaj,* a married woman was unable to escape personal liability for her own medical expenses.[60] The court held that she was liable to the extent of her resources. If her assets were insufficient, her spouse was liable. The same question in reverse was raised in *Bartrom v. Adjustment Bureau, Inc.*[61] The facts were more difficult, because the debt was incurred by a husband whose wife had left him and filed for dissolution on grounds that he had abused her. Eight days later, he was rendered comatose in an auto accident and died later in that state, running up a hospital bill of more than $67,000, which his wife refused to pay. The supreme court took the occasion to modernize the law of necessaries by holding that each spouse is primarily liable for the debts he or she contracts. If that spouse has sufficient funds, the noncontracting spouse is liable only if that spouse has agreed to pay or is liable under the laws of agency. If the contracting spouse's funds are insufficient, a financially superior spouse will have a duty imposed by the law of secondary liability, limited by that spouse's ability to pay at the time the debt was contracted. The common-law rule that misconduct by the indebted spouse canceled the duty of support was still in effect, and the separation of the spouses required creditors to inquire into the facts before extending credit.

The most contentious contemporary dispute involving women and the law in Indiana, as elsewhere, is the right of women to choose to have an abortion. In 1973, the U.S. Supreme Court's decision in *Roe v. Wade* catalyzed an ongoing national debate that shows no signs of abating.[62] It held that life begins at viability of the fetus and forbade state interference with first trimester abortion. Both before and since that decision, the Indiana legislature has attempted to restrict abortion as much as constitutionally possible. Twice the Indiana laws went too far and were held unconstitutional under *Roe.*[63]

A federal district court case that prohibited enforcement of an Indiana "informed consent" law in 2001 was reversed by the Seventh Circuit Court of Appeals in 2003 because it was uncertain how Indiana would enforce the law.[64]

The next Indiana abortion case, *Humphreys v. Clinic for Women, Inc.*, challenged the state Medicaid law, which was required to follow federal rules in order to receive federal funding. The U.S. Supreme Court previously had upheld the Hyde Amendment prohibiting federal funding for any abortion unless lack thereof would place the woman in danger of immediate death or unless the pregnancy was a result of rape or incest.[65] Justice Frank Sullivan, with Chief Justice Randall Shepard and Justice Brent Dickson concurring, held that the Indiana law was not barred by article I, section 23, the privileges and immunities clause of the Indiana constitution. But, with Justices Theodore Boehm and Robert Rucker concurring, Justice Sullivan also held that, under the same Indiana law, the exclusion of funding for women whose pregnancies put them "at serious risk of substantial and irreversible impairment of a major bodily function" is unconstitutional, so long as the state pays to terminate pregnancies that pose a risk of imminent death to the woman or are the result of incest or rape. If the state pays for the incest or rape abortions, it must also pay for the "substantial and irreversible impairment" abortions.[66]

The same Clinic for Women, Inc., challenged the informed consent law under the Indiana constitution's bill of rights. On November 28, 2005, a three-judge majority declined to decide whether the Indiana constitution included a woman's right to choose an abortion but held that, assuming such a right existed, the informed consent law did not violate that right.[67] Justice Brent Dickson concurred on the grounds that the Indiana constitution granted no such right, and Justice Theodore Boehm dissented.

The women's movement has shaped law in Indiana, as it has in other states. It succeeded both because women were forceful in their demands to remove sex-based inequality as enforced in law and because society at large was ready to accept change. Although there is still a gender gap in pay, and a glass ceiling for women in most occupations, parents can be sure their expensively educated daughters will not be prohibited by Indiana law from pursuing their chosen occupations. And Indiana law makes a wife a partner, not a slave, to her husband. Indiana has had one female supreme court justice, one lieutenant governor, four court of appeals judges, one federal district court judge, and numerous trial court judges. The huge influx of women into the law and other professions and into elected and appointed offices (16 percent in the General Assembly's 2004 session) has introduced a new dynamic to lawmaking. It is unclear what will be the ultimate effect on law in Indiana, but it is certain that no longer can anyone can state today, as Justice Joseph P. Bradley did in *Bradwell v. State* in 1873, that women, by their nature, are "too timid and delicate" to practice—or to make—law.

Notes

Eloise Scroggins was research assistant for this chapter.

1. Henneger v. Lomas, 145 Ind. 287, 44 N.E. 462, 463 (1896).

2. Ibid.

3. Williams v. Wilbur, 67 Ind. 42 (1879).

4. Minor v. Happersett, 88 U.S. (21 Wall.) 162, 176–77 (1874) (noting that the right of suffrage was bestowed only on men in all states "save perhaps New Jersey" and that there "the right of suffrage was withdrawn from women as early as 1807").

5. Abigail Adams to John Adams, March 31, 1776, Adams Family Papers Manuscript Collection, Massachusetts Historical Society, Boston.

6. At the turn of the twentieth century, yet another struggle ensued over women's rights: the right, if any, to an abortion.

7. Indiana Territory Act of 1806, repr. in *Indiana State Meeting Report, International Women's Year, July 15–16, 1977*, ed. Donna Bucove (n.p.: Indiana Coordinating Committee for Observance of International Women's Year, 1977), 1–2.

8. Eunice Carmichael Roberts, "Hoosier Women," in *Indiana: A Self-Appraisal*, ed. Donald F. Carmony (Bloomington: Indiana University Press, 1966), 229.

9. Mary M. Huth, *U.S. Suffrage Movement Timeline* (Rochester, N.Y.: Anthony Center for Women's Leadership, 2003), 2.

10. 1846 Ind. Acts 45.

11. Robert Dale Owen was the son of Robert Owen of "Owenite" fame, founder of the utopian colony of New Harmony.

12. Richard William Leopold, *Robert Dale Owen: A Biography* (Cambridge, Mass.: Harvard University Press, 1940), 272–82.

13. Minutes are at the Indiana Historical Society, Indianapolis. This convention was reenacted at Dublin in 2001 by Jill Chambers, of Indianapolis, and her Hoosier colleagues of the National Organization for Women (NOW).

14. Ray Boomhower, comp., Indiana Courts, "Woman's Suffrage Timeline," http://www.in.gov/judiciary/citc/lessons/susan-b-anthony/suffrage_timeline.pdf.

15. 1852 Ind. Acts 373.

16. 1853 Ind. Acts 57.

17. McCarty v. Mewhinney, 8 Ind. 513, 515 (1856).

18. Reese v. Cochran, 10 Ind. 195 (1858).

19. Ibid.

20. Pat Creech Scholten, "A Public 'Jollification': The 1859 Women's Rights Petition before the Indiana Legislature," *Indiana Magazine of History* 72 (December 1976): 347–59.

21. Boomhower, "Woman's Suffrage Timeline."

22. Charles Kettleborough, *Constitution Making in Indiana: A Source Book of Constitutional Documents* (Indianapolis: Indiana Historical Commission, 1916), 117–20.

23. Ibid., 112–20.

24. Bradwell v. State, 83 U.S. (16 Wall.) 130 (1873).

25. Ibid., 141. Bradley presented a classical argument: the inability under the common law for married women like Bradwell to make contracts was evidence that women are incompetent to practice law.

26. Minor v. Happersett, 88 U.S. (21 Wall.) 162 (1874).

27. Zerelda Wallace was the wife of Indiana governor David Wallace and stepmother of Lew Wallace, author of *Ben Hur.*

28. Schilling v. Templeton, 66 Ind. 585 (1879).

29. 1879 Ind. Acts 160–61; 1881 Ind. Acts 527–31.

30. 1881 Ind. Acts 527–31, codified at IC § 31-11-7-1.

31. Weidler v. Floran, 105 Ind. App. 564, 13 N.E.2d 330 (1938).

32. Ray E. Boomhower, *But I Do Clamor: May Wright Sewall, A Life, 1814–1920* (Zionsville: Guild Press of Indiana), 40–41.

33. Pursuant to article XVI of the Indiana constitution, an amendment to the state's constitution must be passed by a majority of each house of the General Assembly twice, in different General Assemblies separated by an intervening election, and then approved by a majority of voters in the next general election.

34. Boomhower, *But I Do Clamor,* 43–47.

35. Kettleborough, *Constitution Making in Indiana,* 117–22.

36. Gougar v. Timberlake, 148 Ind. 38, 40, 46 N.E. 339, 342 (1897).

37. In re Leach, 134 Ind. 665, 34 N.E. 641 (1893).

38. Sharon Hannum Seager, "A Century of Change: Indiana's Women Lawyers," *Traces of Indiana and Midwestern History* 15 (Summer 2003): 15.

39. Boomhower, "Woman's Suffrage Timeline."

40. Ibid.

41. Kettleborough, *Constitution Making in Indiana,* 120.

42. Bd. of Comm'rs v. Knight, 187 Ind. 108, 117 N.E. 565 (1917). In fairness, it must be admitted that *Knight* followed Indiana precedent except with regard to municipal offices.

43. Boomhower, "Woman's Suffrage Timeline."

44. Betty Friedan, *The Feminine Mystique* (New York: Norton, 1963).

45. National Organization for Women, "Chronology of the Equal Rights Amendment, 1923–1996," http://www.now.org/issues/economic/cea/history.html.

46. Civil Rights Act of 1964, 78 Stat. 253, codified at 42 U.S.C. 2000e–2000e-15.

47. 1961 Ind. Acts 500, codified at IC §§ 22-9-1-2 and 22-9-1-3.

48. 1971 Ind. Acts 1444–48.

49. Reed v. Reed, 404 U.S. 71 (1971).

50. Troue v. Marker, 253 Ind. 284, 252 N.E.2d 800 (1969).

51. Beth Van Vorst Gray, "Equal Rights Amendment Ratification in Indiana: Too Little . . . Too Late," (n.p., 2004). Gray, as Beth Greene, was principal secretary of the Indiana Senate from 1970 to 1976.

52. 1974 Ind. Acts 450–53, codified at IC § 22-9-1-3(*l*).

53. 1976 Ind. Acts 69–104, codified at IC § 6-4.1-2-5.

54. 1979 Ind. Acts 320, codified at IC § 6-4.1-3-7.

55. Internal Revenue Code, 95 Stat. 301–2 (1981), codified at 26 U.S.C. §§ 2056.

56. Sheila Suess Kennedy, "American Booksellers Association v. Hudnut," in David J. Bodenhamer and Robert G. Barrows, eds., *Encyclopedia of Indianapolis* (Bloomington: Indiana University Press, 1994), 253.

57. Am. Booksellers Ass'n v. Hudnut, 771 F.2d 323 (7th Cir. 1985).

58. Reilly v. Robertson, 266 Ind. 29, 41, 360 N.E.2d 171, 177 (1977), *cert. denied,* 434 U.S. 825 (1977).

59. Center Township v. Coe, 572 N.E.2d 1350, 1361 (Ind. Ct. App. 1991).

60. Mem'l Hosp. v. Hahaj, 430 N.E.2d 412 (Ind. Ct. App. 1982).

61. Bartrom v. Adjustment Bureau, Inc., 618 N.E.2d 1 (Ind. 1993).

62. Roe v. Wade, 410 U.S. 113 (1973).

63. Arnold v. Sendak, 416 F. Supp. 22 (S.D. Ind. 1976), *aff'd,* 429 U.S. 968 (1976); Indiana Hosp. Licensing Council v. Women's Pavilion of South Bend, 420 N.E.2d 1301 (Ind. Ct. App. 1981).

64. Woman's Choice-East Side Women's Clinic v. Newman, 132 F. Supp. 2d 1150 (S.D. Ind. 2001), *rev'd,* 305 F.3d 684 (7th Cir. 2002), *cert. denied,* 537 U.S. 1192 (2003).

65. Harris v. McRae, 448 U.S. 297 (1980).

66. Humphreys v. Clinic for Women, Inc., 796 N.E.2d 247 (Ind. 2003).

67. Clinic for Women, Inc. v. Brizzi, 837 N.E.2d 973 (Ind. 2005).

NINE

Rebecca S. Shoemaker

THE INDIANA BILL OF RIGHTS

Two Hundred Years of Civil Liberties History

The protection of the civil liberties of individuals has a long and interesting history in Indiana. Early documents that spelled out these guarantees, especially the constitution of 1816, drew extensively on the thinking of the nation's founders and on the governmental framework they established. In the mid-nineteenth century, the second state charter reflected a broader conception of individual rights. Industrialization, immigration, and social reform during the period from 1870 to 1930, as well as antiwar sentiment in World War I and the postwar red scare, brought increased attention to the issue of civil liberties as Hoosiers' political conservatism often clashed with new definitions of liberties.

This struggle continued in the second half of the twentieth century. Prompted by the civil rights movement, the rulings of the Warren Court, and the emergence of civil libertarian groups, such as the Indiana Civil Liberties Union (ICLU), the state entered its own "rights revolution," which paralleled new cultural and legal trends at the national level. This revolution made issues of civil liberties more visible—and more controversial—to the state's residents. At the turn of the century, a renewed national emphasis on federalism brought increased attention and an uncertain future to the protections afforded by the state bill of rights.

Every governmental charter for Indiana, from the Northwest Ordinance of 1787 to the Indiana constitutions of 1816 and 1851, has included protection for individual rights. In the British colonies and later in the newly independent nation, written documents spelled out guarantees of liberties for all to read and consult. The documents that applied to Indiana owed much to this tradition, but more significant is how the state expanded the concept of individual rights. The scope of civil liberties grew with each succeeding document, until the constitution of 1851 contained a list of protections longer and more comprehensive than those guaranteed by the federal Constitution.

The first steps in extending guarantees of individual rights specifically to residents of the region that became Indiana came with the Northwest Ordinance of 1787. Although not as extensive as the later federal or state bills of rights, this document provided assurances to incoming settlers that they had not forfeited their liberties by moving into the new territory. For example, article I guaranteed freedom of religion, promising that "no person shall ever be molested on account of his mode of worship or religious sentiments."[1] This clause marked the first time the U.S. government officially endorsed religious tolerance, although many states already had done so. (The federal Bill of Rights, with its First Amendment guarantee of religious liberty, passed Congress in 1788; ratification by the states occurred three years later.) Among the other protections of the Northwest Ordinance were the right to a writ of habeas corpus, the right to trial by jury, and protection against cruel or unusual punishment.[2]

The protections in the Ordinance, although significant, were lacking in several areas. They did not include, among other things, freedom of press or assembly, assurance of the right to counsel, protection against unreasonable search and seizure, or a prohibition of forced self-incrimination, even though similar guarantees existed in such documents as the Virginia Bill of Rights (1776) and the Massachusetts Declaration of Rights (1780).

The provisions of the federal Bill of Rights, adopted in December 1791, spelled out protection for the liberties of all U.S. citizens, including those who resided in Indiana. The first ten amendments to the federal Constitution included broadened guarantees of freedom of speech and press, protection against unreasonable search and seizure, and prohibition of cruel and unusual punishment, among others. These guarantees prevented encroachment by only the federal government, of course, so no one questioned the need to include a separate bill of rights in the Indiana constitution of 1816 to protect citizens from state interference with their liberties.

When a convention met in Corydon, Indiana, in June 1816 to draft the state's first constitution, one of its early actions was to charge a committee with drafting a bill of rights. None of the committee members were natives of Indiana, most having migrated from states in the east where bills of rights were a valued part of constitutions. In fact, the contents of the document were, in many cases, lifted from or patterned after the constitutions of Pennsylvania, Ohio, Kentucky, and Tennessee. The committee's report, returned after only two days, contained twenty-four provisions, and the final version was approved a few weeks later as the constitution's first article.

The resulting document included an interesting amalgam of guarantees, patterned after the federal Bill of Rights in some places but more detailed in others and touching on a variety of topics not mentioned therein. None of the federal protections were omitted, but only three amendments duplicated exactly the language of their model. The Indiana bill of rights not only protected the free exercise of religion and prohibited government establishment of any church but also barred taxation in support of places of worship. Its provisions for freedom of the press focused particularly on the right of citizens to discuss or criticize the actions of government. It guaranteed individuals the right to own firearms for self-defense as well as for service in the militia. It promised criminal defendants the right to be heard in court and to have their attorneys heard as well. A few provisions, important at the time, quickly lost their relevance, such as the strict limitations on the quartering of soldiers in private dwellings. Other items, such as the one dealing with the imprisonment of debtors, soon were thought to need revision.

The adoption of this document did not eliminate all questions concerning individual rights. Some citizens appeared to esteem the protection of traditional values at least as highly as they did guarantees against government encroachment on individual rights. Few people questioned the intermingling of religion and the state, for example. The early legislature and the governor several times joined forces to invoke public prayer in times of crisis, as in 1821, when the state was in the throes of both an economic crisis and an epidemic of malaria. The legislature passed a resolution calling for a day of public penance on which people were urged to refrain from all work and to attend services of "humiliation, fasting, and prayer."[3] The General Assembly often followed the people's desire that government endorse guidelines for moral behavior, as in 1817, when some legislators proposed a bill calling for strict observance of the sabbath, banning such activities as gambling, quarreling, rioting, and hunting on Sunday. Legislators introduced and frequently passed similar bills during the nineteenth century.[4]

Almost from its enactment, the constitution of 1816 prompted repeated calls for amendment. An early petition called specifically for the abolition of a section providing for the use of grand juries.[5] As in other midwestern states, citizens felt the need to make the document keep pace with rapidly changing political, economic, and social conditions. Finally, in 1850, the Indiana General Assembly responded to a request from Governor James Whitcomb for a convention to revise the state's increasingly inadequate constitution. Although there had been few formal complaints about the bill of rights, the petitions submitted to the convention indicated that citizens were eager for changes in a number of areas having to do with individual rights. The delegates were inundated with calls for attention to the rights of African Americans residing in the state: some groups called for their enfranchisement, and other groups vehemently opposed extending them any rights at all. There were repeated demands that the state outlaw alcoholic beverages. Two petitions asked the convention to incorporate guarantees of the rights of women.

Meeting in Indianapolis in 1851, elected delegates produced a new document whose first article was a bill of rights consisting of thirty-seven sections. This article included most of the provisions of article I of the 1816 document, some of them expanded and others modified. Guarantees of religious freedom, for example, had made up one section in the earlier document: now they were expanded to six, although the actual provisions remained much the same. The section guaranteeing freedom of the press broadened its protection to cover all forms of expression, without the emphasis on political speech contained in the 1816 constitution. The stipulation that the military should be kept strictly subordinate to civilian power was eliminated from the section guaranteeing the right to bear arms. Some modifications reflected changing attitudes on the goals of punishment. Section 18, for example, stated that punishment should "be founded on the principles of reformation, and not of vindictive justice." The new constitution also strictly limited punishment for indebtedness and exempted from seizure items necessary to daily living. It also contained several important new provisions, including acceptance of truth as a defense against libel. Sections 28 and 29 incorporated the federal Constitution's definition of treason. Finally, the last section banned slavery and all forms of indentured servitude from the Hoosier State.

Events of the second half of the nineteenth century raised interesting new challenges to the protection of civil liberties in Indiana. An indication of the sensitivity of some legislators to civil liberties protection came in response to an unusual proposal that would have made serious inroads on religious freedom. A memorial introduced in both houses of the Indiana General Assembly in 1865 called for the adoption of a constitutional amendment "acknowledging Almighty God as the source of all authority and power in civil government, the Lord Jesus as the ruler among nations, and his revealed will as of supreme authority."[6] This resolution bore the signatures of prominent Indianapolis businessman Calvin Fletcher Sr. and 452 other citizens. Numerous citizens, including members of the Jewish community, protested, and members of both houses responded with a variety of recommendations. A majority report from the House Committee on Constitutional Amendments approved the proposal, saying the amendment would "harmonize our form of government with Christianity, state, national, and overall divinely instituted governments of God from whom all power is derived."[7] A minority report by members of the same committee took a quite different stand, however, emphasizing that there were many citizens in Indiana whose opinions did not coincide with those of the petitioners and arguing that adoption of the amendment would be "destructive of natural right, hostile to the true policy and intents of the state and the same is not derived from the people."[8] Members of the Senate Committee on Rights and Privileges rejected the proposal on the grounds that "[a] union of church and state is full of unmixed evil to both organizations."[9] Ultimately, legislators in both houses voted to table the measure, reasoning that its incorporation in the constitution would have the effect of endorsing religious discrimination.

One of the most significant civil liberties cases ever to come from Indiana emerged immediately after the Civil War. *Ex parte Milligan* (1866)[10] involved the arrest and trial of southern sympathizers engaged in an anti-Union conspiracy in Indiana and dealt with the circumstances under which civilians in the United States can be tried by a military tribunal. In 1864, a group of Confederate sympathizers, including one Lambdin P. Milligan, were brought to trial before a military tribunal in Indianapolis on a charge of conspiracy. They had plotted to seize Union arms, free Confederate prisoners held in Illinois, and abduct Indiana governor Oliver P. Morton. In January 1865, the court found Milligan and two associates guilty and sentenced them to be hanged. The case was appealed to the U.S. Supreme Court, which heard arguments early in March 1866. Numerous attorneys, including future president James A. Garfield, presented briefs arguing that the use of military law to try civilians could be done only in case of necessity and when so ordered by Congress.

Justice David Davis read the Court's decision on December 17, 1866; Chief Justice Salmon P. Chase concurred in a separate opinion. The two opinions agreed that the trial of Milligan by military tribunal in a time and place when civilian courts were open and functioning was unlawful and that he should be released. The Bill of Rights was not suspended during wartime, the justices concluded; Milligan had been denied his right to trial by jury as guaranteed by the Sixth Amendment to the U.S. Constitution. The decision in this Indiana case affirmed the guarantee of civil liberties even during times of conflict or strife, a guarantee that was especially important during the postwar reconstruction in the South.[11]

In the late nineteenth and early twentieth centuries, the Indiana General Assembly considered an array of bills to stem the problems arising from increased urbanization and the influx of eastern European immigrants. In the main, these measures sought to put into law the Protestant values of hard work, clean living, church attendance, and temperance. Advocates of traditional morality supported bills to honor the sabbath by banning Sunday baseball, by closing movie houses until after 2:00 PM, and by requiring children to attend church. The same groups, reflecting in part the clash between rural and urban values, worked on occasion with temperance organizations such as the Woman's Christian Temperance Union and the Anti-Saloon League to introduce more than two thousand bills between 1853 and 1917 to regulate or prohibit the manufacture, sale, and consumption of alcohol. Other bills attempted to regulate sexual conduct by requiring blood tests for marriage licenses or restricting the use of hotel rooms by unmarried couples. Although only a small number of these bills became law, the amount of time consumed by such issues demonstrated the belief of many citizens that preserving societal values was the responsibility of democratic government.[12]

In the early twentieth century, the protection of civil liberties was of less importance in the minds of many Hoosiers than was the need to secure the state against real (and perceived) communist activity and other threats emanating from a newly arrived immigrant population having different political views and potentially dangerous loyalties to non-American ideas and activities. Few people in the state voiced any concern about the conviction of native son Eugene V. Debs, head of the national Socialist Party, under the Espionage Act of 1917.[13] To Hoosiers, restrictions on radical speech in wartime were eminently defensible. The General Assembly reacted to the nationwide post–World War I red scare by unanimously adopting an anti-Bolshevik bill in 1919. It banned the display of red flags or other symbols of groups committed to the overthrow of organized governments.[14]

In the 1920s, the political success of the reenergized Ku Klux Klan once again threatened civil liberties in Indiana. During the legislative sessions of 1925 and 1927, Klan-affiliated representatives in the General Assembly introduced so-called Americanism proposals that would have imposed the Klan's Protestant views on the elementary and secondary schools in Indiana. The proposed measures provided for daily Bible reading (King James Version only) in the public schools and permitted two hours' release time per week for religious instruction. Severe restrictions on parochial schools would have been imposed by bills mandating that the same textbooks and licensing procedures for teachers be required in both public and private schools and that only graduates of public schools be licensed as teachers in Indiana. The legislature rejected these bills, the House minority leader and others citing the federal constitutional provision for separation of church and state in opposition to the measures, well before this provision had been made applicable to the states by the U.S. Supreme Court.[15] In 1929, however, the legislature was willing to pass a bill supported by the Daughters of the American Revolution requiring all teachers in Indiana public schools and state universities to take an oath of loyalty to Indiana and to the United States.[16]

Communism and other subversive movements continued to command the attention of many Hoosiers through the middle decades of the twentieth century, especially during the so-called McCarthy era following World War II. In 1949, the General Assembly made it a crime to be a communist.[17] Only Senator Von A. Eichorn voiced objections, arguing that the bill violated constitutional guarantees of freedom of speech and assembly. The constitutionality of the law was challenged repeatedly, but the Indiana Supreme Court ultimately upheld it in 1965.[18] Numerous legislators and lobbyists, especially members of the Indiana Department of the American Legion, campaigned in every session of the General Assembly in the early 1950s for the creation of a state committee to investigate un-American activities.[19] An effort to require teachers in public schools and state universities to take an oath swearing that they were not communists proved unsuccessful, but concerns about the activities of college professors continued. In the late 1940s and early 1950s, both private citizens and patriotic groups such as the American Legion called for the investigation of instructors at Indiana University who taught courses on communist countries or who requested that the university library subscribe to scholarly journals produced in eastern Europe.

Despite the support of many Hoosiers for these restrictions on civil liberties, others focused on protecting individual rights. Legislators only reluctantly created an antisubversive activities committee in 1957 and rendered it ineffectual by refusing to fund it. Indiana University president Herman B. Wells, while acknowledging the concerns of the American Legion and others, took care to protect the academic freedom of his faculty. Despite rhetoric about the dangers of subversive activity in the state, the Communist Party maintained an office in downtown Indianapolis, unmolested, throughout the period. More important for the long term, a small group of Hoosiers created a state affiliate of the American Civil Liberties Union in the fall of 1953.

The Indiana Civil Liberties Union faced substantial opposition from conservative groups around the state, most prominently the Indiana Department of the American Legion. Aroused by national events of the McCarthy era and by restrictions of individual rights at the state and local levels, a group of lawyers, college professors, ministers, and others arranged an organizing meeting in November 1953. They applied for use of a meeting room in the Indiana World War Memorial, a state monument erected to honor veterans of World War I. The Indiana War Memorials Commission, which controlled access to the memorial and was itself controlled unofficially by leaders of the American Legion, refused, setting up a confrontation that continued for more than twenty years and achieved national notoriety when televised nationally by Edward R. Murrow on his program *See It Now.* The debate centered on the legion's contention that the ACLU was made up of communist sympathizers and other disloyal individuals and the ICLU's assertion that its sole intent was to work for the protections guaranteed by the federal Bill of Rights. This dispute was not resolved until the ICLU filed a lawsuit against the commission, charging that its actions were arbitrary and capricious and had denied the ICLU its rights under the First and Fourteenth Amendments. The Indiana Supreme Court eventually agreed and ordered the war memorial opened to the ICLU in October 1973.[20]

During its fifty years of existence, the Indiana Civil Liberties Union has been the most active group in the state in defending the Bill of Rights. Staffed throughout most of its history with a few paid employees and a corps of volunteers, the ICLU operated for years on a meager budget and relied heavily on volunteer attorneys as it defended the civil liberties of Hoosiers through lobbying, advocacy, and negotiated solutions to controversies. The work of the ICLU generally has been guided by the agenda and advice of the American Civil Liberties Union, its parent organization, but the group also has responded to federal legislation and groundbreaking rulings by the U.S. Supreme Court.

Many of the civil liberties issues in the 1950s centered on the religious values of the state's Christian, largely Protestant, majority. A long-running battle over the proper relationship of church and state began in 1955 with a protest filed against the erection of a large, lighted cross on public property in Highland, Indiana. The Knights of Columbus, a Catholic fraternal organization that had sponsored the cross, claimed that it was a memorial intended to honor area veterans. The resulting suit became one of the longest-running civil liberties cases in the state's history. In 1993, forty years after the dispute began, the Seventh Circuit ruled in *Gonzales v. North Township* that the cross must be removed. Similar contention surrounded the state's 1905 Sunday closing law, which continued to be enforced in the 1950s.[21] Responding to lobbying by large chain stores that wanted to do business seven days a week, members of the General Assembly sought to loosen the Indiana law's restrictions throughout the 1960s but met stiff resistance bolstered, ironically, by a Warren Court decision, *McGowan v. Maryland,* upholding the constitutionality of Sunday closing laws.[22] Censorship was another contentious issue. In the 1950s, numerous groups called upon public officials to pass city ordinances banning comic books, considered a contributing factor in the rise of juvenile delinquency, and to take action against a variety of adult reading materials. Although the U.S. Supreme Court in *Roth v. United States* (1957) had provided the standard for judging obscenity—"whether, to the average person, applying contemporary community standards, the dominant theme of the material, taken as a whole, appeals to prurient interest"—Hoosiers were inclined to define the term more broadly.[23] In a highly publicized series of "smut raids" in 1959, private groups such as Citizens for Decent Literature enlisted the aid of law enforcement officers to arrest Indianapolis drugstore owners who were accused of selling girlie magazines. Most charges were dismissed, but one case, in which Judge Richard M. Salb of the Marion County Criminal Court declared Indiana's antismut law unconstitutional, eventually made its way to the state supreme court, which upheld the lower court's ruling.[24] Seven years later, a bookstore owner in the same city was indicted for selling Henry Miller's novel *Tropic of Cancer.* As late as 1967, the women's committee of the chamber of commerce in Anderson sought police help in circulating to retailers lists of objectionable magazines. Movies with questionable subject matter did not escape notice. In spite of the U.S. Supreme Court's restrictions on the censorship of films in cases such as *Burstyn v. Wilson,* police and judges repeatedly had to deal with objections to movies considered unsuitable by residents of various local communities.[25]

One of the most important Indiana victories against censorship during the 1950s was won by Indiana University on behalf of its Institute for Sex Research. Begun in 1941 by Alfred C. Kinsey, the institute had done groundbreaking research in the area of human sexuality, resulting in the publication in 1948 of *Sexual Behavior in the Human Male* and in 1953 of *Sexual Behavior in the Human Female.* The books prompted international discussion and controversy, making it necessary for Indiana University president Herman B. Wells to defend the project to everyone from the parents of university students to then Governor Henry F. Schricker. It was the seizure by U.S. Customs Service officials of shipments of erotica Kinsey had collected overseas, however, that spawned a federal lawsuit that resulted in a victory for opponents of censorship. In November 1957, Indiana University and Kinsey's widow filed suit in federal district court in New York claiming that the customs seizure constituted deprivation of liberty and property without due process of law under the Fifth Amendment.[26] The suit also charged violation of the right of free inquiry under the Ninth and Tenth Amendments. The suit resulted in a ruling favorable to the plaintiffs in November 1958, establishing what one historian has called "a landmark in the freedom of collecting basic research materials and the right of free access and use."[27]

Like the rest of the nation, Indiana was profoundly affected by the wide variety of First Amendment issues in the 1960s. Many of the developments sprang from the so-called rights revolution, the nationalization of the federal Bill of Rights by the U.S. Supreme Court under the leadership of Chief Justice Earl Warren. Many of the cases involved claims by African Americans and other disadvantaged groups that state actions denied their national rights because of race, sex, age, and sexual orientation.

In reviewing the Warren Court's rulings, Indiana attorneys and jurists found their state in the unusual position of having recognized a number of such safeguards years, or even decades, earlier. The Indiana Supreme Court, for example, could point to its 1923 decision in *Flum v. State* that the state constitution required that evidence illegally obtained must be banned from use in criminal trials.[28] The U.S. Supreme Court reached a similar conclusion in *Weeks v. United States* (1914) but applied the exclusionary rule only to federal courts.[29] Not until *Mapp v. Ohio* (1961) did the justices make the rule mandatory in state courts as well.[30]

Similarly, the state supreme court early adopted a liberal reading of the right to counsel clause of article I of the Indiana constitution. In 1854, in *Webb v. Baird,* it held that a poor citizen had a right to representation by an attorney at public expense.[31] In 1891, it ruled in *Hendryx v. State* that appointment of counsel for the indigent was indispensable to the orderly administration of justice.[32] And, in 1920, it guaranteed the right to counsel in pretrial proceedings in *Batchelor v. State.*[33] More recently, the Indiana court has recognized the right to counsel and the right to trial by jury in misdemeanor cases[34] and the right to counsel in juvenile cases.[35] In most of these instances, the state guarantee has exceeded what federal law requires.

Opposition to U.S. involvement in the Vietnam War in the 1960s prompted questions about the extent of constitutional protection for freedom of expression. Although many cases sought definitive rulings on the reach of First Amendment protections, Hoosiers fought an uphill battle in endeavoring to exercise their rights until 1969, when the U.S. Supreme Court extended First Amendment protections to a wide variety of advocacy in *Brandenburg v. Ohio.*[36] In 1962, Indiana State University in Terre Haute expelled six students for leaving campus to attend the White House Peace March in Washington, D.C., and only negotiation with university administrators by the Indiana Civil Liberties Union brought about their reinstatement. In 1966, police arrested antiwar protestors in Indianapolis for refusing to adhere to restrictions on demonstrations during a visit by President Lyndon Johnson. Legal intervention by the ICLU resulted in a dismissal of the charges before trial. In 1967, Indiana State University abruptly fired instructor Scott Chisholm for burning a flag as part of a discussion of methods of protest in one of his classes. University administrators rejected arguments by civil liberties groups that the action was a legitimate expression of Chisholm's political views. A number of protests by high school students during the same period were resolved only after the U.S. Supreme Court's ruling in *Tinker v. Des Moines* that students' rights did not end at the schoolhouse door.[37]

Lawsuits concerning the rights of prisoners in the state's correctional institutions also made an appearance on the state's dockets. Rights advocates argued that the Eighth Amendment protection against cruel and unusual punishment and the guarantees of equal protection in the Fifth and Fourteenth Amendments protected all citizens, including prisoners. Court rulings in cases in New York and Virginia as early as the 1950s had established this principle, and, by the mid-1970s, a significant body of prisoners' rights law had developed nationally.[38] Riots in 1969 at the Indiana State Reformatory at Pendleton prompted debates on this subject and eventually resulted in negotiated agreements for greater prisoner representation on the prison's disciplinary board. Subsequently, the Indiana Civil Liberties Union and Project Justice and Equality filed precedent-setting lawsuits challenging conditions in jails in Lake and Blackford counties. The inmate plaintiffs asked the courts to require officials to provide such basic amenities as blankets, soap, and regular access to showers and to eliminate rodents in cells. More significantly, a second Lake County suit resulted in a court ruling limiting the length of time a suspect could be held before being charged or arraigned.[39]

Issues of women's rights also attracted many supporters, particularly in response to national events in the 1970s. Building on the achievements of the civil rights movement, the publication of Betty Friedan's *Feminine Mystique,* and the formation of the National Organization for Women, the American Civil Liberties Union and other legal advocacy groups filed lawsuits seeking a more comprehensive definition of women's rights. The U.S. Supreme Court's decision in *Reed v. Reed* (1971) marked a turning point in judicial willingness to consider arguments outlining the constitutional grounds for protection of women against discrimination on the basis of sex.[40] The passage of the Equal Pay Act of 1973 and the enforcement of Title VII of the Civil Rights Act of 1964 provided further ammunition for women's rights advocates. On the basis of these developments, in 1971, state senator Robert Garton, of Columbus, successfully sponsored a bill banning discrimination on the basis of sex in hiring, unless sex was a legitimate factor for consideration in a particular job.[41] In 1974, the General Assembly commenced debate of the Equal Rights Amendment, a proposed amendment to the U.S. Constitution that would have banned discrimination on the basis of sex. Three years later, Indiana became the thirty-fifth state to ratify the ultimately unsuccessful amendment.

Abortion and the right to privacy posed a different kind of problem for Indiana leaders, who struggled to find a proper response to the U.S. Supreme Court's decision in *Roe v. Wade* in 1973.[42] The 1905 abortion law on the books in the state at the time was very conservative, permitting abortions only when medically necessary to save the life of the mother. Efforts to broaden the provisions to increase access to abortion had been unsuccessful in 1967, but after *Roe* the General Assembly quickly passed a new law that complied with the Court's ruling. Many legislators were outspoken in their opposition to the new bill, and the text of the bill itself made clear that the legislature was acting only because the recent Supreme Court decision left it no choice.[43] The new statute did not escape challenge, however, and a U.S. Supreme Court ruling in 1976 invalidated that part of the law requiring first trimester abortions to be performed in a hospital or licensed health facility. This struggle between those who would restrict abortion rights and those who advocate preserving at least as much choice as federal law will allow has continued through the ensuing decades, and the state of Indiana generally has restricted access to abortion to the extent that U.S. Supreme Court decisions permit.

The U.S. Supreme Court's rulings in *Tinker v. Des Moines* (1969),[44] in which the justices had first recognized the constitutional rights of students, and *Goss v. Lopez* (1975),[45] in which they began to define due process rights for students, brought the rights of students to a more prominent spot in Indiana jurisprudence in the 1970s. Many of the controversies over the rights of students in Indiana reflected the conservative values of communities and their school officials. For example, in the highly publicized case *Crews v. Cloncs,* the ICLU pursued to the Seventh Circuit Court of Appeals a controversy over school rules mandating the length of the hair of male students.[46] After the federal court found for the student, the ICLU was inundated for months with requests from parents to intervene in similar controversies, a circumstance that suggests the reluctance of many Hoosier schools to protect students' civil liberties in the face of community opposition. In other instances challenging similarly restrictive school policies, the ICLU defended married or pregnant students who faced adverse actions by public school administrators.

New interpretations of the First Amendment's free exercise clause in the 1960s and 1970s also found expression in Indiana courts. An outgrowth of the prisoners' rights movement was the demand that prison officials respect and accommodate the religious beliefs and practices of non-Christian prisoners, particularly black Muslims. In 1976, an ICLU lawsuit on behalf of twelve Muslim inmates at the state reformatory at Pendleton resulted in concessions that made it possible for them to practice their religion while incarcerated.[47] In the mid-1970s, members of the Pentecostal House of Prayer in Terre Haute objected to the state requirement that drivers' licenses display the photographs of their holders. The Indiana Supreme

Court, citing the U.S. Supreme Court's decision in *Wisconsin v. Yoder,*[48] ultimately ruled in 1978 in *Bureau of Motor Vehicles v. Pentecostal House of Prayer, Inc.,*[49] that the group's First Amendment rights outweighed the state's interest in this form of identification.

In 1976, a case reminiscent of the Scopes trial of the 1920s arose in a school district in southwestern Indiana when parents objected to the use in the public schools of a biology textbook that emphasized the teachings of creationism. In spite of the precedent set by the U.S. Supreme Court's ruling in *Epperson v. Arkansas* in 1968,[50] prolonged negotiation with the state textbook commission and, ultimately, a court ruling were necessary to secure the banning of the book as a violation of the establishment clause.[51]

Another significant free exercise question arose when a Jehovah's Witness was denied unemployment benefits after he quit his job because of the dictates of his religion. A man named Thomas, who had worked at a munitions plant, claimed that his work on an assembly line producing gun turrets for tanks conflicted with his religious obligation not to participate in the production of armaments. The Indiana Employment Security Division subsequently denied unemployment compensation because he had quit instead of being let go. Building on its earlier decision in *Sherbert v. Verner,*[52] which held that a Seventh-day Adventist could not be denied unemployment compensation for refusing to work on Saturday, the U.S. Supreme Court ruled in *Thomas v. Review Board of Indiana Employment Security Division* that denial of benefits to a person who had been forced to quit his job to honor his religious belief was a violation of his free exercise rights.[53] Acknowledging that another Jehovah's Witness who was Thomas's coworker had no problem with the assignment, the Court also said that claims under the free exercise clause are not limited to beliefs that are common to all members of a faith.

Other cases from Indiana gave the federal courts an opportunity to refine their earlier rulings on the First Amendment religion clauses. The first controversy of this type challenged the acceptability of seasonal religious displays on public property. After the U.S. Supreme Court had ruled in *Lynch v. Donnelly* that displays including a variety of holiday figures could serve a secular purpose, an Indianapolis citizen sought a ruling on the erection of a Christmas display in the Indianapolis City-County Building.[54] In *Grossbaum v. Indianapolis-Marion County Building Authority,* a federal district court judge concluded that the building was not a public forum and that groups could be denied access if the overall viewpoint of the building's managers was neutral.[55] The judge also repeated the U.S. Supreme Court's conclusion that a Christmas tree should be considered a secular display.

At the end of the twentieth century, a long-running controversy over the display of the Ten Commandments on public property once again became a legal issue. Federal district court judge Allen Sharp ruled in 1999 in *Books v. City of Elkhart* that a monument including the Ten Commandments should be allowed to remain near the entrance to the Elkhart City Hall, saying that it served a secular purpose in contributing to the moral education of young citizens.[56] The Indiana General Assembly strengthened this argument the following year by passing a law allowing the display of the Ten Commandments on public property if it was part of a display of a variety of documents. When Governor Frank O'Bannon announced that he would permit the erection of such a display on the grounds of the State House in Indianapolis, the Indiana Civil Liberties Union promptly sought an injunction to prevent its installation on grounds it would violate the establishment clause of the First Amendment. The federal district court granted the injunction in *ICLU v. O'Bannon,*[57] and the case went on appeal to the Seventh Circuit Court of Appeals in Chicago, which upheld the injunction.[58] The ruling against the monument became binding when the U.S. Supreme Court refused to hear the case. In two cases decided in 2005, *Van Orden v. Perry* and *McCreary County v. ACLU of Kentucky,* the U.S. Supreme Court held that representations of the Ten Commandments could be displayed in public places as long as they were not "overtly religious."[59]

Cases questioning the scope of freedom of expression also appeared on Indiana dockets during the last two decades of the twentieth century. In 1984, the Indianapolis-Marion County City-County Council adopted a new approach to restricting the availability of allegedly pornographic materials. Prompted by a nationwide campaign by legal activist Catharine MacKinnon and others, the ordinance banned the sale of such materials on the grounds that their availability violated the civil rights of women by portraying them in humiliating, subordinate positions that encouraged sex discrimination and violence against women. A variety of groups promptly attacked the ordinance as unconstitutional, and, in *American Booksellers Ass'n v. Hudnut,* federal district court judge Sarah Evans Barker ruled that, although obscenity enjoyed no constitutional protection, the ordinance in question was overbroad and imposed an unwarranted intrusion on freedom of speech.[60] The case eventually reached the U.S. Supreme Court, which left Barker's ruling intact by refusing to hear the case.[61]

Challenges to Indiana's public nudity law in the late 1980s provided an opportunity for the U.S. Supreme Court to emphasize its renewed attention to divisions between federal and state authority, in this case on the issue of freedom of expression. The plaintiff in *Barnes v. Glen Theater, Inc.*, invoked the state law against nude dancing at the Kitty Kat Bar in the city of South Bend even though the U.S. Supreme Court previously had said that nude dancing was a form of expression protected by the First Amendment.[62] The question was whether state law could place any restrictions at all on such performances. In an opinion authored by Chief Justice William H. Rehnquist in 1991, the Court concluded that Indiana had not outlawed nude dancing as such and that its requirements that nude dancers wear pasties and a G-string were within the limits of the state's police power to regulate nudity for moral purposes. The carefully worded opinion came down on the side of the state's right to regulate in such cases.

Since the 1980s, as the Rehnquist Court has invoked the principles of federalism, interpretation of Indiana's bill of rights has become more important. The U.S. Supreme Court held in *Michigan v. Long,* that it generally would not review a decision of a state court if the decision showed "clearly and expressly that it is alternately based on bona fide separate, adequate, and independent grounds."[63] In other words, state jurists wishing to avoid federal review must base their opinions solidly on the state constitution. The opportunities this new theory of federalism presented to state courts were spelled out by Chief Justice Randall T. Shepard in a seminal law review article in 1989. Shepard argued for a historical approach, one spelled out specifically in an opinion in *Ratliff v. Cohn:*[64] "Questions arising under the Indiana Constitution are to be resolved by examining the language of the text in the context of the history surrounding its drafting and ratification, the purpose and structure of our Constitution, and case law interpreting the specific provisions."[65] A brief review of some recent opinions illustrates the results of this approach.

In *Bayh v. Sonnenburg* (1991), the Ohio Supreme Court was asked to determine whether mental patients were entitled to back wages for their labor while committed to state mental facilities.[66] The court's opinion indicates that the justices, in their analysis of article I, section 21, of the state constitution, carefully researched the origins and history of the provision, including the records of the state constitutional conventions, in order to determine its meaning and the intent of the delegates who framed it.

The Indiana Supreme Court's ruling in *Price v. State* in 1993 demonstrated the potential for expanding the protections afforded by the state bill of rights. Price had been convicted for disorderly conduct as a result of her outburst at police investigating a rowdy New Year's Eve party.[67] The majority ruled that Price's words constituted political speech and held that convicting her for doing so violated article I, section 9, of the Indiana constitution, which provides, "No law shall be passed restraining the free interchange of thought and opinion, or restricting the right to speak, write or print freely on any subject whatever." The justices said the conviction "imposed a material burden upon the exercise of political speech."

The court strengthened the use of the state constitution as a basis for litigation in 1997 in *Valentin v. State.*[68] In this case, the court reversed an appellate court ruling based on the state double jeopardy provision, article I, section 14, because the defense had relied only on the federal double jeopardy clause and had not developed and presented a separate argument based on the state double jeopardy clause.

The legal history of civil liberties in Indiana is one of gradual evolution and expansion, in which the meaning of individual rights is shaped by both state and federal actions. For much of the state's history, Hoosiers devoted at least as much attention to the protection of traditional moral and community values as they did to constitutional guarantees of individual rights. Throughout the period, however, the state was reluctant to restrict this right unduly, as was evident in its resistance to the Klan's proposed program of Americanism or the campaigns against so-called subversive activity. In the past half century, the nationalization of the federal Bill of Rights has advanced more liberal definitions of civil liberties, a development that found advocates in groups such as the Indiana Civil Liberties Union.

During recent decades, a variety of factors have created a stronger impetus for legislation and court rulings that provide expanded protections even in controversial areas of individual rights. Since the turn of the twenty-first century, the state has seen renewed debates focusing on prison conditions, protection for the public meetings of the Ku Klux Klan, and the constitutionality of Indiana's death penalty statute. State jurists and attorneys have responded to the U.S. Supreme Court's renewed emphasis on a philosophy of federalism, which has prompted fresh consideration of the state constitution and its bill of rights as a tool in the defense of civil liberties. The outcome of these debates is unclear, but it is certain that the protection of civil liberties will continue to be an important chapter in the history of Indiana law.

Notes

1. Land Ordinance of 1787, *Journals of the Continental Congress, 1774–1789,* ed. Worthington Chauncey Ford, vol. 32 (Washington, D.C.: Government Printing Office, 1936), 334–43..

2. Henry Steel Commager, *Documents of American History* (Englewood Cliffs, N.J.: Prentice-Hall, 1973), 128–32; Paul Finkelman, "A Constitution for an Empire of Liberty," in *Pathways to the Old Northwest: An Observance of the Bicentennial of the Northwest Ordinance* (Indianapolis: Indiana Historical Society, 1988), 7.

3. 1821–22 Ind. Acts 171.

4. See, for example, *Journal of the Senate of the State of Indiana,* 34th Gen. Ass. (1848–49), 295.

5. 1816–17 Ind. Acts 165–68.

6. Charles Kettleborough, *Constitution Making in Indiana: A Source Book of Constitutional Documents with Historical Introduction and Critical Notes* (Indianapolis: Indiana Historical Bureau, 1975), 2:62.

7. Ibid., 2:63.

8. *Journal of the House of Representatives of the State of Indiana,* 43d Gen. Ass. (1865), 640.

9. *Senate Journal,* 43d Gen. Ass. (1865), 434.

10. Ex parte Milligan, 71 U.S. (4 Wall.) 2 (1866).

11. William H. Rehnquist, *All the Laws but One: Civil Liberties in Wartime* (New York: Alfred A. Knopf, 1998), 130–37.

12. Justin E. Walsh, *The Centennial History of the Indiana General Assembly, 1816–1978* (Indianapolis: Indiana Historical Bureau, 1978), 290–301.

13. Debs v. U.S., 249 U.S. 211 (1919).

14. 1919 Ind. Acts 588.

15. See, for example, the U.S. Supreme Court's ruling in *Pierce v. Society of Sisters,* 268 U.S. 510 (1925), in which Justice James McReynolds overturned a law restricting parents' freedom to send their children to parochial schools but based his opinion on the protection of property rights.

16. Walsh, *Centennial History,* 395.

17. 1949 Ind. Acts 1016.

18. State v. Levitt, 246 Ind. 275, 203 N.E.2d 821 (1965).

19. The American Legion, whose national headquarters is located in downtown Indianapolis, played a central role in Indiana during several decades of the twentieth century. For example, both Governor Paul V. McNutt (1933–37) and Governor George N. Craig (1953–57) were former commanders of the American Legion who had risen to power through, and were strongly influenced by, a political machine operated by the legion.

20. ICLU v. War Memorials Commission, 260 Ind. 36, 291 N.E.2d 888 (1973).

21. Gonzales v. North Township, 4 F.3d 1412 (7th Cir. 1993).

22. McGowan v. Maryland, 366 U.S. 420 (1961).

23. Roth v. U.S., 354 U.S. 476, 488–89 (1957).

24. State v. Kuebel, 241 Ind. 268, 172 N.E.2d 45 (1961).

25. Burstyn v. Wilson, 343 U.S. 495 (1952).

26. U.S. v. 31 Photographs, 156 F. Supp. 350 (S.D.N.Y. 1957).

27. Thomas D. Clark, *Years of Fulfillment,* vol. 3 of *Indiana University, Midwestern Pioneer* (Bloomington: Indiana University Press, 1977), 279.

28. Flum v. State, 193 Ind. 585, 590, 141 N.E. 353, 354–55 (1923).

29. Weeks v. U.S., 232 U.S. 383 (1914).

30. Mapp v. Ohio, 367 U.S. 643 (1961).

31. Webb v. Baird, 6 Ind. 13 (1854).

32. Hendryx v. State, 130 Ind. 265, 29 N.E. 1131 (1891).

33. Batchelor v. State, 189 Ind. 96, 125 N.E. 773 (1920).

34. Bolkovac v. State, 229 Ind. 294, 98 N.E.2d 250 (1951); State ex rel. Rose v. Hoffman, 227 Ind. 256, 85 N.E.2d 486 (1949).

35. Speight v. State, 239 Ind. 237, 155 N.E.2d 752 (1959).

36. Brandenburg v. Ohio, 395 U.S. 444 (1969).

37. Tinker v. Des Moines, 393 U.S. 503 (1969).

38. Samuel Walker, *In Defense of American Liberties* (New York: Oxford University Press, 1990), 310–12.

39. Dommer v. Hatcher, 427 F. Supp. 1040 (N.D. Ind. 1975); Dommer v. Crawford, 638 F.2d 1031 (7th Cir. 1980); Dommer v. Crawford, 653 F.2d 289 (7th Cir. 1981).

40. Reed v. Reed, 404 U.S. 71 (1971).

41. Walsh, *Centennial History,* 619.

42. Roe v. Wade, 410 U.S. 113 (1973).

43. 1973 Ind. Acts 1740.

44. Tinker v. Des Moines, 393 U.S. 503 (1969).

45. Goss v. Lopez, 419 U.S. 565 (1975).

46. Crews v. Cloncs, 432 F.2d 1259 (7th Cir. 1970).

47. Ibid.

48. Wisconsin v. Yoder, 406 U.S. 205 (1972).

49. Bureau of Motor Vehicles v. Pentecostal House of Prayer, Inc., 269 Ind. 361, 380 N.E.2d 1225 (1978).

50. Epperson v. Arkansas, 393 U.S. 97 (1968).

51. Hendren v. Campbell (Sup. Ct. No. 5, Marion County) (April 14, 1977).

52. Sherbert v. Verner, 374 U.S. 398 (1963).

53. Thomas v. Review Bd. of Indiana Employment Sec. Div., 450 U.S. 707 (1981).

54. Lynch v. Donnelly, 465 U.S. 668 (1984).

55. Grossbaum v. Indianapolis-Marion County Bldg. Auth., 870 F. Supp. 1450 (S.D. Ind. 1994).

56. Books v. City of Elkhart, 79 F. Supp. 2d 979 (N.D. Ind. 1999).

57. ICLU v. O'Bannon, 110 F. Supp. 2d 842 (S.D. Ind. 2000).

58. Books v. City of Elkhart, 235 F.3d 292 (7th Cir. 2000).

59. Van Orden v. Perry, 125 S. Ct. 2854 (2005); McCreary County v. ACLU of Kentucky, 125 S. Ct. 2722 (2005).

60. Am. Booksellers Ass'n v. Hudnut, 771 F.2d 323 (Ind. 1984).

61. Am. Booksellers Ass'n v. Hudnut, 106 U.S. 1172 (1986).

62. Barnes v. Glen Theater, Inc., 501 U.S. 560 (1991).

63. Michigan v. Long, 463 U.S. 1032 (1983).

64. Ratliff v. Cohn, 693 N.E.2d 530 (Ind. 1998).

65. Randall T. Shepard, "Second Wind for the Indiana Bill of Rights," *Indiana Law Review* 22, no. 2 (1989): 586.

66. Bayh v. Sonnenburg, 573 N.E.2d 398 (Ind. 1991), *cert. denied,* 502 U.S. 1094 (1992).

67. Price v. State, 622 N.E.2d 954 (Ind. 1993).

68. Valentin v. State, 688 N.E.2d 412 (Ind. 1997).

TEN

Martha McCarthy and Ran Zhang

THE UNCERTAIN PROMISE OF FREE PUBLIC SCHOOLING

If a nation expects to be ignorant and free, in a state of civilization, it expects what never was and never will be.

—*Thomas Jefferson*

Education is not mentioned in the U.S. Constitution, so it is not a fundamental right of American citizenship. Providing for education is among the powers reserved to the states or to the people under the Tenth Amendment; thus, education policies reflect the unique culture of each state. In Indiana, this culture is moderately conservative. The state's history is not characterized by radical changes or revolutions; instead, political and social changes generally have been evolutionary. Historian James H. Madison's observation that Indiana's population traditionally has been cautious and not prone to rapid innovations certainly has been true in the school arena.[1] In addition, the early settlers in Indiana came from both New England and the South, so the state's culture is a blend of the northern ideology of capitalism, Protestantism, and republicanism with southern conservative views from the plantation economy.[2] During the early years of statehood, there was more support for free schools in the northern counties and more support for private education in the southern part of the state. Of course, this division was not absolute; some northerners opposed tax-supported public schools, and some southerners embraced public education as a way to improve local conditions.[3]

Evolution of Education in Indiana: An Overview

> Few areas of life [have] reflected major concerns and conflicts of Indiana's citizens more clearly than public education.
>
> *James H. Madison,* Indiana through Tradition and Change

Initial Federal Incentives

Despite being a state enterprise, education in Indiana has, from the beginning, paralleled and been shaped by national developments. These have included, but not been limited to, policies of the federal government, which have influenced educational priorities through the government's power to tax and spend for the general welfare and to enact legislation implementing constitutional guarantees.[4]

Federal assistance for education started before Indiana became a state, with the enactment of the federal Northwest Ordinances. The Land Ordinance of 1785 provided that the proceeds from certain federal lands (lot sixteen of each township) be used for maintaining schools,[5] and the Ordinance of 1787 stated that "religion, morality, and knowledge being necessary to good government and the happiness of mankind, schools and the means of education shall forever be encouraged."[6] Although these ordinances were designed to attract settlers, their declarations regarding education influenced subsequent state constitutions in the Midwest and elsewhere and often appeared in early education litigation.[7] These ordinances are sometimes called "the founding documents of public education in the Old Northwest."[8]

Notwithstanding their symbolic influence, it appears that the Northwest Ordinances had "very little effect on the actual support of schools" because the land rentals did not produce much revenue in an era of abundant cheap land, and the funds that were collected often were mismanaged.[9] Given these problems, public schools developed slowly in Indiana.[10] Some churches operated parochial schools, and, in fact, the first schools in the state were Sunday schools.[11] Moreover, early public schools were not necessarily free; common schools were instead "common pay schools."[12] In most instances, parents pooled funds to build schoolhouses and paid tuition to hire teachers. So, in a sense, these schools were both public and private.[13]

Early Years of Statehood

Federal incentives and voluntary local action characterized the initial development of education in Indiana. At the time Indiana adopted its first constitution and became a state in 1816, the major concern was making the transition to statehood instead of ensuring an educated citizenry. Nonetheless, the Indiana constitution of 1816 reflected concern for education, at least rhetorically. Article IX placed a duty on the General Assembly to improve the federal lands granted for the use of schools and to apply funds raised from such lands to educational purposes. The constitution also stipulated: "It shall be the duty of the General Assembly, as soon as circumstances will permit, to provide by law for a general system of education, ascending in a regular gradation from township schools to a state university, wherein tuition shall be gratis, and equally open to all."[14] Indiana's sweeping education article was unprecedented among state constitutions and drew praise from school reformers nationally.[15]

The General Assembly, however, did not implement the constitution's education provision in any serious way, despite the efforts of Governor Jonathan Jennings. He urged Indiana lawmakers to implement this provision, declaring that "the dissemination of useful knowledge" is necessary "as a support to morals and a restraint to vice."[16] As in many other states, a huge gap existed between the lofty constitutional ideals and educational realities.[17] In addition to the need to establish a state government, a number of other factors—such as sparse population, emergent economic needs of early pioneers, the belief that education was primarily the responsibility of families or churches, and the depression of 1839—contributed to the low priority given education by early Indiana policymakers.[18] School funding was quite tenuous and consisted primarily of proceeds from federal lands and donations or voluntary taxes. Cash-strapped farmers were reluctant to support taxes for a number of public services, including education. The constitutional directive that the General Assembly provide for a general system of education "as soon as circumstances will permit" was so flexible that there was little significant progress toward providing for such a system.[19] But at a time when many states were establishing pauper schools, the constitution of 1816 at least promised free public education for everyone, even though this promise was not realized.[20]

There was—and remains to some extent—high regard for local control and community autonomy in educational matters. Despite the citizenry's strong faith in the value of education, many people opposed the imposition of taxes to support schools.[21] Some wanted schools reserved for a chosen few, but most opponents of tax-supported schooling feared government controls.[22] Still, a number of laws pertaining to education were enacted during the thirty years following the ratification of the 1816 constitution, most significantly in 1824 and 1833.

The law of 1824 was the first effort to create a plan for an egalitarian state school system: it divided congressional townships provided by the Ordinance of 1785 into local districts and empowered township trustees to appoint school district trustees who employed teachers. To be eligible for employment, individuals had to be granted teaching certificates by the township trustees.[23] The elaborate law of 1833 had 205 sections. It provided for elected trustees and increased their number to three per district. It also allowed local voters to decide to have schools for specified months, to authorize contributions to build schools, and to collect taxes to support them. But citizens could not be taxed against their wishes and could not be taxed unless they benefited from the schools.[24] Little was accomplished toward a general system of free public education because these and other laws of this period generally were not binding; having nonbinding laws was especially troublesome in connection with financing schools. In short, there was "an elaborate code" but "few schools."[25]

Increasing industrialization, urbanization, and immigration in the mid-nineteenth century focused more attention on establishing a system of state-supported education. The common school movement, led by people like Horace Mann in Massachusetts and Henry Barnard in Connecticut and Rhode Island, influenced the growth of public education in Indiana from the 1830s through the 1860s and energized Hoosier leaders. Most notable was Caleb Mills, who led Wabash College for many years and wrote eloquently about the importance of free, tax-supported education. Through his writings, he was instrumental in marshaling support for public education in Indiana.[26] In building the case for free public education, Mills and others emphasized that Indiana had the worst literacy rate among northern states.[27]

The first of a series of Indiana common school conventions was held in 1847, and these meetings became influential in determining subsequent education legislation.[28] A referendum to establish free schools was passed by 56 percent of the voters in 1848 (two-thirds of the counties opposing the measure were in the southern half of the state).[29] The following year, legislation authorized a series of taxes—property, poll, and insurance—to fund common schools, although local voters had to approve collection of these taxes.[30] About one-third of Indiana counties, again disproportionately southern, chose not to do so, thus declining to fund public education.[31]

Struggle over a General and Uniform Educational System

The debates on education in the constitutional convention in 1850–51 were quite different from those in 1816. Indiana had experienced a frustrating failure in its expensive 1836 initiative to improve transportation and to bolster the state's economy, which caused the state to default on some of its debt. This fiscal catastrophe was an impetus for the 1851 constitution, as was interest in a common school system that would be less costly than the existing voluntary local school system.[32] Also, the citizenry was becoming disenchanted with state laws that applied only to specified jurisdictions, so-called special legislation, in contrast to laws of general application.[33] The new charter reflected a commitment to education as necessary to preserve a free government and morality among citizens, although language from the 1816 constitution proposing a system of free education through the college level was eliminated. Article VIII, section 1, stipulated: "Knowledge and learning, generally diffused throughout a community, being essential to the preservation of a free government; it shall be the duty of the General Assembly to encourage, by all suitable means, moral, intellectual, scientific, and agricultural improvement; and to provide, by law, for a general and uniform system of Common Schools, wherein tuition shall be without charge, and equally open to all."[34]

In 1852, the Free School Law provided for a general and uniform system of common schools and school libraries. It imposed state property and poll taxes to support schools and delegated authority to township voters to adopt local property and poll taxes.[35] The law also provided for a state superintendent of public instruction to be elected for a two-year term[36] and established the first state board of education.[37] The Free School Law made the provision of education mandatory, a shift from the permissive laws of the early period that *allowed* towns to tax for schooling "as soon as circumstances will permit" to mandatory directives that *required* free schooling and provided for state supervision.[38] Indiana's common school movement had faced many obstacles, and this legislation was widely regarded as its "ultimate accomplishment," finally awakening "the public mind" to take public responsibility for universal common schooling.[39]

This landmark legislation was quickly challenged, however, and, in 1854, two significant Indiana Supreme Court decisions invalidated important elements of it. In *State v. Springfield Township,* the court prohibited distributing the proceeds from the use of federal lands (congressional township funds) to support schools throughout the state on a per-pupil basis, reasoning that the federal lands had been granted to the inhabitants of the townships rather than to the state as a whole.[40] Responding to this decision, in 1855 the General Assembly consolidated all the other education funds except the congressional township funds. The consolidated common school funds then were to be distributed unequally to compensate the townships that had large populations but few congressional township funds.[41]

The second decision, *Greencastle Township v. Black,* invalidated the provisions of the Free School Law that allowed township voters to impose a property tax for financing schools after state funds had been expended.[42] The court reasoned that it was solely the state's obligation to provide for a uniform school system. In the next decade, there were several efforts in the General Assembly to counteract the negative impact of *Greencastle,* but the proposals were not successful. The *Indianapolis Journal* in 1858 criticized the "foolish and ridiculous uniformity" required by the Indiana constitution that prevented "the passage of a proper and efficient school law."[43]

Indiana did not establish an actual system of free public schools until after the Civil War. In 1865, township trustees finally received the power to levy a special tax for constructing and equipping schools, although the tax levy still could not be used for tuition.[44] Two years later, the legislature finally authorized property taxes and poll taxes to support public education.[45] Almost two more decades passed before the Indiana Supreme Court in 1885 recognized the state legislature's general power to delegate its taxing authority to local governments without tailoring the legislation to different local circumstances.[46]

The General Assembly adopted the first compulsory education law in 1897, requiring children ages eight to fourteen to attend school for twelve consecutive weeks per year.[47] Early in the twentieth century, the law was changed to require children ages seven to sixteen to attend school for the entire six-month school year.

Bureaucratization and Professionalization of Education

In the twentieth century, there was a slow but steady trend away from complete local autonomy in educational matters in Indiana and toward more state support and regulation. Education became more centralized, and professionals increased their influence. There was a movement to make the school curriculum more uniform, structured, and sequenced. The government monopoly became not only more bureaucratic but also more insulated from parents.[48] Particularly in urban areas, the "rather mechanical form of public bureaucracy, which was permeated with 'illegitimate' lay influence," was replaced "with a streamlined 'professional' bureaucracy in which lay control was carefully filtered through a corporate school board."[49]

Indiana policymakers, like those in other states, found it more efficient to enact state policies pertaining to certain topics (e.g., textbook adoptions, compulsory education, equal opportunities, minimum wages and qualifications of teachers).[50] A decrease in the number of school districts in the state paralleled the trend toward greater state involvement in funding schools.[51] Considerable school district consolidation took place as a result of the first Reorganization Act passed under the constitution of 1851; the number of city, town, and township school districts dropped from approximately nine thousand in the early 1800s to about one thousand by mid-century.[52] Consolidation has continued, and Indiana has fewer than three hundred school districts today.

During the first half of the twentieth century, urban public schools were considered far superior to other schools. This opinion was typical across states at the time but seems almost incomprehensible today. In 1923, the Indiana Education Survey Commission's report concluded that Indiana's small rural schools were inferior because, compared to urban schools, they had inexperienced, less qualified, and poorly paid teachers; a shorter school year; and run-down buildings.[53] The report attributed the problems to the decentralized structure, precluding statewide leadership.[54] The Indiana School Study Commission echoed the same sentiment in the 1940s.[55] Urban schools drew students who were economically advantaged compared to students attending rural schools, and large city schools were more likely to hire certified teachers and to run schools efficiently. This situation changed dramatically by the latter part of the twentieth century, as city conditions declined and as urban schools competed with other social services for local tax revenues and served a disproportionate number of students with special needs.

Individual Rights and Social Justice

Indiana's population traditionally has been racially homogeneous. Well into the twentieth century, less than 5 percent of the state's population was African American or born outside the state; indeed, of all the states, Indiana had the largest percentages of Caucasian and native-born residents in 1920.[56] But during the 1920s and 1930s, the African American population increased in Gary, East Chicago, and Indianapolis—urban areas that accounted for about three-fifths of the state's minority population.[57] Many racist practices were evident in the 1900s, and membership in the Ku Klux Klan was prevalent in the 1920s and considered respectable in some Indiana communities well beyond the middle of the century.

Indiana was one of the four northern states that allowed separate schools for African American children at the time of World War II.[58] Finally, in 1949, the General Assembly declared that Indiana's public schools no longer would be segregated.[59] This was five years before the U.S. Supreme Court established a national standard in *Brown v. Board of Education,* invalidating state laws that imposed school segregation.[60] Although the 1949 Indiana law did not impose penalties for failure to desegregate schools, most school corporations interpreted it as requiring desegregation.[61] Nonetheless, many Indiana schools remained racially segregated long after 1949 because of housing patterns and certain government actions that channeled minority students to particular school districts and schools.[62]

Legal challenges to school segregation in Indiana did not become prevalent until after 1973, when the U.S. Supreme Court held that unconstitutional school segregation could be found in states other than those that had mandated segregation by law at the time of the *Brown* decision.[63] Several urban school corporations in Indiana generated desegregation litigation, but the most notable case has involved the Indianapolis Public Schools. This litigation resulted in an order for one-way busing of minority children to suburban school corporations in Marion County in the early 1980s.[64] After almost two decades, the federal judiciary finally allowed the school corporations to begin phasing out the busing plan.[65]

Desegregation has been just one way in which the federal government has played an important role in promoting social justice in schools. Although Congress always has been a minor player in financing public schools, federal categorical grant programs have influenced educational priorities, particularly the focus on civil rights in the 1960s and 1970s.[66] Federal legislation coupled with judicial rulings were significant in obligating public schools to reduce discriminatory practices and provide compensatory services for students with special needs.

When Congress enacted the Elementary and Secondary Education Act (ESEA) of 1965,[67] federal aid to education tripled, and Title I of the ESEA focused considerable attention on improving educational opportunities for economically and educationally disadvantaged children.[68] Subsequent federal civil rights laws protected individuals against discrimination based on race, ethnicity, sex, religion, age, and disabilities and made some federal aid available to combat injustices, particularly against vulnerable minority groups. Indiana, like other states, has enacted civil rights provisions paralleling the federal laws that have influenced educational policies. The state also has targeted some of its own funds to offset the additional costs associated with educating children with special needs.

Influence of Athletics

Indiana traditionally has not generated a significant body of school-related litigation, but high school athletics provide an exception. As illustrated by the movie *Hoosiers,* high school basketball, especially in small, rural Indiana towns, has been "central to the culture of schools and communities and a source of identification and pride for the state and the region."[69] The focus on basketball, and not on other sports, is attributable to the relatively small team size, the season between harvest and planting, and the fact that it can be played indoors in inclement weather.

Support for the local team traditionally has transcended social class and united communities. In fact, communities' identification with their high school basketball teams and their belief that they would lose community ownership in larger schools hampered school consolidation in Indiana. The concern for school efficiency and economies of scale eventually brought about considerable high school consolidation, but there is a growing recent movement to return to smaller schools.

School consolidation has not been the only point of controversy. For example, there has been tension between athletics and academics, and some educators have lamented that the preoccupation with having winning teams has overshadowed academic needs, a dilemma played out in *Hoosiers.* Moreover, the notion of uniting behind the home team has not affected all communities equally. Until 1941, schools for African American students were excluded from interscholastic competition regulated by the Indiana High School Athletic Association (IHSAA), a voluntary, not-for-profit corporation. Yet, discriminatory practices persisted beyond that date.[70] Also, athletic opportunities for women did not receive serious attention until after passage of Title IX of the Education Amendments of 1972 that barred sex discrimination in schools and colleges receiving federal funds.[71] The IHSAA held the first state tournament for women in 1976, but opportunities for women remained depressed for more than a decade.[72]

Significant school litigation in Indiana has focused on transfer regulations and residency requirements. Perhaps this should not be surprising, given the fierce interscholastic athletic competition that causes IHSAA to monitor transfers that appear athletically motivated. In general, courts have upheld the IHSAA rule that students transferring to a member school are not eligible for interscholastic athletics for a year after enrollment.[73] In some situations, however, courts have required exceptions for students who clearly changed schools for academic, financial, or other nonathletic reasons.[74] In the absence of such special circumstances, the IHSAA has considerable discretion to regulate transfers and other aspects of interscholastic athletic competition. For example, students are eligible to compete interscholastically for four years after entering the ninth grade and only if under age twenty by the date of the state finals in the sport.[75]

Despite the general reluctance of Hoosiers to initiate federal constitutional litigation, some of the most significant federal court cases pertaining to drug testing of student athletes have originated in Indiana. These cases merit attention because they illustrate the interplay between federal and state judicial interpretations of U.S. and state constitutional guarantees.

The U.S. Court of Appeals for the Seventh Circuit led the way in upholding an Indiana school district's random drug testing program as a condition of participation in interscholastic athletics, finding no impairment of the Fourth Amendment's prohibition of unreasonable searches.[76] The U.S. Supreme Court subsequently adopted this position in 1995.[77] The Seventh Circuit later condoned random drug testing of students who participate in any extracurricular activities,[78] a principle that the nation's high court embraced in 2002.[79] These rulings emphasized that participation in athletics and other extracurricular activities is a privilege and not a right, so drug-screening programs apply only to students who are involved voluntarily in these activities. In 1998, however, the Seventh Circuit struck down an Indiana school district's policy requiring drug and alcohol testing of all students suspended three or more days for violating any school rule.[80] The court found an insufficient connection between suspension and drug use, noting that, unlike students who elect to participate in extracurricular activities, the students who are suspended have not voluntarily consented to be tested.

Even without a federal constitutional bar to random drug testing of student athletes, states still can provide protection to students greater than that required under the Fourth Amendment. In 2000, an Indiana appeals court struck down a policy requiring student drivers or participants in extracurricular activities in grades seven through twelve to consent to random urinalysis.[81] The court interpreted the Indiana constitution as providing greater protection against unreasonable searches than the Fourth Amendment, although both provisions have virtually identical language, and concluded that the state constitution requires individualized suspicion before students can be subjected to drug testing or other types of searches. As a result, some Indiana school districts suspended their drug-testing programs for student athletes and drivers until the Indiana Supreme Court reversed this decision in 2002.[82] The state's high court held that the contested urinalysis policy was reasonably related to the school's legitimate purpose of ensuring student health and safety, bringing Indiana back in line with the national standard.

The two-pronged impact of athletics in generating litigation and fostering community pride in the local high school is still felt throughout Indiana. Athletics traditionally have enjoyed a disproportionate share of the school spotlight, but significant educational reforms in the past few decades have drawn widespread attention.

Accountability and Assessment

National trends have influenced Indiana's education system, and state and local policies have reflected such trends. The U.S. Department of Education's report issued in 1983, *A Nation at Risk,* asserted that the quality of American education had declined significantly since the early 1960s, weakening the nation's economy. It further emphasized that state governments, not the federal government, must lead the effort to reform schools.[83] The 1980s witnessed a rapid expansion of the state's leadership role in school reform, and education became prominent on political agendas. As in most states, Indiana's governor and legislature put hundreds of reform measures in place during the next two decades.[84]

The A+ Program for Educational Excellence, enacted by the General Assembly in 1987, was the most comprehensive educational reform package passed in Indiana until that time and clearly positioned the legislature as the central agent of school change in the state. Prior to A+, an average of eight education provisions were enacted each year; since 1987, the average has jumped to more than twenty education reform measures annually.[85] Among the A+ initiatives were Indiana Statewide Testing for Educational Progress (ISTEP), performance-based school accreditation, a beginning teacher internship, mandatory staff evaluation, and a longer school year (changed from 175 to 180 days).

The state's system for financing schools has been controversial since 1973, when the General Assembly imposed state property tax controls and began setting annual maximum general fund property tax levies for each school corporation. Few have understood the complicated funding formula, and, despite efforts in the mid-1980s to reduce disparities across school corporations by adopting a per-pupil equalization provision, school revenues have not been equal. Fifty school corporations filed suit in 1987, alleging that the state's school funding system violated the Indiana constitution's equal protection clause and its mandate that the General Assembly provide a "general and uniform system of common schools."[86] The state subsequently changed the school funding formula, and the school districts agreed to drop the lawsuit in 1992 because of the state's efforts to address the revenue disparities.

The school funding formula adopted in 1993 is designed in part to eliminate the effect of a school corporation's property wealth on its operating revenue and to increase funding to corporations having more disadvantaged students. It also increases per-pupil revenue and the state's share of total school revenue.[87] In fact, the state-to-local funding ratio shifted from 1:2 in the early 1970s to 2:1 by the late 1990s, and the state continues to provide at least two-thirds of all public school revenues in Indiana.[88] It remains to be seen, however, whether the progress in equalizing revenue and property tax assessments will be sufficient to keep the lawsuit dormant.

In addition to school finance reforms, several significant education provisions since 1987 have focused primarily on school accountability and performance-based licensure for teachers and school leaders. In 1992, the General Assembly created the Indiana Professional Standards Board to govern preparation and licensure of educational personnel in the state. The board has adopted standards and licensure exams for teachers and administrators and is holding universities accountable for addressing the standards in their preparation programs.[89] Although the standards board originally was established to function independently of the Indiana Department of Education, in 2005 the board was moved into the department and now is known as the Division of Professional Standards.[90]

Whereas educational accountability traditionally has focused on school inputs (e.g., number of books), the current reforms measure accountability by school outcomes, primarily student performance on statewide tests. Such accountability is at the core of the federal No Child Left Behind Act of 2001 (NCLB, reauthorizing the Elementary and Secondary Education Act of 1965).[91] The NCLB Act reflects a conceptual shift in implementing annual student testing based on academic standards and in holding states, school districts, and schools more accountable for the achievement of *all* students. It is intended to narrow the test-score gap between advantaged and disadvantaged students and to ensure that all teachers are of high quality. The NCLB Act requires states to report student achievement data by income level, race, ethnicity, disability, and degree of English proficiency to guarantee that no group of students is left behind. Schools that do not meet their annual yearly progress (AYP) objectives toward 100 percent student proficiency in basic skills ultimately may face reorganization, with parents provided other educational options for their children. Critics have faulted this law because of its unfunded mandates and the large number of schools that cannot meet AYP for every student group.[92]

Indiana enacted school accountability legislation prior to the NCLB Act, and it has since modified its requirements to align them with the federal mandates. The Indiana accountability law is fairly typical of legislation across states in including standards-based assessments and school improvement strategies and requires dissemination of performance report cards.[93] The heart of the Indiana accountability system is annual statewide student testing in specified grades.[94] Like most other states, Indiana has adopted a graduation exam that students must pass to receive a high school diploma.[95] It is not an overstatement to say that high-stakes tests are driving school reform initiatives nationally, notwithstanding the mounting criticism of the overemphasis on such testing programs.[96]

The Education Roundtable has become a very important force in determining educational policies in Indiana. The Roundtable, formalized in 1999, advises the governor, state superintendent of public instruction, General Assembly, and state board of education. Most Roundtable members are appointed by the governor and the superintendent of public instruction. They represent businesses, policymakers, educators, and nonprofit agencies throughout the state. The president pro tempore of the Senate appoints two members from different political parties, as does the speaker of the House of Representatives.[97] The Roundtable has made important policy recommendations pertaining to charter schools and professional licensing that subsequently have been incorporated into state law.

A recent topic addressed by the Roundtable is the P-16 initiative, which focuses on a seamless system of education from preschool through the college level. Implementing P-16 as a single, coherent system has been called "the next great education reform."[98] Possibly, the current P-16 initiative will bring educational practices more in line with the lofty aims of a coordinated educational system that first appeared in the Indiana constitution almost two centuries ago.

Legal Developments in Selected Areas

> In the long run if the child suffers, so does the entire state.
> —*General Education Board,* Public Education in Indiana

In certain areas, the law has been particularly volatile and has influenced educational developments far beyond the schoolhouse door. Three areas that deserve special attention are church-state relations involving schools, educational choice, and special education. Legal activity in each of these areas, particularly strategies to increase educational choice, will likely have an important impact on schooling in Indiana in the future.

Church-State Relations Involving Schools

In Indiana and other states, education and religion historically were entwined. The Ordinance of 1787 listed "religion" and "morality" ahead of "knowledge" in describing the purposes of public support for education. Although the U.S. Constitution was unique among nations at that time in banning governmental establishment of religion, the First Amendment prohibition was directed only toward Congress. The amendment did not include James Madison's proposed restriction on state interference with religious liberty, because other framers of the Bill of Rights were not willing to place such constraints on state action.[99] It was not until the mid-twentieth century that the U.S. Supreme Court interpreted the Fourteenth Amendment as incorporating most of the protections of the Bill of Rights and applying them to state action as well.[100]

Religious concerns provided the impetus for early education in the American colonies. Indeed, the first compulsory education law, enacted in Massachusetts in 1642, sought to ensure that children learned to read and understand religious principles. Several years later, Massachusetts provided for the creation of public schools because one of the "chief projects of the old deluder, Satan, [is] to keep men from the knowledge of the scripture."[101] The *New England Primer,* used through the 1700s and early 1800s, taught the alphabet with biblical examples, such as "A—in Adam's fall, we sinned all."[102]

Sunday schools, a Protestant innovation, first appeared in the United States in the 1790s.[103] They were an important force in Indiana to provide basic literacy instruction during the early 1800s and remained so even after the 1851 constitution. Sabbath schools were supposed to pave the way for common schools.[104] As public schools became more prevalent and took over the function of general education, the involvement of Sunday schools in general education waned. Nonetheless, during much of the nineteenth century, Sunday schools and public schools functioned as "a partnership on which thousands of Hoosier communities counted as primary bearers of their faith and culture."[105]

Protestantism exerted a strong influence on the public school curriculum well into the twentieth century. For example, *McGuffey's Eclectic Readers,* written by a Protestant minister, were read widely in public schools from the 1830s until the 1920s and greatly influenced students' moral codes.[106] School reformers characterized the public school program as nonsectarian, but Protestant influences were prevalent,[107] despite objections from Catholics and fundamentalist Christians.[108] Laws mandating religion in the public school curriculum were defended as necessary to teach moral values and protect the general welfare.[109]

The Indiana constitution reflects a fundamental ambiguity regarding the role of religion in education, an ambiguity that is ironic but common across states. Most state constitutions are more elaborate than the First Amendment to the U.S. Constitution in guaranteeing the free exercise of religious beliefs and precluding state support of religion. The 1851 Indiana constitution stipulates that no laws shall control the free exercise of religious opinions or interfere with the rights of conscience or give preferences to any creeds or modes of worship.[110] In addition, citizens cannot be required to support any place of worship against their consent or take religious tests for public office, and the constitution prohibits the use of public funds to benefit any religious institution.[111] But the 1851 constitution does not suggest a complete separation of church and state. The first section begins: "WE DECLARE, That all people are created equal; that they are endowed by their CREATOR with certain inalienable rights." Also, by indicating that "all people shall be secured in the natural right to worship ALMIGHTY GOD, according to the dictates of their own consciences,"[112] the 1851 constitution reflects a preference for Judeo-Christian religious traditions. This preference has continued to influence Hoosier lawmakers. In fact, an Indiana law enacted in 1865, in force for more than a century, stipulated that "the Bible shall not be excluded from the public schools of the State."[113]

Religious influences in public schools have not been as dominant in Indiana as in the southern Bible belt, but prayers and Bible reading still were common in many Hoosier schools when the U.S. Supreme Court invalidated such practices under the establishment clause of the First Amendment in the early 1960s.[114] These practices reflected what remains a fairly strong sentiment in Indiana that local school boards, not the federal judiciary, should make decisions governing the public school program, including the role of religion in the curriculum. Thus, Indiana school patrons, especially in rural areas, often have not been receptive to judicial pronouncements that certain religious practices, such as baccalaureate services, no longer can be sponsored by the public school.

Both federal and state constitutions allow some degree of religious accommodation in education. For example, the Indiana Supreme Court rejected a state constitutional challenge to a law that allows dual enrollment, under which students in religious schools can take public school courses on the private school premises.[115] The law counts private school students in the school corporation's entitlement to state aid in proportion to the amount of time the students are instructed by public school teachers.[116] The court was not persuaded that this law violates the Indiana constitution's prohibition on the use of public funds to benefit religious institutions, concluding that only incidental benefits accrue to parochial schools under the dual enrollment program.

Indiana law also authorizes school corporations to direct teachers to call for a moment of silence for meditation or prayer at the beginning of the school day, as long as prayer is not promoted.[117] In addition, public school students can participate in voluntary, student-initiated devotionals during *noninstructional* time, although the school cannot sponsor such events. Under federal law and U.S. Supreme Court precedent, student religious groups in secondary schools must be treated like other noncurriculum groups in terms of access to public school facilities before and after school.[118] Also, public schools cannot discriminate against community religious groups if the school provides a forum for other community groups to meet.[119]

Church-state controversies continue to generate considerable litigation. Many legal conflicts focus on the tension between protecting individuals' free speech rights to express their religious beliefs and values and the right to be protected from governmental advancement of religion. Some courts have held that student initiation of religious activities does not immunize the public school from violating the establishment clause, because students should not be allowed to lead devotionals that school personnel would be precluded from directing.[120] But other courts have reasoned that the free speech clause is violated if student religious expression is treated differently from other types of *private* expression in public schools.[121]

Given recent Supreme Court decisions, this tension is not likely to be resolved in the near future.[122]

The delicate balance regarding religious issues in the schools is evident in litigation and legislation about release-time programs, under which students receive religious instruction off public school grounds. In 1952, the U.S. Supreme Court established the precedent that such voluntary release-time programs represent a permissible accommodation of religion as long as the religious education takes place off public school premises and does not involve public school personnel.[123] Thus, many states, including Indiana, have legislation authorizing such release-time programs.[124] In 2001, however, an Indiana federal district court enjoined several features of a release-time program in the Metropolitan School District of Perry Township (Marion County). The program operated in trailers brought onto public school property, with utilities supported by the school district, and students were discouraged from remaining in the classroom during the release-time program.[125] Recognizing the legality of release-time programs, the court nonetheless found establishment clause violations in the school district's effort to encourage participation and in the use of school property for the religious classes.

Similar to developments in several states, some recent legal disputes in Indiana have focused on religious displays. In 2000, the General Assembly enacted a law authorizing the posting of the Ten Commandments along with other historical documents on state-owned property.[126] The Seventh Circuit subsequently struck down two such displays as promoting religion in violation of the establishment clause.[127] In 2005, the U.S. Supreme Court declined to review a Sixth Circuit decision striking down school displays of the Ten Commandments[128] the day after it rendered two decisions that provided mixed guidance on the constitutionality of similar courthouse displays.[129] Thus, future efforts to post the Ten Commandments on public school property in Indiana are not likely to survive judicial scrutiny, although the constitutionality of courthouse displays remains somewhat uncertain.

Recitation of the version of the Pledge of Allegiance that includes the phrase "one nation under God" also has been controversial. The Seventh Circuit in 1992 rejected an establishment clause challenge to an Illinois law requiring the daily recitation of the pledge in public schools, as long as students are not *required* to participate. The court ruled that the phrase, "one nation under God," does not change this patriotic observance into a religious exercise that would abridge the establishment clause, reasoning that in this patriotic observance, the "'ceremonial deism' . . . has lost through rote repetition any significant religious content."[130] But the Ninth Circuit attracted national attention in 2002 when it reached an opposite conclusion, declaring that recitation of the pledge in public schools abridges the establishment clause by endorsing a belief in monotheism.[131] The Supreme Court in 2004 sidestepped the establishment clause issue, reversing the Ninth Circuit's decision because the plaintiff noncustodial parent did not have standing to challenge the practice. Thus, the constitutionality of public school students' saying "under God" in the pledge remains unresolved.[132]

In addition to controversies over religious influences in public schools and governmental support of religious schools, Indiana has witnessed legal disputes regarding the role of religion in the school curriculum. One especially controversial area involves teaching evolution and creation science in public schools. In 1977, an Indiana superior court struck down the decision by the Indiana State Commission on Textbook Adoption to include a creationist text, *Biology: A Search for Order in Complexity,* on its approved list.[133] The court rejected the asserted purpose of presenting a balanced argument about the origin of life, finding the book's focus on fundamentalist Christian doctrine violated the establishment clause. There was no appeal, but the families who challenged the book were harassed, and in the next legislative session a bill was introduced (though not enacted) to require a balanced treatment of evolution and creationism in textbooks.[134] The U.S. Supreme Court subsequently invalidated a Louisiana statute that mandated "equal time" for creation science when evolution was taught and required school boards to make available curriculum guides and other materials on creation science.[135] Instruction about the origin of humanity continues to generate legal disputes, and Indiana so far has escaped the recent movement—so volatile in several other states—to eliminate the required teaching of evolution in public schools and allow introduction of alternative theories.[136]

Legislators regularly introduce bills to curtail various aspects of the public school instructional program for religious reasons, such as requiring sex education classes to teach abstinence as the only certain way to prevent out-of-wedlock pregnancy and sexually transmitted diseases. One such program, Indiana Respect, developed in 1988, provides funds for various in-school and after-school programs and other activities to teach abstinence.[137] Some citizen groups have sought state legislation to increase parental rights in controlling materials and activities for their children, and several proposals have mimicked the federal Protection of Pupil Rights Amendment that gives parents the right to have their children excused from certain federally funded instructional activities.[138] Controversies over what will be taught in public schools also have fueled calls for more parental choice in deciding *where* their children will be educated. In short, if parents cannot secure policies to tailor the public school program to their religious preferences, they often press for the use of public funds to pay for private education for their children under the rubric of educational choice.

Educational Choice

There has been interest in private education since the colonial period. In Indiana, private academies provided most secondary education until the twentieth century.[139] Secondary education in these academies focused to a large extent on a classical curriculum to prepare students for college. In the late 1800s, Indiana had three educational systems: the common schools for elementary education, the private secondary academies, and the universities.[140]

In two of the earliest school cases to reach the U.S. Supreme Court, the justices acknowledged the constitutionally protected right for private schools to exist and for parents to satisfy compulsory education laws by sending their children to private schools.[141] The Court recognized the state's general welfare interest in mandating school attendance but ruled that the state could not standardize children by requiring that they all attend public schools. In short, the state controls whether, but not where, children are educated.

Besides sanctioning private school education as satisfying compulsory education laws, all states allow children to receive equivalent instruction at home.[142] Indiana classifies home education programs similarly to nonpublic, nonaccredited schools.[143] Parents selecting homeschooling need not secure permission from public school authorities, but they must keep records so they can verify attendance upon request of the state superintendents of public instruction.[144] Home instruction must be equivalent to that offered in public schools,[145] and students must be taught for the same number of days public schools are in session.[146]

As public education grew in the latter part of the twentieth century, interest in private schooling and home education waned somewhat. Private school enrollments have remained fairly stable since the 1970s (about 11 to 12 percent of all K–12 students). Reflecting the national average, approximately 11.6 percent (133,437) of all school age children in Indiana attended private schools in 2004–5.[147] Despite this overall stability, the Catholic school percentage has declined,[148] and enrollments in independent private schools (those not affiliated with a religious sect) and in evangelical Christian academies have increased since the 1970s.[149]

The most significant change has been in home education, which started enjoying renewed interest in the 1960s as some parents became dissatisfied with public schools for various reasons (e.g., secularization of the curriculum, perceived lack of rigor, desegregation mandates, student violence). Home education has experienced steady growth for the past thirty years; about fifteen thousand students were homeschooled nationally in the 1970s, compared to estimates of 1.1 million students in 2003.[150] The number of Indiana children being educated at home more than tripled from 1997–98 to 2005–6 (from 7,140 to 23,455).[151]

Indiana is relatively lax in regulating nonaccredited private schools, including home education; these programs are exempt from curriculum and program requirements that public schools must meet.[152] Courts in Indiana have been reluctant to assess their equivalency to public schools.[153] The General Assembly similarly has declined to impose many regulations on private schools or on home education. This approach is consistent with the national trend of a decline in state requirements (e.g., personnel qualifications, curriculum standards) that must be met by nonaccredited alternatives to public schools.[154] States instead use outcome measures (e.g., statewide tests) to determine whether nonaccredited private programs are adequately educating specific children.

Current education policy decisions may provide an impetus for growth in private school enrollments. As school reform efforts have shifted from equity and access to accountability, students must be provided educational options if they are assigned to schools repeatedly rated as deficient (a status based primarily on test scores). These options may include students transferring to private schools at public expense. Thus, the marketplace may become increasingly prominent in guiding school improvement initiatives. Education researcher Frederick Hess has observed that "the hard-and-fast lines we have drawn between 'public' and 'private' are a lot blurrier and a lot less useful than we pretend."[155]

There is a national movement to provide educational choice for families, and, in the abstract, it is difficult to oppose family choice in educational matters. The basic assumption is that parents will select effective schools, and inferior schools will go out of business, so the marketplace offers salvation for ailing public schools. Advocates of privatizing education assert that voucher programs, under which parents can redeem state-supported vouchers of a specified amount at public or private schools, give poor families choices that only the wealthy traditionally have enjoyed.[156]

Yet, some fear that the ideal of the common school focusing on the general welfare of the citizenry will be lost if education becomes a marketplace commodity based on consumer interests. Taken to an extreme, choice can allow schools to become homogeneous by ideology, economic status, and student background, further marginalizing some groups, as freedom of choice plans have done in the school desegregation context.[157]

In 2002, the U.S. Supreme Court in *Zelman v. Simmons-Harris* removed the establishment clause barrier to state voucher programs that allow public funds to flow to religious schools.[158] Of course, voucher programs including religious schools might still abridge state prohibitions against the use of public funds for religious purposes, and the Supreme Court in 2004 held that, in this regard, states can impose requirements more stringent than those demanded by the establishment clause.[159] Thus, the legality of voucher proposals will be resolved on a state-by-state basis. About half of the states currently are considering some type of voucher program to provide options for specific groups of children, such as those attending failing public schools or those from economically disadvantaged families. Such limited voucher plans are viewed as less expensive than some other school reform strategies, such as reducing class size.

Indiana has experimented with intradistrict open enrollment plans for a couple of decades. Also, students or their parents can request transfers to other school corporations because of crowded conditions or the desire to enroll in high school curricular offerings that are not available in their home districts.[160] Some targeted public voucher programs have been proposed,[161] but the only operational voucher programs allowing public school students to attend private schools in Indiana are privately funded. After the General Assembly rejected a proposal for a publicly supported voucher program, Golden Rule Insurance Company established Indiana's Educational Choice Charitable Trust in 1991 to provide partial scholarships for low-income students to attend private schools. This program received considerable national attention as a model for privately funded voucher programs.[162]

Some view charter schools as a back-door approach to vouchers. Because the schools remain public, they are far more politically palatable than broad-scale voucher programs. The state finances charter schools, but does not require compliance with some public school regulations. Before Indiana enacted a charter school law, there was debate for several years about what entities would be authorized to grant the charters, how the schools would be funded, and what state regulations would be relaxed for these schools. Finally, in 2001, Indiana became the thirty-eighth state to adopt charter school legislation; the Indiana law was revised in 2003.[163] State universities, school districts, and the mayor of a consolidated city each can charter a limited number of nonsectarian schools per year.

Indiana's charter school law does not allow for-profit entities to hold charters, but school districts can contract with private companies to provide instructional services or to manage schools, including charter schools.[164] Several Indiana school boards have entered into such contracts with for-profit groups. Financially strapped school corporations find these arrangements enticing because they pay the companies only if they meet their goals, usually in terms of student achievement gains. Organizational expert Peter Senge has recognized that business is the "locus of innovation in an open society" because it has "a freedom to experiment missing in the public sector and, often, in nonprofit organizations."[165]

However, questions are being raised about whether the emphasis on private gain will overshadow concerns for education as a social enterprise.[166] For example, if a company's contract is based on raising student test scores in reading and math, other aspects of the curriculum and citizenship preparation may be de-emphasized or eliminated altogether. Similarly, if schools must recruit students to ensure their existence, marketing strategies may overshadow educational concerns. Despite the controversies surrounding large-scale private management experiments involving Educational Alternatives and the Edison Project, private companies continue to seek contracts.[167] These companies view charter schools as particularly attractive because such schools are exempt from some state regulations.

Indiana is in the middle, between states having highly regulated charter schools and states that put very few constraints on such schools and do not cap the number of charters that can be granted. Several virtual charter schools have been established in which students are educated primarily online; the participation of students from different states in such schools raises interesting legal issues. These current initiatives to privatize schooling could alter the educational landscape in the state and nation in significant ways.

Special Education

Historically, persons with disabilities were denied fundamental legal rights and basic human dignities. In the nineteenth century, however, there was a gradual movement away from reliance on "private benevolence" and toward government sponsorship of special institutions for disabled persons.[168] The state became involved in this field as a part of social welfare programs. Disabled children were viewed as charity recipients and often were isolated in special institutions (perhaps as much to protect others as to help the disabled). They also were exempted from compulsory school attendance laws.[169] In the first quarter of the twentieth century, courts still upheld the exclusion of children with disabilities from public schools because of the "nauseating effect" they had on teachers and other children.[170]

Compared with other states, Indiana began providing education for students with disabilities relatively early. In the 1840s, the General Assembly established state residential public schools for deaf and blind children. In 1849, it made education of deaf-mutes and the blind free,[171] and the 1851 constitution subsequently reflected this sentiment by specifying: "It shall be the duty of the General Assembly to provide, by law, for the support of institutions for the education of the deaf and dumb, and of the blind; and also for the treatment of the insane."[172] In 1897, the Indianapolis public schools implemented a special class for disturbed and delinquent adolescent boys,[173] and, in 1909, Indiana was among the first states to compel school attendance of deaf and blind children.[174]

Gradually, some public schools started to establish special ungraded classes for children with disabilities.[175] A number of Indiana laws in the second quarter of the twentieth century allowed school corporations to provide nonresidential special education classes and authorized some state reimbursement to schools offering such classes. In 1961, the General Assembly provided reimbursement for excess costs of psychological services and special education administration and for securing more meaningful diagnostic information.[176] But the state provisions were not mandatory until the federal government took the lead in articulating specific rights of children with disabilities.

Federal and state legislation began to codify changing attitudes toward educating children with disabilities in the 1970s, influenced in part by the broader civil rights movement. Whereas the earlier emphasis had been on providing school access and instructing such children in segregated classes, attention shifted to integrating such children into regular education classrooms and assuring their *entitlement* to free, appropriate public schooling. The Individuals with Disabilities Education Act of 1990 (IDEA, formerly the Education for All Handicapped Children Act of 1975) includes detailed specifications that school districts must meet to qualify for reimbursement of a portion of the excess costs of educating children with disabilities.[177] Indiana, like other states, has extensive requirements that parallel those in the IDEA.

All Indiana school corporations now must provide services for children with disabilities either through the individual district or in a joint school services program.[178] In addition, state law specifies how reimbursement from the state will be calculated and obligates the state board to adopt rules for the proper administration of special education programs. Thus, Indiana has elected to prescribe the specific requirements for the education of children with disabilities in Article 7 of the State Board of Education rules instead of through state legislation.[179] Article 7, like the IDEA, requires the development of individualized education programs by case conference committees to ensure an appropriate public education for various categories of children with disabilities. Such children must be placed in the least restrictive environment, provided related services necessary for them to benefit from the educational program, and assured procedural safeguards in placement and disciplinary decisions.[180]

The increasingly specific federal and state mandates about special education services have strong supporters as well as harsh critics. These mandates expose competing values, and Indiana has not avoided these conflicts. Most people applaud the progress in identifying children with disabilities and providing appropriate services for them, and some assert that the required individualized education programs are extremely positive and should be provided for all children. But others raise concerns about the exorbitant costs of special education services, particularly for the most severely disabled students. Critics contend that other social service agencies, not public schools, should support programs for children with significant physical and psychological problems.[181] There are also disputes regarding the merits of inclusion, a strategy that entails bringing support services to the child with disabilities in the regular classroom instead of providing those services in segregated settings. A number of lawsuits have focused on the criteria applied in determining whether a given child should be placed in an inclusive setting.[182]

The participation of children with disabilities in high-stakes testing programs also has generated litigation. Such children cannot be denied the opportunity to take such tests to qualify for regular high school diplomas, but the scope of necessary accommodations remains controversial. An Indiana appeals court ruled that children with disabilities who were scheduled to take the test necessary for earning a diploma three years after the requirement was instituted had received sufficient notice. It further held that school districts do not have to provide accommodations that would jeopardize the validity of the test (e.g., reading to the student for a test measuring reading comprehension).[183] This issue has become particularly volatile because children with disabilities, with a few exceptions, must participate in the mandatory testing program under the NCLB Act.

One of the most highly contested topics in this area is disciplinary practices. Critics say the IDEA has created a double standard because schools may terminate educational services for regular education students but not for children with disabilities. In 1992, an Indiana school corporation challenged a U.S. Department of Education interpretation of the IDEA as requiring the continuation of services for children with disabilities who have been removed from the classroom for disciplinary reasons. The Seventh Circuit reasoned that the department's letter specifying that services could not be terminated for such children was an interpretation, not an attempt to legislate, and thus was exempt from the formal notice and comment process required for legislative acts.[184] The federal judiciary has recognized that educational and related services for children with disabilities cannot be terminated for disciplinary reasons, although, in some instances, services can be provided in a more restrictive setting.[185]

Nationally, litigation involving the rights of children with disabilities is the fastest-growing area of school law, and legal activity in Indiana supports this trend. Some fear that the legalization of special education may result in a backlash against providing services for such children, and, without question, legal activity in this arena will continue to influence school policies and practices in Indiana and elsewhere.

Themes and Tensions

> Law has always been an important instrument in shaping public schooling as well as a mirror of its goals, structures, and processes.
>
> —*David Tyack, "Toward a Social History of Law and Public Education"*

This essay has portrayed the legal history of education in Indiana by emphasizing important themes instead of by documenting each historical event in chronological order. Of course, such a portrayal is simply one view of the evolution of schooling in Indiana. We had envisioned concluding with a set of trends but found more tensions than trends. The following generalizations characterize the legal history of Indiana schools and suggest how the law may shape future directions.

There has been interplay and, often, conflict among the federal, state, and local governments in providing incentives and requirements for education. Federal influence dominated the days leading to statehood: the proceeds from some federal lands were earmarked for education, but this incentive was as much to stimulate settlement of the territories as to encourage education. Then, for a lengthy period of time, education was primarily a matter of local preferences, with minimal state guidance and support. During this period, Indiana's system of education was weak, as was generally true across states.

The 1960s witnessed renewed federal interest in education, particularly in providing categorical aid that was influential in shaping educational programs for children with special needs and disadvantages. But establishing national priorities does not necessarily locate educational responsibility at the federal level. Throughout U.S. history, a national interest in education has been salient, but the federal government has deferred to local implementation.[186] For example, federal and state accountability laws reflect a national concern with ensuring student achievement and charge individual schools with carrying out the accountability mandates.[187]

Despite the influence of the federal government in setting educational priorities, primarily state and local governments have regulated and supported public education. In fact, the federal government has never provided more than 10 percent of public school funds. States steadily have increased their financial support, contributing about half of public school revenues across states by 2002, and Indiana reflects this trend.[188] Accompanying the growth in state education aid have been increasing state regulations and constraints on local prerogatives. State legislatures have plenary, or complete, power to enact laws governing education as long as they respect federal and state constitutional rights and federal civil rights laws. Indiana is not alone in the struggle to find the appropriate state-local balance in educational governance, and wide variations exist among states. Indiana falls between highly centralized and decentralized state systems, but the trend over time in Indiana has been toward greater centralization of educational governance.

Conflicts between local school districts and state legislatures in determining the curriculum and other specific aspects of educational offerings have been apparent in Indiana and many other states. Many citizens express fear that education decisions are becoming too centralized, negating local preferences. Given the long history of local control of education in the United States and the commitment to giving a voice to people affected by policy decisions, it is not surprising that there has been some resistance to statewide academic standards, testing programs, accountability mandates, and other features of a centralized, standardized system.

However, if all education decisions were left to local discretion and control, resource disparities across school districts would increase. Some educators feel strongly that progress in equalizing educational opportunities and narrowing the achievement gap between advantaged and disadvantaged students can occur only through greater state control.[189] Whether local control or state regulation will lead to more equitable and effective educational programs continues to provoke volatile debate.

There has been a tension between encouraging private decisions in educational matters and ensuring an educated citizenry to promote the general welfare and the common good. This tension between private and public interests has been evident since before statehood. The pioneer spirit embodied a desire to be independent of government controls, even though citizens benefited from government programs.[190] Parents assumed much of the early financial responsibility for their children's education and, in turn, had the authority to select who would teach their children and what the curriculum would entail. As state support and professional control of public schools increased during the twentieth century, some parents, particularly in urban areas, felt they had little influence in educational matters.

During the past two decades, the renewed attention on family choice and parental rights in educational decisions has prompted various proposals to open education to the marketplace and greatly reduce the public education bureaucracy. In fact, some groups would like to dismantle public schools and provide vouchers that families could redeem at the private schools or home education programs of their choice.[191] These proposals shift the emphasis from the common good to a focus on individual enhancement.

The question of whether the marketplace or the government should serve the primary regulatory function for education remains the source of considerable controversy in Indiana and elsewhere, and the final outcome in this debate could affect the future of schooling in the state and nation. The distinction between state and market control of education is not simply a governance issue: "It is also a statement about what we value in education and about how we weigh the claims of the individual and the community in a democratic society."[192]

There has been a tension between embracing and rejecting judicial resolution of educational disputes. Traditionally, public schools in Indiana reflected the dominant values of the local community, such as moral values (e.g., opposition to homosexuality) and religious values (support for Christianity). Perhaps as a result, Hoosiers rarely turned to courts to resolve educational disputes.

Yet, as the state's citizenry became increasingly diverse in the twentieth century, especially in urban areas, a clear consensus on religious, moral, and social values could not be assured. Thus, some people began to question the role of the public school in institutionalizing such values. Moreover, attention focused on the role of law in protecting vulnerable minorities disadvantaged by majority rule.[193] Starting with the landmark desegregation decision, *Brown v. Board of Education,* federal courts became more assertive in applying constitutional provisions to protect minority rights, and federal and state civil rights laws began to be applied in school settings.[194] Judicial interpretations of federal constitutional and statutory rights has had an important impact on school practices.

Judicial and legislative activism in public education is not universally supported, however, and this tension is certainly present in Indiana. With a few exceptions, Hoosiers have not been as litigious as have citizens in some states in challenging school policies and practices.[195] The sentiment remains strong in some Indiana school corporations that the local community, not the judiciary, should determine the public school structure and content. But others argue fervently that legal intervention is necessary, especially in communities where the local preferences are at odds with national priorities.

The tension between educational equity and excellence has influenced school improvement efforts since the mid-twentieth century. Initial school reform activities in Indiana often focused on attaining educational equity in terms of school access (e.g., racial minorities, children with disabilities) and on equalizing the disparities in school fiscal resources that arise from disparities in local districts' property values. Many federal categorical grant programs and state equalization strategies have been designed to advance such equity goals.

Starting in the late 1980s, attention shifted away from equity in school resources to accountability for student performance. The standards movement in Indiana and elsewhere reflects this focus on excellence (or at least adequacy) as measured by student achievement on statewide tests. The federal No Child Left Behind Act also rests on the belief that equity will be achieved by increasing school accountability to ensure that all students reach specified standards. Attaining equity goals is still important, but such goals are now viewed through the lens of accountability for student achievement on standards-based tests. It is still uncertain whether this approach actually will reduce the achievement gap and level the playing field as envisioned.

The law governing education often has reflected lofty aims that have not been translated into reality. Developments in Indiana vividly illustrate the disparity between legal rhetoric and educational practices. Both the 1816 and 1851 Indiana constitutions reflect an exalted position for education, but one that has never been fully realized. Indiana is not unique in this regard: education clauses across state constitutions contain "exhortation to virtue or justificatory prose" more than any constitutional provisions other than declarations of individual rights.[196] Part of the dilemma is the gap between the vision of a uniform state educational system, which many say they endorse, and the reverence for local control in educational decisions, which has been a strong tradition in Indiana.

Even beyond the chasm between rhetoric and reality in constitutional promises, reforms prescribed by state laws often have not been realized, partly because of budget shortfalls. For example, Indiana's appropriations for professional development and mentoring have never fulfilled legislative promises. Like state legislatures, Congress often has authorized funding that has not been forthcoming. For example, the federal government has never appropriated its promised share (40 percent) of the excess costs to educate children with disabilities.[197] Educators have become accustomed to legal enactments that are not funded or otherwise supported, a circumstance that encourages indifference. School personnel often refer to the latest legislative reforms with the phrase, "this too will pass," because when the champions of particular initiatives leave office, the policies and priorities may change as well.

The gap between political rhetoric and reality is particularly troubling in education because policymakers have asked more from schools than they reasonably can deliver. They expect schools to remedy problems that society as a whole has not been able to address successfully, such as racial discrimination, teenage pregnancies, and socioeconomic disparities. Unrealistic demands are illustrated painfully in the area of school desegregation, where mandated school integration was expected to resolve society's racial conflicts in spite of segregated neighborhoods and prevalent employment discrimination.[198]

Future Directions

It is important periodically to look backward to provide a context regarding where we have been and to offer insights regarding where we may be heading.[199] Historian David Tyack's observation that school laws have both mirrored and shaped public education has certainly been true in Indiana.[200] Developments in education have reflected the Hoosier tendency to be cautious and conservative. Although Indiana has not experienced the volatile legal controversies evident in some states, legal action in areas such as desegregation and church-state relations have influenced general public policy in the state.

Notwithstanding the wide disparity between legal rhetoric and reality, it also is true that laws voicing ideals shape education to some extent, even if only to change the nature and terms of the conversation. The road to a uniform state system of education has not been an easy one, and many challenges still lie ahead. Few would argue that Hoosiers have lived up to the ideals for education outlined in the 1816 and 1851 constitutions, but efforts continue toward the goal of achieving an equitable and effective statewide educational system. The school accountability movement focusing on student outcomes is the latest strategy designed to ensure that all Hoosiers receive an adequate education to prepare them for citizenship. Whether its promise will be realized remains to be seen.

It is possible that the current emphasis on enhancing family choice in education and using public funds to support private school options, including religious schools, portends a major structural and substantive change in education nationally. Indeed, subjecting education to the marketplace could become the most significant transformation since the common school movement in the mid-1800s. However, even if major education changes are on the horizon nationally, Indiana is not likely to take the lead in the transformation, given the pragmatism that characterizes Hoosiers. If Indiana remains true to its history, educational changes in the state will continue to take place deliberately and in small steps.

Notes

The authors want to thank Professor Donald Warren, Indiana University, for offering helpful suggestions on an early draft of this chapter.

1. James H. Madison, *The Indiana Way: A State History* (Bloomington: Indiana University Press and Indiana Historical Society, 1986), xiii.

2. Carl Kaestle, *Pillars of the Republic: Common Schools and American Society, 1780–1860* (New York: Hill and Wang, 1983), 183; John Meyer, David Tyack, Joane Nagel, and Audri Gordon, "Public Education as Nation-Building in America: Enrollments and Bureaucratization in the American States, 1870–1930," *American Journal of Sociology* 83 (November 1979): 591–613.

3. Carl Kaestle, "The Development of Common School Systems in the States of the Old Northwest," in *". . . Schools and the Means of Education Shall Forever Be Encouraged": A History of Education in the Old Northwest, 1787–1880*, ed. Paul Mattingly and Edward Stevens (Athens: Ohio University Libraries, 1987), 31–43.

4. For a discussion of the distinction between educational funding laws and civil rights laws, see Nelda Cambron-McCabe, Martha McCarthy, and Stephen Thomas, *Public School Law: Teachers' and Students' Rights*, 5th ed. (Boston: Allyn and Bacon, 2004), 14–17. State and local governments can opt out of federal funding programs, but they must comply with civil rights laws.

5. Land Ordinance of 1785, *Journals of the Continental Congress, 1774–1789*, ed. Worthington Chauncey Ford et al., vol. 28 (Washington D.C.: Government Printing Office, 1933), 375–406. See Clement Malan and James Robinson, *Indiana School Law* (Indianapolis: C. E. Pauley, 1935), 4.

6. Northwest Ordinance of 1787, art. 3, *Journals of the Continental Congress*, ed. Worthington Chauncey Ford et al., vol. 32 (Washington, D.C.: Government Printing Office, 1936), 334–43.

7. Richard Boone, *A History of Education in Indiana* (New York: D. Appleton, 1892), 3.

8. Scott Walter, "Awakening the Public Mind: The Dissemination of the Common School Idea of Indiana, 1787–1852," in *Hoosier Schools: Past and Present*, ed. William Reese (Bloomington: Indiana University Press, 1998), 6. The dedication of land rentals to educational purposes was a time-honored English custom, so it was not surprising that this practice was common in colonial America. See Kaestle, *Pillars of the Republic*, 184.

9. Kaestle, *Pillars of the Republic*, 183–84. See also Harold Negley, "Indiana," in *Education in the States: Historical Development and Outlook*, ed. Jim Pearson and Edgar Fuller (Washington, D.C.: National Education Association of the United States, 1969), 371–97.

10. Indiana Department of Education, Indiana Superintendent of Public Education, Suellen Reed, "Questions and Answers," http://ideanet.doe.state.in.us/reed/reed_qanda/qa1.html.

11. Walter, "Awakening the Public Mind," 5. See also L. C. Rudolph, *Hoosier Faiths: A History of Indiana Churches and Religious Groups* (Bloomington: Indiana University Press, 1995), 357.

12. Kaestle, preface to *Pillars of the Republic*, xi–xii.

13. Negley, "Indiana," 373. See also Reed, "Questions and Answers."

14. Indiana const. of 1816, art. IX, § 2.

15. Walter, "Awakening the Public Mind," 7.

16. Boone, *History of Education*, 13.

17. See David Tyack, Thomas James, and Aaron Benavot, *Law and the Shaping of Public Education, 1785–1954* (Madison: University of Wisconsin Press, 1987), 30.

18. Donald Carmony, *Indiana, 1816–1850: The Pioneer Era* (Indianapolis: Indiana Historical Bureau and Indiana Historical Society, 1998), 363; Justin Walsh, *The Centennial History of the Indiana General Assembly, 1816–1978* (Indianapolis: Select Committee on the Centennial History of the Indiana General Assembly, 1987), 139.

19. It was somewhat akin to the phrase "with all deliberate speed" in the landmark *Brown v. Board of Education* desegregation case that some scholars have faulted as delaying immediate and effective school desegregation.

20. Boone, *History of Education,* 24.

21. Kaestle, preface to *Pillars of the Republic,* x.

22. During the General Assembly's discussion of taxation for school purposes in 1837, one delegate said: "When I die I want my epitaph written, 'Here lies an enemy to free school.'" Boone, *History of Education,* 87.

23. 1824 Ind. Acts 379 (January 31, 1824). See also Walter, "Awakening the Public Mind," 7.

24. 1833 Ind. Acts 78 (February 2, 1833). See also Carmony, *Indiana,* 367–70.

25. Boone, *History of Education,* 87.

26. Andrew Cayton and Peter Onuf, *The Midwest and the Nation: Rethinking the History of an American Region* (Bloomington: Indiana University Press, 1990), 60. Robert Dale Owen was another prominent educational leader in Indiana. He championed secular education and the Workingmen's Party and he established an educational experiment that challenged traditional educational institutions and mainstream Protestant and capitalist ideology. Although this experiment at New Harmony failed, Owen had a significant influence on the development of public schools in Indiana. See Fassett Cotton, *Education in Indiana* (Bluffton, Ind.: Progress Publishing, 1934), 451–52; Kaestle, *Pillars of the Republic,* 142–46.

27. The 1840 decennial census indicated that Indiana ranked sixteenth among the twenty-six states in literacy; only one in seven people in the state was able to read or write. Boone, *History of Education,* 87–89.

28. Ibid, 96.

29. Kaestle, "Development," 34. See also Boone, *History of Education,* 105–7.

30. 1849 Ind. Acts 123 (January 17, 1849). See also Boone, *History of Education,* 112–19.

31. Boone, *History of Education,* 123.

32. Barclay Thomas Johnson, "Credit Crisis to Education Emergency: The Constitutionality of Model Student Voucher Programs under the Indiana Constitution," *Indiana Law Review* 35, no. 1 (2001): 196–200.

33. Ibid.

34. Ind. const. of 1851, art. VIII, § 1. The original version of Indiana's constitution of 1851 can be found in Charles Kettleborough, *Constitution Making in Indiana: A Source Book of Constitutional Documents with Historical Introduction and Critical Notes* (Indianapolis: Indiana Historical Commission, 1916), 1:346. The wording of this section was changed slightly in 1972.

35. 1852 Ind. Acts 439 (June 14, 1852). See also Cotton, *Education in Indiana,* 320–21; Boone, *History of Education,* 143–64; Malan and Robinson, *Indiana School Law,* 381.

36. The state constitutional specification in article VIII, section 8, of a two-year term for the state superintendent was eliminated by a constitutional amendment adopted November 7, 1972. The superintendent's term was set at four years in 1974 (1974 Ind. Acts 337 [February 13, 1974]).

37. The governor appoints the state board members. In 1945, the General Assembly divided the board into three fairly independent commissions (general education, textbook adoption, and teacher training and licensing) with six members each (1945 Ind. Acts 1529 [March 9, 1945]). In 1984, legislation changed the board's composition from the three commissions to an integrated board of ten members plus the state superintendent of public instruction, who chairs the board (1984 Ind. Acts 279, § 22 [March 5, 1984]).

38. Kaestle, *Pillars of the Republic,* 186.

39. Walter, "Awakening the Public Mind," 21–22.

40. State v. Springfield Township, 6 Ind. 67 (1854).

41. Walsh, *Centennial History,* 248; Boone, *History of Education,* 151–52. In 1856, the Indiana Supreme Court held that this equalization strategy conformed to "the spirit" of the Indiana constitution. Quick v. White-Water Township, 7 Ind. 454, 460 (1856).

42. Greencastle Township v. Black, 5 Ind. 557 (1854). See also Negley, "Indiana," 375.

43. Kettleborough, introduction to *Constitution Making in Indiana,* 1:cli.

44. 1865 Ind. Acts 3 (March 6, 1865). See also Negley, "Indiana," 375.

45. 1867 Ind. Acts 30 (March 9, 1867). See also Cayton and Onuf, *Midwest and the Nation,* 60; Negley, "Indiana," 375.

46. Robinson v. Schenck, 102 Ind. 307, 1 N.E. 698 (1885). See also Negley, "Indiana," 375.

47. 1897 Ind. Acts 248 (April 14, 1897). See also Malan and Robinson, *Indiana School Law,* 390; Negley, "Indiana," 376. The topic of compulsory attendance generated heated debate about state power and parental rights during the last quarter of the nineteenth century. Walsh, *Centennial History,* 248–49.

48. Joseph Murphy, *The Privatization of Schooling: Problems and Possibilities* (Thousand Oaks, Calif.: Corwin, 1996). See also Kaestle, *Pillars of the Republic,* 117. Despite the dominance of public education, there was an active, although small, private school movement.

49. David Tyack, *The One Best System: A History of American Urban Education* (Cambridge, Mass.: Harvard University Press, 1974), 168.

50. Negley, "Indiana," 378.

51. Indiana is unique in calling school districts "school corporations." Throughout this chapter, the terms "school district" and "school corporation" are used interchangeably.

52. Negley, "Indiana," 378. The School Corporation Reorganization Act of 1959 accelerated the consolidation of school corporations (1959 Ind. Acts 451 [March 12, 1959]).

53. James H. Madison, *Indiana through Tradition and Change: A History of the Hoosier State and Its People, 1920–1945* (Indianapolis: Indiana Historical Society, 1982), 267–68.

54. General Education Board, *Public Education in Indiana* (Report of the Indiana Education Survey Commission) (New York: General Education Board, 1923), 265.

55. William Reese, "Urban Schools in Postwar Indiana," in Reese, *Hoosier Schools,* 145–72. It should be noted that these reports were dominated by "administrative progressives" who sought centralization of school control to increase efficiency. See Tyack, *One Best System,* 126–29.

56. Madison, *Indiana through Tradition and Change,* 3, 7.

57. Ibid., 7–8.

58. Maureen Reynolds, "The Challenges of Racial Equality," in Reese, *Hoosier Schools,* 179.

59. 1949 Ind. Acts 603 (March 8, 1949).

60. Brown v. Bd. of Educ. of Topeka, 347 U.S. 483 (1954).

61. Reynolds, "The Challenges of Racial Equality," 179.

62. When city and county services were combined into Uni-Gov in Marion County in 1968, school corporations were not merged, keeping more minority students in the Indianapolis Public Schools. Ibid., 186.

63. Keyes v. Sch. Dist. No. 1, 413 U.S. 189 (1973).

64. U.S. v. Bd. of Sch. Comm'rs of Indianapolis, 677 F.2d 1185 (7th Cir. 1982).

65. See U.S. v. Bd. of Sch. Comm'rs of Indianapolis, No. IP68-C-225 (S.D. Ind. June 21, 1998).

66. The federal contribution reached its highest level of 9.8 percent of school revenues in 1978. See National Center for Education Statistics, U.S. Department of Education, *Digest of Education Statistics, 2004* (Washington, D.C.: Government Printing Office, 2004).

67. Elementary and Secondary Education Act of 1965, 79 Stat. 27 (1965) (codified as amended at 20 U.S.C. §§ 6301 et seq. [2005]).

68. Cambron-McCabe, McCarthy, and Thomas, *Public School Law,* 14–16.

69. David G. Martin, "Gymnasium or Coliseum? Basketball, Education, and Community Impulse in Indiana in the Early Twentieth Century," in Reese, *Hoosier Schools,* 121–44, quote at 121.

70. Ibid., 140–42.

71. 86 Stat. 373 (1972) (codified as amended at 20 U.S.C. § 1681 [2005]).

72. Herb Schwomeyer, *Hoosier HERsteria: A History of High School Girls Basketball* (Greenfield, Ind.: Mitchell-Fleming, 1985), 287.

73. See, for example, Robbins v. Ind. High Sch. Athletic Ass'n, 941 F. Supp. 786 (S.D. Ind. 1996); Anderson v. Ind. High Sch. Athletic Ass'n, 699 F. Supp. 719 (S.D. Ind. 1988); Ind. High Sch. Athletic Ass'n v. Carlberg, 694 N.E.2d 222 (Ind. 1997).

74. Crane v. Ind. High Sch. Athletic Ass'n, 975 F.2d 1315 (7th Cir. 1992) (student's move from his divorced father's home to live with his mother in another district warranted an exception as it was not athletically motivated); Ind. High Sch. Athletic Ass'n v. Durham, 748 N.E.2d 404 (Ind. Ct. App. 2001) (holding that a student qualified for a hardship exception because a change in his family's financial circumstances caused him to transfer from a private to a public school); Ind. High Sch. Athletic Ass'n v. Carlberg, 661 N.E.2d 833 (Ind. Ct. App. 1996) (requiring an exception to the transfer policy for a student who changed schools for academic and financial, not athletic, reasons).

75. IHSAA Rules C-4-1; C-12-2 (2005).

76. Schaill v. Tippecanoe, 864 F.2d 1309 (7th Cir. 1988).

77. Vernonia Sch. Dist. 47J v. Acton, 515 U.S. 646 (1995).

78. See Joy v. Penn-Harris-Madison Sch. Corp., 212 F.3d 1052 (7th Cir. 2000); Todd v. Rush County Schools, 133 F.3d 984 (7th Cir. 1998).

79. Bd. of Educ. v. Earls, 536 U.S. 822 (2002).

80. Willis v. Anderson Cmty. Sch., 158 F.3d 415 (7th Cir. 1998).

81. Linke v. Northwestern Sch. Corp., 734 N.E.2d 252 (Ind. Ct. App. 2000), *rev'd*, 763 N.E.2d 972 (Ind. 2002).

82. Linke v. Northwestern Sch. Corp., 763 N.E.2d at 972.

83. Barry Bull, "School Reform in Indiana since 1980s," in Reese, *Hoosier Schools*, 194–217.

84. A significant feature of Indiana's educational governance is that the superintendent of public instruction and the governor are elected independently and have been from different political parties for more than two decades. A study released in 2001 by the National Association of State Boards of Education and the National Governors' Association urged Indiana to change to a system in which the governor appoints the state superintendent. See Mary Ann Zehr, "Indiana Urged to Switch to Appointed State Schools Chief," *Education Week*, February 14, 2001, 25.

85. Indiana Education Policy Center, *Education in Indiana: An Overview* (Bloomington: Indiana University, 1994), 24. See generally the Indiana School Boards Association *Legislative Bulletin* (published twice monthly during legislative session).

86. Lake Central v. Indiana, No. 56 C01-8704-CP81 (Newton Cir. Ct. 1987).

87. Robert Toutkoushian and Robert Michael, *Demystifying School Funding in Indiana*, Education Policy Brief vol. 3, no. 2 (Bloomington, Ind.: Center for Evaluation and Education Policy, 2005).

88. This shift is more dramatic in Indiana than in many other states, but it reflects the national movement toward greater state aid to and control of public education.

89. See Indiana Professional Standards Board, *Comprehensive Standards Document* (Indianapolis: Indiana Professional Standards Board, 1999). Teachers were licensed in Indiana by taking an examination prior to 1921, and specific university coursework was not required. Although graduation from an accredited university program is now a prerequisite, licensure again is conditioned on test passage.

90. See Indiana Department of Education, "About the Indiana Professional Standards Board," http://www.doe.state.in.us/dps/visitors/aboutipsb.html.

91. No Child Left Behind Act, 115 Stat. 1425 (2001) (codified as amended at 20 U.S.C. §§ 6301 et seq. [2005]).

92. See James Popham, "The 'No Child' Noose Tightens—But Some States Are Slipping It," *Education Week*, September 24, 2003, 48.

93. IC §§ 20-31-1-1 et seq. (2005).

94. IC §§ 20-32-5-1 et seq. (2005).

95. IC §§ 20-32-4-1 et. seq. (2005).

96. See generally Gerald Bracey, *Put to the Test: An Educator's and Consumer's Guide to Standardized Testing* (Bloomington, Ind.: Phi Delta Kappa, 1998); W. James Popham, *Testing! Testing! What Every Parent Should Know about School Tests* (Boston: Allyn and Bacon, 2000).

97. IC §§ 20-19-4-1 et seq. (2005). Another recent initiative is the Indiana Urban Schools Association (IUSA), a coalition of thirty-four districts with about two-fifths of the state's student population. IUSA was established in 1993 in part to monitor the state's progress in addressing the special needs of urban schools and to lobby for legislation. Personal correspondence with Charles Little, Executive Director of IUSA, November 12, 2003 and November 17, 2003.

98. Education Commission of the States, "'P-16': The Next Great Education Reform," *State Education Leader* 20 (Winter 2002), available online at http://www.ecs.org/clearinghouse/35/37/3537.htm#ten. As of 2002, at least half the states reported multifaceted P-16-type initiatives.

99. Walter Berns, *The First Amendment and the Future of American Democracy* (New York: Basic Books, 1976), 3–6, 33.

100. See, for example, Cantwell v. Connecticut, 310 U.S. 296 (1940), and explanation in note 114.

101. R. L. Finney, *A Brief History of the American Public School* (New York: Macmillan, 1946), 4.

102. Leo Pfeffer, *Church, State and Freedom* (Boston: Beacon Press, 1967), 325. A revised version of the *Primer* was reintroduced in 1996 for homeschooled children.

103. Anne Boylan, *Sunday School: The Formation of an American Institution, 1790–1880* (New Haven, Conn.: Yale University Press, 1988), 6.

104. Robert Lynn and Elliott Wright, *The Big Little School: Two Hundred Years of the Sunday School,* rev. ed. (Birmingham: Religious Education Press, 1980), 55.

105. Rudolph, *Hoosier Faiths,* 357.

106. Ellwood Cubberley, *Public Education in the United States: A Study and Interpretation of American Educational History,* rev. ed. (Boston: Houghton Mifflin, 1934), 294.

107. This was referred to as common faith, civil religion, or public religion, as contrasted with denominational or ecclesiastical religion. See James Carper and Brian Ray, "Religion, Schooling, and Home Education: Past and Present," in *Religion, Education, and American Experience: Reflections on Religion and American Public Life,* ed. Edith Blumhofer (Tuscaloosa: University of Alabama Press, 2002), 223, 227.

108. B. Edward McClellan, *Moral Education in American: Schools and the Shaping of Character from Colonial Times to the Present* (New York: Teachers College Press, 1999), 35–43.

109. Otto Hamilton, *The Courts and the Curriculum* (New York: Teachers College Press, 1927), 113.

110. Ind. const. of 1851, art. I, §§ 2, 3, 4.

111. Ibid., art. I, §§ 4, 5, 6.

112. Ibid., art. I, §§ 1, 2 (emphasis in original).

113. Boone, *History of Education,* 233.

114. See Sch. Dist. of Abington Township v. Schempp, 374 U.S. 203 (1963); Engel v. Vitale, 370 U.S. 421 (1962). The establishment clause is applicable to the states through the Fourteenth Amendment, which specifically restricts state interference with citizens' fundamental liberties. See Cantwell v. Connecticut, 310 U.S. 296 (1940).

115. Embry v. O'Bannon, 798 N.E.2d 157 (Ind. 2003).

116. IC § 21-3-1.6-1.2 (2005).

117. IC § 20-30-5-4.5 (2005). Indiana's law is similar to statutes in Arizona, Kansas, New York, and Pennsylvania. See Education Commission of the States, "School Prayer, Moment of Silence, Other Policies Concerning Religion," available online at http://www.ecs.org/clearinghouse/13/38/1338.htm.

118. Equal Access Act, 98 Stat. 1302 (1984) (codified at 20 U.S.C. § 4071 [2005]) (prohibiting secondary schools that have established a forum for noncurriculum student groups to meet during noninstructional time to discriminate based on the religious, philosophical, or political content of the meetings); Bd. of Educ. v. Mergens, 496 U.S. 226 (1990) (rejecting an establishment clause challenge to the EAA).

119. See Good News Club v. Milford Cent. Sch., 533 U.S. 98 (2001); Lamb's Chapel v. Center Moriches Union Free Sch. Dist., 508 U.S. 384 (1993).

120. See ACLU of N.J. v. Blackhorse Pike Reg'l Bd. of Educ., 84 F.3d 1471 (3d Cir. 1996); Harris v. Joint Sch. Dist. No. 241, 41 F.3d 447 (9th Cir.1994), *vacated*, 515 U.S. 1154 (1995).

121. See Chandler v. Siegelman, 230 F.3d 1313 (11th Cir. 2000); Jones v. Clear Creek Indep. Sch. Dist., 977 F.2d 963 (5th Cir. 1992).

122. Compare Santa Fe Indep. Sch. Dist. v. Doe, 530 U.S. 290 (2000) (striking down elections to allow student-led prayers before sporting events because the school policies were designed to promote prayer), with Good News Club v. Milford Cent. Sch., 533 U.S. 98 (2001) (finding a free expression right for religious groups to hold devotional meetings in public schools after school hours if other community groups were allowed such access, even though the devotional meetings target elementary children attending the school).

123. Zorach v. Clauson, 343 U.S. 306 (1952). Four years earlier, the Court had struck down a release-time program in which clergy came into the public school to provide the religious instruction, McCollum v. Bd. of Educ., 333 U.S. 203 (1948).

124. IC § 20-33-2-19 (2005).

125. Moore v. Metro. Sch. Dist., No. IP 00-1859-C-M/S, 2001 U.S. Dist. LEXIS 2722 (S.D. Ind. February 7, 2001).

126. IC § 4-20.5-21-2 (2005).

127. ICLU v. O'Bannon, 259 F.3d 766 (7th Cir. 2001), *cert. denied*, 534 U.S. 1162 (2002); Books v. City of Elkhart, 235 F.3d 292 (7th Cir. 2000), *cert. denied*, 532 U.S. 1058 (2001). See also Kimbley v. Lawrence County, 119 F. Supp. 2d 856 (S.D. Ind. 2000). More than two decades ago, the Supreme Court struck down a Kentucky law requiring the posting of the Ten Commandments in public schools, Stone v. Graham, 449 U.S. 39 (1980), but this decision did not curtail the legal activity as anticipated.

128. Baker v. Adams County/Ohio Valley Sch. Bd., 86 Fed. Appx. 104 (6th Cir. 2004), *cert. denied*, 125 S. Ct. 2989 (2005).

129. Van Orden v. Perry, 125 S. Ct. 2854 (2005) (upholding a monument with the Ten Commandments on the Texas state capitol grounds that it was part of a historical display); McCreary County, Kentucky v. ACLU of Kentucky, 125 S. Ct. 2722 (2005) (striking down courthouse displays of the Ten Commandments that had the purpose of advancing religion).

130. Sherman v. Cmty. Consol. Sch. Dist. 21, 980 F.2d 437, 446 (7th Cir. 1992). The right to be excused from saying the pledge for religious or philosophical reasons was recognized by the Supreme Court in 1943 in West Virginia St. Bd. of Educ. v. Barnette, 319 U.S. 624 (1943).

131. Newdow v. U.S. Congress, 328 F.3d 466 (9th Cir. 2002), *rev'd sub nom.* Elk Grove Unified Sch. Dist. v. Newdow, 124 S. Ct. 2301 (2004).

132. Indiana is not one of the thirty-five states that requires the Pledge of Allegiance to be recited in public schools.

133. Hendren v. Campbell, No. S577-0139 (Superior Ct. No. 5, Marion County, Indiana, April 14, 1977). See Jerry P. Lightner, ed., *A Compendium of Information on the Theory of Evolution and the Evolution-Creationism Controversy,* rev. ed. (Reston, Va.: National Association of Biology Teachers, 1978), 31–41.

134. Rudolph, *Hoosier Faiths,* 664–65. Similar measures have been proposed, but not seriously considered, into the twenty-first century.

135. Edwards v. Aguillard, 482 U.S. 578 (1987).

136. See Cambron-McCabe, McCarthy, and Thomas, *Public School Law,* 55–56. Proposals are being considered in numerous states to change science standards to include criticism of evolution and introduction of Intelligent Design (ID). Advocates of ID contend that human beings, given their complexity, must be the product of a powerful force, but they do not name the designer. The critics of evolution have adopted a smart approach in arguing that public schools have an obligation to "teach the controversy," and even President Bush has advocated teaching ID along with evolution. However, most scientists consider ID a religious belief and contend that there is no *scientific* controversy. See Claudia Wallis, "The Evolution Wars," *Time*, August 15, 2005, 27–35.

137. IC § 20-30-5-13 (2005). A cross-state comparison of abstinence-only programs is available at Teenpregnancy.org, "State Information," http://www.teenpregnancy.org/america/statisticsDisplay.asp?ID=1&sID=617.

138. 88 Stat. 574 (1974) (codified as amended at 20 U.S.C. § 1232h [2005]).

139. Cotton, *Education in Indiana,* 397–99. In 1918, the Indiana Supreme Court held that high school was a part of common school and subject to the compulsory attendance law in *State v. O'Dell,* 187 Ind. 84,118 N.E. 529 (1918).

140. In the 1870s, the university shifted away from the classical curriculum to a more liberal curriculum. Negley, "Indiana," 376. Of course, there also were some private, primarily religious, elementary schools as well.

141. Pierce v. Soc'y of Sisters, 268 U.S. 510 (1925) (striking down an Oregon law requiring students to attend *public* schools); Meyer v. Nebraska, 262 U.S. 390 (1923) (invalidating a Nebraska law that required all children to be instructed in English below the eighth grade as impairing the Fourteenth Amendment liberty rights of private school parents to select an individual to teach their elementary school children in German).

142. See Mary Jo Dare, "The Tensions of the Home School Movement: A Legal/Political Analysis" (Ed.D. diss., Indiana University, 2001). See also State v. Peterman, 32 Ind. App. 665, 70 N.E. 550 (1904) (recognizing that home education can satisfy Indiana compulsory education mandates).

143. IC § 20-33-2-8 (2005).

144. IC § 20-33-2-21 (2005).

145. See Mazanec v. N. Judson-San Pierre Sch. Corp., 614 F. Supp. 1152 (N.D. Ind. 1985). See also IC § 20-33-2-28 (2005). But Indiana law does not define equivalency of instruction.

146. IC § 20-33-2-5 (2005).

147. Indiana private enrollment data are available at Stats Indiana, "Private School Enrollment by County," http://www.stats.indiana.edu/web/county/prischenroll0405.html; Indiana total enrollment data are available at Stats Indiana, "Total School Enrollment," http://www.stats.indiana.edu/web/county/total_enrollment2005.html.

148. Whereas Catholic schools initially were established because of the pervasive Protestant influence in public education, as the public school curriculum became more secular in the latter part of the twentieth century, Catholic school enrollments declined.

149. Independent private schools represent 16 percent of private school enrollments nationally. See U.S. Department of Education, National Center for Education Statistics, *A Brief Profile of America's Private Schools* (Washington, D.C.: Government Printing Office, 2002).

150. See National Center for Education Statistics, U.S. Department of Education, *1.1 Million Homeschooled Students in the United States in 2003* (Washington, D.C.: Government Printing Office, 2004).

151. Indiana Department of Education, Home School Enrollment, http://mustang.doe.state.in.us/TRENDS/trends1.cfm?var=henr.

152. IC § 20-33-2-12(a) (2005). See also Home School Legal Defense Association, "State Laws," http://www.hslda.org/laws/default.asp. See also Brian Ray, *Worldwide Guide to Homeschooling* (Nashville, Tenn.: Broadman and Holman, 2002).

153. See Mazanec v. N. Judson-San Pierre Sch. Corp., 614 F. Supp. 1152 (N.D. Ind. 1985).

154. See Dare, "Tensions of the Home School Movement," 85–137. Home-educated students can take part in public school educational or extracurricular activities with the permission from local school board or superintendent. IC § 20-33-2-12(b) (2005). However, to participate in interscholastic sports, the home-schooled child must enroll in three public school classes per day and otherwise comply with the bylaws of the Indiana High School Athletic Association. For information on the relationship between public schools and homeschools in Indiana, see Indiana Department of Education, "The Relationship between Public Schools and Home Schools in Indiana," http://ideanet.doe.state.in.us/sservices/hsefaq.htm.

155. Frederick Hess, "What Is 'Public' about Public Education?" *Education Week*, January 8, 2003, 56.

156. See John Chubb and Terry Moe, *Politics, Markets, and America's Schools* (Washington, D.C.: Brookings Institute, 1990); Joe Nathan, "Possibilities, Problems, and Progress," *Phi Delta Kappan* 78 (September 1996): 18–24.

157. See Frances Fowler, "The Shocking Ideological Integrity of Chubb and Moe," *Journal of Education* 173, no. 3 (1991): 119–29; Gary Orfield, "Housing and the

Justification of School Segregation," *University of Pennsylvania Law Review* 143 (May 1995): 1397–1406. Some critics of vouchers are concerned that choice programs "make it easier for families to exit the schools to which African Americans had only recently gained access." Frederick Hess, "'Trust Us,' They Explained: Racial Distrust and School Reform," *American Experiment Quarterly* 6 (Spring 2003): 31.

158. Zelman v. Simmons-Harris, 536 U.S. 639 (2002).

159. Davey v. Locke, 540 U.S. 712 (2004) (rejecting a free exercise clause challenge to the state of Washington's prohibition on the use of opportunity scholarships for students to pursue a ministry degree, even though the state prohibition reaches beyond establishment clause restrictions).

160. IC § 20-26-11-5 (2005). In 1987, the General Assembly enacted the Postsecondary Enrollment Options Act, IC §§ 20-30-11-1 et seq. (2005), which allows certain high school students to enroll in college courses for both high school and college credit.

161. A bill submitted in 1999 (S.B. 89) would have provided vouchers equal to the state's per-pupil funding to students in Indianapolis to attend a public school outside their attendance zone or an accredited private school, but the bill died in committee.

162. This trust was founded by J. Patrick Rooney, then chairman of the Golden Rule Insurance Company in Indianapolis. See the Heritage Foundation, "School Choice: Indiana," http://www.heritage.org/Research/Education/Schools/indiana.cfm; "Fighting the Golden Rule" (editorial), *Wall Street Journal,* September 6, 1991, 8.

163. IC §§ 20-24-1-1 et seq. (2005). As of October 2005, forty states and the District of Columbia had authorized charter schools. See U.S. Charter Schools, "State Information," http://www.uscharterschools.org/pub/uscs_docs/sp/index.htm.

164. In addition to companies that want to manage public schools, some companies, such as Sylvan and Berlitz, have been quite successful in securing contracts to provide remedial or other specialized instructional services.

165. Peter Senge, *The Fifth Discipline: The Art and Practice of the Learning Organization* (New York: Doubleday, 1990), 15.

166. Note, "The Hazards of Making Public Schooling a Private Business," *Harvard Law Review* 112 (January 1999): 695–712.

167. See Frederick Hess, "Breaking the Mold: Charter Schools, Contract Schools, and Voucher Plans," in *American Educational Governance on Trial: Change and Challenges,* ed. William Lowe Boyd and Debra Miretzky (Chicago: University of Chicago Press, 2003), 114–35.

168. The nation's first institution providing education for individuals with certain disabilities was the Asylum for the Education and Instruction of Deaf and Dumb Persons established in Hartford, Connecticut, in 1817. Margaret Winzer, *The History of Special Education: From Isolation to Integration* (Washington, D.C.: Gallaudet University Press, 1993), 136.

169. John Richardson, *Common, Delinquent, and Special: The Institutional Shape of Special Education* (New York: Falmer Press, 1999), 26.

170. See State ex rel. Beattie v. Bd. of Educ., 169 Wis. 231, 172 N.W. 153 (1919).

171. Boone, *History of Education,* 111.

172. Ind. const. of 1851, art. IX, § 1. This original version cited here can be found in Kettleborough, *Constitution Making in Indiana,* 1:350. The wording of this section was changed slightly in 1984.

173. Negley, "Indiana," 389.

174. Winzer, *History of Special Education,* 323.

175. Ibid, 314; Richardson, *Common, Delinquent, and Special,* 47–69.

176. Negley, "Indiana," 389–90.

177. 104 Stat. 1103 (1990) (codified as amended at 20 U.S.C. §§ 1400 et seq. [2005]). In 2004, the Individuals with Disabilities Education Improvement Act was passed and became effective on July 1, 2005, 118 Stat. 2647 (2004) (codified at 20 U.S.C. §§ 1400 et seq. [2005]). This law made changes in the way public schools identify, evaluate, serve, and discipline students with disabilities. The law brings the IDEA into alignment with the No Child Left Behind Act for students with disabilities. See Melinda Baird and Julie Weatherly, *IDEA '04 Professional Development Workshop: How the Marriage of IDEA '04 and NCLB Affects You* (Horsham, Penn.: LRP Publications, 2004).

178. IC §§ 20-35-1-1 et seq. (2005). Even though there is some Medicaid support available and some federal and state aid for the excess costs of educating children with disabilities, such children still are considerably more costly for local school districts.

179. See 511 Ind. Admin. Code tit. 7, rr. 17-1 et seq. (2005).

180. See Evans v. Evans, 818 F. Supp. 1215 (N.D. Ind. 1993) (Indiana Department of Education procedures, which delayed implementing individualized educational programs for students with disabilities, violated the IDEA).

181. See generally, Laura Rothstein, *Special Education Law,* 3d ed. (New York: Longman, 2000).

182. See, for example, Beth B. v. Clay, 282 F.3d 493 (7th Cir. 2002); Blackmon v. Springfield R-XII Sch. Dist., 198 F.3d 648 (8th Cir. 1999).

183. Rene v. Reed, 751 N.E.2d 736 (Ind. Ct. App. 2001), *trans. denied,* 774 N.E.2d 506 (Ind. 2002).

184. Metro. Sch. Dist. of Wayne Township v. Davila, 969 F.2d 485 (7th Cir. 1992).

185. See Honig v. Doe, 484 U.S. 305 (1988); S-1 v. Turlington, 635 F.2d 342 (5th Cir. 1981).

186. Richard F. Elmore, "Education and Federalism: Doctrinal, Functional, and Strategic Views," in Kirp and Jensen, *School Days, Rule Days,* 166–86.

187. See 115 Stat. 1425 (2001) (codified as amended at 20 U.S.C. §§ 6301 et seq. [2005]); IC §§ 20-31-1-1 et seq. (2005).

188. See National Center for Education Statistics, *Digest of Education Statistics, 2004* (Washington, D.C.: Government Printing Office, 2004); Thomas Sergiovanni, Paul Kelleher, Martha McCarthy, and Frederick Wirt, *Educational Governance and Administration,* 5th ed. (Boston: Allyn and Bacon, 2004), 359–60.

189. Plaintiffs have made this argument in some challenges to state school funding systems that rely heavily on local property taxes to support schools. For a review of these cases, see John Dayton, "*Serrano* and Its Progeny: An Analysis of

Thirty Years of School Funding Litigation," *Education Law Reporter* 157 (2001): 447–64.

190. See James H. Madison, "Indiana's Pioneer Heritage and the End of the Twentieth Century," *Indiana History Bulletin* 67 (June 1996): v–vi.

191. See generally, Chubb and Moe, *Politics, Markets, and America's Schools.*

192. Hess, "Breaking the Mold," 132.

193. Tyack, James, and Benavot, *Law and the Shaping of Public Education,* 195.

194. Brown v. Bd. of Educ. of Topeka, 347 U.S. 483 (1954).

195. See the discussion of drug testing cases in connection with extracurricular activities accompanying notes 76–82.

196. Tyack, James, and Benavot, *Law and the Shaping of Public Education,* 30.

197. 89 Stat. 776 (1975) (codified as amended at 20 U.S.C. § 1411 [2005]).

198. Orfield, "Housing and the Justification of School Segregation," 1397–1406.

199. Madison, "Indiana's Pioneer Heritage," ii.

200. Tyack, "Toward a Social History of Law and Public Education," 212.

PART V

Bench and Bar

ELEVEN

Elizabeth R. Osborn

INDIANA COURTS AND LAWYERS, 1816–2004

The story of Indiana's courts and bar reflects the same emphasis on local control that marks the state's culture. In both the nineteenth and twentieth centuries, Hoosiers continually resisted efforts to create a unified court system. They also favored open admission to legal practice until well into the twentieth century. This tendency to keep law and legal practice close to the people has roots in the earliest days of statehood.

Courts

The Northwest Ordinance of 1787, sections 3 to 5, provided for the judicial organization of the Indiana territory. Congress appointed three judges to a general court with both appellate and original jurisdiction. It had exclusive jurisdiction in only two instances: capital cases and petitions for divorce. The judges and the territorial governor were jointly responsible for promulgating all the laws for the new territory.[1] The Ordinance required this group to select laws from those already in existence, but in practice they modified the adopted laws to fit the needs of a frontier society.[2] Population growth and dispersion brought a new system of lower courts, including county courts of common pleas, quarter session courts, circuit courts, orphan courts, and justice of the peace courts, among others.[3]

By 1816, Indiana already had been through several cycles of creating, consolidating, and abolishing a variety of trial courts, and it entered the union with a judicial system divided into three parts: justice of the peace courts, circuit courts, and the General Court. The new state constitution retained many similarities to the territorial system. Article V provided that "[t]he judiciary power of this state, both as to matters of law and equity, shall be vested in one Supreme Court, in Circuit Courts, and in such other inferior courts, as the General Assembly may from time to time, direct and establish." The governor, with the advice and consent of the Senate, appointed the three judges of the supreme court to seven-year terms "if they shall so long behave well." Each circuit court, similarly, had three judges. The two houses of the legislature appointed the president of the circuit; the voters of the circuit elected the other two judges. The voters of each township elected justices of the peace.[4]

Within two years, the legislature began tinkering with the structure of the judicial branch. In 1818, it added probate courts and shortly thereafter created more circuits. In 1829, reflecting the growing sensitivity to perceived differences in social standing, the legislature removed the requirement that probate judges be lawyers. They had only to be deemed "qualified."[5] In 1849, the common pleas courts were brought back to life. By 1850, Indiana's court system was once again relatively unorganized. It had expanded in a piecemeal manner, meeting the needs of particular situations instead of following a larger plan.

The widespread faith of Jacksonian democrats in the ability of all men to participate equally in government and the economy eventually led to multiple constitutional reforms, both in Indiana and around the nation. Jacksonians desired, for example, that all public officials—including judges—be popularly elected and accountable to the people; the reform of the judiciary often featured prominently in calls for a constitutional convention.[6]

The constitution of 1851 restated the basic structure of the courts adopted by the 1816 version, establishing a supreme court and circuit courts and allowing the legislature to create other inferior courts. The supreme court was given room for growth, allowing expansion from three to five judges as needed. Supreme court judges were to be popularly elected on party ballots for six-year terms instead of being appointed by the governor. The state was to be divided into roughly equal districts and one judge elected from each. The constitution also provided for the election of a clerk of the supreme court; under the old constitution, the court had chosen its own clerk. The constitution required the publication of all of the court's written opinions and specified that the reporter not be a member of the court, thus ending the work of Judge Isaac Blackford who single-handedly had undertaken the first publication of the court's opinions in *Blackford's Reports*. In the years before the constitutional convention, this publication had evoked a bit of controversy, in part because Blackford's painstaking attention to detail frequently delayed publication and in part because Blackford chose which opinions to report.[7]

The 1851 constitution abolished the old circuits, and the legislature created new ones—forty-three altogether—in 1852. The constitution provided for the election of circuit court judges and supreme court judges to six-year terms, on good behavior. It also required that circuit judges live in their geographic circuits. Justices of the peace continued to be elected at the township level, but their terms were shortened to four years.[8] In a final gesture demonstrating the people's displeasure with even the appearance of privilege, the convention inserted into the judicial article a provision allowing "every person of good moral character" to be admitted to the practice of law.[9]

No sooner had the 1851 constitution gone into effect than the legislature began to tinker with the system once again. It created new varieties of courts and judicial officers and abolished others on a regular basis. For example, it abolished probate courts and reestablished courts of common pleas. It routinely changed the jurisdiction of these common pleas courts. In 1865, the legislature dismantled the recently created courts of conciliation, for example, and replaced them with criminal courts. In 1871, it created superior courts for certain jurisdictions and, in 1873, it once again eliminated the common pleas courts and added more superior courts.

The General Assembly created or abolished whole groups of courts as area needs changed, instead of simply expanding or contracting the number of judges in the existing court system. As a result, Indiana developed an extremely diverse trial court system. In the nineteenth and twentieth centuries, when many states were seeking to create a unified court system (one that provided flexibility for growth or contraction as needed), Hoosiers continued to cling to their nonuniform and highly individualized system.[10] In some ways, this legacy is still alive.

Presently, there are four different types of trial courts in Indiana: circuit courts (the only trial courts mentioned in the constitution), superior courts, county courts, and city or town courts. Although these courts have different names, they are more alike than they are different. The variation in names is a product of the piecemeal legislation that created the courts, not substantive differences in their functions. The General Assembly created superior and county courts as local needs outstripped the capacity of the initial circuit courts to handle the case load. After the establishment of the Indiana county court system in January 1976, most county courts eventually were eliminated in favor of superior courts. Floyd, Madison, and Montgomery counties, however, have retained their county courts with expanded duties. In addition to circuit and superior courts, some Indiana municipalities created city and town courts by local ordinance.[11] Since 1851, judges of these courts have been elected by local voters.

The election of judges complicated further the highly individualized mixture of trial and appellate courts. In order to continue in their positions on the bench, judges were forced to spend considerable time away from their courtrooms campaigning. One effect was a slow but steady buildup of a backlog of cases at all levels of the system. The legislature continued to create and rearrange trial courts to meet this need, but these efforts did not help the supreme court with its work load. Dealing with that problem required other options.

The first attempt to reduce the growing logjam in the state's only appellate court was simply to expand the size of the court. In 1852, a fourth judge was added to the court and, in 1872, a fifth, but cases continued to accumulate. The constitution made no provision for any kind of an intermediate appellate court, but in 1881 the legislature, in an effort to expedite the court's case load, created a temporary Supreme Court Commission. Each of the five supreme court judges appointed a commissioner. These commissioners received the same salary as the judges, but they could write opinions only for the court to take under consideration. In 1885, the two-year backlog had been cleared away, and the General Assembly allowed the statute on commissioners to expire. By 1889, cases again had accumulated, and the legislature tried to reappoint commissioners itself instead of allowing the court to do so. In this instance, however, the court ruled that the legislation was an unconstitutional infringement of the legislative branch into the judiciary.[12]

In 1891, the General Assembly helped the supreme court with its case load by creating a temporary appellate court. No real distinction was made between the supreme court and the appellate court; the appellate court simply heard the overflow cases from the supreme court docket.

This appellate court had been expected to last for about six years, but in 1897 the General Assembly voted to keep the court for an additional four years. Because the number of cases kept growing, the appellate court became a permanent part of the judicial branch in 1901. Thereafter, its role began to change to that of an intermediate appellate court to which cases would come on first appeal, before reaching the Indiana Supreme Court. In 1972, the old appellate court was replaced with the current court of appeals through an amendment to the Indiana constitution. This amendment specified that all Hoosiers were entitled to a single appeal and that, except in the case of a sentence of death, life imprisonment, or a sentence of more then ten years, that appeal would originate in the new court of appeals.[13] The voters of Indiana approved the amendment on November 3, 1970, and the Indiana Court of Appeals began hearing cases on January 1, 1972. Today, few people outside the legal profession realize that the court of appeals was ever anything other than an intermediate appellate court.[14]

When the court of appeals was created, the General Assembly established three districts—northern, central, and southern. Three judges from each district made up the original court. Over time, because of the huge number of cases handled by the court of appeals, new districts were established, and the number of judges increased. Currently, there are five districts and three judges from each district. The members of the court choose one of their colleagues to be chief judge for a three-year term.

The 1970 constitutional amendment brought other changes to the judicial branch as well. All appellate judges are now selected for the bench through a merit process supervised by the Indiana Judicial Nominating Commission instead of popular elections. The commission screens judicial applicants and forwards its recommendation to the governor for the final selection. For the most part, court of appeals judges need not live in their district after they are appointed, but they must have lived there at the time of their appointment. Once a candidate takes office, Indiana voters on a nonpartisan ballot have the opportunity to decide after an initial two-year term—and once every ten years thereafter—whether to retain each appellate judge.[15]

A third appellate-level court, the Indiana Tax Court, was established on July 1, 1986, by the General Assembly. The Indiana Tax Court holds most of its hearings in Indianapolis (Marion County), where it is located. However, a taxpayer can choose to have a hearing in one of six other counties: Allen, Jefferson, Lake, St. Joseph, Vanderburgh, or Vigo. Most of the cases heard by the Indiana Tax Court are appeals of decisions made by the Indiana government agencies that decide the amount of tax to be paid. There are two characteristics of the tax court that set it apart from Indiana's other two appellate courts. The Indiana Tax Court sits as both an appellate court and a trial court, depending on the type of case it is hearing, and it is the only appellate court with only one judge. Thomas G. Fisher is the judge of the Indiana Tax Court and has served since it was created in 1986. The governor chooses the judge of the Indiana Tax Court, using recommendations by the Judicial Nominating Commission, just as he selects judges for the other appellate courts.

Legal Practice

While Hoosiers modified their state court structure, the lawyers appearing before those courts shared much in common with fellow practitioners in neighboring Ohio and Illinois and elsewhere around the country. Lawyers came to think of themselves as more than workers filling a job; they believed they played a special role in the advancement and perpetuation of the whole republican experiment. In nineteenth-century America, as legal historian Michael Grossberg observes, "the law existed as a relatively autonomous domain within American society. That is, over time the American legal system developed its own characteristic language, institutions, assumptions, professional ideology, and rituals. . . . Consequently, the law was not just one more occupation; it was a distinctive endeavor with a special place and power in the republic."[16] The practice of law produced many of the great political leaders of the day, including two presidents with ties to Indiana: Abraham Lincoln and Benjamin Harrison. Some even argue that the practice of law has been the perfect training ground for American political leaders. It provided an aspiring public servant like Lincoln the opportunity "to hone his rhetorical and analytical skills, communicate with a wide range of . . . citizens, gain exposure to the larger world of developing corporations and professions, cultivate valuable political contacts, and earn a comfortable income."[17]

The practice of law was physically and intellectually demanding in the pre–Civil War era. In Indiana, Ohio, and Illinois, judges "rode the circuit," moving from place to place to hold court. Lawyers, of course, moved along with the judges. Setting the circuit court schedule was usually one of the first orders of business in each legislative session. Each circuit court generally met twice a year for a two- or three-week session. When circumstances warranted, the legislature might allow for a special session.

Lawyers had to follow the rhythm and schedule of the court. Lawyers and judges spent a considerable amount of time on horseback, moving toward the next courthouse and the next prospective clients. The experience of Abraham Lincoln, in neighboring Illinois, was not different from his Indiana counterparts. He worked with three different law partners from 1836 to 1861; during that time, he and his partners handled about fifty-one hundred cases covering every conceivable criminal or civil situation. Each spring, Lincoln spent three months following the circuit court as it moved from place to place. He worked the federal court circuit during the summer before heading back to the local circuit for another three months in the fall.[18] In between, he handled other legal matters in his local community. There was none of the legal specialization that came to characterize the practice of law in the twentieth century; every lawyer took on just about every kind of case that appeared on his doorstep. When Benjamin Harrison began practicing law in Indianapolis in 1854, he too spent much of his time outside the state's capital. It was not unusual for Harrison "to mount a hard trotting horse and ride through muddy roads ten miles into the country to try a case for a five-dollar fee."[19]

Riding the circuit brought lawyers and judges into close contact with each other over a considerable period of time. They rode from town to town together; by day they faced each other in the courtroom; and they passed the time together at night in whatever boardinghouse or tavern was available to them. Part of being a lawyer was participation in this social and professional milieu.[20]

The company of fellow lawyers and judges not only helped to pass the time far from home, but it was also a way to keep abreast of changes in the law. Lacking established law libraries—a law library had to fit in a saddlebag—and laboring under the grind of a peripatetic court existence, lawyers and judges found the task of staying apprised of new laws and changes in existing laws to be an ongoing challenge. Periodically in Indiana and in surrounding states, the legislature would go to considerable effort to update and distribute, or even just reprint, the current general laws. These digests, or revised statutes, were a crucial means of maintaining contact between lawmakers and legal practitioners. Sometimes they were compiled by clerks appointed to the duty, sometimes by prominent state lawyers, or, as in 1838 in Indiana, by the state supreme court itself.

No matter who created the texts, it was the job of the state supreme court to certify their accuracy. In Indiana, Ohio, and Kentucky, early digests reprinted not only current laws but also important legal documents, such as the Northwest Ordinances, the U.S. Constitution, and individual state constitutions. Later versions provided notes about court decisions, state or national, to help lawyers and jurists understand current interpretations of the law. To aid in the orderly and consistent dispensation of justice, the texts often included examples of documents issued by justices of the peace and county clerks as well as tables of allowable fees.[21] These books served as texts for prospective lawyers who were teaching themselves the law. When Abraham Lincoln was still living in Indiana and just beginning his course of self-study in the law, he borrowed and read everything available to him within a reasonable walking distance; the *Revised Statutes of Indiana* was one of the books he read, along with the *Commentaries* of William Blackstone and a history of the United States.[22]

By the late 1800s, when Benjamin Harrison returned to Indianapolis and the practice of law, the days of riding the circuit were already a thing of the past. Like other cities around the nation, Indianapolis saw substantial commercial and manufacturing growth following the Civil War; and where goes business, there also goes the law. More and more lawyers attended law school instead of "reading the law" in a lawyer's office, and many were turning to more specialized legal practice, especially commercial law, instead of the general law practiced in the antebellum period or the part-time lawyering of the Revolutionary generation. But the fraternity that had been built during the circuit-riding era did not disappear: it just changed form.

Despite growing differences in the daily practices of individual lawyers, there were significant efforts to preserve the ritual and community of an earlier period. Fraternal orders such as the Masons and the Odd Fellows served this purpose for some men, and lawyers formed their own organizations. Benjamin Harrison was a key player in this area. In the 1870s, he was a part of the early movement to professionalize the practice of law in Indiana and to preserve the special relationships built between lawyers and judges while riding the circuit. In November 1878, Harrison joined with about forty other Indianapolis area lawyers (including future vice president Charles W. Fairbanks) to found the Indianapolis Bar Association. Any lawyer having an office in Indianapolis or having been admitted to practice in the geographic area covered by the U.S. Circuit Court for the District of Indiana could join for an initial fee of $2 and annual dues of $5. This organization is still an active part of the Indianapolis legal community; dues today range from $95 to $225 but include a subscription to the biweekly publication the *Indiana Lawyer.*

Bar associations and similar fraternal organizations preserved the close-knit community of the law. Members policed themselves and promoted a positive view of the profession. In Indiana, the bar association was one of the groups most active in advocating the requirement of a formal bar admission exam. The association wanted to make sure that all lawyers who practiced in Indiana were qualified to do so and would bring no dishonor to the group as a whole. In 2004, the mission of the state's multiple bar associations remains essentially the same: to educate the public about the law and to ensure that all Indiana lawyers are excellent representatives of the field as a whole.[23]

Admission to Practice Law

Changes in the judicial branch under the 1851 constitution were not limited to the internal structure of the Indiana Supreme Court or to the election of judges. The new constitution, drafted under the weighty influence of Jacksonian democracy and its dislike of anything that smacked of privilege, also changed the way the men who argued before the bar entered their chosen profession.

In the early nineteenth century, lawyers were mostly self-taught. Aspiring lawyers read law books on their own or under the supervision of an established attorney. If an apprenticeship was established, its length, price, and expected outcome were negotiated solely between the parties involved. The formal apprenticeship usually concluded with the young lawyer's admission to the bar.[24] The conditions for admission varied from court to court, but most jurisdictions required some sort of statement from the supervising lawyer concerning the candidate's preparation and moral character, and several required some sort of examination. This exam, however, was usually oral and relatively casual.[25] Massachusetts, in 1855, was the first state to give a written exam.[26]

The Indiana constitution of 1816 made no particular mention of attorneys, but the legislature quickly enacted statutes requiring all lawyers to obtain a certificate attesting to their good moral standing and to receive a license from two judges of the supreme court or two judges of a circuit court. The licensure procedure was left to the discretion of individual judges, so the degree of legal knowledge necessary to receive the license might vary widely from jurisdiction to jurisdiction.[27] Between 1816 and 1851, the legislature changed these requirements from time to time, but the intent remained essentially the same. One change required attorneys, like other public officials, to take an oath swearing they had not participated in any part of a duel since January 1, 1819. The penalty for dueling included fines, jail time, and permanent disqualification from office holding, jury service, and voting. Although the oath remained in effect for supreme court judges and other public officials, it was removed for attorneys within a few short years.[28]

The 1851 constitution brought democratic changes both to court structure and to the practice of law. Even though approximately one-third of the 150 delegates were lawyers or future judges, the convention wiped away what might be perceived as a vestige of privilege—legal education as a prerequisite for admission to the practice of law.[29] The new constitution dropped the requirement of examination for licensure by members of a court and simply provided that "every person of good moral character, being a voter, shall be entitled to admission to practice law in all courts of justice."[30] Indiana did not again impose any educational requirements on attorneys until 1931.

During this eighty-year period (1851–1931), the determination of an applicant's moral character fell primarily to local jurisdictions. Remnants of this obligation still survive today in local traditions. In Monroe and Elkhart counties, for example, when new lawyers are admitted to the bar, the proceedings sometimes include a formal presentation of the candidates to the assembled group, a listing of the candidates' qualifications, and the presiding officer's call for objections.

Indiana lawyers realized very quickly, however, that this low "bar" to the admission into their profession was not at all desirable. Lawyers often were the target of negative stereotypes, even without the added fuel of a bunch of poorly trained and qualified advocates.[31] Led by Benjamin Harrison, Indiana lawyers began to push for changes in the qualifications for bar admission as early as 1881. In 1896, the Indiana State Bar Association began to work in earnest for the repeal of article VII, section 21, of the 1851 constitution. They sought—without success—a constitutional amendment, the so-called Lawyer's Amendment, in 1897, 1899, 1903, 1905, 1907, 1909, and 1929.[32]

The supreme court's 1901 interpretation of the Indiana constitution's amendment process hampered these efforts. The justices determined that the constitution required a majority of all voters casting ballots in the election—not just a majority of those casting votes on the constitutional question—to vote in favor of any proposed amendment in order for it to pass. This was an incredibly difficult hurdle for proponents of any amendment to overcome.

A movement in the 1920s, spurred by the American Bar Association's endorsement of a required bar examination, led the Indiana State Bar Association to pass its own resolutions and rules requiring successful completion of an examination to join the association. The association wrote exam questions covering fifteen different topics and sent them out to the circuit judges to distribute to members of the county bar, who administered the exam. Counties circumvented the constitution by interpreting the "good moral character" clause to mean that, if an applicant had not passed an exam and demonstrated thereby a thorough understanding of the law, the applicant was obviously of "bad moral character."[33] When meaningful change finally was achieved, it came through legislation, not through a constitutional amendment.[34]

In March 1931, the General Assembly passed legislation giving the Indiana Supreme Court jurisdiction regarding the admission of attorneys to the practice of law under any rules it saw fit to establish.[35] The court immediately adopted rules requiring the successful completion of a written exam and created a board of law examiners to oversee its implementation. But not everyone was willing or eager to accept this relatively late professionalization of the field.[36] Lemuel Todd, a voter and man of good moral character, filed a lawsuit contending that he could not constitutionally be barred from the practice of law. In deciding *In re Todd,* the court reversed its previous decision regarding ratification of amendments by the voters and thus found the 1932 vote on the Lawyer's Amendment to have repealed article VII, section 21, of the 1851 constitution.[37] Those who were having difficulty passing the new exam were not happy with this result. For the next eight years, they worked to achieve legislative control over the admission process, but to no avail.[38] The bar exam, it appeared, was a settled question.

The format of the instrument itself engendered considerable debate over the last decade of the twentieth century. As a result of this debate, the Indiana test underwent a significant revision in 2001. For seventy years, from 1931 to 2001, the state bar exam consisted of a series of essay questions exclusively focused on Indiana law. The exam, administered in Indianapolis under the supervision of the board of law examiners, generally took two days—from 8:00 AM until 6:00 PM, with an hour-and-a-half lunch break each day. The first exam, administered on October 5 and 6, 1931, featured a mix of short-answer essays and longer, more detailed essays for a total of fifty questions. All of the questions focused on questions of Indiana law. Only modest variations were made in this format over the next seventy years. In 2001, however, the examiners revamped the test completely. In response to concerns about subjectivity in grading, the debate over national standards, and a desire to add a more practical element to the test, the bar exam became an opportunity for potential lawyers to demonstrate the breadth of the total knowledge they had acquired during their three years in law school, not just their knowledge of Indiana law.

The new exam, first administered in February 2001, includes three sections: the Multistate Performance Test (MPT), the Multistate Bar Exam (MBE), and essays on Indiana law and practice. The MPT requires the applicant to accomplish two tasks of the sort that lawyers perform on a daily basis. The applicants are presented with a selection of documents and might be asked, for example, to write a brief, prepare documents necessary to help a judge resolve a case, or draft a memorandum about a client's problem based on the materials provided. This section allows the test-taker to demonstrate that he or she has developed the appropriate writing and analytical skills necessary to be a good lawyer. Once the MPT is completed, applicants take a break and then return in the evening to answer a set of six essay questions prepared and graded by the board of law examiners. The questions may cover any subject and are tailored to probe the writer's knowledge of specific elements of Indiana law. Each essay may contain elements that reach across multiple subject areas, requiring that the applicant demonstrate breadth as well as depth of knowledge.

The final element of the exam is the MBE. The MBE contains two hundred multiple-choice questions. Applicants are given one hundred questions in the morning and a second hundred in the afternoon. These questions are written and scored by a national organization and are administered across the entire nation at the same time. Although many examiners believe that a single uniform exam will increase the objectivity of the scoring and provide a more consistent national standard, not everyone agrees. The most common objection is that a national exam would not allow states to test on law specific to their jurisdictions.[39] While the experts ponder the pros and cons of a completely nationalized and objective exam, Indiana remains on a middle path: administering two elements of a national exam while retaining its own set of essay questions developed and graded at the state level.

Law Schools

By 1940, the question of the legitimacy of passing an exam in order to be admitted to the bar was settled. Compulsory graduation from a law school in order to take that exam, however, was a different question, and one that was not yet formally resolved.

In some ways, attendance at law school as a requirement for admission to the bar was a hurdle even more difficult than the bar exam itself. Since statehood, there never had been any formal requirement regarding the sort of legal education that was necessary for admission to the bar. Not until the 1940s did rules governing eligibility for the bar eliminate a course of study in a law office under the supervision of an attorney as an option for legal education.[40]

Throughout the colonial, antebellum, and postbellum periods, American law schools had met with very little success.[41] Instead, potential lawyers received their training through self-education and an apprenticeship with a willing senior attorney. Indiana lawyer and future state supreme court justice Jesse Holman read law in Henry Clay's office; lawyer and future governor Conrad Baker studied under the supervision of the abolitionist Thaddeus Stevens; and prominent lawyer and businessman Calvin Fletcher recorded events in his ever-present diary about his experiences both as a lawyer and as a supervisor of aspiring lawyers. The apprenticeship was a well-entrenched tradition that went well beyond the mere study of law; it contained a series of rites of passage to manhood as well as the preparation for a profession.[42] When the apprenticeship was concluded and the required certificate of good moral standing was obtained or the licensing exam completed, a new attorney simply hung out his shingle and set up practice.

During the antebellum period, Americans stubbornly clung to this tradition of "reading" the law, in striking contrast to their acceptance of the growing professionalization of the medical field. Most people believed that any hardworking and diligent young man should be able to become a lawyer and enter this masculine fraternity.[43] And, as was demonstrated by the Indiana constitution of 1851 and the Harvard Law School's decision to eliminate the requirement for a college degree for admission, some gatekeepers lowered the level of achievement necessary to enter the profession.[44] This attitude lingered well into the twentieth century in some places; those defending this tradition cited Abraham Lincoln's success using this mode of preparation.[45]

As a result, law schools rested on a shaky and insecure foundation. Numerous law schools in Indiana and around the nation—for example, Notre Dame, Indiana University, and Harvard—closed their doors at one point or another in the 1800s. Others, like the law department of Asbury College (now DePauw), shut down and never reopened. Of the twelve law schools that existed in Indiana in the 1800s, only four survive to the present: Indiana University Bloomington (1842), Notre Dame (1869), Valparaiso (1879), and Indiana University Indianapolis (1894).[46]

The Indiana law schools, despite divergent origins, share much in common. All of the schools struggled with low enrollments; Indiana University's first graduating class, for example, comprised only five students, and Notre Dame's only three.[47] Attracting and keeping students was a problem faced by law schools nationwide, despite the astronomical growth in the overall number of lawyers.[48] In 1833, for example, there were only 150 students recorded in attendance at law schools nationally, and by 1875 that number had grown to only 1,600 law students enrolled in thirty-one schools.[49] Around the country, law schools and the lawyers that supported this formalization and professionalization of the field embarked on a high-profile marketing campaign extolling the superiority of law schools over apprenticeship. An emphasis on the law as a rational science was a key element in this campaign.[50]

Law schools initially were unable to impose any real admission requirements beyond being of good moral character, the minimum required for admission to the bar. It was not until 1889 that Indiana University expanded its admission standards to include a minimum age of eighteen, success on a proficiency test in written and spoken English, and a basic grade school education. Notre Dame imposed the same requirements, but a prospective student had to be only seventeen years old. Many schools initially had required some previous college education but quickly saw the futility. Even the requirement of a high school diploma only gradually became general practice, and it was not until well into the twentieth century that all law schools began to require previous college work as a condition of admission. The founding of the American Bar Association spurred an increase in the rigor of course offerings and the adoption of more stringent admission requirements. Indiana University's law school was one of the original twenty-five member schools to meet the necessary requirements for accreditation by the Association of American Law Schools.[51]

The cost of tuition and room and board was another barrier potential law students had to overcome.[52] The program of a typical law school, or law department as they were often called, lasted about two years; most students arrived for class with no previous college education and often with "secondary" level preparation that can only be termed "inadequate." At Indiana University there was no tuition in the liberal arts program, but law students paid $12.50 per term and a $5.00 diploma fee.[53] Tuition costs were always a problem for law students at Notre Dame. The school received no funds from the state government and did not institute any sort of financial assistance program for students until Dean Joseph A. O'Meara asked the alumni organization to help raise funds in 1952.[54] Occasionally, the Indiana Law School, which eventually became Indiana University School of Law–Indianapolis, began to offer evening classes to accommodate working students.[55]

Making collegiate and professional education accessible to a larger population was a primary goal of the founders of what became Valparaiso University. Large numbers of the students who attended Northern Indiana Normal School, now Valparaiso University, were from the urban working class, rural farm families, and immigrants. These students had to pay for their own education, and they worked at a variety of jobs in town and around campus to raise the necessary funds, including working in the fields during harvest and planting season. To keep fees low, there were none of the usual luxuries associated with eastern colleges: student social activities and collegiate athletics.[56] The law students at Valparaiso in the late nineteenth century paid $10.00 for each ten-week term, or a dollar per week, a princely sum for many but a bargain compared to the nearby University of Chicago Law School, whose tuition alone was $86.00 per term.[57] Valparaiso offered the opportunity of higher education to a large number of students who otherwise never would have had access to it. Guided by this philosophy, Valparaiso's law school became one of the nation's largest by 1910.[58]

The two world wars and the Great Depression brought yet another challenge to student recruitment. Notre Dame was particularly innovative and creative in keeping the school open, even while other law schools were forced to shut down temporarily. Administrators rented the law school classrooms to other university colleges to help the school break even on its costs and revenues. This vigilance was rewarded when enrollments jumped from 50 to 225 students in the two years following World War II.[59] To increase their ability to attract and retain students, Indiana Law School and Benjamin Harrison Law School operated as a single school from 1914 to 1944, offering both day and evening courses.[60]

Finding students was not the only challenge law schools faced in the nineteenth century and early twentieth century. It took Indiana University's trustees seven years from the time they decided to open a law department (1835) until the first students entered the classroom (1842). These seven years were spent searching for a professor willing to take on the task of opening and running the school. Judge Isaac Blackford of the Indiana Supreme Court was one of the many candidates who turned the trustees down before circuit court judge David McDonald finally accepted the position. Only four years later, the university, facing financial difficulties, stopped paying the law professor a regular salary. In lieu of a salary, he was provided with a furnished room, firewood, and a percentage of the students' tuition.[61]

Opening about thirty years later (1879), Northern Indiana Normal School (Valparaiso) faced a similar challenge. Local lawyer Mark DeMott agreed to lead the law school, but only after he struck a deal with the university founders Henry Baker Brown and Oliver Perry Kinsey. DeMott was not only the primary instructor of the law school but essentially the owner, as well. DeMott collected the students' tuition and then paid a percentage back to the university. At least initially, he even conducted classes in the law office where he continued to run his private practice. It was not until 1906 that the university bought out DeMott upon his retirement and that the law department formally came under the school's jurisdiction.[62]

Faculty recruitment for the new law school in Indianapolis came at the price of another school's failure. The original core of professors at the Indiana Law School (Indianapolis) was recruited from the recently defunct law department of DePauw University that had closed in 1894. Noted Indiana Law School professor and DePauw University trustee (not to mention U.S. senator and, later, vice president) Charles Fairbanks surely facilitated the relocation of this group of gifted legal minds from Greencastle to Indianapolis. The cadre included William Fishback, Byron and William Elliot, and John Griffiths. The influence of former president Benjamin Harrison and Indianapolis resident Eli Lilly, both of whom served on the Indianapolis school's first board of trustees, was probably another useful recruitment tool.[63]

Once faculty and students were in place, Indiana law schools followed the general curriculum patterns of other American institutions. At Notre Dame Law School, the oldest Roman Catholic law school in the United States, and at Indiana's other law schools, the degree awarded at the end of the two-year undergraduate program was an LL.B. The Indiana Law School for a time combined the remnants of the traditional apprentice system with the new classroom-based program. Their two-year program included credit for law office training.[64] As noted earlier, it was not until the 1940s that the supreme court dropped credit for a legal apprenticeship from its rules regarding bar examination qualifications. As it turned out, the tradition of legal apprenticeship outlasted the more hotly contested issue of a bar exam by more than a decade.

Over time, Notre Dame and the other law schools expanded their programs to include three years of coursework, a master in law (LL.M.), and eventually the J.D. Originally, a J.D. required additional research and writing beyond the standard coursework, but, by the middle of the twentieth century, most law schools made this their standard degree. Both in Indiana and in law schools around the country, the coursework of the middle to late 1800s consisted primarily of lectures, reading, and recitation, but by the end of the nineteenth century the case study method was gaining prominence. Elective courses, moot court, practice court (a Notre Dame innovation to provide students with practical experience in the trial courts), and international study opportunities, all part of today's law school landscape, had found their way into law school curricula by the 1960s.

Over the last two hundred years, Indiana's courts, law schools, and law admission practices changed greatly as Indiana transitioned from a territorial frontier to a modern industrial state. The work is by no means complete. As Indiana moves toward its bicentennial in 2016, several key questions have come to receive considerable attention from the Indiana Supreme Court, the General Assembly, and the public: 1) how best to organize the courts to serve the state's population, 2) how best to educate future lawyers, and 3) how to adapt bar admissions to serve a global community. While Hoosiers charged with overseeing the world of courts and lawyers look at ways to meet the demands of the twenty-first century, they also remain firmly committed to the best parts of Indiana's past. In Indiana, communities still retain extensive control over their local courts, and the bar exam still contains a section devoted completely to Indiana law. In spite of national trends toward uniform systems, don't expect Hoosiers to remove completely these ties to their past.

Notes

The author wishes to thank Terri Ross and Kim Schwant of the Indiana Supreme Court Law Library for their invaluable assistance in tracking down obscure rules and references.

1. Northwest Ordinance of 1787, *Journals of the Continental Congress*, ed. Worthington C. Ford et al., vol. 32 (Washington, D.C.: Government Printing Office, 1936), 334, 336. For further discussion of this topic, see Elizabeth Rose Osborn, "The

Influence of Culture and Gender on the Creation of Law in Antebellum Indiana, Ohio, and Kentucky" (Ph.D. diss., Indiana University Bloomington, 2004).

2. John G. Baker, "The History of the Indiana Trial Court System and Attempts at Renovation," *Indiana Law Review* 30, no. 1 (1997): 238.

3. Ibid., 239.

4. Indiana const. of 1816, art. V.

5. Baker, "History of the Indiana Trial Court System," 244.

6. Governor Whitcomb's speech to the legislature on December 6, 1848, exhorted the legislature yet again about the need for a constitutional convention in order to bring some much needed reforms. Excerpts from this speech are reprinted in Charles Kettleborough, *Constitution Making in Indiana: A Source Book of Constitutional Documents, with Historical Introduction and Critical Notes* (Indianapolis: Indiana Historical Commission, 1916), 1:185–89.

7. Mrs. Edward Franklin White, "The Publication of the Supreme Court Reports," *Indiana Law Journal* 1 (June 1925): 42–43.

8. 1852 Revised Statutes of the State of Indiana, vol. 2, ch. 8, § 3.

9. Indiana const. of 1851, art. VII, § 21.

10. Baker, "History of the Indiana Trial Court System," 245–48. The county court system was created by legislative act in 1975. P.L. 305 § 48, 1975 Ind. Acts 1683, eff. Jan. 1, 1976. County courts were abandoned as circuit and superior courts were granted the same powers. In 2005, the General Assembly passed an act specifically retaining the county courts in Floyd, Madison, and Montgomery counties. See P.L. 2, § 88, 2005 Ind. Acts 1031, eff. April 25, 2005 (codified at Ind. Code Ann. § 33-30-2-1 [West supp. 2005]). Montgomery County will lose its county court in 2006, and the other counties may lose theirs if certain conditions are met. P.L. 237, § 1, 2005 Ind. Acts 4218, eff. Jan. 1, 2006.

11. Baker, "History of the Indiana Trial Court System," 248–53.

12. Robert H. Staton and Gina M. Hicklin, "The History of the Court of Appeals of Indiana," *Indiana Law Review* 30, no. 1 (1997): 203–8; Hovey v. Noble, 118 Ind. 350, 21 N.E. 244 (1889).

13. Indiana const. of 1851, art. VII, § 4.

14. Staton and Hicklin, "History of the Court of Appeals," 208–14.

15. Indiana const. of 1851, art. VII, § 11.

16. Michael Grossberg, "Institutionalizing Masculinity: The Law as a Masculine Profession," in *Meanings of Manhood: Constructions of Masculinity in Victorian America*, ed. Mark C. Carnes and Clyde Griffen (Chicago: University of Chicago Press, 1990), 134.

17. Daniel W. Stowell, ed., *In Tender Consideration: Women, Families, and the Law in Abraham Lincoln's Illinois* (Chicago: University of Illinois Press, 2002).

18. Ibid., 1.

19. Charles W. Taylor, *Biographical Sketches and Review of the Bench and Bar of Indiana* (Indianapolis: Bench and Bar Publishing, 1895), 213.

20. Grossberg, "Institutionalizing Masculinity," 137.

21. See, for example, Salmon P. Chase, *The Statutes of Ohio and of the Northwestern Territory, Adopted or Enacted from 1788 to 1833 Inclusive: Together with the Ordinance of 1787; the Constitutions of Ohio and of the United States, and Various Public Instruments*

and Acts of Congress: Illustrated by a Preliminary Sketch of the History of Ohio; Numerous References and Notes and Copious Indexes, 3 vols. (Cincinnati: Corey and Fairbank, 1833–1835); *Revised Statutes of the State of Indiana* (1838); *A Digest of the Statute Laws of Kentucky, of a Public and Permanent Nature, Passed since 1834 . . .*, (Frankfort, Ky.: A. G. Hodges, 1842).

22. William Lee Miller, *Lincoln's Virtues: An Ethical Biography* (New York: Alfred Knopf, 2002), 51–53.

23. James Ogden, "State Bar Heads Approve Uniform Admission Plan," *Indiana Law Journal* 1 (November 1925): 71; "Examinations for Admission to the Bar," *Indiana Law Journal* 1 (February 1926): 85. Indiana State Bar Association, Articles of Incorporation of the Indiana State Bar Association (in possession of the author), art. II: "The Association is formed to foster and advance the profession of law; [and] to encourage and promote reforms in the law."

24. Christine Ann Fidler, "'Young Limbs of the Law': Law Students, Legal Education, and the Occupational Culture of Attorneys, 1820–1860" (Ph.D. diss., University of California–Berkeley, 1996), 56–66. Indiana lawyer and businessman Calvin Fletcher supervised a variety of apprentices in his Indianapolis law office. See, Gayle Thornbrough, ed., *Diary of Calvin Fletcher* (Indianapolis: Indiana Historical Society, 1972), especially volume 1 covering the years 1817–38. Fletcher frequently made comments on the aptitude of his students and his involvement with them. He regularly noted in his diary things like "Simon Yandes recited one lesson in Black Com" (June 16, 1835) or "In the eve heard S. Yandes recite" (June 24, 1835).

25. In colonial South Carolina, for example, the supreme court controlled all admission to the bar, whereas in North Carolina, New Jersey, and New York, the royal governor admitted attorneys—usually with the help of local judges. In most areas, both before and after the Revolution, however, each court examined and admitted its own attorneys. Julius C. Travis, "Report of the Committee on Legal Education in the Proceedings of the Twenty-ninth Annual Meeting of the Indiana State Bar Association, July 8–9, 1925," *Indiana Law Journal* 1 (December 1925): 90.

26. Randall T. Shepard, "On Licensing Lawyers: Why Uniformity Is Good and Nationalization Is Bad," *New York University Annual Survey of American Law* 60 (Summer 2004): 453.

27. W. W. Thornton, "Admission to the Bar in Indiana," *Indiana Law Journal* 1 (June 1926): 334. For statutes regarding the practice of law, see, for example, 1818 Laws of the State of Indiana, ch. 64, §§ 1–2; 1824 Revised Laws of Indiana, ch. 8, §§ 1–2.

28. 1817 Laws of the State of Indiana, ch. 39, § 4; 1820 Laws of the State of Indiana, ch. 15.

29. In October 1850, Indiana printers Baker and McFarland listed the following occupations for members of the convention: sixty-four farmers, forty-one lawyers, five printers/editors, eighteen doctors, eleven merchants/traders, three teachers, two bankers/accountants, two manufacturers, ten tradesmen (carpenter, tailor, miller, bricklayer, etc.), and one county employee. Indiana State Library, Indiana Div., broadsides coll. In the 1920s, as debate raged among members of the Indiana bar regarding the institution of a bar examination, there was much discussion of what exactly the lawyers at the convention had intended in the language of art. VII,

§ 21. See, for example, the essay by Indiana University School of Law professor James J. Robinson, "Admission to the Bar as Provided for in the Indiana Constitutional Convention of 1850–51," *Indiana Law Journal* 1 (March 1926): 209–17; Brent E. Dickson, Thomas A. John, and Katherine A. Wyman, "Lawyers and Judges as Framers of Indiana's 1851 Constitution," *Indiana Law Review* 30, no. 1 (1997): 397–408.

30. Indiana const. of 1851, art. VII, § 21.

31. Fidler, "Young Limbs of the Law," 135–83; Michael Grossberg, "Fighting Faiths and the Challenges of Legal History," *Journal of Social History* 25 (Fall 1991): 191–201.

32. S. Hugh Dillon, "The Origin and Development of the Indiana Bar Examination," *Indiana Law Review* 30 (Winter 1997): 391–93.

33. For a complete explanation of this process and for a reprint of the letter sent to local judges with these exams, see James Ogden, "The Movement for Uniform Admission Rules," and "State Bar Heads Approve Uniform Admission Plan," *Indiana Law Journal* 1 (November 1925): 53–54, 71–72; "Examinations for Admission to the Bar," *Indiana Law Journal* 1 (February 1926): 85.

34. In re Denny, 156 Ind. 104, 59 N.E. 359 (1901).

35. 1931 Ind. Acts ch. 64, § 1.

36. Even within the ranks of the Indiana State Bar Association there was some discomfort with what was seen as efforts to circumvent the intent of the 1851 constitution. The January 1932 edition of the *Indiana Law Journal* contains a series of four exchanges between Indiana University School of Law professor Bernard Gavit and Thomas J. Hurley, a lawyer from Gary, Indiana. Not surprisingly, Gavit supported the legislation giving the supreme court the authority to create rules for admission to the bar, whereas Hurley argued that there was little ambiguity in the framers' sole requirement that lawyers "be of good moral character." *Indiana Law Journal* 7 (January 1932): 205–8, 209–22, 223–25, 226–29.

37. In re Todd, 208 Ind. 168, 193 N.E. 865 (1935).

38. Dillon, "Origin and Development of the Indiana Bar Examination," 391–95.

39. Shepard, "On Licensing Lawyers," 457n21. In 2004, Louisiana and Washington were the only jurisdictions not requiring the MBE.

40. The court's published rules for 1943 contain the law office exception for taking the bar, but this section is not present in the 1946 edition. Rule 3-14a, Rules of the Supreme Court of Indiana, 1943 rev.; Rule 3-14, Rules of the Supreme Court of Indiana, 1946 rev.

41. Fidler, "Young Limbs of the Law," 81–84. Fidler reports that, in 1820, there were only five law schools all located in eastern states; in 1860, there were twenty-one.

42. John P. Coburn, "Sketch of the Old Supreme Court," in *Biographical Sketches and Review of the Bench and Bar of Indiana,* ed. Charles W. Taylor (Indianapolis: Bench and Bar Publishing Company, 1895), 33; Randall T. Shepard, "Conrad Baker, 1865–66, 1867–73," in *Biographical Directory of Indiana Governors,* ed. Linda C. Gugin and James E. St. Clair (Indianapolis: Indiana Historical Society Press, forthcoming, 2006); Thornbrough, *Diary of Calvin Fletcher*, 1:254, 257, 295, 426; 3:67, 99; Grossberg, "Institutionalizing Masculinity," 133–51.

43. Grossberg, "Institutionalizing Masculinity," 133–51.

44. Michael I. Swygert, "Valparaiso University School of Law, 1879–2004: A Contextual History," *Valparaiso University Law Review* 38 (Spring 2004): 659.

45. Grossberg, "Institutionalizing Masculinity," 139.

46. Swygert, "Valparaiso University School of Law," 662. References to each law school are by current name only. Both Valparaiso and Indiana University–Indianapolis law schools operated under different names between their founding and the present.

47. Colleen Kristl Pauwels, "Inferior to None," *Bill of Particulars* 15 (Fall 1992): 15; Philip S. Moore, *A Century of Law at Notre Dame* (Notre Dame, Ind.: University of Notre Dame Press, 1969), 5.

48. Fidler, "Young Limbs of the Law," 84. Fidler finds that, in 1822, there were only 6,000 lawyers in America but that, by 1850, that number had grown to 21,979. In Indiana there was on average, in 1850, one lawyer for every 1,069 people.

49. Ibid., 83; Swygert, "Valparaiso University School of Law," 699.

50. Fidler, "Young Limbs of the Law," 74–134. Fidler spends an entire chapter in her dissertation examining "The Marketing of Legal Education in Antebellum America."

51. Pauwels, "Inferior to None," 20. The AALS was founded in 1900. The initial requirements for receiving accreditation included the following: incoming students must have a high school diploma; the program must be at least two years long; and the school's students must have access to a library containing both the state and federal reporters. These standards steadily increased in the ensuing years.

52. Fidler, "Young Limbs of the Law," 86–90. Fidler estimates that it cost a student from the Midwest about $300 per year to attend an eastern law school in the years before the Civil War. Tuition at Harvard Law School in 1844 was $100; Yale charged $80. This did not include, of course, room and board or the considerable transportation costs.

53. Ibid., 88; Pauwels, "Inferior to None," 18–19. To place these tuition costs in perspective, Fidler estimates that, in this same period, a full-time agricultural worker's average earnings were $158 per year—62 percent of that total was needed for basic food and shelter.

54. Moore, *Century of Law at Notre Dame,* 125.

55. Richard W. Polston, "History of the Indiana University School of Law–Indianapolis," *Indiana Law Review* 28, no. 2 (1995): 161.

56. Richard Baepler, *Flame of Faith, Lamp of Learning: A History of Valparaiso University* (St. Louis: Concordia Publishing House, 2001), 63–69.

57. Swygert, "Valparaiso University School of Law," 675.

58. Baepler, *Flame of Faith,* 69.

59. Moore, *Century of Law at Notre Dame,* 88–89.

60. Polston, "History of the Indiana University School of Law–Indianapolis," 164–65.

61. Pauwels, "Inferior to None," 15–16.

62. Baepler, *Flame of Faith,* 50–52.

63. Polston, "History of the Indiana University School of Law," 161–62.

64. Ibid., 174.

TWELVE

Robert J. Maley and John R. Maley

MORE THAN ARBITERS OF CASES AND CONTROVERSIES

The Growing Impact of the Judiciary on Indiana's Legal Culture

In Anglo-American jurisprudence, courts exist to resolve legal disputes among adverse parties. The U.S. Constitution, for instance, expressly links judicial power to "cases" and "controversies" among parties.[1] Although Indiana's constitution lacks the "case or controversy" clause of its federal counterpart, the separation of powers language of the Indiana constitution[2] "fulfills an analogous function" in Indiana judicial activity.[3] As a result, absent a case or controversy, Indiana courts cannot act.[4] Yet, even with this restriction, some courts—typically because of the personality of a particular judge—have had an impact on legal culture beyond the four corners of particular cases. In the last fifty years, and especially during the last fifteen years, courts in Indiana have had a dramatic impact on the state's legal culture and its practice of law despite growing and increasingly complex case loads.

The primary reason for this influence of the courts is progressive judicial leadership, especially by the Indiana Supreme Court. Through energetic leadership, bold initiatives, and dogged persistence, Indiana courts have significantly and positively shaped the practice of law and Indiana's legal culture. Furthermore, because the legislative and executive branches of government seem not to be much interested in these areas, courts and the judiciary likely will continue to play a prominent role in shaping Indiana's legal culture for the foreseeable future.

The Indiana Supreme Court's Enhanced Influence on the Practice of Law

No court has had more impact on the practice of law or the state's legal culture than the Indiana Supreme Court. Among its key areas of influence are the admission, discipline, and legal education of attorneys; rulemaking; lawmaking; state constitutional jurisprudence; pro bono legal services; and diversity within the bar.

Admission to the Bar

The area of Indiana legal culture with the longest history is admission to the practice of law. The constitution of 1816, like the federal Constitution, mentioned neither attorneys nor the practice of law. The earliest Indiana Supreme Court decision in this area is *Blake's Case,*[5] in which an applicant for admission as an attorney before the supreme court objected to taking the oath prescribed by the act of the General Assembly entitled "An act more effectually to prevent dueling." In the opinion, Justice Jesse Holman wrote, "The office of counsel and attorney at law is of Legislative and not of Constitutional creation, and therefore the oaths necessary to be taken before the exercise of that office are policy questions and as completely subject to Legislative provision as the age, place of residence, character or legal acquirements of such officers, unless the Constitution has prohibited such legislative provision."[6] The court ruled that Blake had to take the oath before being permitted to practice law before the Supreme Court. The concept of judicial control of the practice of law had not begun to develop.

Although the Indiana Constitution of 1816 did not even mention attorneys, article VII, section 21, of the constitution of 1851 provided that "[e]very person of good moral character, being a voter, shall be entitled to admission to practice law in all courts of justice."[7] This language reinforced the local nature of antebellum Indiana society but fragmented the state's legal culture. Qualification for and admission to the bar varied from county to county. The procedure for admission of attorneys was established by each court, and the local bar took its personality from the elected circuit court judge and from the lawyers admitted to practice before that county court.

The universal admission language of article VII, section 21, influenced the practice of law in Indiana from 1851 until 1931. For more than eighty years, the state's courts had no real central authority to require any proficiency in the law for any citizen who wished to be admitted to practice law. Any voter "of good moral character" could hang out a shingle and offer legal services to the unsophisticated public.

During this period, lawyers often formed county bar associations and developed their own ways of determining "good moral character." Some counties, noted federal judge S. Hugh Dillin, "actually conducted an adversary hearing in which the applicant had the burden of proving the quality of his character with questions of law deemed germane to the proceeding."[8] Other counties insisted upon an examination before a committee on admission appointed by the court or an examination in open court by members of the bar, and still others permitted a jury trial on the issue of good moral character. As one writer of the time observed, "Each of these and other provisions simply harassed the applicant and tended to deter those who had no knowledge of law whatsoever in seeking to exercise their constitutional prerogative to practice law."[9]

Attorneys admitted to the bar under the provisions of article VII, section 21, were known as "constitutional" lawyers. Clifford M. Haworth, prosecutor for Wayne County in the 1920s, with whom the senior author began practice, was one such attorney. His experience is illustrative. Lacking a college education, he had read law in a lawyer's office, running errands for the privilege. His proficiency in the law was examined in open court by three prominent and skeptical local lawyers, all law school graduates, after which examination he was admitted to practice law in the Wayne Circuit Court. In those days, a change of venue was available for the asking. A trial lawyer therefore would practice not only in the courts of the counties surrounding his home county but also, upon subsequent changes in venue, in the counties adjacent to those counties. Haworth was required to present a certificate from the Wayne Circuit Court to be admitted to practice before the courts in other counties.[10]

Haworth knew the lawyers and judges in east-central Indiana and often commented that the quality of each county bar was a direct reflection of the quality of the circuit court judge, who controlled and set the tone of the local legal culture. In several of those counties, the practice of law was undisciplined. Haworth related several experiences in which arguments before the court ended in the exchange of fisticuffs between opposing counsel, a challenge he did not shy away from.

Many lawyers admitted to practice before nisi prius courts did not seek admission to practice before the Indiana Supreme Court. Although admission to the highest court was available to anyone admitted to any county circuit court, during that period the higher courts had little impact in shaping legal culture throughout the state. The debate, and often open controversy, over what educational qualifications, if any, should be required of lawyers to practice law raged in the several trial courts, the local bar associations, and among legal scholars.

The constitution required lawyers to be voters in order to practice their craft. Prior to 1921, women could not vote in state elections in Indiana: did this mean that women could not be licensed attorneys? This issue came before the supreme court in 1893 in the case of *In re Leach*.[11] A woman had applied for admission as a member of the bar of the Greene Circuit Court, which found her to be a citizen of the state, over the age of twenty-one, and of good moral character. The trial court also found that she possessed sufficient knowledge of the law to qualify her to practice, although the record is silent as to how that determination was made. The trial court found, however, that the woman was not a voter as required by article VII, section 21, of the constitution and should be denied admission.

On review, the Indiana Supreme Court noted that the legislature had enacted a statute that repeated the words of the constitution and provided a procedure for admission.[12] The court decided that, although the constitution and the statute secured the right of the voter of good moral character to practice law, neither was a *limitation* upon the right of membership. The court held that neither prescribed a denial of such right to women. Having searched in vain for any expression from the common law excluding women from the profession of law, the court ruled that women were not excluded from the practice, despite the fact they were not voters, and reversed the lower court's denial of admission.

Three years after *Leach,* former President Benjamin Harrison, then practicing law in Indianapolis, gathered a group of lawyers to join him in organizing the Indiana State Bar Association. After he became its president, the bar association adopted as one of its main objectives the repeal of article VII, section 21. It was a project that would consume many years.

In 1897, the General Assembly passed a joint resolution to amend the Indiana constitution to provide that "[t]he General Assembly shall by law prescribe what qualifications shall be necessary for admission to practice law in all courts of justice." The same resolution was again adopted by the General Assembly in 1899 and submitted to the voters at the general election in 1900. The amendment passed by nearly a two-to-one margin (240,031 to 144,071), although the total number of votes cast on the amendment issue fell far short of the total 655,965 ballots cast in the election for state offices.

Assuming that the amendment had been adopted, the Marion Circuit Court established rules for admission and appointed a board of bar examiners. Subsequently, a Mr. Denny applied to be admitted to practice law in the Marion Circuit Court on the only qualifications that he was a person of good moral character and a voter. He declined to submit to an examination, and the circuit court ruled that he was not entitled to admission. Denny appealed to the state supreme court on the grounds that the amendment had not received the required number of votes and was therefore invalid.

The supreme court agreed. In the case of *In re Denny,* the justices noted that article XVI, section 1, controls the process for amending the Indiana constitution.[13] After an amendment is twice passed by a majority vote of two succeeding sessions of the General Assembly, it is submitted to the electors of the state, whereupon it must be ratified by "a majority of said electors." In 1880, the Indiana Supreme Court had held in *State v. Swift* that an amendment must be ratified by a majority of all votes cast at the election, not merely a majority of all votes cast on that particular amendment.[14] The court was constrained to follow the ruling in *Swift* and judged that the amendment had failed to pass. Accordingly, the court ordered that Denny be admitted to practice law without taking the examination.

The General Assembly adopted the same amendment in 1903 and 1906 and submitted it to the voters in the general election of 1906. It received more than three-fourths of the votes cast on the amendment but again failed to secure a constitutional majority. In 1907 and 1909, the General Assembly once again enacted the joint resolution, which went before the voters in the general election of 1910. Thereafter, Charles W. Boswell applied for admission to the Marion County bar. The circuit court held a trial and found that Boswell met all the constitutional requirements; but, acting on the assumption that the amendment had been adopted and that the court was free to provide additional qualifications, it denied admission to Mr. Boswell. The supreme court, in the case of *In re Boswell,*[15] found that 60,357 votes had been cast in favor of the so-called Lawyer's Amendment and only 18,494 against it (77 percent for and 23 percent against) but that 627,133 votes had been cast for the office of secretary of state. The court followed the rulings in *Swift* and *Denny* and reversed the decision of the circuit court.

After these unsuccessful efforts to change the constitution, the issue lay dormant until 1931, when the General Assembly passed a statute giving the supreme court "exclusive jurisdiction to admit attorneys to practice law in all courts of the state under such rules and regulations as it may prescribe," to take effect on July 1, 1931.[16] Soon thereafter, Chief Justice Clarence P. Martin signed the order creating Rules of Supreme Court on Roll of Attorneys and Admission to Bar.[17] The rules required applicants to take an examination to determine their professional fitness to practice law. The court appointed a five-member board of law examiners with one member from each supreme court judicial district and instructed it to hold three examinations each year. The first exam was held in October 1931. The Supreme Court had taken a giant step to reshape the legal culture of the state.

The supreme court's establishment of the bar exam was not met with total approval. A classic debate occurred between Thomas J. Hurley, of the Gary bar, and Bernard C. Gavit, a professor of law at Indiana University. Writing in the *Indiana Law Journal,* Hurley argued that the phrase "entitled to admission" in article VII, section 21, could not be interpreted to mean "entitled to take an examination on learning in the law" and that ignorance has never been a factor in moral character.[18] Professor Gavit responded that it was not necessary to amend article VII, section 21, asserting that a proper judicial interpretation of "good moral character" as a requisite to practice law necessarily included educational requirements.[19]

Then, in 1932, the electorate passed by a large majority (65 percent) a constitutional amendment to allow the General Assembly to prescribe qualifications for the practice of law. Three years later, an appeal reached the supreme court from a Mr. Todd, who had been denied admission to practice law without taking the prescribed bar exam.[20] The court found the vote on the 1932 amendment to have been 439,919 for adoption and 236,613 against. As in earlier attempts to pass the amendment, however, the number of voters favoring adoption was much less than half the number of voters who voted for political candidates at the general election. To hold that the amendment had been adopted, it would be necessary to overrule *Swift, Denny,* and *Boswell.* The court began a lengthy analysis by observing: "When the overruling of previous decisions involves only a question of public interest in no way affecting private interests the rule of *stare decisis* does not control."

The court then overruled the prior decisions, affirming that the constitution had been amended and denying Todd's petition to be admitted without examination. The court held that the "majority of electors" provided for in article XVI, section 1, means a majority of persons who vote on a proposed amendment.[21] The 1932 amendment was valid and article VII, section 21, was eliminated.

The practice of law thus came fully under the control of the Indiana supreme court, and an organized and unified bar emerged. There were further legislative attempts to take control of bar admission away from the Supreme Court and to do away with the bar exam. In 1939, for example, bills were introduced in the General Assembly to abolish the state board of law examiners and to place admission to practice law with a so-called judicial council. This major political effort by the antiexamination movement proved to be its culmination, as both bills were defeated.[22]

Not all lawyers admitted to practice in local trial courts went through the formal process of admission to the supreme court. Indeed, many preeminent lawyers and judges, including some on the supreme court itself, were never so admitted, "so uselessly formal was the process."[23] After enactment of the statute of 1931, many of these lawyers found statewide admission attractive, so they applied and were admitted. Control of the bar and the shaping of Indiana's legal culture finally had shifted to one body, the Indiana Supreme Court.

When the supreme court appointed the first five members of the board of law examiners in 1931, it also appointed for each supreme court judicial district a committee on character and fitness, consisting of the member of the board from that district and one member of the bar from each county in the district. The committees were to "inquire into the question as to whether or not the applicant is possessed of those requisites of good moral character [other than a knowledge of the law] necessary to qualify him to serve as an attorney."[24] The supreme court also prescribed the oath to be taken by all upon being admitted to practice law in the state of Indiana.[25]

Challenges to the validity of the bar exam process had not disappeared completely. The deans of many law schools continued to argue that admission to the practice of law should be granted to any and all graduates of approved law schools without further ado. For at least the last twenty-five years, the State Board of Law Examiners has met annually with the deans of the Indiana University Bloomington, Indiana University Indianapolis, Valparaiso, and Notre Dame law schools for a somewhat vigorous discussion of the role each should play in the determination of the qualifications of those who would be licensed to offer legal services to the citizens of this state. In 1977, the supreme court, upon urging by then Chief Justice Richard Givan, amended Rule 13 of the Rules of Admission, to require each applicant for the bar exam to present a certificate from the dean of the law school attesting that the applicant had successfully completed specified core courses in the law. This rule was extremely unpopular with the law schools. Givan was reacting to the criticism that law students were taking courses in "Urban Law," "Sports Law" and similar subjects to the exclusion of the basic courses traditionally required. This attempt to shape the quality of applicants for the bar exam was enforced until it was revoked in 1996 by a supreme court order under Chief Justice Randall Shepard.

The discussions between the law school deans and the bar examiners have not been limited to curriculum. The examination of applicants for the bar exam by the supreme court's committees on character and fitness resulted in the referral of an ever-increasing number of applicants for hearings before the full Board of Law Examiners on matters of character and fitness. Many of these questions were revealed under the strenuous and thorough investigation of each applicant's background by the staff of the law examiners. Many of the incidents giving rise to character and fitness questions predated the applicant's acceptance to law school and yet were determined to be a serious detriment to the admission of the applicant to the practice of law in Indiana. In other cases, such incidents occurred during law school.

In a process still in effect, applicants for the bar examination first are required to appear before a member of the character and fitness committee for examination upon their character and fitness and their familiarity with and willingness to abide by the Indiana Rules of Professional Conduct. The staff of the State Board of Law Examiners provides the examining committee member with a complete file on each applicant to be examined. The committee member must certify in writing the approval or disapproval of the applicant. Thereafter, the staff arranges an interview before the full board of law examiners for applicants whose fitness was in doubt. On occasion, the staff discovers matters in the applicant's file serious enough to be submitted directly to a hearing before the full board. The board has found it necessary to deny admission to a growing number of applicants who fail to establish character and fitness.

The supreme court has taken an active interest in ensuring that those coming to the bar are of good moral character. Recent amendments to the Rules of Admission to the Bar and the Discipline of Attorneys have given the board the authority and the procedure to better control and supervise those applicants whose character and fitness examinations reveal significant problems not sufficiently severe to prohibit their taking the bar exam, particularly in view of the great investment the applicants already have made in legal education. Conditional admission with supervision is now possible. Other recent rule changes seek to improve control over admission of lawyers from foreign jurisdictions and corporate business lawyers. Also, beginning with the February 2001 bar examination, the court modified the traditional two-day, twenty-essay exam format by including portions of the Multistate Bar Examination. Furthermore, in the last decade the court has revised the potential test areas to include topics such as Indiana family law and Indiana constitutional law.

The Indiana Supreme Court has used the State Board of Law Examiners, its Committee on Character and Fitness, its direction of the bar examination, and its rules on admission to enhance the quality of those who are permitted to take the sacred oath to practice law in the state of Indiana. The applicants are screened for character and fitness, the scope of their study of law is influenced and shaped by the matters upon which they will be tested on the Indiana State Bar Examination, and attention is given to their education in and familiarity with ethics and the Rules of Professional Conduct by the administration of the Multistate Professional Responsibility Exam.

In short, the Indiana Supreme Court over the past seventy-five years has become increasingly active in shaping the legal culture of the state from the very beginning of the lawyer's practice. The court is firmly entrenched as *the* singular branch of government regulating admission to the Indiana bar, a dramatic change from the first 115 years of the state's history. Through this final screening process, the court indirectly influences not only who practices in Indiana but what subjects they take in law school to prepare for the exam.

Discipline

Lawyer discipline was without any central regulatory structure or format for most of Indiana's legal history. Much has changed in the last thirty years.

During the nineteenth century, when admission to the practice of law in Indiana was largely unregulated, so too was discipline. In this respect, Indiana was hardly alone. The first known code of legal ethics in the United States can be traced to Alabama in 1887.[26] The American Bar Association (ABA) did not even exist until 1878 and did not get into the business of promulgating ethics codes until the early twentieth century.[27] Although the Indianapolis Bar Association, like the ABA, dates to 1878,[28] the Indiana

State Bar Association did not come into existence until nearly two decades later, in 1896.[29]

There does appear to have been some modest effort to structure attorney discipline in the latter half of the nineteenth century in Indiana. An 1867 decision from the Indiana Supreme Court, *Ex parte Smith,* involved an appeal by Jeremiah Smith from the Randolph Circuit Court's decision disbarring him from practice in that court.[30] At the time, an Indiana statute provided that

> any court of record may suspend an attorney from practicing therein for any of the following causes:
>
> 1. Where he has been convicted of a felony, or of a misdemeanor involving moral turpitude; in either of which cases the record of conviction is conclusive evidence;
> 2. When he is guilty of a willful disobedience or violation of the court requiring him to do or forbear an act connected with or in course with his profession; and
> 3. For a willful violation of any of the duties of an attorney, as herein before prescribed.[31]

The statute also directed the mode of procedure in such cases, requiring five days' notice to the attorney. The trial court had summarily suspended Smith, but, on review by the supreme court, the judgment was reversed and remanded for failure to comply with the specified procedure.

Later, in 1879, the supreme court decided *Ex parte Trippe,* which also involved a suspended attorney's appeal from a circuit court.[32] The supreme court reversed because of the trial court's failure to follow procedure. What is most notable about *Trippe,* however, is its recitation of an 1876 statute[33] describing the duties of attorneys, which, remarkably, included many of the provisions of today's Oath of Attorneys found in Rule 22 of the Indiana Rules of Admission to the Bar and the Discipline of Attorneys.

Another early reference to attorney discipline in Indiana is a statute enacted in 1881, which provided as follows:

> The proceedings to remove or suspend an attorney may be commenced by direction of the court or on motion of an individual. In the former case, the court must direct some attorney to draw up and prosecute the accusation; in the latter case, it may be drawn up by any person, and sworn to by the person making it.

> Such accusation may be filed in any court in which the attorney practices; and after five days' notice of the filing, the attorney shall be bound to appear and plead to the same, or suffer judgment by default. If he appear, pleadings may be filed and trial had as in other cases.[34]

Except for these scattered cases, the discipline of lawyers simply did not occur in Indiana until well into the twentieth century, long after the American Bar Association had adopted its Canons of Professional Ethics in 1908.[35] The ABA canons, however, never were adopted in Indiana.[36] As one Indiana commentator noted in 1970:

> In 1908, the American Bar Association adopted the original thirty-two canons of professional ethics. They were supplemented from time to time, until there was a total of forty-seven canons. While these canons were the official rules of the American Bar Association, they were not official rules in many jurisdictions. They had never been adopted formally by the legislature or by the Supreme Court of Indiana. It is doubtful if they had any official status or if they could have been enforced in Indiana.
>
> Even if they were enforceable, they did not constitute a system which could serve as a reasonable guide to lawyers. They were simply individual rules adopted at random over a period of time, and could not be considered either well organized or comprehensive.[37]

In 1969, the House of Delegates of the American Bar Association approved a proposed code of professional responsibility. The Indiana State Bar Association studied the code and recommended that it be adopted.[38] In 1971, the state supreme court did so, making Indiana the twenty-eighth state to adopt such codes of ethics.[39]

But what of the period from 1900 through 1971 in Indiana? Although the history is murky, prior to the 1931 statute giving the Indiana Supreme Court power over admission of attorneys, the court does not appear to have been particularly active in attorney discipline. Disbarment opinions from 1903,[40] 1910,[41] and 1924[42] are available, but in each instance the supreme court or the appellate court was acting as a reviewing appellate court.

By 1937, the legislature had passed a statute on attorney discipline. It provided that any circuit or superior court of the county in which an attorney resides shall revoke the admission of such attorney to practice law in the state of Indiana in a proceeding brought in conformity with the provisions of the statutes of Indiana, whenever

> First. He has been convicted of a felony in any jurisdiction wherein the crime for which he was convicted is designated as a felony, or of a misdemeanor involving moral turpitude, in either of which cases, the record of conviction is conclusive evidence; or
>
> Second. He has committed a felony or a misdemeanor involving moral turpitude; or
>
> Third. He has willfully violated any of the duties of an attorney, as prescribed by statute; or
>
> Fourth. He has willfully violated his oath of an attorney.[43]

A 1943 opinion reflects the state attorney general's prosecution of an attorney for violation of this statute.[44] It was not until ten years later that court opinions began to appear involving prosecutions by the Indiana Supreme Court Disciplinary Commission for violation of this statute. For instance, in the 1953 decision of *In re Harrison,*[45] the Indiana Supreme Court ruled that it had power, along with the circuit or superior courts, to enforce the attorney discipline statute and disbarred Mr. Harrison for conviction of a felony. The first decision involving a prosecution by the Disciplinary Commission is a 1952 case, *In re Lucas,*[46] which notes that the commission was appointed pursuant to the supreme court's 1949 admission rule numbered 3-21.[47]

In 1971, when the Indiana Supreme Court adopted the Code of Professional Responsibility, the court also reorganized its Disciplinary Commission and provided for a full-time staff to investigate and prosecute disciplinary cases.[48] The court funded the commission through an annual assessment on licensed Indiana attorneys, a fee that remains in place today.[49]

As an arm of the Indiana Supreme Court, the commission has been more active in the last thirty years in the regulation of Indiana lawyers. The Disciplinary Commission's purpose and procedures are now detailed in Indiana Admission and Discipline Rule 23. The court adopted a new set of Rules of Professional Conduct in 1987, and several amendments have occurred over the years since. The commission, governed by seven lawyers and two nonlawyers, has a substantial staff and operating budget.[50] During the 2002–2003 fiscal year, it received more than fifteen hundred grievances regarding Indiana attorneys.[51] The commission's staff attorneys regularly write and speak on issues of lawyer ethics and discipline.

In short, after nearly 150 years of relative inaction, the Indiana Supreme Court and its Disciplinary Commission have effected a dramatic change in the regulation of Indiana attorneys in the last thirty years. A formal entity with rules, procedures, staff, and a significant budget now actively regulates Indiana lawyers. The growth in the size of the bar and the number of disciplinary violations that still occur (including almost one hundred instances of attorney discipline from the Indiana Supreme Court from 2002 to 2003), indicate that this level of oversight is necessary and, perhaps, still inadequate to the task.[52]

Continuing Legal Education

One of the most sweeping changes in Indiana legal culture and the legal profession has been the state's adoption of mandatory continuing legal education (CLE) for attorneys. Historically, Indiana lawyers had no such requirement. In 1976, the Indiana Supreme Court created the Indiana Judicial Council on Legal Education and Competence at the Bar.[53] One of the council's express purposes was to "make recommendations concerning the need for and the implementation of continuing legal education for lawyers and judges."[54]

Effective October 1986, the supreme court adopted Admission and Discipline Rule 29, which, for the first time in Indiana, established "minimal continuing legal education requirements for each attorney admitted to the Bar of the State of Indiana."[55] The comprehensive rule created the Indiana Commission for Continuing Legal Education as a new arm of the Indiana Supreme Court and charged it with regulation and administration of Indiana's continuing legal education processes. The rule also established minimal requirements for CLE on annual and three-year bases.

Nearly twenty years later, CLE is now a mainstay of the Indiana legal culture, as in most other states. The commission has a full-time staff and eleven appointed commissioners. In fiscal year 2001–2002, it reviewed more than 6,000 CLE courses and recorded more than 199,000 hours of CLE credits among Indiana attorneys, of which more than 28,000 were ethics credits.[56] The culture of CLE has spawned an entire subindustry of CLE providers, providing boosts for state and local bar associations, new writing and speaking opportunities for Indiana lawyers, and countless offerings across the state on a wide variety of substantive, procedural, and ethical topics.

Rulemaking

Rulemaking is another area in which the Indiana Supreme Court has had a tremendous impact on the profession, the practice of law, and legal culture during the last thirty years. Prior to 1970, Indiana civil actions were governed not by a set of court-adopted rules of procedure but instead by statutory code pleading.

In the late 1960s, the Indiana Civil Code Study Commission created by the legislature looked into the possible adoption of rules of civil procedure patterned after the Federal Rules of Civil Procedure.[57] The legislature passed the rules, and the supreme court studied, modified, and finally promulgated them in 1969 as the Indiana Rules of Trial Procedure to be effective January 1, 1970.[58] Those rules were then, and still are, substantially similar to the Federal Rules of Civil Procedure, for which there exists a substantial body of interpretive law. This close conformity with the federal rules enhanced, and still enhances, the practitioner's understanding of Indiana's rules.[59]

Debate took place over the effect of the court's rules, but the court itself pronounced in 1973 that "[a]lthough a Supreme Court adopted trial rule is not a statute, it has the same binding force as any formally promulgated statute. The Supreme Court has the inherent power to create rules of procedure and that right has been recognized by the Indiana General Assembly."[60] Moreover, the court has ruled that, where incompatibility exists between court rules and a statute, the court rules prevail.[61]

The court's timing in adopting the trial rules roughly coincided with the 1970 amendment to article VII, section 4, of the Indiana constitution. This amendment "completely revise[d]" the judicial article of the constitution.[62] The amendment gave the court original jurisdiction over "supervision of the exercise of jurisdiction by the other courts of the State" and other express powers not previously enumerated in the constitution.[63]

The trial rules have had a tremendous impact on civil litigation, the practice of law, and Indiana's legal culture. The rules are orderly, predictable, and modified and amended with regularity to reflect contemporary practice. Indeed, the court has a formal Committee on Rules of Practice and Procedure that meets regularly to study possible changes to procedural rules.

The court's impact through the rulemaking process has not been limited to civil procedure. Indeed, in the last decade, the court has dramatically changed the legal landscape through the following new rules:

Rules for Alternative Dispute Resolution (1992)
Rules of Evidence (1994)
Parenting Time Guidelines (2001)
Rules of Appellate Procedure (2001), completely revised
Jury Rules (2003)

That all these rules were adopted within a single ten-year period is significant in itself, but each of these packages also blazed new trails in Indiana jurisprudence. Indiana was a leader in adopting its alternative dispute resolution (ADR) rules in 1992.[64] The federal courts, by contrast, were not required to have ADR programs until Congress passed the Alternative Dispute Resolution Act of 1998. As a result of the act, the U.S. District Court for the Southern District of Indiana first adopted local ADR rules in 2000.[65] Because of the Indiana Supreme Court's leadership and the structure provided by the ADR rules, mediation has become a central component of Indiana civil litigation. Indeed, many potential cases are resolved through voluntary presuit mediation.

Similarly, the Rules of Evidence changed the entire culture of evidence rulings in Indiana courts. Since the beginning of Indiana litigation, trial judges made evidentiary decisions within the often vague and fact-specific pronouncements of limited appellate precedent. Since the enactment of the Indiana Rules of Evidence, judges and practitioners alike have enjoyed more certainty and predictability in evidentiary rulings.

In 2001, the supreme court exercised its rulemaking authority to establish the Parenting Time Guidelines, a remarkable step into an arguably substantive area. A problem existed in determining how to assess visitation in divorce cases, and the court's Parenting Time Guidelines reflect active intervention by the court to address the issue. The Domestic Relations Committee of the Judicial Conference of Indiana developed these guidelines after reviewing the literature concerning visitation, the visitation guidelines of other jurisdictions, and input from family law practitioners and child development experts.[66] The guidelines are an excellent example of a subject that other branches of government could have addressed; but the courts were uniquely situated to have the most immediate interest, experience, and impact on the subject.

Finally, the Jury Rules are extraordinary in their own right for addressing issues untouched by most jurisdictions. The Jury Rules, for instance, allow jurors to submit questions in writing.[67] Very few jurisdictions in the United States expressly allow this, several prohibit it, and most are silent on the subject.[68] By analyzing jurors' roles and rights in the trial process and then promulgating specific rules addressing these issues, Indiana's Supreme Court once again was active in an area that, in Indiana and elsewhere, simply has been ignored.

The court's recent activism in rulemaking is, at least to these authors and presumably to most in the bar, a welcome development. Lawyers, bar associations, and even the general public have an interest in the subjects addressed, but only the supreme court has the inherent interest, talent, and authority to effect truly prompt and positive change in these matters.

Lawmaking

Historically, the Indiana Supreme Court was limited in its decisions addressing substantive legal issues affecting citizens and businesses. The court's docket was composed primarily of direct criminal appeals and left little time for discretionary transfer review of civil cases.

In recent years, however, the supreme court twice has lobbied for and succeeded in bringing about amendments to the Indiana constitution's provisions for its mandatory direct appeal jurisdiction. The court did so for the express purpose of opening its docket to hear more civil transfer cases.[69]

The court has followed through on its stated purpose, taking on and hearing a wide variety of important civil issues ranging from liability of gun manufacturers for crime in the *City of Gary* case,[70] to validity of written adoption consents,[71] to the liability of a president of a home renovation firm for faulty work done by the company.[72] The court also has been interested in and willing to take a fresh look at established substantive common law to determine whether it is in need of modification to reflect changed times.[73] Moreover, recent data suggest that the court is, in fact, accepting transfer in substantially more civil than criminal matters (granting 16 percent of the civil requests in fiscal year 2003, compared to 6 percent of the criminal).[74]

Rebirth of the Indiana Constitution

In the last fifteen years, through Chief Justice Shepard's leadership, the court has renewed its interest in and focus on the Indiana constitution, long the forgotten stepchild to the U.S. Constitution.[75] This renewal has manifested itself in several ways.

First, the court, through its State Board of Law Examiners, publicizes Indiana constitutional law as a potential testing subject on the Indiana Bar

Examination.[76] This has the natural effect of motivating law schools to offer, and law students to take, an Indiana constitutional law course. At Indiana University School of Law–Indianapolis, for instance, the counsel to the governor currently teaches such a course. Bar exam review courses, such as the one offered by the Indianapolis Bar Association, now teach an Indiana constitutional law section, thus leading to a growing number of Indiana lawyers having a working knowledge of the state constitution. Moreover, programs focusing on the Indiana constitution have become a regular feature on the CLE circuit.[77]

Second, the court has openly discussed its interest in Indiana constitutional law, both in public forums and in published opinions and articles.[78] This has the natural effect of causing practitioners to study the Indiana constitution and advocate its provisions on behalf of clients.

Third, the court has accepted jurisdiction in numerous cases raising Indiana constitutional law issues.[79] For instance, the court has addressed important litigation on transfer regarding the timing of the governor's return of vetoes, an issue rooted solely in the text of the Indiana constitution.[80]

All this activity, to be sure, would not have occurred without leadership from the Indiana Supreme Court. The long-range impact remains to be seen; it is perhaps too early to assess the court's work in this "new" area. One distinguished writer on the subject, Jon Laramore, concludes that progress to date in the individual rights area is slow, observing:

> The modern era in Indiana constitutional law began in 1989, when Chief Justice Shepard published "Second Wind for the Indiana Bill of Rights" in this law review. His invitation to revivify Indiana constitutional law has been taken to heart by the bar and many of the chief justice's judicial colleagues. But progress over the fourteen years since the article was published has not followed the pattern the chief justice forecast.
>
> New individual rights—beyond those guaranteed by the U.S. Constitution—have not been the primary product of the last fifteen years of state constitutional development. Although much litigation has addressed article I of the Indiana Constitution, the portion of the constitution covering individual rights, the Indiana Supreme Court has expanded individual rights beyond the federal standard in only a few cases. Rather, the most significant Indiana constitutional decisions have come from articles III through X, the provisions dealing with separation of powers, the responsibilities

> of the branches of government, and state institutions and finance. Indiana's appellate courts *have* brought new attention to the Indiana Constitution, but the largest impact on everyday Hoosiers has not come from decisions applying article I.[81]

There is merit, to be sure, to this observation, and it is beyond the scope of this chapter to analyze each recent decision interpreting the Indiana constitution. What seems certain at this stage, however, is that the legal culture has changed. The junior author of this chapter graduated in 1988 and after law school and the bar exam process, knew nothing of the Indiana constitution. Today's new lawyers, by contrast, know this document and its interpretation, and they study it for the bar exam. Thousands of Indiana lawyers have the tools to advance Indiana constitutional arguments. Indiana constitutional law is now a viable subject of litigation. The coming decades will reveal the extent to which everyday Hoosiers are impacted by this renewed interest in the Indiana constitution.

Pro Bono Work

The Indiana Supreme Court has had a significant impact on the delivery of pro bono legal services in Indiana in the last decade. A creature of amended Rule 6.5 of the Indiana Rules of Professional Conduct, the new Indiana Pro Bono Commission has the following express purposes:

> [It] will strive to promote equal access to justice for all Indiana residents by facilitating the integration and coordination of existing services; fostering the development of new pro bono programs; supporting and improving the quality of existing pro bono programs; fostering the growth of a public service culture within the Indiana Bar which values pro bono publico service; promoting the ongoing development of financial and other resources for pro bono organizations in Indiana; and enabling Indiana attorneys to discharge their professional responsibility to provide pro bono services.[82]

Since its inception, the commission has helped foster a culture and environment supportive of legal pro bono. The court and the commission have been helped by the availability of funds earned through Interest on Lawyer Trust Accounts (IOLTA), lawyer trust accounts that formerly did not earn interest.[83] It is too early in this venture to assess fully the court's impact in this area, but early results—renewed interest in and publicity of pro bono work—are promising.

Diversity

The court has embraced two measures aimed at increasing the diversity of the Indiana bar. First, in 1997, the Indiana Conference for Legal Education Opportunity (ICLEO) was established by the legislature at the urging of the court.[84] The program was created to assist minority, low-income, or educationally disadvantaged college graduates in pursuing a law degree and a career in the Indiana legal profession. In the short time since its creation, ICLEO has assisted several hundred students in entering law school, succeeding in law school, and entering the practice. Recently, an ICLEO alumnus was appointed to a judicial position, a single but important indication of the potential for this program.[85]

Meanwhile, in 1999, the court established a commission on race and gender fairness to "study and make recommendations on race and gender issues in Indiana's judicial system."[86] The commission is also "charged with the task of investigating ways to improve race and gender fairness in the courts, legal system, among legal service providers, state and local government, and among public organizations."[87] The commission already has issued a detailed, comprehensive report with findings and recommendations and the commission will have a significant impact on the profession in the future.[88]

The Influence of the Indiana Court of Appeals on Legal Culture

The Indiana Supreme Court has had a wide and significant impact on the Indiana legal profession and Indiana legal culture, particularly in the last fifteen years. The role of the Indiana Court of Appeals beyond individual cases and controversies is more limited, serving as the primary appellate court of review in Indiana. But it has influenced Indiana legal culture in at least two areas. First, the court of appeals has, in the last decade, established an unprecedented record of prompt disposition of Indiana appeals. Indeed, with an average time to disposition of less than two months from ripeness, the court of appeals is believed to be the most efficient and prompt among any appellate courts in the country in deciding appeals.[89] This has led to predictability among Indiana practitioners about the costs and time involved in taking and defending appeals.

Second, and perhaps as an inevitable downside of the court's speed in disposition, oral argument is the exception rather than the rule in Indiana appellate practice. For instance, in the last fiscal year, only 61 oral arguments were heard by the court of appeals out of a total of 1,980 appeals decided.[90] This extraordinarily low rate of oral argument—3 percent of all appeals—stands in stark contrast to the approximate 50 percent argument rate in the U.S. Court of Appeals for the Seventh Circuit. Reasonable minds can differ as to whether oral argument is necessary, economical, and of assistance to the court on appeal. What is certain, however, is that the art of appellate oral advocacy is not practiced with any regularity in Indiana.

The Role of Indiana's Trial Courts in Legal Culture

The Indiana trial courts—the locus of everyday litigation—have tremendous influence on the state's legal profession and legal culture. This impact, however, is typically on a case-by-case basis and not through systemic initiatives such as those pursued by the Indiana Supreme Court.

To be sure, some Indiana trial judges have left their mark on their local bar and the local legal culture. Before joining the Indiana Court of Appeals, for instance, Judge Sanford Brook dramatically enhanced the caliber of trial practice in St. Joseph County (and beyond) through his leadership in trial advocacy programs with the National Institute for Trial Advocacy.

The state's trial bench has been supportive of the Indiana Supreme Court's initiatives. Indeed, a sitting trial judge chairs each of the Pro Bono Districts created through the Indiana Pro Bono Commission. Indiana trial judges have been instrumental in the study, analysis, and drafting of many of the Indiana Supreme Court's recent rules initiatives. Working collaboratively with and through the Indiana trial bench, the Indiana Supreme Court has had a more profound and dramatic impact on legal culture through its many agents of change.

The Future

Much has changed in the last fifteen years, and it is expected that this new level of reform and initiatives will continue for the foreseeable future for the following three reasons.

First, the Indiana Supreme Court is staffed with energetic, dynamic, and dedicated justices with a demonstrated interest in legal reform. Furthermore, many of the justices have prior leadership and service experience in other sectors and thus know how to get things done. Probably most important, Chief Justice Shepard has been a consistent leader in Indiana legal reform, and his prominence nationally ensures that new ideas will emerge in the future.

Second, the legal profession—the trial bench and bar, as well as bar associations—seems receptive to the reforms that have occurred in recent years. Indeed, these groups have been necessary and willing partners in many of the initiatives. The legal community has become accustomed to leadership, initiative, and creativity from the court; the trust thus engendered makes future projects easier to jumpstart and see through to fruition.

Finally, there is and likely will remain a demand for leadership in the legal profession and in developing legal culture. The legislative and executive branches show no signs of stepping boldly in this field, and the need for reform and creativity likely will increase as society, economy, and indeed our state continue to change. Whether it is automating courts through the Indiana Supreme Court's Judicial Technology Committee, implementing non-county-based judicial structures, limiting the unauthorized practice of law, or enhancing resources for the third branch, much remains to be done. If the last fifteen years are any indicator, the future will present many opportunities and challenges requiring leadership from the Indiana judiciary. The authors look forward to watching the next chapter of Indiana legal history unfold, for the future is bright.

Notes

1. U.S. Const. art. III, § 2.

> The judicial Power shall extend to all Cases, in Law and Equity, arising under this Constitution, the Laws of the United States, and Treaties made, or which shall be made, under their Authority;—to all Cases affecting Ambassadors, other public Ministers and Consuls;—to all Cases of admiralty and maritime Jurisdiction;—to Controversies to which the United States shall be a Party;—to Controversies between two or more States;—between a State and Citizens of another State;—between Citizens of different States;—between Citizens of the same State claiming Lands under the Grants of different States, and between a State, or the Citizens thereof, and foreign States, Citizens or Subjects.

2. Ind. const. art. III, § 1.

3. Indiana Dep't of Envtl. Management v. Chem. Waste Management, Inc., 643 N.E.2d 331, 336–37 (Ind. 1994).

4. City of Indianapolis v. State Bd. of Tax Comm'rs, 261 Ind. 635, 308 N.E.2d 868 (1974). The Indiana Supreme Court does, of course, have original jurisdiction over specific matters such as admission and discipline of lawyers. Ind. const. art. VII, § 4. Moreover, the Indiana Supreme Court does not always feel constrained by "case or controversy" concepts. As the court explained in a 1999 decision addressing the ethics of in-house lawyers for insurance companies representing insureds:

> There is no case or controversy requirement limiting the jurisdiction of this Court as Article III of the U.S. Constitution restricts the jurisdiction of federal courts. Nevertheless, in many circumstances this Court has refrained from addressing issues that may be mooted by procedural or other threshold issues, even if there is no constitutional requirement to do so. See, e.g., *Price v. State,* 622 N.E.2d 954, 958 (Ind. 1993). However, this case does not involve invalidating an action of another branch of government or otherwise challenging the action of a co-equal branch. Rather it addresses issues that are indisputably within the power of the judiciary and specifically within the power of this Court.

Cincinnati Ins. Co. v. Willis, 717 N.E.2d 151n2 (Ind. 1999).

5. Blake's Case, 1 Blackf. 483 (Ind. 1818).

6. Ibid.

7. Ind. const. art. VII, § 21 (repealed 1932).

8. S. Hugh Dillin, "The Origin and Development of the Indiana Bar Examination," *Indiana Law Review* 30, no. 1 (1997): 391.

9. Lenn J. Oare, *A Study of Bar Examinations in Indiana,* 8 Notre Dame Lawyer (January 1933): 123, 125.

10. The senior author was a colleague of Haworth and learned Haworth's history through this relationship.

11. In re Leach, 134 Ind. 665, 34 N.E. 641 (1893).

12. R.S. 1881, § 962.

13. In re Denny, 156 Ind. 104, 59 N.E. 359 (1901).

14. State v. Swift, 69 Ind. 505 (1880).

15. In re Boswell, 179 Ind. 292, 100 N.E. 833 (1913).

16. 1931 Ind. Acts 150.

17. Revised Rules of Supreme and Appellate Courts of Indiana, Rule 41, Roll of Attorneys and Admission to Bar (1933).

18. Thomas J. Hurley, "Learning in the Law and Admission to Practice," *Indiana Law Journal* 7 (January 1932): 205, 206.

19. Bernard C. Gavit, "Learning in the Law and Admission to Practice—A Reply," *Indiana Law Journal* 7 (January 1932): 209, 218–20.

20. In re Todd, 208 Ind. 168, 172, 193 N.E. 865, 866 (1935).

21. Ibid., 187, 193 N.E. at 872.

22. Dillin, "Origin and Development," 394.

23. Oare, "Study of Bar Examinations in Indiana," 123, 124.

24. Rule 17 of the Revised Rules of the Supreme and Appellate Courts of Indiana [1936 rev.].

25. Currently, the Indiana State Board of Law Examiners consists of ten members, two from each Supreme Court Judicial District. Bar exams consisting of essay questions written and graded by the examiners were given in February and in July of each year.

26. James R. Elkins, professor of law, West Virginia University, "Practical Moral Philosophy for Lawyers" (December 1998),www.wvu.edu/~/lawfac/jelkins/pmpl99/course/rules.html.

27. American Bar Association, "Brief History of the American Bar Association," http://www.lectlaw.com/files/att05.htm.

28. Alicia Carlson and Sandra Cline, *Law in America's Crossroads—A History of the Indianapolis Legal Profession* (2001), 58–59.

29. Jack Lyle, "Indiana State Bar Association: A Century of Service to the Public and Profession," *Res Gestae*, September 1996, 8.

30. *Ex parte* Smith, 28 Ind. 47 (1867).

31. James Gavin and Oscar B. Hord, *Statutes of the State of Indiana Revisions of 1852* (1870), 2:329. Cited in *Ex parte Smith,* 28 Ind. 47 (1867).

32. *Ex parte* Trippe, 66 Ind. 531 (1879).

33. Edwin A. Davis, *Statutes of the State of Indiana, Revisions of 1876* (1876), 2:304. Cited in *Ex parte Trippe,* 66 Ind. 531 (1879).

34. 1881 Ind. Acts 386, as reported in *In re Darrow,* 175 Ind. 44, 92 N.E. 369, 370 (1910).

35. See Alfred P. Carlton Jr., president, American Bar Association, letter to Securities and Exchange Commission (December 18, 2002), http://www.sec.gov/rules/proposed/s74502/apcarlton1.htm.

36. Frederick E. Rakestraw, "The Code of Professional Responsibility," *Res Gestae,* May 1970, 22.

37. Ibid., 23.

38. Ibid.

39. Jerome L. Withered, *Hoosier Justice: A History of the Supreme Court of Indiana* (1998), 109.

40. In re Griffin, 33 Ind. App. 153, 69 N.E. 192 (1903).

41. In re Darrow, 175 Ind. 44, 92 N.E. 369 (1910).

42. Buhler v. Trick, 195 Ind. 190, 144 N.E. 840 (1924).

43. 1937 Ind. Acts 452.

44. Beamer v. Waddell, 221 Ind. 232, 45 N.E.2d 1020 (1943).

45. In re Harrison, 231 Ind. 665, 109 N.E.2d 722 (1953).

46. In re Lucas, 230 Ind. 254, 102 N.E.2d 909 (1952).

47. Ibid.

48. Withered, *Hoosier Justice,* 109.

49. Ibid., 110.

50. For instance, during fiscal year 2002–2003, the commission had a $1.6 million expense budget. Indiana Supreme Court, *Annual Report, 2002–2003,* 17.

51. Ibid.

52. Ibid.

53. Indiana Admission and Discipline Rule 28 (1976).

54. Ibid.

55. Indiana Admission and Discipline Rule 29 (1986).

56. Indiana Supreme Court, *Annual Report, 2001–2002,* 17.

57. Withered, *Hoosier Justice,* 103.

58. Ibid.

59. This same phenomenon replicated itself in 1994 when, as discussed below, the Indiana Supreme Court adopted the Indiana Rules of Evidence, patterned substantially after the longstanding Federal Rules of Evidence.

60. State ex rel. Bicanic v. Lake County Comm'rs, 260 Ind. 73, 292 N.E.2d 596 (1973).

61. Neeley v. State, 261 Ind. 434, 305 N.E.2d 434 (1974).

62. Roeschlein v. Thomas, 258 Ind. 16, 280 N.E.2d 581 (1972).

63. Ind. const. art. VII, § 4.

64. The authors are unaware of any state with formal, court-promulgated ADR rules prior to Indiana.

65. See S.D. Ind. Local Rules of Alternative Dispute Resolution (adopted Dec. 1, 2000).

66. Preamble, Indiana Parenting Time Guidelines (2001).

67. Indiana Jury Rule 20.

68. "Jurors exercise new right to ask questions," nwitimes.com, available at http://www.nwitimes.com/articles/2003/12/08/news/region_and_state/6dbaac28c98f45ed86256df600145469.txt.

69. See, e.g., Randall T. Shepard, "Second Wind for the Indiana Bill of Rights," *Indiana Law Review* 22, no. 2 (1989): 575, 580.

70. City of Gary v. Smith & Wesson Corp., 801 N.E.2d 1222 (Ind. 2003).

71. In re Adoption of Baxter, 799 N.E.2d 1057 (Ind. 2003).

72. Greg Allen Constr. Co. v. Estelle, 798 N.E.2d 171 (Ind. 2003).

73. See, e.g., Randall T. Shepard "The Importance of Legal History for Modern Lawyering," *Indiana Law Review* 30, no. 1 (1997): 2–3 (noting with approval an oral argument in which one advocate explained with some persuasiveness the reasons for adopting a new rule for a line of cases dating from the 1880s, while the appellee's counsel stated without positive effect, "We'd like the court to follow the law").

74. Douglas Cressler, "Appellate Procedure," *Indiana Law Review* 37, no. 4 (2004): 907, 926.

75. See, e.g., Shepard, "Second Wind," 575.

76. See Indianapolis Bar Association, "Indiana Bar Exam Information," http://www.indybar.org/barexam.cfm.

77. See, e.g., What Makes Indiana Special? Indiana Constitution CLE, 81st Annual Indiana History Conference of the Indiana Historical Society, November 3, 2001.

78. See, e.g., Shepard, "Second Wind," 575.

79. Jon Laramore, "Indiana Constitutional Developments: The Wind Shifts," *Indiana Law Review,* 36, no. 2 (2003): 361.

80. D&M Healthcare, Inc. v. Kernan, 800 N.E.2d 898 (Ind. 2003).

81. Laramore, "Indiana Constitutional Developments," 361.

82. Indiana Pro Bono Commission, "About the Indiana Pro Bono Commission," http://www.in.gov/judiciary/probono/about.html.

83. Indiana State Bar Association, "IOLTA Fact Sheet," http://www.inbar.org/content/iolta/ioltaqa1.asp.

84. See 1997 Ind. Acts. 2911, codified at IC §§ 33-2.1-12-1, et seq.

85. Indiana State Bar Association, "Indiana CLEO Fellow Tapped for City Court Bench," http://www.inbar.org/content/news/new.asp?art=436.

86. Indiana Supreme Court, "Commission on Race and Gender Fairness," http://www.in.gov/judiciary/fairness/index.html.

87. Ibid.

88. Indiana Supreme Court Commission on Race and Gender Fairness, "Executive Report and Recommendations," http://www.in.gov/judiciary/fairness/pubs/fairness-final-report.pdf.

89. Indiana Court of Appeals, "2002 Annual Report," http://www.state.in.us/judiciary/appeals/docs/2002report.pdf.

90. Ibid.

THIRTEEN

John G. Baker

INDIANA JUDGES

A Portrait of Judicial Evolution

Indiana's judicial history consists of three distinct eras linked to the method of selecting judges and marked by the character of individuals who served on the bench. At first, Indiana judges were appointed. The environment in which they practiced law—a state on the American frontier—forced them to be adaptable generalists. They came from diverse backgrounds: James Lemon served under General George Rogers Clark during the Revolutionary War; John Boone was brother to famed huntsman Daniel Boone; and Ezra Ferris was a minister and physician in addition to serving in the state's judiciary. In the second era, political operatives led the state judiciary and, at times, simultaneously ran major political parties. This situation arose from the outburst of Jacksonian democracy that deeply affects Indiana to this day. It was during this era that men such as Samuel Bigger and Abram Hammond moved easily from the bench to the governor's mansion. In the third era, the bench became more stable and more professional. Each of these periods resulted directly from changes in the state's political and legal environment.

Remarkably, the legacy of the Indiana judicial system came from men and women who often were underpaid when compared to jurists in other states or to practicing lawyers. In the 1840s, "only one state paid circuit judges less than Indiana."[1] This characteristic has been a constant one for Hoosier jurists. Until recently, only one state paid its trial court judges less than Indiana.[2] Effective July 1, 2005, the Indiana General Assembly passed into law the first adjustment to judicial salaries in ten years.[3]

When Indiana was still a territory—and even after its admission into the Union—attorneys and judges would literally "ride the circuit" on horseback, traveling from town to town to hold court. The 1816 constitution made the governor responsible for the appointment of judges, subject to the General Assembly's consent. Often the men who served as judges had worked the circuit as lawyers with the governor and legislators, most of whom also practiced law. The result was a tightly knit legal community. Whatever else might be said about the early bench, it seems clear that the abilities of prospective state judges at the time of their appointments had been observed in court as well as "in the wilds" of the territory.

The 1851 constitution radically changed the judiciary: it provided for popular election of supreme court and circuit court judges.[4] Jacksonian democracy's leveling principle of equality among all men extended to the courts.[5] Because of these changes, judges became more overtly political, openly seeking office in a way that had been unnecessary under the first state charter.

A 1970 amendment to the Indiana constitution again changed the process of judicial selection. Candidates for supreme court justices and court of appeals judges now apply to the Indiana Judicial Nominating Commission, composed of attorneys, nonattorneys, and the chief justice of the Indiana Supreme Court. The commission forwards to the governor the names of three candidates, from which list the governor makes an appointment. This depoliticized the selection process: political parties previously had chosen their judicial candidates at a state convention. Although circuit and superior court judges still faced elections, the Code of Judicial Conduct precluded sitting judges from taking leadership roles in political parties or becoming subservient to political party chairmen.[6] As a result, the judiciary has become much more of a career in itself and less of a way station in a legal career.

No collective biography of the Indiana judiciary—over time or during any period—currently exists, but it is possible to gain a sense of their character and contributions from individual portraits. Judges necessarily impact the judicial philosophy of the era in which they live. The five judges presented here demonstrate the evolution of the judiciary over time.

Indiana's Renaissance Man: Jesse L. Holman

Early state supreme court justice Jesse Lynch Holman had a reputation as "an all-around man."[7] In addition to practicing law, he was a novelist, poet, city planner, and preacher. Holman had for a mentor a man of extraordinary political acumen and oratory talent: Kentuckian Henry Clay. It was under Clay (who became Speaker of the U.S. House of Representatives) that Holman became conversant in the law.

Holman moved to the Indiana Territory in 1808, settling in Dearborn County on the banks of the Ohio River.[8] The following year, Governor William Henry Harrison appointed Holman prosecuting attorney for Dearborn County. Dearborn County in the early 1800s bore little resemblance to the county of that name today. In 1808, it included not only the present Dearborn County but also land from what would become all or parts of Jefferson, Franklin, Wayne, Switzerland, and Ohio counties.[9]

In 1810, Holman built his home overlooking the Ohio and dubbed it "Veraestau," a reference to the Latin words for spring, summer, and fall.[10] The Latin word for winter was noticeably absent: Holman's plan was that "the winter outside of the house was never reflected within."[11]

The year 1814 was a monumental one for Holman: he won election to the lower chamber of the territorial legislature and became its speaker. Later that year, he received an appointment as circuit court judge, traveling a great southeastern expanse of the Indiana Territory.[12] As one writer described riding the circuit, early Indiana lawyers and judges could not be fainthearted:

> In passing from one county seat to another it was often necessary to spend ten or twelve consecutive nights in the wilderness. The party usually consisted of the three Judges, a clerk . . . and from five to ten attorneys. . . . The attorneys carried their books and papers in old-fashioned leather saddlebags. In swimming the streams they put these around their necks to keep the papers dry. They usually carried provisions for themselves and horses for the entire trip, and slept in the open air, with their saddles for pillows and their cloaks for coverings.[13]

On the circuit, attorneys formed political alliances and friendships that propelled them to success. Both Jonathan Jennings and William Hendricks followed circuit judges across the state, and each achieved political success on the basis of the contacts he made.[14] Indeed, "of the first eight governors elected to office by the voters, all but one were professional lawyers of the circuit-riding kind."[15]

In 1816, Governor Jennings appointed Holman, then thirty-two years old, to the first Indiana Supreme Court. Holman's selection was the subject of much controversy. In 1816, James Noble, William Hendricks, and Jonathan Jennings were "generally regarded as the most powerful men in the state."[16] Although not always allies, the three men evidently made a pact to secure high office for themselves in the state's first election—Jennings as governor, Hendricks as congressman, and Noble as U.S. senator.[17] Then, the three power brokers chose their friends and supporters for spots on Indiana's highest court: Jennings chose James Scott, Noble tapped Holman, and Hendricks selected John Johnson.[18]

During his tenure as supreme court justice, Holman heard one of the most contentious issues of the era: the question of slavery in the new state of Indiana. The 1820 case—which was heard during the court's second term—involved a mixed-race female slave named Polly, brought into Indiana by her owner. The Knox Circuit Court held Polly to be the property of her owner, and Polly appealed to the Indiana Supreme Court. The court held that, although the Virginia deed of cession and Ordinance of 1787 did not exclude slavery from the Indiana Territory, the 1816 constitution firmly prohibited the practice. Holman joined in Justice Scott's opinion, which held that the 1816 constitution's statement that "there shall be neither slavery nor involuntary servitude in this State" expressed the will of the citizenry that "slavery can have no existence in the State of Indiana."[19]

After John Johnson died in 1817, Isaac Blackford joined Holman and Scott on the supreme court, and this trio became arguably the most influential grouping in the history of Indiana constitutional law. Besides ruling that the Indiana constitution categorically prohibited slavery, they also established that indentured servitude—then rampant—was allowable only as long as the state of servitude remains voluntarily.[20] Equally important was their decision to uphold a death sentence for James Hudson, the first white man prosecuted for killing an Indian, a heavily weighted sign of impartiality that, regrettably, was not common on the American frontier.[21]

In 1819, Holman joined with other men in Dearborn County to form the Aurora Association for Internal Improvements.[22] Holman himself held land in trust for the association and created the plat of the town. On January 30, 1819, Holman recorded the plat before the Dearborn County recorder and christened the town "Aurora," because "the aurora comes before the rising sun."[23] Rising Sun was another municipality located nine miles south—downriver—of Aurora.

Not content with merely founding a city, Holman helped establish the First Baptist Church of Aurora in 1820.[24] Holman was a deeply devout man who "manifested with a boldness and consistency of character, that satisfied everyone that he was not ashamed of the Cross of Christ."[25] Near the end of his life, Holman cofounded the Indiana Bible Society—which distributed four hundred bibles throughout the state—and underwrote one-fourth of its total costs.[26]

Holman was a champion of education and advocated the creation of the Aurora Public Library.[27] He cajoled wealthy donors to contribute funds to build the Aurora Seminary.[28] Holman's commitment to education culminated in his service as superintendent of Dearborn schools from 1832 through 1835.[29]

During the presidential election of 1824, Holman was an elector for the state of Indiana and thus had to choose for whom he should cast his electoral vote. The candidates for president were Andrew Jackson, John Quincy Adams, William Crawford, and Henry Clay, Holman's mentor. Andrew Jackson had received a plurality of the Indiana popular vote, topping both Adams and Clay.[30] Holman cast his electoral vote for Adams instead of Clay. Because no candidate had received a majority of the electoral votes the election was sent into the U.S. House of Representatives; the House chose John Quincy Adams, for whom Clay had marshaled support.[31]

Holman wrote to Clay after the election, explaining his reasons for voting for Adams instead of his mentor. After receiving Holman's letter, Clay replied in a most respectful manner:

> For the friendly sentiments expressed in your letter I am very thankful. I have not been an indifferent spectator of your progress in life, which I have, on the contrary, witnessed with much gratification. As to the part taken by you, in the late presidential election, with which I was acquainted, you would have been unworthy of the esteem which I entertain for you, if you had not have independently formed and acted on your own judgment. The reasons which you assign for your preference of another have great force, and being satisfactory to you, are entirely so to me.[32]

Although not receiving a vote from his protégé may have stung, Clay still held Holman in high esteem.

In 1830, Governor James Ray refused to reappoint Holman to a third term on the court, possibly because Holman had not supported Ray's senatorial run.[33] Holman became a private citizen until 1835, when President Andrew Jackson nominated him to the U.S. District Court for the District of Indiana. Holman served as judge of that court until his death in 1842.

Jesse Holman was an excellent jurist, yet an examination of his legal career only scratches the surface of a deeper soul. He was a man of faith, a man committed to education, and a man who founded a city. Like a number of other jurists of his day, but perhaps more than most, he accomplished much in a number of areas. He was, above all, a Renaissance man.

The War Hero: John Coburn

Forty-three years after the Indiana Supreme Court's decision in Polly's case barred slavery in Indiana, delegates to a special South Carolina convention unanimously voted to secede from the United States. A monumental armed struggle ensued, in which nearly half a million American soldiers[34]—including nearly twenty-five thousand Hoosiers[35]—would die. During this conflict, an Indiana judge named John Coburn gallantly led troops from the 85th and 33rd Indiana Infantry Regiments, the 19th Michigan Infantry Regiment, and the 22nd Wisconsin Infantry Regiment.[36] These four regiments were known collectively as Coburn's Brigade.[37]

Coburn was born in Indianapolis in 1825.[38] In 1846, he graduated from Wabash College[39] and, in 1850, won election to the General Assembly.[40] In 1859, Coburn became a judge in the court of common pleas of Marion County, presiding over probate matters and civil cases involving less than one thousand dollars in controversy.[41] He served until the outbreak of the Civil War[42] in 1861.[43] He resigned the bench and received command of the 33rd Indiana Volunteer Infantry Regiment.[44]

On October 21, 1861, the 33rd clashed with Confederate forces at Camp Wildcat in Kentucky. Although outnumbered, the Hoosiers had the high ground and held on until the Confederates' ammunition was spent. Coburn went on to serve as a brigadier general until Confederate cavalry general Nathan Bedford Forrest took him prisoner in 1863.[45] He returned to the Union forces in 1864 as part of a prisoner exchange and—instead of settling down after his combat service—resumed fighting for the Union until the end of the conflict.

In 1866, Coburn won a race for the U.S. House of Representatives, where he served until 1875. During this service, John Coburn delivered one of the most stirring speeches in support of a bill to suspend the right of habeas corpus in areas where the Ku Klux Klan was active:

> The laws to suppress the Ku Klux may be enforced, but other organizations will spring up. The writ of habeas corpus may be suspended and peace be restored, but it will not be permanent. So long as there are demagogues, so long as there are designing men, so long as party spirit runs high, so long will this dangerous and uncertain condition of society prevail. I would use the remedies named, but only as temporary and provisional. Nothing but the light of intelligence will rob a few southern leaders of their power and endow the southern people with the true attributes of sovereignty. I would at all hazards maintain the peace, and I would with all the power of the Government provide for the education of the people.[46]

Coburn realized that putting an end to the Klan's terror by force of law was only a temporary solution. To Coburn, education was the answer to the hatred that was tearing the South apart during Reconstruction.

Coburn returned to the bench in February 1884, when President Chester A. Arthur appointed him to the U.S. District Court for the Territory of Montana.[47] Unfortunately for the Republican Coburn, Grover Cleveland, a Democrat, won the presidential election of 1884 and removed him from the bench in 1885 for "offensive partisanship."[48] Coburn returned to Indianapolis, where he practiced law until his death in 1908.

Coburn's story illustrates that the efforts made by Indiana judges to ensure freedom for Hoosiers are not necessarily confined to the bench. John Coburn exchanged black judicial robes for Union blue. He championed the struggle for equality while a congressman. Coburn's efforts to better the lives of *all*—whether in the courtroom, at the front of a legislative chamber, or on the battlefield—show him to be a paragon of justice and a beacon for all Hoosiers.

The Teacher: Ora L. Wildermuth

Judges are always learning. They must keep abreast of new decisions from higher courts and become wise in the ways of managing people. Like all attorneys, they must continually study their craft so as to not be left behind. The truly remarkable judge, however, is the one who loves learning for its own sake. Ora L. Wildermuth was such a judge.

Wildermuth became a judge at a time when the judiciary was but a detour an attorney took during the course of his career. The state's elected judges played a role in electoral politics and political parties. What is truly remarkable is that somebody as civic-minded and scholarly as Ora L. Wildermuth was able to take part in the political fray without debasing his principles.

Wildermuth grew up in Pulaski County and attended a one-room schoolhouse. He had to travel to Star City for high school and, by his final year, he was the sole student remaining in his class. After finishing high school, Wildermuth became a teacher for a year before enrolling at Indiana University, from which he received a law degree in 1906.

Wildermuth moved to Gary and immediately became the young town's first teacher.[49] To supplement his income, he established a small law office that doubled as his residence. He also stored the school's books in his law office, thereby making him Gary's only teacher and librarian.[50]

In 1908, Wildermuth voiced concern that Gary did not have a public library. The statutes of the time authorized local library boards with taxing power but required board members to have five years of residency in the city in which they served.[51] Gary had been founded in 1906, so no resident qualified to be a board member.[52] There was a loophole: a school board could appoint a library board to operate under its auspices, apparently for the benefit of the school system. Ingeniously, Wildermuth persuaded the Gary school board to appoint him to the library board and thereafter purchased books of interest to all Gary residents, not just students. After Gary celebrated its fifth anniversary, the city established a "normal" library board with Wildermuth at its head.[53] The first Gary library was grossly underfunded and had to rely on volunteer staff. Reflecting on those early years, Wildermuth noted, "Books were listed, not by the Dewey system, but by the trial and error system."[54]

Wildermuth became a trustee of Indiana University in 1925, and he used a ceremony introducing Herman B Wells as the university's new president to tell the crowd how meaningful he found his appointment to the university board.[55] Wildermuth encouraged building projects on the Bloomington campus to ensure that the university became a premier learning center; he was the first to float the idea of a satellite campus in Gary, though it would be years before Indiana University Northwest was created.[56] So great were Wildermuth's contributions that Indiana University renamed the Bloomington campus's Old Field House the Ora L. Wildermuth Intramural Center in 1971.[57]

Wildermuth was not only a man who championed learning but also an advocate of civic involvement. He was a Democrat in Lake County, then a Republican stronghold. He became chairman of the Lake County Democratic Party in 1909, and through hard work he helped elect Gary's first mayor, Thomas Knotts.[58] As a reward, Knotts appointed Wildermuth Gary's first city judge, a position he held for three years. He continued to work actively for the election of Democrats in Gary and other Lake County municipalities.

Wildermuth's involvement in local politics reflected the broader trend of political involvement in the Indiana judiciary. Republican Leander J. Monks—who wrote the history of *Courts and Lawyers of Indiana*—was another example of a masterful politician who became a judge. He won election to the Indiana Supreme Court in 1894 by an astounding forty-five thousand votes, ousting a Democratic incumbent.[59]

Wildermuth's political involvement in Lake County ended in 1940. At a public speech attended by a "spillover" crowd, Wildermuth began, "Many of my Democratic friends tried to dissuade me from making this speech and maybe I'll be purged for doing so."[60] He went on to endorse Republican candidate Wendell Willkie's presidential run against Franklin Roosevelt. Wildermuth's concern was that a third presidential term—which had never been sought before—would set the stage for dictatorship. Wildermuth steadfastly denied that he was joining the Republican Party but stated, "My obligations to my country are beyond my obligations to my party."[61] He never returned to the political scene.

Still an advocate of education, Wildermuth wrote an essay that was distributed to members of the Indiana University Board of Trustees regarding "The Role of the Universities in the War Effort."[62] With uncanny insight, he noted that "[t]his war is different from any previous war. Marching and drilling are of less importance, technical knowledge and skill are of far greater importance."[63]

A lover of education: that is how Ora L. Wildermuth is remembered. Like many others who served as judges during this era, his judicial service was intertwined with a broader political career. He was also a man of principle, choosing to honor his obligation to his country over that to his political party, no matter what the cost.

The judges discussed so far did not have what one would call a "judicial career." Although Jesse Holman served for fourteen years on the Indiana

Supreme Court, his tenure was secured by constitutional provision. Moreover, much of his time was spent developing the city of Aurora.[64] John Coburn resigned from the state bench to fight in the Civil War and later lost his federal judgeship because of political wrangling. Ora Wildermuth was a city judge in Gary for only three years before moving on to other causes. The environment in which these judges operated—one featuring partisan election or partisan appointment—largely dictated this rather heavy turnover rate. The average tenure for a supreme court justice tells the story. From 1816 until Indiana's new constitution was adopted in 1851, a supreme court justice served an average of 11 years. After the judiciary became an elected branch of government, the average tenure of a supreme court justice dropped to 6.4 years.[65] Changes were in the offing that would transform the judiciary.

Some historians trace these momentous changes to the *Mass Transportation Authority of Greater Indianapolis* case (MTA).[66] In 1967, the General Assembly enacted legislation allotting a percentage of the state's inheritance tax revenue to the MTA. Both houses passed the bill on the final day of the session and presented it to Governor Roger Branigin that same day. Governor Branigin did not sign the bill, yet he did not veto it. In 1968, the MTA demanded the funds due under the bill, but Governor Ed Whitcomb and State Auditor Trudy Etherton—both from outside of the Indianapolis area—refused. The MTA filed an action in Marion Superior Court to compel payment, charging that the bill had become a law because Governor Branigin had not vetoed it. The state officers argued that Governor Branigin had exercised a pocket veto. Before the Marion Superior Court could hold a hearing, the case moved to the appellate court in accordance with special statutory authority. The appellate court ordered payment of the funds, but Etherton refused to issue a warrant to the MTA and instead asked the Indiana Supreme Court to hear the case.

The court declined to accept the case, dividing along party lines. Republican justices James Hunter and Norman Arterburn argued that the governor had no pocket veto and presented arguments from the 1850 constitutional convention to back their claim.[67] Democratic justices Roger DeBruler and Amos Jackson voted to hear Etherton's appeal, noting that the practice of assuming that a pocket veto had occurred was longstanding.[68] Justice Richard Givan—appointed to the court in 1968—did not take part in the decision, because he had been counsel for the MTA. The court was deadlocked—two justices for accepting jurisdiction and two against—so the appellate court's decision stood.

The impasse created by the partisanship within the supreme court led some to wonder whether the courts—at least at the appellate level—should be depoliticized. Indeed, when the appellate court later held a contempt hearing—Etherton was still refusing to issue a warrant—rumors had been floating around the State House that Governor Whitcomb had ordered plainclothes Indiana State Police officers into the courtroom to prevent Etherton from being taken into custody.[69] Two years after the *MTA* case, the voters amended the constitution to select appellate judges by merit. The result was Indiana's modern, less partisan judiciary.

The Pioneer: V. Sue Shields

Like many judges of keen ability, Sue Shields did not begin her college education seeking to become an attorney. Instead, she began at Ball State University intending to become a nurse but later changed the focus of her studies to government and history.[70] A law school recruiting panel, however, caught Shields's attention, so she went to law school.

After law school, Shields began her career as an attorney for the Internal Revenue Service in 1961 and later as a deputy attorney general in 1962. In 1964, she and her husband opened a law office in Hamilton County. When Republican Party leaders asked Shields—then twenty-five years of age—to become a candidate for a newly created superior court in Hamilton County, she believed herself too young to run for the bench. She did believe, however, that it would be an excellent way to drum up clients for her law office: attorney advertising was still prohibited in 1964.[71] To her surprise, she won the May primary and was unopposed in the general election.[72] Thus, she became Indiana's first female trial court judge.[73]

Judge Shields presided over many interesting matters while on the bench. She once had to divide Christmas tree decorations piece by piece in a divorce proceeding and in another had to calm the litigants down while they squabbled over visitation rights to a dog.[74] While presiding over an attempted murder trial in the dead of winter, she had the Indiana State Police use helicopters to bring in jurors when the roads were too treacherous to drive.[75] Judge Shields showed her true mettle, however, when she was pregnant with her first son. Knowing that she was due at any time, she wanted to ensure that the evidence in a civil case was presented and that the final instructions were settled so that the instructions needed only to be read to the jury. She actually finished the trial and went into labor the next morning.

On July 1, 1978, Judge Shields joined the Indiana Court of Appeals, where she was—again—the first woman on the court. Her chambers were initially in the building now known as the National City Center, but she relocated her offices to the Indiana State House in 1980. All Indiana Court of Appeals judges with chambers in the State House have brass nameplates to hang above their doors. Apparently, the State Department of Administration had been surprised that Justice Alfred Pivarnik—and not Judge Shields—had been appointed to the Indiana Supreme Court in 1977: Judge Shields's nameplate read "Justice Shields." In 1994, Shields once again proved to be a pioneer when she was appointed the first female federal magistrate judge in Indiana.[76]

By the late 1970s and early 1980s, Indiana trial courts had serious problems. A county could have, in addition to a circuit and superior court, "county courts, municipal courts, magistrate courts, probate courts, and juvenile courts."[77] Each court, moreover, had its own staff and cases, which could not be transferred to other courts in the event of overcrowded court calendars. In assessing the effects of this arrangement, the Indiana Judges Association observed that "some courts suffer from overcrowded dockets, while other courts function only part-time because of a lighter caseload."[78] To add to this confusion, the jurisdiction of courts could differ from county to county. For example, some courts of general jurisdiction were prohibited from exercising juvenile jurisdiction.

To address the problems of the trial courts, the Indiana Judges Association created the Judicial Reform Committee, and Shields cochaired this committee along with then Jasper Circuit Court judge Michael Kanne.[79] The committee issued its report on June 5, 1978. The report's centerpiece was an explanation of the benefits to be gained from a uniform trial court system. When the committee issued its report, however, the outcry was tremendous, and some called for Shields's removal as cochair of the committee.[80] The greatest resistance came from trial court judges themselves, who were shocked at the prospect of working in a county to which they had no ties and who resented the idea of having cases reassigned to them simply because some of their colleagues did not work as efficiently.[81]

Another key component of the committee's report was the proposal that Indiana trial court judges be appointed by the governor from a list prepared by a judicial nominating commission instead of being elected.[82] Like the unified court proposal, this provision caused considerable consternation among trial court judges, who pointed out that the idea went against the Jacksonian ideal of opening the electoral process to as many as possible.[83] The committee had concluded that a merit selection was preferable because only the best at running a political campaign—not necessarily the best people—were currently being elected.[84] In the end, the committee's report suggested that judges be elected but provided a compromise: the voters could select among the three judicial candidates recommended by the nominating commission.[85] Judge Shields opposed this compromise on the basis that the association should not attempt to hedge its beliefs.[86] Perhaps she was correct: the association's proposal was never implemented.

In 2004, Sue Shields still served as magistrate judge for the U.S. District Court for the Southern District of Indiana. A pioneer for her gender, she has challenged prevailing attitudes in the legal community that had held that a woman was not well-suited for the bench and has served well at all levels in the judiciary of the state.

The Reformer: John L. Kellam

At first blush, one would look at John L. Kellam's ten years of undergraduate studies and say that he—just as much as Ora L. Wildermuth—was a devotee of education. In reality, like many people in their late teens and early twenties, Kellam just did not know what career he wanted. He began as a prelaw student at Indiana University in Bloomington but then switched to a premedical track. Dissatisfied, he changed his major to accounting. Finally, after spending a decade as an undergraduate, Kellam graduated and entered law school.

After graduating from law school, Kellam clerked for Joseph Carson, an elected Republican judge of the Indiana Court of Appeals, from 1967 until 1970. It was as a clerk that Kellam first began to see the need to reform the judiciary. In 1970, he attended the Republican State Convention, an integral part of the way court of appeals judges were elected. He noted that the judicial candidates were nominated by the convention based on horse trading among party chairmen. Although many of the judges eventually elected by the voters were capable, some were not. Their selection had more to do with geography—with an eye toward balancing a party ticket—than with judicial merit.[87]

After five years as a deputy prosecutor, Kellam ascended to the bench in Henry County as that county's first county court judge. In 1980, he succeeded Wesley Ratliff as judge of the Henry Circuit Court when Judge Ratliff was appointed to the Indiana Court of Appeals.

Kellam's first judicial post was the product of the county court law passed by the General Assembly in 1975.[88] The legislature abolished the justice of the peace courts and the city and town courts, though the General Assembly then gave municipalities the authority to create their own city or town courts.[89] It vested the functions of the courts abolished by the act in new county courts. In some counties in which the legislature did not create a county court, the act sent the matters previously heard by justice of the peace, city, and town courts to the circuit court or—if the community had superior courts—to an additional superior court.[90] Kellam says that this law transformed the judicial branch from a stop along a legal career to a career in and of itself.[91] The number of younger judges—some in their twenties—rose dramatically.[92] After the replacement of lay justices of the peace by law-trained county court judges, the courts became more professional and more creative in crafting remedies.[93] A tidal wave of new judges arrived with new ideas to reform the judiciary and to ensure more efficient operations within the court system.

At the same time, the more professional judiciary became more insulated from political life. On November 3, 1970, the voters adopted article VII, section 9, eliminating the direct election of judges of the Indiana Court of Appeals and justices of the Indiana Supreme Court. Finally, the Indiana Supreme Court adopted the Code of Judicial Conduct, which further shielded judges from political activity. Kellam believed that this growing disconnect between the judiciary and political life led judges to be less involved political affairs, as the judicial corps sought to protect its appearance of impartiality.[94] A career in the judiciary meant that fewer former judges would be part of the General Assembly, a situation made permanent by a statute that required judges to give up their pensions while serving as an employee of the state.[95]

Judge Kellam took the helm of the Indiana Judges Association in 1986, a moment when relations between the judiciary and legislature were acrimonious at best.[96] In 1980, state senator Martin Edwards, who had been president pro tempore of the Indiana Senate and had been one of the legislators who backed issues favored by judges, was convicted in the U.S. district court for corruption.[97] The remaining legislative personnel left Indiana with a General Assembly led by legislators who were ill-disposed toward the Judges Association.

The work done by the Judicial Reform Committee—cochaired by Judges Shields and Kanne—made Kellam aware of the desperate need for reform. Because of the inability to transfer cases between courts—the lack of a unified court—some courts' dockets were overflowing while others were bare. Indeed, Kellam was appalled when members of the General Assembly in less-populous counties told him that, when they went to their county courthouse, the sitting judge was nowhere to be found.[98] Moreover, the state received a net revenue stream from fees and fines, while local governments suffered a net expense, forcing the "judiciary [into] a position of competing with the departments of local government" for funds.[99]

Kellam realized that if he was to persuade the General Assembly to take up important judicial reforms, he would have to ensure that both branches of government at least spoke to each other. First, he met with legislators and asked them to tell him their concerns. Only after the legislators had vented their frustrations with the judiciary did Kellam approach them with ideas and suggestions. Through this strategy of open-channel communication, he persuaded the legislature to create a commission on trial courts to investigate the lack of uniformity among Indiana's lower courts and the problems posed by local funding of those courts.

Judge Kellam's chief concern was that courts could not transfer cases to alleviate backlogs "simply because [they did not] have proper subject matter jurisdiction,"[100] a problem exacerbated by the fact that "general jurisdiction" meant something different in each county. He also was concerned about financing Indiana's lower courts, observing that "the quality of justice often depends upon the county's tax base."[101] Moreover, he was alarmed by the salaries paid to Indiana judges, arguing that "judges' salaries should at least allow the attorney who becomes a judge to maintain a standard of living that does not amount to financial punishment."[102] Finally, Judge Kellam was troubled by the automatic change of venue rule in civil trials: many significant civil cases from metropolitan areas were being transferred to rural counties, straining the judicial budgets of those counties.[103]

The eventual report of the Commission on Courts reflected Judge Kellam's concerns. It confirmed the disadvantages of funding courts largely by local government and highlighted the lack of uniformity in case management.[104] In his capacity as president of the Indiana Judges Association, Kellam produced a legislative proposal to improve Indiana's trial courts. The so-called Kellam Plan included important ideas for reform, including (1) the creation of a unified court system; (2) the shifting of costs of trial courts to the state and away from local government; and (3) an increase in judicial pay to attract and keep competent attorneys on the bench.[105]

One goal of the proposal was to establish a unified judiciary by eliminating the multiplicity of general and limited jurisdiction courts. The plan called for the establishment of circuits and districts.[106] The General Assembly would create the circuits, presumably one per county. Districts would consist of groups of circuits.[107] A presiding judge elected by all the judges in the district would head each district. The presiding judge would have the authority to reassign judges to circuits whose dockets were overcrowded, thereby allocating judicial resources where they were most needed.[108] In this way, cases could be transferred easily from one court to another if the first court's case load was too great.

The second prong of the Kellam Plan was to move the operating costs of trial court from local to state government. Kellam believed this shift was necessary for several reasons, among them the fact that local trial courts usually were called on to enforce laws passed by the General Assembly, the legislative body of the state of Indiana.[109] Moreover, Kellam was concerned that a citizen in a wealthy county would have greater access to justice than one in a poorer county.[110] Finally, there was the paradox that the state received a net income from the trial court fines and fees, while the courts themselves were a net drag on local government budgets.[111] If the state funded the trial courts, Kellam reasoned, these problems would disappear.

Kellam's third idea was to increase judicial salaries. Low salaries induced judges to manage cases in ways that generated more income. A "special judge," for example, collected a fee for his or her extra services, but only if that judge had to travel to another court to hear the case. Judges once again rode the circuit on Fridays, going to other counties to collect special fees and leaving behind an empty court room for other judges to use for their own "special judge" cases. A second problem was that judges' base salaries were among the lowest in the United States.[112] This led many able attorneys to select a career in private practice instead of joining Indiana's judicial corps.

Judge Kellam pushed and cajoled until his plan was introduced in the General Assembly as Senate Bill 12. Unfortunately, the bill did not make it through the legislature. The statewide unification of trial courts apparently would have caused disruptions in the judiciary. Moreover, the idea of judicial districts disconcerted some members of the public who were concerned that a judge for whom they had not had the opportunity to vote would judge their case. Financial concerns on the part of the state, coupled with alarm from county officials that a move to state funding would divest them of "contact" with local judges, sank the proposal to move trial courts to state funding.[113]

The General Assembly did not force all trial courts to unify. However, the circuit and superior courts in Monroe County practiced a type of de facto unification—for example, Monroe Superior Court and the Monroe Circuit Court consolidated budgets and shared personnel—from 1981 until 1990, when judicial and local legislative leaders produced formal unification by enacting Indiana Code section 33-4-10-1. Delaware County's legislative and judicial leaders later obtained the same option. The results in Monroe and Delaware counties demonstrated that unification would work and that parochialism could be overcome.

Undaunted by the modest gains achieved in the legislative sphere, Judge Kellam worked on improving the state's judicial system. He chaired the Judicial Administration Committee of the Indiana Judicial Conference, which drafted Indiana's Child Support Guidelines. The guidelines revamped the entire concept of providing for children; whereas family courts at one time had been essentially financial counselors, the primary focus shifted to providing financially for children.[114] Since his retirement in 2001, Judge Kellam has taken part in the Judicial Technology and Automation Committee charged with establishing a comprehensive electronic case management system.

Indiana has been fortunate to have Judges Kellam and Shields leading the efforts to improve our judiciary. Shields's ideas as part of the Judicial Reform Committee launched judicial reform by stressing the need to change a Byzantine system of overlapping jurisdictions. Through his indefatigable work before, during, and after his presidency of the Indiana Judges Association, Judge Kellam was able to persuade the legislature to take note of the problems at the trial court level. His diplomatic skill won over members of the legislature at a time when relations were strained.

The ideas of Judges Shields and Kellam have borne fruit in the Indiana Supreme Court. The supreme court's requirement that local courts devise case management plans is an outgrowth of Kellam's plan to deal with overcrowded dockets. Likewise, the statutory provisions allowing certain courts to unify are descendants of Shields's recommendations for reform. These judges' ideas set a course for judicial reform that are still in development.

The Indiana judiciary has come a long way. At first, those who rode the circuit would serve a stint on the bench but then continued their legal careers. Later, the judiciary entered a political phase, pushed by the leveling wind of Jacksonian democracy. Finally, the judiciary has come to be composed of professionals who seek to serve the public on the bench during the whole of their legal career.

The reasons for these phases are discernible. In territorial times, the governor was familiar with the character of the lawyers with whom he "rode the circuit," so a new governor led to new judges. The 1851 constitution instituted an elected judiciary, so involvement in party machinery became important. Since changes in the Indiana constitution and statutes in the 1970s, the state's judiciary has achieved a new level of professionalism. Thus, the judiciary has become more stable. This disengagement has had its drawbacks, as relations with other branches of government have suffered. Fortunately for Hoosiers, though, this stability means that the vast judicial experience gained by these men and women will continue to be at work, doing justice in our courthouses.

Notes

1. Donald F. Carmony, *Indiana, 1816–1850: The Pioneer Era* (Indianapolis: Indiana Historical Bureau, 1998), 248.

2. National Center for State Courts, *Survey of Judicial Salaries* 29, no. 2 (2004).

3. 2005 Ind. Acts 2351–53.

4. Ind. const. of 1851, art. VII, §§ 3, 9.

5. Indiana Judges Association, *Indiana Trial Court System: Recommended Improvements* (Alabama: Indiana Judicial Center, 1978), 20.

6. Canon 5 of the Indiana Code of Judicial Conduct reads, in relevant part: "[A] judge or a candidate for election or appointment to judicial office or retention in judicial office shall not: (a) act as a leader or hold an office in a political organization."

7. Leander J. Monks, Logan Esarey, and Ernest V. Shockley, eds., *Courts and Lawyers of Indiana* (Indianapolis: Federal Publishing, 1916), 1:187. One cannot be surprised that the author, a native son of Aurora, Indiana, chose Jesse L. Holman as a subject of this chapter. Judge Holman wanted Aurora to be the county seat for Dearborn County and even named one of the downtown streets "Judiciary Street." This lore was well-known to me, as I grew up in a home at the corner of Fifth and Judiciary streets.

8. C. W. Taylor, comp., *Biographical Sketches and Review of the Bench and Bar of Indiana. . . .* (Indianapolis: Bench and Bar Publishing, 1895).

9. Northeastern Genealogy Online, "Indiana County Formation Maps," http://www.negenealogy.com/in/in_maps/in_cf.htm.

10. Veraestau still exists today, and this historic home may be visited. For more information, contact the Hillforest Foundation at (812) 926-0087 or at http://www.hillforest.org.

11. Israel George Blake, *The Holmans of Veraestau* (Oxford, Ohio: Mississippi Valley Press, 1943), 6.

12. Ibid., 10.

13. Monks, Esarey, and Shockley, *Courts and Lawyers,* 1:8–9.

14. Ibid., 1:78.

15. Ibid., 1:80.

16. Suzann Weber Lupton, "Isaac Blackford: First Man of the Court," *Indiana Law Review* 30, no. 1 (1997): 319, 322n23.

17. Monks, Esarey, and Shockley, *Courts and Lawyers,* 1:183.

18. Ibid., 1:184.

19. Sandra Boyd Williams, "The Indiana Supreme Court and the Struggle against Slavery," *Indiana Law Review* 30, no. 1 (1997): 305, 306; Lasselle v. State, 1 Blackf. 60, 62 (Ind. 1820).

20. Jerome L. Withered, *Hoosier Justice: A History of the Supreme Court* (Lafayette, Ind.: J. L. Withered, 1998), 18.

21. Ibid., 21.

22. City of Aurora, "Welcome to Aurora!" http://www.aurora.in.us/hist1.htm.

23. Blake, *Holmans of Veraestau,* 34.

24. First Baptist Church of Aurora, "Church History," http://aurorabaptist.org/history.html.

25. Blake, *Holmans of Veraestau,* 36.

26. Ibid., 38.

27. Ibid., 34.

28. Ibid.

29. Ibid., 35.

30. Multieducator, Inc., "Presidential Elections, 1824," http://www.multied.com/elections/1824.html.

31. U-S-History.com, "The Election of 1824," http://www.u-s-history.com/pages/h262.html.

32. James Duvall, "Two Letters from Henry Clay to Judge Holman," http://www.geocities.com/ boonehistory/clay2holman.html.

33. Blake, *Holmans of Veraestau,* 22.

34. Department of Veterans Affairs, *America's Wars Fact Sheet* (Washington, D.C.: Department of Veterans Affairs, 2002).

35. Kristopher Ligget and Larry Ligget, "Indiana in the Civil War," http://www.indianainthecivilwar.com/.

36. During the Civil War, the Union's regiments had approximately one thousand troops, and brigades had about four thousand. A division typically had three brigades for a total of twelve thousand soldiers. A Union corps had three divisions, or about thirty-six thousand troops. National Park Service, "Army Organization in the Civil War," http://www.nps.gov/gett/gettour/armorg.htm.

37. Frank Welcher and Larry Ligget, *Coburn's Brigade: The 85th Indiana, 33rd Indiana, 19th Michigan, and 22nd Wisconsin in the Western Civil War* (Carmel: Guild Press of Indiana, 1999), 1.

38. Ligget and Ligget, "Indiana in the Civil War, John Coburn: 1825–1908," http://www.indianainthecivilwar.com/hoosier/coburn.htm.

39. Welcher and Ligget, *Coburn's Brigade,* 14.

40. Civil War Indiana, "John Coburn," http://civilwarindiana.com/biographies/coburn_john.html.

41. John G. Baker, "The History of the Indiana Trial Court System and Attempts at Renovation," *Indiana Law Review* 30, no. 1 (1997): 233, 246.

42. Much disagreement remains about the name of the internal conflict between the states of the Union that took place between 1861 and 1865. See Benham v. State, 622 N.E.2d 982, 984n9 (Ind. Ct. App. 1993) (referring to the "War Between the States"), and Benham v. State, 637 N.E.2d 133, 138n1 (Ind. 1994) (Sullivan, J., dissenting) ("correcting" the name of conflict to the "Civil War"). Though some old southern Indiana Democrats would term the conflict "the War of Northern Aggression," this essay uses the term "Civil War" because the state supreme court has termed it thus.

43. Indiana in the Civil War, "John Coburn, 1825–1908."

44. Ibid.

45. The TN GenWeb Project, "The Civil War in Williamson County, Tennessee," http://www.noelm.com/williamson/civwarTS.html.

46. *Congressional Globe,* 42d Cong., 2d sess., 482–83 (January 22, 1872).

47. Indianapolis and Marion County History Preservation Society, "General John Coburn," http://www.countyhistory.com/doc.marion/383.htm.

48. Ibid.

49. Letter to unknown recipient, Indiana University Bloomington Archives, collection no. C130.

50. Prepared speech for lunch at the Gary Public Library, Indiana University Bloomington Archives, collection no. C130.

51. Ibid.

52. Ibid.

53. Ibid.

54. Ibid.

55. Speech at Herman B. Wells's inaugural, Indiana University Bloomington Archives, collection no. C130.

56. Notes on an Indiana University extension in Gary, Indiana University Bloomington Archives, collection no. C130.

57. Indiana University Office of the Chancellor, "Campus History," http://www.iub-chancellor.indiana.edu/pg/chrono.shtml. The Old Field House, which would have been known to my parents as simply the Field House and which now is named for Wildermuth, is not to be confused with the Harry Gladstein Field House, a building just east of Assembly Hall.

58. *Gary Post-Tribune,* October 15, 1909.

59. Withered, *Hoosier Justice,* 64.

60. *Gary Post-Tribune,* October 1, 1940.

61. Ibid.

62. "The Role of Universities in the War Effort," Indiana University Bloomington Archives, collection no. C130.

63. Ibid.

64. Jesse Holman served as a judge for the U.S. District Court for the District of Indiana for six years, although the federal judiciary had constitutional protections not afforded to Indiana judges.

65. After the 1970 amendment to the Indiana constitution providing for appointment by a judicial nominating commission and subsequent retention by the voters, the average term for a supreme court justice rose to 14.3 years. The data to compute these averages was obtained from Minde C. Browning, Richard Humphrey, and Bruce Kleinschmidt, "Biographical Sketches of Indiana Supreme Court Justices," *Indiana Law Review* 30, no. 1 (1997): 329, 383–89.

66. State ex rel. Mass Transp. Auth. of Greater Indianapolis v. Ind. Revenue Bd., 251 Ind. 607, 244 N.E.2d 111 (1969).

67. Ibid., 611, 244 N.E.2d at 113.

68. Ibid., 631, 244 N.E.2d at 124.

69. Patrick J. Sullivan, judge of the Indiana Court of Appeals, interview by author, Indianapolis, February 24, 2004.

70. V. Sue Shields, magistrate judge, U.S. District Court for the Southern District of Indiana, interview by author, Indianapolis, October 9, 2003.

71. Betty Barteau, "Thirty Years of the Journey of Indiana's Women Judges, 1964–1994," *Indiana Law Review* 30, no. 1 (1997): 113.

72. Shields interview.

73. Garcia-Jean Meyer, "YLS Seeks to Identify, Honor First 100 Women Lawyers," *Res Gestae,* April 2000.

74. Shields interview.

75. Ibid.

76. Barteau, "Thirty Years," 114.

77. Indiana Judges Association, *Recommended Improvements,* 5.

78. Ibid.

79. Judge Kanne served as a judge on the U.S. District Court for the Northern District of Indiana from 1981 to 1987. In 1987, Judge Kanne was appointed to serve on the U.S. Court of Appeals for the Seventh Circuit, with principal offices in Chicago. Judge Kanne's Indiana office is located in Lafayette, Indiana.

80. Shields interview.

81. Ibid.

82. Indiana Judges Association, *Recommended Improvements,* 17.

83. Shields interview.

84. Indiana Judges Association, *Recommended Improvements,* 28.

85. Ibid., 31.

86. Shields interview.

87. John L. Kellam, former judge of the Henry County, Indiana, Superior Court, interview by author, Indianapolis, September 30, 2003.

88. 1975 Ind. Acts 1638.

89. 1981 Ind. Acts 2295. This statute remains in effect today.

90. This was the case in Vanderburgh, Allen, and St. Joseph counties.

91. Kellam interview.

92. The fabled "Class of 1976" included young judges such as Nicholas Schilralli, of the Lake Superior Court; David Johnson, of the Greene Circuit Court; and Frank Guthrie of the Jackson Superior Court, all of whom continue to serve on the bench. I, too, was part of this cohort. When we first became judges, none of us had yet reached the age of thirty.

93. In 1980, the General Assembly once more provided for lay judges in some city and town courts. 1980 Ind. Acts 334. However, the Indiana Commission for Continuing Legal Education requires that lay judges receive periodic legal training.

94. Kellam interview.

95. 1974 Ind. Acts 594–95.

96. Kellam interview.

97. U.S. v. Edwards, 672 F.2d 1289 (7th Cir. 1982).

98. Kellam interview.

99. John L. Kellam, "The Indiana Judicial System: An Analysis of Change," *Indiana Law Review* 21, no. 1 (1988): 273, 279.

100. Ibid., 278.

101. Ibid., 279.

102. Ibid., 286.

103. Kellam interview.

104. Ind. Legislative Services Agency, *Final Report of the Commission on Trial Courts* (Indianapolis: Indiana Legislative Services Agency, 1988), 1.

105. Indiana Judges Association, *A Proposal for Reform of the Indiana Trial Court System* (Alabama: Indiana Judicial Center, 1986), 1.

106. Ibid., 2.

107. Ibid.

108. Ibid., 3.

109. Ibid., 7.

110. Ibid.

111. Ibid.

112. Ibid., 11.

113. Kellam interview.

114. 1995 Ind. Acts 4062–4101.

FOURTEEN

George T. Patton Jr.

POLITICAL PRAGMATISM AND COMMON SENSE

Leading Cases of the Indiana Supreme Court

Since its creation in 1816, the Indiana Supreme Court has been resolving Hoosier disputes, but its nearly two-hundred-year record of jurisprudence does not neatly or immediately offer up overarching themes because the law, by its nature, involves individual parties and separate cases. Every couple of decades, however, some decision transcends individual disputes, moves beyond the realm of judges and lawyers, and becomes a public case, a legal landmark to the people of Indiana.

Although the decisions might seem unremarkable to the twenty-first-century mind, these cases were quite forward-looking for their times. The legal principles and outcomes Hoosiers take for granted today had to be established and woven into Indiana society. As a whole, these cases show Indiana justice as pragmatic, practical, straightforward, intuitive, unpretentious, and respectfully deferential to the other branches of state government.

These cases also tell of an Indiana Supreme Court that was, at times, ahead of courts in other midwestern states. The justices were sometimes near the forefront in their thinking about legal developments of their times; although not necessarily the first adopters of change, they usually embraced larger national trends quickly and gave them currency in Indiana law. They tended to defer to the decisions of the people of Indiana as they spoke through the legislative and executive branches. Although usually deferential, the court at times had to remind Hoosiers and their elected representatives of state constitutional principles. In the final analysis, these cases tell stories of an Indiana Supreme Court remarkably faithful to its duty to promote justice for all citizens.

Slavery

State v. Lasselle (1820) placed before the state courts the issue of slavery. At stake was the 1816 constitutional prohibition of slavery in Indiana, a proscription that mimicked a similar clause in the Northwest Ordinance of 1787. The opinion was brief, direct, and unequivocal—it now seems unremarkable, but the outcome was hardly foreordained, at least not in political terms.

The Knox Circuit Court in Vincennes had ordered Polly, a woman of color, to the custody of Hyacinthe Lasselle, a French settler who had purchased Polly's mother as a slave from Indians in the Northwest Territory prior to the Treaty of Greenville and the transfer of the territory to the United States. Those representing Polly's interest, attorneys listed in *Blackford Reports* only as Kinney, Tabbs, and McDonald, appealed to the Indiana Supreme Court. Amory Kinney was a prominent lawyer in Vincennes who had "read law in Vermont under Samuel Nelson . . . later . . . a Justice of the United States Supreme Court."[1] Colonel George McDonald was the son-in-law of Charles Carroll, of Carrollton, one of the signers of the Declaration of Independence.[2] Little is known about Tabbs.

Judge James Scott wrote the opinion for the court. He began directly: "The question before this Court is, as to the legality of Lasselle's claim to hold Polly as his slave."[3] He noted the "elaborate research" presented by both parties "into the origin of our rights and privileges, and their progress until the formation of our State government, in 1816."[4] Polly argued that the Northwest Ordinance of 1787 and the Indiana constitution prohibited slavery in Indiana. Lasselle claimed that when Virginia gave up its claims to the Northwest Territory, it reserved the "the privilege of holding slaves" to those settlers who professed to be citizens of Virginia and that this "right" was vested and could not be taken away by any subsequent constitutional provision.

The justices felt no need to resolve the competing historical claims. Relying on such English common-law authorities as Coke, Blackstone, and

Bacon, the court said that the Indiana constitution had charted a new course. "A Convention, chosen for the express purpose, and vested with the full power to form a constitution," Scott reasoned, had the power "in forming our Constitution, to prohibit the existence of slavery in the State of Indiana."[5] Looking to that document, the court noted the declarations "That all men are born equally free and independent" and "There shall be neither slavery nor involuntary servitude in this State."[6] The Indiana constitution "intended a total and entire prohibition of slavery in this State," the court wrote, "and we can conceive of no form of words in which that intention could have been more clearly expressed."[7] Scott concluded that "under our present from of government, slavery can have no existence in the State of Indiana, and . . . the claim of . . . Lasselle can not be supported."[8] The court reversed the judgment of the Knox Circuit Court and discharged Polly.

Although the national debate on slavery continued for more than forty years, the Indiana Supreme Court forcefully and simply enforced the state constitutional prohibition on the practice. The short opinion admitted no reservations in implementing the straightforward constitutional language. In tackling such a difficult question in this fashion, the justices ensured that Indiana would remain in the company of states unreceptive to slavery.

The outcome for slavery in the United States makes the decision by the Indiana Supreme Court appear unexceptional, but, in fact, it contrasts sharply with the territorial governor's approach under article VI of the Ordinance of 1787, which also prohibited slavery and involuntary servitude in the Northwest Territory.[9] As legal historian Paul Finkelman has noted, "[T]he Northwest Ordinance did not end slavery in what would become Indiana and Illinois. Nor did the Illinois Constitution of 1818 lead to an immediate end to slavery in the state. Indeed, not until 1845 would the Illinois Supreme Court be willing to free the slaves (or their descendants) born in the Northwest after adoption of the Ordinance of 1787."[10]

Two years after the creation of the Indiana Territory in 1800, a convention of settlers presided over by territorial governor William Henry Harrison asked Congress to relax the antislavery article of the Ordinance.[11] Although this attempted move toward de jure slavery was unsuccessful, de facto slavery developed by 1807 as residents in the territories discovered a new method of living under the Ordinance and owning slaves.[12] Governor Harrison, a Virginian and a slave owner, "was able to use his power to circumvent the ordinance [by] . . . adopting laws that allowed slavery to grow in Indiana."[13]

When Congress created the Illinois Territory in 1809, proslavery interests in Indiana lost many allies to the state's newly organized neighbor. Simultaneously, opposition to slavery was growing along with the influx of settlers from the North and Northeast.[14] These new settlers understood that the implementation of article VI required popular support, and they pressured the territorial government to explore the Ordinance's prohibition.[15] After the adoption of the Indiana constitution in 1816, many slave owners left Indiana. Slave owners who remained no doubt assumed that, the new state constitution notwithstanding, that nothing would change.[16] The state supreme court's decision upholding the state constitutional ban on slavery "turned out to be far more effective than implementation of the ordinance" had been.[17] By 1830, slavery had virtually ceased in Indiana: the federal census listed only three slaves in the state.[18]

Right to Counsel

Almost twenty-five years later, in 1854, the court confronted the question of the right to counsel for a criminal defendant who was a pauper unable to afford a lawyer.[19] The state had indicted Thomas Wickens on a charge of burglary in the Tippecanoe Circuit Court at Lafayette. Wickens was destitute and lacked the means to employ counsel for his defense. The trial court ordered attorney Baird to defend Wickens and ordered the county auditor Nathan Webb to pay for the legal defense.

Webb appealed to the Indiana Supreme Court, arguing that the trial court had no authority to order Baird to defend Wickens at the expense of the county. The court, in an opinion by Judge William Stuart, first concluded that Baird's services as an attorney in defending Wickens must be compensated: "To the attorney, his profession is his means of livelihood. His legal knowledge is his capital stock. His professional services are no more at the mercy of the public, as to remuneration, than are the goods of the merchant, or the crops of the farmer, or the wares of the mechanic."[20] But the decision of the court went far beyond the issue of compensation:

> It is not to be thought of, in a civilized community, for a moment, that any citizen put in jeopardy of life or liberty, should be debarred of counsel because he was too poor to employ such aid. No Court could be respected, or respect itself, to sit and hear such a trial. The defense of the poor, in such cases, is a duty resting

> somewhere, which will be at once conceded as essential to the accused, to the Court, and to the public."[21]

The court concluded that the duty to pay should be fixed on the county: "It seems eminently proper and just, that the treasury of the county, which bears the expense of his support, imprisonment and trial, should also be chargeable with his defense."[22] The court allowed attorneys to sue the county directly for the fees incurred in representing those too poor to hire counsel in criminal cases.

The legal basis upon which the court acted is murky. It cited, but did not rely upon, the provision in article I, section 21 of the newly ratified Indiana constitution: "no man's particular services shall be demanded without just compensation."[23] It concluded that the statute on which the lower court had acted applied only to civil suits; so the decision, in effect, created a means to enforce the constitutional injunction, a task normally performed by the legislature.[24] The court also reasoned that failure to provide compensation meant that the state, in essence, was requiring lawyers to contribute a free service. Such "gratuitous services from a particular class, in effect, imposes a tax to that extent upon such class—clearly in violation of the fundamental law, which provides for a uniform and equal rate of assessment and taxation upon all the citizens."[25] Ultimately, the court relied on its inherent discretionary authority to decide what services are necessary to run a legal tribunal and how they were to be paid.

The Enrolled Act Rule: Deference to the Legislature

In both *State v. Lasselle* and *Baird v. Webb*, the supreme court acted in the absence of legislation by the General Assembly. When the legislature did act, however, the court typically deferred to its authority, as when adopting the Enrolled Act Rule (1869).[26] The issue arose when attorney Thomas M. Browne sought $1,500 for his service on the Morgan Raid Commission, created by the legislature in 1867. Browne filed an action against John D. Evans, the auditor of the state, for the money. Evans refused to pay, asserting that the law allowing for the appropriation had passed without a quorum in the house of representatives. He relied upon the *Journal of the House* as his evidence. The Marion Common Pleas Court in Indianapolis awarded the money to Browne; Evans appealed.

The Indiana Supreme Court framed the question on appeal as follows: "Where a statute is authenticated by the signatures of the presiding officers of the two houses of the legislature, the courts will not search further, to ascertain whether such facts existed as gave constitutional warrant to those officers to thus authenticate the act as having received legislative sanction in such manner as to give it the force of law?"[27] In other words, would the court look beyond the enrolled act? The justices decided that they would accept the signatures of the presiding officers and that to inquire further would impinge on the legislative branch. Judge James Frazer wrote that "it is not becoming that one co-ordinate department of the government should . . . condemn another" and that "it would seem scarcely fit . . . that the courts should be at liberty to enter into that investigation" because it would be "invading the field which belongs exclusively to the legislature."[28] Regardless of whether courts "can look behind the official authentication made by the proper officers of the two houses," they "should be very careful not to invade the authority of the legislature."[29] "No person charged with official duties under the judicial department shall exercise any of the functions of the legislative department," he noted.[30]

The court acknowledged the possibility of corrupt presiding officers. "It is not fit that the judiciary should claim for itself a purity beyond others; nor has it been able at all times with truth to say that its high places have not been disgraced."[31] But to make that judgment was not the role of courts. The judiciary "cannot . . . look beyond the authentication, because of the constitution itself."[32] The separation of powers doctrine embedded in the 1851 charter meant that, in the end, "governments must repose confidence in officers . . . , [and] courts cannot look beyond the enrolled act and its authentication."[33] In reaching this decision, the court adopted a deferential stance that historically has marked its relationship to the legislature and executive. By this deference, the court acknowledged the role that the people, through their elected representatives, play in shaping the laws and policies that govern them. This is ironic because the judiciary in Indiana, from 1851 to 1970, likewise was democratically elected.[34]

The deferential approach of the Enrolled Act Rule contrasts to the aggressive approach taken by the Indiana Supreme Court in the slavery and right to counsel cases. The slavery case involved construction and application of clear language in the Indiana constitution to provide an answer when the legislature had not acted. The right to counsel rested on the court's legal authority to conduct proceedings in a manner it deemed consistent with the constitution, a matter within its sphere of authority. The Enrolled Act Rule arose out of an action by the legislature, a coordinate state branch of government, which the justices accepted under the separation of powers doctrine.

Admission of Women to the Bar

Within its sphere of influence, the court charted its own path, often a course more progressive than the popular culture suggested was possible. A prime example occurred in 1893, when the Indiana Supreme Court first declared that women could be admitted to the Indiana bar.[35] Antoinette Dakin Leach applied to the Greene Circuit Court for admission to the bar. At the time, any voter could become a lawyer under a provision of the Indiana constitution that read, "Every person of good moral character, being a *voter,* shall be entitled to admission to practice law in all courts of justice,"[36] and a statute that provided, "[E]very person of good moral character, being a *voter,* on application, shall be admitted to practice law in all the courts of justice" (emphases added).[37] As a woman, Leach could not vote in Indiana; accordingly, the circuit court judge denied her application because she did not meet the constitutional and statutory criteria for admission to the bar. Leach appealed.

The Indiana Supreme Court interpreted the substantive law differently, observing that neither the Indiana constitution nor state statutes excluded women from the practice of law (i.e., *voter* does not mean *only voters*).[38] The court noted that, at common law, as a matter of custom women were not lawyers but concluded that the changing role of women made many of these practices obsolete.[39] The justices reasoned by analogy to other professions: "The other learned professions of this state are open alike to the sexes. There is no reason for an exception of the legal profession."[40] "If nature has endowed woman with wisdom," Judge Leonard Hackney asked rhetorically, "if our colleges have given her education, if her energy and diligence have led her to a knowledge of the law, and if her ambition directs her to adopt the profession, shall it be said that forgotten fiction must bar the door against her?"[41]

Other states—Illinois, Wisconsin, Oregon, Maryland, and Massachusetts—took the view that, in the absence of an express grant of authority, women could not be attorneys. Harkening to the words of the Declaration of Independence, the Indiana court wrote that the theory of our political institutions was that all people have certain inalienable rights, that among these are life, liberty, and the pursuit of happiness, including the freedom to pursue all avocations, honors, and positions.[42] "Before the law this right to a choice of vocations can not be said to be denied . . . on account of sex," the court said in reaching a conclusion well ahead of its time.[43]

The justices viewed this decision as being within their authority under the state constitution. The court acted just as it had in the slavery and right to counsel cases, asserting judicial power to decide.[44] The supreme court reversed the lower court's decision with instruction to admit Leach to the bar.

The Exclusionary Rule

In the twentieth century, the Indiana Supreme Court continued to chart a progressive legal course. In 1923, the court adopted the exclusionary rule, which made any evidence seized under an invalid search warrant inadmissible in criminal trials.[45] A grand jury in Elkhart County had indicted Edward Callender for possession of whiskey during the age of Prohibition. Callender pleaded not guilty. After a trial, a jury convicted him but petitioned the trial court to suspend his jail sentence during good behavior. The trial judge imprisoned Callender for sixty days.

On appeal, Callender challenged the evidence that he had intoxicating liquors, pointing out that it had been procured by a search of his premises under an unauthorized warrant. He claimed that no affidavit had been filed before a neutral judicial officer authorized to issue a warrant and that the warrant itself had been signed by the chief of police, not by a judge or mayor as required by law. The state argued that the Prohibition Law of 1917 had authorized seizures with such warrants and that the U.S. Supreme Court had recognized their use for seizing contraband.[46]

The court decided that "[i]f the property was secured by search and seizure under the pretext of a search warrant, which was invalid for any reason, then the property so seized could not be used as evidence against [him] and its admission over his objection was prejudicial error."[47] The court relied upon the state constitutional provision that mirrored language in the U.S. Constitution: "The right of the people to be secure, in their persons, houses, papers, and effects, against unreasonable search or seizure, shall not be violated; and no warrant shall issue, but upon probable cause, supported by oath or affirmation, and particularly describing the place to be searched, and the person or thing to be seized."[48]

The justices reversed the conviction and issued an instruction to grant a motion for new trial because there was "no evidence to support the verdict except that procured by the illegal search warrant, and improperly admitted, it is not supported by sufficient evidence and is contrary to law."[49]

The decision tracked closely a 1914 decision of the U.S. Supreme Court, *Weeks v. United States,* that broke with common-law precedent and ordered the exclusion from federal trials of evidence obtained through unconstitutional search. *Weeks* was a landmark decision, but its limitation was apparent. It did not apply to the states. If state or local police conducted the search and turned over otherwise illegally obtained evidence to federal officials, the evidence would be admissible. The practice became known as the "silver platter" exception to the exclusionary rule and became a routine method of investigation for federal officials.[50] *Weeks* also meant that local prosecutors could introduce illegally seized evidence in trials under state law as long as state constitutions or laws allowed it. Most states permitted the practice. The Indiana Supreme Court in *Callender vs. State* decided that Indiana would not be among them.[51]

Between 1920 and 1960, half the states had allowed pertinent evidence into criminal proceedings on a case-by-case basis, even if it was obtained illegally. The remaining states followed the federal lead. The twenty states that adopted an exclusionary rule in the 1920s did so to soften the impact of Prohibition. Indiana was in the vanguard of these early adopters. In this instance, the state's penchant for individual privacy and for protection against overbearing government overrode its reputation as a state tough on crime.[52]

Stamping out the Klan

During the early 1920s, the Ku Klux Klan dominated Indiana politics and controlled much of state and local government. Hoosier D. C. Stephenson was the most notorious, most powerful, and most feared leader of the Ku Klux Klan in mid-America. He made and unmade legislators, judges, mayors, and governors. "I am the law" in Indiana he said most famously[53]—and he was, at least until convicted of second-degree murder in 1925.

In 1932, the Indiana Supreme Court upheld Stephenson's conviction.[54] In hindsight, this might seem a simple matter. The legal issue presented by the case was straightforward, if capable of producing disagreements: is a kidnap and rape victim who takes poison in her distress and dies later, after her tormentor stands by to let the poison work, someone who has committed suicide or someone who has been murdered? The larger context of the role of the Klan in Indiana politics in the 1920s made the case a difficult one and provides insight into the court's role in stamping out the Klan's influence.

On March 16, 1925, Stephenson took Madge Oberholtzer, a State House secretary, against her will to a room in a Pullman car on a train bound from Indianapolis to Chicago. Stephenson assaulted and raped Oberholtzer around 6:00 AM on March 17 as the train approached Hammond, Indiana. He then forced her to leave the train for a Hammond hotel, where she attempted suicide by taking poison. Stephenson refused to furnish her with an antidote or to take her to a doctor. In the afternoon and night of March 17, Stephenson drove Oberholtzer back to Indianapolis, and, until noon of March 18, he held her in his garage without providing an antidote or physician. He eventually sent her home. Dr. John Kingsbury found her there later, lying in bed in a state of shock, pale and cold with a rapid pulse. Her clothing was disheveled, and she had a bruise on her chest. When Kingsbury pressed her to tell him what happened, she told him what Stephenson had done. Oberholtzer died on April 14.[55]

The grand jury in Marion County charged Stephenson with murder. A jury found him guilty of murder in the second degree as charged, fixing his punishment as life imprisonment. The trial court entered judgment in accord with the jury's verdict on November 16, 1925.

Stephenson was carried off to the state prison at Michigan City, and there began a six-year legal struggle featuring tussles about appellate briefing and multiple habeas corpus proceedings. Although lawyers and judges were interested in the evidentiary issue of Oberholtzer's dying declaration, for the people of Indiana the important decision was upholding the criminal conviction of a leader of the Klan. The Indiana Supreme Court affirmed his conviction in January 1932.

The court voted 3 to 2 to affirm the conviction; Justices Clarence R. Martin and Walter E. Treanor, one of each party, dissented. The majority declared: "To say that there is no causal connection between the acts of [Stephenson] and the death of Madge Oberholtzer would be a travesty on justice. The whole criminal program was so closely connected that it should be treated as one transaction."[56] The dissenters argued that Oberholtzer had purchased and consumed the poison on her own, without Stephenson's participation, and with the intent of suicide.[57]

The rule of law announced by the majority, the *Indianapolis Star* opined, "will be far-reaching long after Stephenson and Stephensonism have been forgotten."[58] Not completely forgotten in today's legal circles is the fact that the majority's opinion did not carry the name of its author, being instead an opinion "per curiam." The supreme court had chastised the state's intermediate judges for this practice, but it proved useful in the Stephenson appeal: crossing the Klan could be hazardous to a judge's political or personal health. This judicial action, albeit delayed for a number of years, helped stamp out the influence of the Klan in state government.

In the 1920s, society's struggles over the Klan and over Prohibition were deeply divisive battles that played out in both law and politics. At the Indiana Supreme Court, this meant a mountain of liquor litigation, long delays in dispositions, and turnover in court membership due to the political turmoil. By the time the court acted in 1932, only David A. Meyers and Julius C. Travis remained from the five justices who had received the appeal in 1926. Republican Clarence R. Martin had arrived in 1927, and Democrats Curtis W. Roll and Walter E. Treanor had come in 1931.

The interplay between the political world and the legal world, especially with elected justices, is an interesting story beyond the scope of this chapter: but the important point of this case was that no person was above the law.

The Bar Examination

A few years later, in 1935, the supreme court addressed a challenge to the then new bar examination.[59] In July 1931, the justices had adopted rules requiring applicants who wished to join the bar to take an examination to determine their professional fitness. Lemuel S. Todd filed a petition challenging the court's authority to require bar applicants to take an examination to test professional fitness.

The Indiana State Bar Association petitioned the court to dismiss Todd's challenge. The association argued that the court rules were a reasonable means of assessing "good moral character." It also pointed out that a recent state constitutional amendment had clarified the court's power to make and enforce the rules for bar admission that Todd complained about. Todd replied that the constitutional amendment was not valid because it had not been ratified by the people; although more voters had voted "yes" than "no" on the amendment issue, the "yes" votes did not represent more than half of all voters who had cast ballots on election day. Todd cited *State v. Swift* (1880), *In re Denny* (1901), and *In re Boswell* (1913), all of which had held that this was what ratification required.[60]

The court dismissed Todd's petition and overruled the prior opinions. It said there was no reason to assume that nonvoters were favorably or unfavorably disposed toward the proposed amendment and that the only practical way to measure the public will was by counting the ballots actually cast. This act showed the court's flexibility when applying rules developed in another time that no longer made sense. The court also pushed forward the cause of making the Indiana bar more professional by setting minimum state standards.

Judicial Review

In addition to improving the quality of Indiana lawyers, the court protected the right of the people to judicial review and oversight of the decisions of the executive branch.[61] Jacob K. Warren filed a worker's compensation claim against the Indiana Telephone Company, which the Industrial Board denied. The intermediate appellate court affirmed the board's decision. Warren attempted to take his case to the Indiana Supreme Court, even though the statutory scheme did not provide for further appeal.

The court wrote

> The matters presented challenge us to consider some very serious and important questions, among which may be mentioned, the place of the Supreme Court in the judicial system of the state; the power of the General Assembly with respect to administrative agencies; the constitutional guaranties of due course of law for injury done to the person; and the inviolate right to trial by jury in civil cases.[62]

The court then created the framework for judicial review:

> Strictly speaking, there is no such thing as an appeal from an administrative agency. It is correct to say that the orders of an administrative body are subject to judicial review; and that they must be so to meet the requirements of due process. Such review is necessary to that the end that there may be an adjudication by a court of competent jurisdiction that the agency has acted within the scope of its powers; that substantial evidence supports the factual conclusions; and that its determination comports with the law applicable to the facts found.[63]

These standards protect the people of Indiana from arbitrary and capricious action by administrative bodies.

The court found that, although the

> General Assembly vested exclusive jurisdiction in the Appellate Court to review the proceedings of the Industrial Board, it did not provide any procedural machinery for an appeal or review. This presents a serious situation. . . . Uniformity in the interpretation and application of the law is the keystone of our system of jurisprudence. . . . [I]t was the positive intention of the framers of our Constitution that the laws of this state should be general and uniform so far as it is possible to make then so. Such uniformity cannot be attained or preserved if the courts that interpret and apply the laws are not required to take their controlling precedents from some common source.[64]

Having laid out the harm that such a regime would inflict, the court said, "We therefore disapprove of the language contained in many cases which seem to suggest that the right of appeal to this court exists only by the grace of the legislative branch of the government."[65] The importance of this ruling for the people of Indiana is the court's establishment of a uniform rule to apply to all Hoosiers, one removing distinctions so that every person has the potential to have the Indiana Supreme Court decide his or her case.

Indiana is a state relatively inhospitable toward claimants like Warren. This case, however, was not about workers' rights per se but about protecting access to judicial review.

Protecting Injured Workers

Following up on the right of judicial review in worker's compensation cases, the Indiana Supreme Court in 1973 refused to allow employers to discharge workers in retaliation for filing a worker's compensation claim.[66] Although hesitant to file a worker's compensation claim for fear of losing her job, Dorothy Frampton did so. One month later, she was fired without reason. She brought an action claiming that her employer had improperly fired her. The lower courts dismissed her suit.

On appeal, the Indiana Supreme Court wrote that "the employee must be able to exercise his right in an unfettered fashion without being subject to reprisal." "If employers penalize employees for filing workmen's compensation claims," the justices reasoned, it would undermine an important public policy.[67] The court laid out a tough approach: "Retaliatory discharge for filing a workmen's compensation claim is a wrongful, unconscionable act and should be actionable in a court of law. Although we know of no other case in this or in any other jurisdiction holding that such is actionable, there has been parallel development in landlord tenant law. . . . Retaliatory discharge and retaliatory eviction are clearly analogous."[68] The court concluded that "when an employee is discharged solely for exercising a statutorily conferred right an exception to the general rule must be recognized."[69] Courts in other states noted this case and began to cite it in support of similar decisions. Here, the Indiana Supreme Court was a half-step in front of a national trend.

Although Indiana has a strong employer-oriented political culture, this decision shows the Indiana Supreme Court stepping in to protect the right of workers to raise claims in administrative and judicial forums without fear of retaliation. Such a ruling does not dispel the sovereign's inclination, but it demonstrates the court acting in its judicial role to protect individuals raising a violation of constitutional rights, statutory laws, or administrative regulations meant to protect them.

Fair Redistricting, Fair Elections

The final case, from 2003, deals with the redistricting of the City-County Council of Indianapolis and Marion County.[70] The opinion is a ringing endorsement of judicial independence and neutrality. As frequently happens in jurisdictions in which political parties are narrowly separated, redistricting results in litigation. This happened when the Republicans, long in control of the council, adopted a redistricting plan that a rising Democratic minority challenged in the Marion Superior Court. There, it was heard en banc by more than two dozen judges, a majority of whom were Republicans. On a party-line vote, the court adopted the Republican plan.

On appeal, the Indiana Supreme Court held that the decision did not conform to applicable principles of judicial independence and neutrality. The court wrote in a section entitled "The Judiciary's Duty of Independence and Neutrality" that "all parties to the dispute champion judicial independence, free of partisan political decision-making."[71] Although the dispute had its origin in partisan politics, the justices agreed that "Indiana judges must consider only the factors required by applicable federal and State law."[72] Furthermore, the court said, "Whatever role politics may legitimately play in decisions and maneuvering of the legislative and executive branches, if those branches cannot reach a political resolution and the dispute spills over into an Indiana court, the resolution must be judicial, not political. Thus, Indiana judges may not consider the partisan political consequences of redistricting plans because this is not among the constitutional and statutory factors that inform a judicial decision."[73] Because time was of the essence, the court redrew the district in such an evenhanded manner that one council district was decided by a mere three votes and the longtime political minority party won control of the council by a single seat.

The court's independent, nonpartisan resolution is the fruit of a state constitutional amendment in 1970 providing for "merit selection" and appointment of the justices. But throughout the court's history, the justices on the bench have attempted to hold the balance even, level, and true. In deciding this redistricting matter in such a fashion, the Indiana Supreme Court has pushed the political branches to resolve such redistricting matters without court intervention.

As these cases suggest, the Indiana Supreme Court, at times, has been more progressive than other state or federal courts. The court led the way on slavery, aid to the poor, and women's rights. The most remarkable feature of these decisions is that they represent a consistent trend over nearly two hundred years. The opinions show the Hoosier traits of independence, pragmatism, and fairness rooted in the fundamental principle that all people are equal in the eyes of Indiana government. Although some of the decisions rest respectably within larger national trends, in hindsight they mostly look like good, practical, common sense.

Notes

I thank my wife, Eileen M. Ambrose, for reviewing and revising a draft of this chapter; summer associate Curtis Jones for assisting me in selecting these cases; and my assistant Linda S. Cooper for her help.

1. Jerome L. Withered, *A History of the Supreme Court of Indiana* (manuscript, February 1983), 46.
2. Ibid.
3. State v. Lasselle, 1 Blackf. 60 (Ind. 1820).
4. Ibid., 61.
5. Ibid.
6. Ibid., 62, quoting Ind. const. of 1816, art. I, § 1; Ind. const. of 1816, art. XI, § 7.
7. Lasselle, 1 Blackf. at 62.
8. Ibid.

9. Paul Finkelman, "Evading the Ordinance: The Persistence of Bondage in Indiana and Illinois," *Journal of the Early Republic* 9 (Spring 1989): 21.

10. Ibid.

11. Ibid., 30.

12. Ibid., 34.

13. Ibid., 34–35, citing, e.g., "A Law concerning Servants," adopted in 1803.

14. Ibid.

15. Ibid., quoting Peter S. Onuf, *Statehood and Union: A History of the Northwest Ordinance* (Bloomington: Indiana University Press, 1987), 118.

16. Ibid., 40.

17. Ibid.

18. Ibid.

19. Webb v. Baird, 6 Ind. 11 (1854).

20. Ibid., 17.

21. Ibid., 18.

22. Ibid., 19.

23. Ibid., 15, quoting Ind. const. of 1851, art. I, § 21.

24. Ibid., 15.

25. Ibid., 17.

26. Evans v. Browne, 30 Ind. 514 (1869).

27. Ibid.

28. Ibid., 522.

29. Ibid., 523.

30. Ibid.

31. Ibid., 526.

32. Ibid.

33. Ibid., 526–27

34. The decision in *Evans v. Browne,* springboard for this doctrine of deference, may itself have also been influenced by the fact that Indiana's ratification of the Fourteenth and Fifteenth Amendments likewise occurred without legislative quorums being present, Democratic members having resigned their offices in an effort to block ratification. The Indiana Supreme Court that decided *Evans v. Browne* was an all-Republican court, and Republicans supported these federal amendments.

35. In re Leach, 134 Ind. 665, 34 N.E. 641 (1893).

36. Ind. const. art. VII, § 21.

37. 1881 Ind. Acts 383.

38. In re Leach, 134 Ind. at 665, 34 N.E. at 641.

39. Ibid., 667, 34 N.E. at 641 ("Such . . . fictions as became part of the law of this country are rapidly disappearing, and few, if any, of them exist in Indiana").

40. Ibid., 668, 34 N.E. at 641.

41. Ibid.

42. Ibid., 669, 34 N.E. at 642.

43. Ibid.

44. Ibid., 671, 34 N.E. at 641–42.

45. Callender v. State, 193 Ind. 91, 138 N.E. 817 (1923).

46. Weeks v. U.S., 232 U.S. 383 (1914).
47. Callender, 193 Ind. at 96, 138 N.E. at 818.
48. Ibid., 96–97, quoting Ind. const. art. I, § 11.
49. Ibid., 99, 138 N.E. at 819.
50. Lustig v. U.S., 338 U.S. 74, 79 (1949).
51. David J. Bodenhamer, *Fair Trial: Rights of the Accused in American History* (New York: Oxford University Press, 1992), 77–78.
52. See Yale Kamisar, "The Exclusionary Rule in Historical Perspective," *Judicature* 62 (February 1979): 337.
53. Stephenson v. State, 205 Ind. 141, 174, 179 N.E. 633, 644 (1932).
54. Ibid., 193–94, 179 N.E at 651.
55. Ibid., 165–79, 179 N.E at 641–45.
56. Ibid., 189, 179 N.E at 649.
57. Ibid., 200–247, 179 N.E at 651–67.
58. *Indianapolis Star,* January 20, 1932, 8.
59. In re Todd, 208 Ind. 168, 193 N.E. 865 (1935).
60. State v. Swift, 69 Ind. 505 (1880); In re Denny, 156 Ind. 104, 59 N.E. 359 (1901); In re Boswell, 179 Ind. 292, 100 N.E. 833 (1913).
61. Warren v. Indiana Tele. Co., 217 Ind. 93, 26 N.E.2d 399 (1940).
62. Ibid., 100–101, 26 N.E.2d at 402.
63. Ibid., 105, 26 N.E.2d at 404.
64. Ibid., 108–10, 26 N.E.2d at 405–6.
65. Ibid., 111, 26 N.E.2d at 406.
66. Frampton v. Cent. Indiana Gas Co., 260 Ind. 249, 297 N.E.2d 425 (1973).
67. Ibid., 251, 297 N.E.2d at 427.
68. Ibid., 252–53, 297 N.E.2d at 428.
69. Ibid., 253 297 N.E.2d at 428.
70. Peterson v. Borst, 786 N.E.2d 668 (Ind. 2003).
71. Ibid., 672.
72. Ibid.
73. Ibid., 672–73.

FIFTEEN

Allen Sharp

THE U.S. SUPREME COURT ON CIRCUIT IN INDIANA, 1837–1891

The Pioneer Period

When one reads the simple, but cryptic, language of Article III of the Constitution of the United States, one gains very little sense of the original intent of the drafters about the function of the federal judiciary in general and about its function below the level of the Supreme Court of the United States in particular. There is really nothing in those few words authorizing the creation of one Supreme Court and other, "inferior courts" that in any way describes what the federal judiciary became in the twentieth century.

Today, it is hard to envision a Supreme Court justice instructing grand juries, conducting jury trials, and dealing with local lawyers and litigants, but the Judiciary Act of 1789 authorized it all. The last Federalist Congress tried to end these practices by creating permanent federal appellate courts in the Judiciary Act of 1801, commonly known as the Midnight Judges Act. The act, however, was repealed by the Jeffersonian Congress in 1802. In fact, in that statute, Congress cancelled a session of the Supreme Court. The practice of Supreme Court justices riding circuit thus lasted until 1891.

Indiana became a state in 1816, and Benjamin Parke became its first U.S. district court judge. The enabling statute created a federal circuit court, but it did not assign a Supreme Court justice to come to Indiana. At that time, the task undoubtedly would have fallen to Justice Thomas Todd, of Kentucky, who was nearby, but his health was known to be frail in his last years on the court. His successor, Robert Trimble, also from Kentucky, served only two years and, as far as can be ascertained, never came to Indiana or was assigned here. In 1837, Congress amended the statute, and Justice John McLean, of Ohio, began coming to Indiana on circuit.

A recent writer has described Justice McLean's circuit riding in Indiana, a hazardous duty because of the primitive modes of travel:

> In his report to the Senate, Justice John McLean added: "on no inconsiderable part of my route through Indiana in May, last, the road was so deep as to be almost impassable to a carriage of any description. The mails and passengers had to be conveyed in common wagons." Most justices traveled via stagecoach or steamboat, depending on the region and the time of the year. They also took advantage of the railroad as it developed.[1]

Indiana in 1837 was in its pioneer period. John Bartlow Martin provides a vivid, but brief, description of that time:

> Even after the Indians were gone, pioneering was a life of few comforts, rare pleasure, great drudgery, much sickness. Roads were few, impassable morasses in winter, choked with dust in summer. Ill fortune dogged the settler's every pursuit. . . . After the trees were cut and the cabin built and the brush cleared and the stumps uprooted and the rails split, and the rail fence built and, at long last, the earth broken with the plow and the first crop gathered, a land speculator would turn up and prove that he owned the title.[2]

At the time, there were virtually no railroads. Later, as the population grew and rail lines were extended, McLean received an annual railroad pass, but in 1837 the mode of travel was horse or coach. Pulitzer Prize–winning historian R. C. Buley, while painting a somewhat romanticized picture of circuit riding, still conveys the gist of what must have been an arduous job:

> Judges and lawyers on circuit carried their libraries in their saddlebags, plenty of anecdotes and jokes in their heads. Jogging along in the mud, they practiced stump speeches on each other, held

> moot courts, imitated preachers, and at least once rested their horses while they tried a 'possum for trespass on a public highway. Lawyers in general had a reputation of being heavy drinkers, but since this was true of other vocational groups also, the charge may be dismissed.[3]

So why did Supreme Court justices come to Indiana as circuit riders? Article III of the Constitution of the United States gives only the briefest sketch of what the new federal judiciary should look like. It speaks only of a Supreme Court and leaves the number of justices to the discretion of Congress, as it does the creation of so-called inferior courts.

The Senate committee that considered the Judiciary Act of 1789 borrowed the idea of circuits from the British practice of sending judges of the central courts at Westminster to conduct jury trials throughout the country. States already had experimented with traveling judges. William Paterson, a key member of the Constitutional Convention that fashioned Article III and of the Senate that adopted the Judiciary Act, stated that the essential idea was for the people to have "law to their Homes, to their very Doors!" Another key member, Roger Sherman, also a senator in 1789, said, "Judges can acquire a knowledge of the rights of the people of these states much better by riding the circuit, than by staying at home reading British and other foreign Laws."[4]

So the First Congress in 1789 put some meat on these bare constitutional bones. In addition to establishing a Supreme Court, it created a separate circuit court federal judiciary. Congress originally required Supreme Court justices to ride circuit twice a year but soon modified the practice to once a year.

The early federal circuit courts were courts of original jurisdiction, so circuit riding placed the Supreme Court justices directly at the trial of most of the earliest federal cases. For example, Congress vested the circuit courts with exclusive jurisdiction in all criminal matters involving violation of federal statutes. But more important was the belief that circuit riding by Supreme Court justices would keep them in touch with local communities and would bring home to the people in every state a sense of the national judicial power through their presence. One technique for making this connection was the judge's charge to the grand jury, which was widely circulated in early newspapers.

There was a strong feeling that favorable public opinion was necessary to ensure the survival of the young republic and that the visible presence of justices would help foster loyalty to the new form of government. As a member of the U.S. House of Representatives, James Buchanan, of Pennsylvania, later the fifteenth president, argued strongly in favor of the circuit-riding provision. He said, "If the Supreme Court should ever become a political tribunal, it will not be until the judges shall be settled in Washington, far removed from the people, and within the immediate influence of the power and patronage of the executive."[5]

When Indiana became a state in 1816, Benjamin Parke was the sole U.S. district court judge and, at the time, he was the sole representative of the federal courts in Indiana, inasmuch as no Supreme Court justice had been assigned to the state. That changed in 1837, when, at the very end of the second administration of Andrew Jackson, the Congress again turned its attention to the federal judiciary. It first added two members to the Supreme Court, then at seven, raising the number to nine. Congress also created nine federal circuits; the two new ones were in the West and Southwest. Eight states, including Indiana, were added to the circuit system, and it was the duty of each Supreme Court justice to ride circuit at least once per year for each district within a circuit.[6] Thus, Justice John McLean came to Indiana on circuit for the first time in 1837 under that mandate.

Before becoming a Supreme Court justice, McLean had sat briefly on the Ohio Supreme Court, served a term in the U.S. House of Representatives at the outset of the War of 1812, and acted as the postmaster general during the entirety of the administrations of James Monroe and John Quincy Adams. By the time Andrew Jackson was elected president in 1828, the post office system had acquired an extensive patronage system, which the new president wanted for his own supporters. Some believe that Jackson appointed McLean as a political maneuver. A recent biographer of John Marshall has ably put McLean's appointment in historical context:

> Two days after the inauguration, Jackson startled his more clamorous supporters by nominating John McLean of Ohio to fill Trimble's seat on the Court. McLean was a moderate Whig who . . . had remained on good terms with Jackson throughout the 1828 campaign, and it was widely believed that he harbored presidential ambitions four years hence. He was also known to be opposed to the political spoils system. So long as he remained in the cabinet, it would be impossible to restaff the post office with reliable Democrats. By elevating McLean, Jackson demonstrated the adroitness

> that made him so formidable. With one stroke, he was shelving a potential presidential opponent, opening the post office to his supporters, rewarding a foe of his old enemy Henry Clay, and disarming the Whigs with a judicial appointment they could only applaud.[7]

Early in December 1837, Justice McLean arrived in Indianapolis to hold federal circuit court. It was the beginning of many travels to the state. Annually he traveled twenty-five hundred miles through Illinois, Indiana, Michigan, and Ohio. At the time and throughout the tenure of Chief Justice Roger B. Taney, members of the Supreme Court spent more than half their time traveling and attending to their circuit duties.

When McLean came to Indiana, the state was in building boom, constructing canals and other public improvements. This was part of the Whig program of internal improvements at federal expense expounded by Henry Clay and others under the so-called American system. One of the products of this effort was the White Water Valley Canal in southeastern Indiana, and a case handled by Justice McLean dealt with an injunction and a request for a receiver for this project.[8] By 1847, the bubble had burst on most of the canal projects—the state had declared bankruptcy in 1837 because of its debts incurred to finance canals—and their political attractiveness had disappeared.

In this period, there also remained serious legal disputes with regard to the title to real estate. In a case involving early conveyances that purported to be from the town of Clarksville, Indiana, Justice McLean rejected deeds dating from 1794 and 1817 on what would appear to be somewhat technical grounds (such as failure to prove that the clerk acknowledging the deed was in fact clerk at the time).[9] Ownership of land was at the heart of frontier development, and land titles presented problems so widespread and weighty that even federal circuit justices were drawn into their resolution.

In 1849, Justice McLean presided in a trademark case about a medicine called "Chinese Liniment," which was sold in small bottles with a label. Patent medicines were an important aspect of the culture, and disputes regarding them often found their way into federal court.[10] The manufacturer of Chinese Liniment contended that the manufacturer of a similar product, "Ohio Liniment," had infringed his trademark. McLean's decision has a modern ring to it. He basically said that, where the same mark or label is used, which recommends the article to the public by the established reputation of another who sells a similar article, and the spurious article cannot be distinguished from the genuine one, the courts will grant an injunction even though there was no intentional fraud.[11]

During the pre–Civil War period, the sale of public lands in Indiana remained a significant federal activity, and the federal Land Office handling those sales was in Crawfordsville. In 1845, a case came before the federal circuit court involving the U.S. marshal for the District of Indiana and a receiver in the Land Office in Crawfordsville. The plaintiff alleged that the receiver had engaged in defalcation, misappropriation, or failure to account for funds that had come into his hands as a fiduciary. As a result, the marshal seized goods, chattels, lands, and tenements that belonged to the receiver under a warrant issued by the solicitor in the U.S. Treasury Department. This warrant was a version of Treasury Department warrants created under an act of Congress of May 25, 1820, which authorized the procedure in question, especially the provision dealing with certain federal officers who received money prior to its payment into the U.S. Treasury.

McLean looked carefully at the authority of the federal judiciary under Article III and at the Seventh Amendment with regard to trial by jury. He upheld the actions taken to recover monies due the Treasury Department, but expressed concerns that the statute in question might have done an end run around the Seventh Amendment's protection of civil jury trials. In fact, he decided to disagree and to certify the case to the Supreme Court of the United States; but that certification was never completed, and the Supreme Court never acted on the issue. This case involved more than $40,000, a goodly sum at the time. Disputes of this sort in the modern era usually center on Treasury Department and Internal Revenue Service procedures involving federal tax liens.[12]

Much of Justice McLean's circuit work involved fugitive slave issues under Article IV, Section 2, Clause 3, of the federal Constitution and the Fugitive Slave Acts of 1793 and 1850. In 1840, McLean heard a case in which the facts were a mirror image of those in the later *Dred Scott* case, but in which he reached an opposite decision.[13] The owner of a slave family consisting of Sam, Mariah, and their son Hendrick moved himself and the slaves from Kentucky, a slave state, into Illinois, a free state. Their owner kept the group in Illinois for an extended period and then moved them to Missouri, a slave state. The slaves escaped, ending up in Hamilton County, Indiana. The alleged owner came to Indiana to reclaim his property and ran into a legal buzz saw before McLean on the federal circuit court. McLean held a jury trial on the issue, and the legal conclusion is captured in a single sentence:

> Having been brought to the state of Illinois, which prohibits slavery, by their master, from the state of Kentucky, and kept at labor for six months, under a declaration of the master that he intended to become a citizen of that state, and who actually exercised the rights of a citizen by voting, there can be no doubt that the slaves were, thereby, entitled to their freedom.[14]

Sam, Mariah, and their child remained free in Indiana. Years later, McLean continued to subscribe to this rationale and was one of the two dissenters in *Dred Scott* in 1857.

In 1849, Justice McLean dealt with another family of runaway slaves from Kentucky. There were five members of the family, Caroline and her four children—Francis, John, Amanda, and Henry. In October 1847, they escaped from Kemble County, Kentucky, where they had been owned by a man named Ray. The next day, they were discovered near Clarksburgh, Indiana, where a man named Clark took them into his house and secreted them. Clark claimed he had sent a messenger to Ray, although Ray disputed it. The next day, Caroline and her family escaped.

Ray sued Clark in federal court for concealing Carolyn and her family and for helping them escape. He sought compensation for the value of the slaves, not the penalty provided for in the Fugitive Slave Act of 1793. The issue was whether the party sued was involved in removing the fugitives or aiding in removing them. Following a jury verdict against Clark, McLean awarded Ray $1,500 in damages as permitted under the 1793 act, which provided a $500 penalty against one who secreted a fugitive from labor, that is, a slave.

Justice McLean was obviously perplexed in this pre–Civil War opinion. He described the debate over slavery as "an exciting topic" and argued that the power to establish slavery should not belong to the federal government. He stated, nevertheless, that it was the right of a state to establish slavery and further opined that he must follow the mandates of the constitutional provision in Article IV of the federal Constitution:

> we must stand firmly by the principles of the Constitution and maintain the rights secured by it, to citizens of the states respectively and, whatever may be the excitement and turmoil in other places we must here act calmly and deliberately, free from all influences which do not arise from the facts and the law in the case.[15]

In 1850, McLean confronted another Indiana runaway slave case, *Norris v. Newton*.[16] This time, however, he came out on the other side. Although the manner in which he handled the *Norris* case in the circuit court seems to belie his private antislavery convictions, he was constrained to follow a U.S. Supreme Court precedent, *Prigg v. Pennsylvania* (1842), that basically federalized the fugitive slave recovery process.[17] Even though McLean himself had dissented in *Prigg*, he was bound by its precedent.

Norris owned a relatively small farm with a few slaves on the Kentucky side of the Ohio River near Lawrenceburg, Indiana. His slaves included the Powell family, consisting of a husband, wife, and two young sons. Apparently, Norris was lenient and permitted the family to sell produce from their garden across the Ohio River in Indiana. One night, they disappeared into the southern Indiana wilderness. Norris looked for them extensively. Approximately two years passed before Norris learned that they had moved to a location just across the Indiana state line in Michigan, north of South Bend, and had been able to purchase and tend a small tract of land there. Norris and seven armed compatriots raided the Powell home and took the family as prisoners, intending to return them to Kentucky. The posse got only as far as South Bend, where an abolitionist lawyer, Edwin Crocker, intervened and obtained an order from a local judge preventing the Powells from being returned to slavery in Kentucky. Norris stormed back to Kentucky, threatening to sue all who had participated in this antislavery exercise, including Crocker, the local judge named Egbert, the local sheriff, and a good number of other people who acted as witnesses or ran interference for the Powell family.

Norris filed a series of damage lawsuits against Crocker and others in the U.S. circuit court in Indianapolis. In an extended and convoluted series of proceedings, including a trial by jury, a technical question arose with regard to the applicability of some provisions of the 1850 Fugitive Slave Act that conflicted with the Fugitive Slave Act of 1793. The case attracted a number of the prominent Hoosier lawyers, including Oliver Hampton Smith, who had served in both branches of the Congress and wrote one of the early descriptions of lawyers, courts, and law practice in antebellum Indiana. The case finally made its way to the Supreme Court of the United States. There, the interest of the Powell family was argued in the Supreme Court by then Ohio's U.S. senator, Salmon Portland Chase, later chief justice of the United States. The Court issued a narrow, technical decision permitting the Powell family to remain free.[18]

In the 1850s, a significant expansion of rail facilities took place in Indiana. It is therefore not surprising that, in 1857, Justice McLean received a case involving the railroad being constructed between New Albany on the Ohio River and Michigan City on Lake Michigan. In dispute was a forty-three-mile section of the line from Gosport to Indianapolis. The railroad company had borrowed $500,000, secured by bonds of $1,000 each payable semiannually in New York City at 10 percent. It could not pay or, at least, did not, and the bonds came due. The facts reflect some very interesting economic history. The estimated cost of this trans-Indiana railroad at the time was approximately $16 million, but substantially less than that had been expended. The entire length of the road was 288 miles, which had been built for $7.5 million. In many ways, the case was simply a huge debt collection involving the infant railroad industry. A receiver was appointed, a practice that was commonplace then and afterward in similar litigation.[19] This type of case became a growth cottage industry of railroad litigation for several decades.[20]

By 1856, McLean had disposed of more cases than the five southern circuits combined. As Carl B. Swisher, a leading twentieth-century historian of the Supreme Court, noted, "Justice McLean's circuit had grown into an empire, and was too large for one judge to give more than nominal attendance."[21]

But this heavy work load did not keep McLean from engaging in presidential politics while in Indiana. The justice often engaged in extensive socialization while on circuit in aid of his presidential ambitions.

Of course, McLean also participated in important Indiana cases while sitting in Washington. One of the most dramatic involved land granted by Congress to Vincennes University in 1806 and 1807. While Indiana was a territory, Congress had granted some twenty thousand acres for the creation of a seat of higher learning, which became Vincennes University. After statehood, the legislature decided to direct some remaining part of the Vincennes land grant to the purpose of sustaining the new state university at Bloomington. Ruling for the Vincennes trustees, McLean wrote that the congressional grant count not be countermanded by the Indiana General Assembly.

Presidents from Jackson through Buchanan populated the Supreme Court with slave-owning southerners or so-called doe-faced northerners (northerners with southern views on slavery). Jackson's appointment of

McLean and Millard Fillmore's appointment of Benjamin Curtis are exceptions. Both dissented in the *Dred Scott* case. McLean died in 1861, giving Lincoln one of his five appointments to the Supreme Court. In addition to his central role in railroad and slavery cases, McLean's prodigious record while riding circuit in Indiana demonstrated that this work did indeed keep justices close to the local scene, even the political scene.

War and Dissent

In *Lincoln's Supreme Court,* David Silver has a chapter entitled "Dual-Role Justices," in which he spells out the very important activities of justices on circuit during the Civil War. He observes that "a number of the justices—Davis, Miller, Field, and Grier—not only were very energetic in holding circuit court during the war, but delivered a large number of important written opinions as well. It is these written opinions that give insight into their feelings on numerous war-related subjects, many of which did not come before the Supreme Court itself."[22]

The first justice on Silver's list, David Davis, of Illinois, followed McLean as circuit justice. He was, by his physical presence and personality, considerably different. Davis had attended Kenyon College in Ohio and the law department of Yale University. He had been a lawyer and then a state trial judge in the Eighth Circuit in central Illinois. He became a wealthy landowner with hundred of acres of rich farmland in the area of Bloomington. He was a huge man, standing well more than six feet tall and weighing more than three hundred pounds. It often was said when he purchased a suit of clothes that they didn't measure him—they surveyed him![23] For a decade, he was the presiding trial judge on a state court circuit in central Illinois where Abraham Lincoln and Stephen A. Douglas practiced regularly. He became a close friend of Lincoln, and Lincoln passed over a number of other highly qualified prospects to appoint Davis directly from a state trial court to the Supreme Court of the United States. He was the only justice ever to make that trip directly.

Davis was personally and politically loyal to Lincoln, but his closeness to the president did not keep him from having serious reservations about some wartime practices and policies. He apparently had harbored such reservations as early as 1863, when he first came to Indianapolis to hold circuit court in both May and November, and on another circuit visit in 1864, when he sat with U.S. district court judge Caleb B. Smith, a Hoosier who had served earlier as secretary of the interior in Lincoln's cabinet. Davis had some difficulty with an order of General Ambrose E. Burnside in June 1863 that suspended the publication of the *Chicago Times.* U.S. district court judge Thomas Drummond granted an injunction against that military action, a decision that Judge Davis indicated that he fully supported.

While serving in Indiana, Davis confronted issues regarding antiwar activities. These were difficult cases, but his experiences as a trial judge served him well while riding the circuit. This is evident by the very first grand jury instructions he gave in Indianapolis:

> Gentlemen of the Grand Jury: We meet in a time of great national peril—in the midst of a war, unexampled for its time of its wickedness and magnitude. . . . Our own honor—the treasure that has been spent—the blood that has been shed—the memories of the past, and the hopes of the future *demand* that this rebellion shall be crushed, the union of these States restored, and the authority of law recognized. . . . We may, and will differ, in any great war, on the right manner of conducting it, and the wisdom of the policy pursued, but no man, who is not a traitor at heart, will ever suffer that difference to lead him by speech or writing to counsel resistance to law. . . . It is charged that there are secret organizations . . . with "grips, signs and passwords" having for their objects—resistance to Law, and the overthrow of the Government. . . . If anywhere in this State bad men have combined together for such wicked purposes, I pray you, bring them to light and let them receive the punishment due to their crime.[24]

Riding the circuit led to a strange procedure once the justices returned to the Supreme Court bench. After the justices had made decisions on circuit, they were still allowed to participate in the final review of those same decisions on the Supreme Court bench. This is precisely what Justice Davis did in *Ex parte Milligan.*[25]

Lambdin P. Milligan was not a member of the military. He lived in the far northern part of Indiana, which was not in a war zone. In Fort Wayne, before a large crowd, he advocated violent resistance to the Conscription Act of 1863. The federal government charged him with a civilian offense that normally would have triggered the right to a trial by jury, as mandated by Article III and the Sixth Amendment of the U.S. Constitution. He received no such trial. Instead, Milligan was tried for sedition before a twelve-member military commission late in 1864.

The prosecutor invoked this procedure pursuant to a string of legislation created in response to the Civil War. Early in the war, when Congress was not in session, Lincoln suspended the writ of habeas corpus in Maryland in the face of an actual secession movement and pro-Confederate military activities in the state. Under Lincoln's suspension of habeas corpus, the military arrested John Merryman and incarcerated him at Fort McHenry. Merryman had been organizing soldiers to fight for the Confederacy and been involved in the sabotage of bridges. Chief Justice Roger Taney, on circuit, granted a writ of habeas corpus that General George Cadwallader, who was in command of troops at Fort McHenry, refused to obey. Taney then issued a scathing opinion attacking the Lincoln administration for ignoring his writ, a decision that Lincoln ignored. Later, Congress passed the Habeas Corpus Act in 1863. It appeared to authorize such suspension of the writ but did not specifically authorize trials by military commissions. In fact, it envisioned the continuing function of federal grand juries. Under that statute, Major General Alvin P. Hovey, commander of the Union Army in Indiana, issued Special Order 129 on September 17, 1864, creating the military commission before which Milligan and others were tried later that year.

The constitutionality of trying civilians by military tribunal came before the U.S. circuit court, consisting of Justice David Davis and Judge David McDonald, when Lambdin P. Milligan brought an action for habeas corpus after he had been convicted and sentenced by the military commission for subversive activities. The circuit court heard the case in October 1864, when the outcome of the war still was in doubt.

Some earlier decisions by Davis suggested what direction his judicial compass might take in *Milligan*. In March 1863, four deserters had been arrested in Charleston, Illinois. The local Democratic judge, Charles Constable, released the deserters and held those who had arrested them as kidnappers. A Union army unit from Indiana surrounded the Coles County (Illinois) Courthouse, arrested Judge Constable, and took him to Indiana as a federal military prisoner. The federal court there released the judge, who returned to hold court in Charleston. Soon there was a clash between Union soldiers and the Knights of the Golden Circle, an anti-Union secret society, in which several people were killed. There were more military arrests. Lincoln asked Judge Davis for advice, and Davis recommended that the prisoners be turned over to civil authorities. Lincoln acted accordingly, and none of the prisoners was convicted.

Other evidence comes from a late nineteenth-century biography of Oliver P. Morton, Indiana's Civil War governor. While riding on circuit in Indianapolis, David Davis went for a Sunday buggy ride with the governor, whom he had known earlier through politics.[26] Morton supported the trial of civilians before military commissions to put down what he perceived as acts of sedition. Davis asserted his feelings that the trial of civilians before military commissions for civilian offenses, when the state courts were open and operating, was a violation of the U.S. Constitution. It's not totally clear what Morton's immediate response was to Davis on this buggy ride, but he did soon write urging then President Andrew Johnson to commute the death sentences imposed by the commission.

In the *Milligan* case, Judge McDonald took the view that the military commission and its activities regarding Lambdin P. Milligan did not violate the Constitution. Davis took the contrary view. Under the prevailing statute, such disagreement between the two federal circuit judges was enough to remove the case to the U.S. Supreme Court,[27] where Davis wrote the principal majority opinion that generally is cited in *Ex parte Milligan,* with Chief Justice Salmon P. Chase concurring, though more narrowly. The Supreme Court was unanimous in finding that Milligan should be released from the state prison in Ohio, where he had been held pending his execution. It was by far the most expansive and important opinion written by Justice Davis. He recognized the importance of this decision: "No greater question was ever considered by this court," he wrote, "nor one which more nearly concerns the right of the whole people." Davis offered a plain statement of the value of the rule of law and the role of courts in it: "By the protection of the law human rights are secured; withdraw that protection, and they are at the mercy of wicked rulers, or the clamor of an excited people. If there was law to justify this military trial, it is not our province to interfere; if there was not, it is our duty to declare the nullity of the whole proceedings."[28]

Parallel with the problems of *Milligan* in Indiana were those involving Clement L. Vallandigham, a leader of the antiwar movement in Ohio. Justice Davis had been involved in the Ohio proceedings surrounding General Burnside's arrest of Vallandigham. Cases like *Milligan* and *Vallandigham* posed special challenges for people like Indiana's two Democratic Party leaders, Thomas A. Hendricks and Daniel W. Voorhees. Hendricks, later governor, and Voorhees, a Democratic congressman from western Indiana who later served a lengthy postwar tenure in the U.S. Senate, had to walk a tightrope between opposing the war and facing accusations of disloyalty. After Justice Davis had been involved in the Vallandigham proceedings in Ohio, he came to Indianapolis to hold federal court. His biographer records the following event: "At dinner that night, the Judge, at the head table, called to Daniel W. Voorhees, who was collaborating with Vallandigham: 'Voorhees, you had better look out. They have got down to the Vs.'"[29]

Davis's opinion in *Milligan* largely overshadowed his other activities as a circuit justice. He heard many other interesting cases, including two on patents. In the first case, he invalidated an Indiana law that required patent holders to file a copy of the patent with an Indiana clerk and sign an affidavit of ownership before selling or even offering to sell a patent.[30] Davis held that this law was preempted by the Patent Act of 1836. Later, in 1872, he had to determine whether an invention that allowed guards to bolt prison doors while keeping the guards from coming into contact with prisoners infringed a patent on another device with a similar purpose but a different design.[31]

In 1877, Davis resigned from the Supreme Court and served one term as the U.S. senator from Illinois. He had abandoned the Republican Party by then and served as an Independent throughout the remainder of his career in the Senate. He more than filled the chairs of the Senate chamber; as Benjamin Harrison's biographer noted, "Judge David Davis . . . had difficulty squeezing into the largest armchair in the chamber."[32] (Harrison was senator from Indiana at that time.) Later, as president pro tempore of the Senate (1881–83), David Davis was literally a heartbeat away from the presidency while President Chester Alan Arthur was quite ill.[33]

Rebuilding and Expansion

The third and last justice to ride circuit in Indiana was John Marshall Harlan, of Kentucky, who succeeded Davis both on the Supreme Court and as circuit justice. He served from 1877 to 1911 and was considered a real workhorse. The circuit boundaries he inherited in 1877 reflected the present-day arrangement: Indiana, Illinois, and Wisconsin.

The first Harlan—his grandson John Marshall Harlan II was an associate justice of the Supreme Court from 1955 to 1977—was one of the greatest justices in the entire history of the Court. Before 1860, Harlan was a Kentucky Whig. He and his family were very small slave owners for a time. In the 1860 election, he supported John Bell, of Tennessee, candidate of the Constitutional Union Party, which was the home of the viable remnants of the die-hard Whigs. He served briefly as a Union army officer, but resigned when his father died in 1863. In 1864, Harlan again supported another candidate over Abraham Lincoln, this time backing General George B. McClellan for president. Immediately following the Civil War, he opposed the adoption of the Thirteenth and Fourteenth Amendments.

In the 1870s, he practiced law in Kentucky and served as attorney general, elected to that post as a Republican. He argued a major church property case involving a schism in the Presbyterian Church before the U.S. Supreme Court.[34] He was a key person in the nomination of Rutherford B. Hayes for president at the Republican National Convention in 1876. Accordingly, when Justice Davis resigned, Hayes immediately had a nomination for the Supreme Court and he appointed Harlan.

Harlan regularly came to Indianapolis to hold court, and, of course, also sat in Springfield and Chicago, Illinois. It appears that he also held court at least on occasion in Evansville, which was closer to his home in Harrodsburg, Kentucky. He heard a number of important election cases. Walter Quinton Gresham was the U.S. district judge in Indiana at that time, having been appointed to the post by President Ulysses S. Grant in 1868.

The Indiana that Justice Harlan observed around 1880 was vastly different from the one Justice McLean witnessed in 1850. Indiana historian Emma Lou Thornbrough captures the essence of these changes in a few sentences:

> At mid-century Indiana was at the threshold of a revolution in transportation. . . . In 1850 there were only about two hundred miles of complete track in the state. By 1880 there was a network of over four thousand miles, reaching into almost every county and connecting Indiana with both the east and west coast. Railroads brought new settlers, broke down rural isolation, transformed villages into cities, brought far-reaching changes in agriculture and everyday life, and hastened the beginnings of mining and industry. Railroad corporations wielded great political power and successfully sought favors from government. After a few years a clamor for government regulation developed.[35]

Moreover, Indiana's population doubled between 1850 and 1880, from nearly a million to nearly two million, and industrialization was beginning to challenge agriculture for primacy in the state's economy.

In the post–Civil War period, the economic importance of the railroad industry was reflected on the docket of the federal courts in Indiana. Much tort law, creditor-debtor law, and insolvency law grew up in litigation surrounding the railroad interests. One of the key Indiana cases handled by Justice Harlan involved a number of railroads represented by prominent lawyers.[36] The lawyers included two former governors of Indiana, Conrad Baker and Thomas A Hendricks. Hendricks later became a senator and vice president of the United States. The lawyers in the case also included William Evarts, who had been secretary of state and a U.S. senator, and Joseph H. Choate, one of the great lawyers of the time. Justice Harlan waded into this highly complex dispute and wrote what was, literally, a textbook regarding railroad finance, upholding the validity of a railroad lease upon which more than $15 million of financing was based. This case came as the railroad industry was recovering from the effects of a huge, massive labor strike in the 1870s.

Harlan also dealt with a federal election fraud case involving a clerk named Simeon Coy, of Indianapolis. The case attracted widespread attention. Simeon Coy was charged in the U.S. district court in Indiana with a conspiracy to induce election inspectors to give their tally sheets to someone else for counting of the votes in a contest for criminal judge in Marion County, Indiana. There was no charge that Coy had interfered in the election of federal officials, although a candidate for U.S. House of Representatives was also on the ballot. When the case first came to the federal circuit court on appeal of a district court interpretation of the statute, Judge Walter Q. Gresham ruled that, because only the state election was concerned, federal courts had no jurisdiction. Soon thereafter, U.S. district court judge William A. Woods, who had just been appointed to the federal bench in Indiana, ruled otherwise on a similar but legally different question, and Coy was tried and convicted. Coy filed a petition for habeas corpus. Acting on circuit, Harlan issued an extended opinion denying the habeas petition and upholding Coy's conviction.[37] Senator Daniel W. Voorhees and a cocounsel named McNutt took the appeal to the Supreme Court, and the Supreme Court affirmed.[38]

The decision regarding Coy, who was a Democrat, came back to challenge both Judge Woods and Justice Harlan in a case that involved the aftermath of the 1888 election, in which Benjamin Harrison narrowly was elected president (with a minority of the popular vote). The matter became known as the Blocks of Five case. It grew out of a letter said to have been written by W. W. Dudley, treasurer of the National Republican Committee. Dudley's letter proposed that Indiana Republicans "divide the floaters into blocks of five, and put a trusted man with necessary funds in charge of these five and make him responsible that none get away and that all vote our ticket." After Harrison became president, the U.S. attorney in Indiana brought an indictment, which involved a considerable interplay between Judge Woods and Justice Harlan. No one was ever tried on this indictment, although there was considerable consternation and correspondence passing between Justice Harlan and Judge Woods because of Woods's ruling that attempts at bribery, as opposed to acts of bribery, were not indictable under federal law.

In the middle of the controversy, a vacancy occurred in the office of the U.S. attorney, and, in that time under those circumstances, Justice Harlan had the appointive power and selected Judge Solomon Claypool, a Democrat.[39] Eventually, real warfare broke out between Woods and Claypool. Woods basically instructed a grand jury that no indictment could issue against Dudley. Although it was out of character, Harlan equivocated on this question. He first thought that an indictment was appropriate and later changed his mind "reluctantly." This put him on the same page as Judge Woods. Woods later sued Claypool for libel, but Justice Harlan refused to allow his letters to Woods be used, saying, "It has often occurred in my judicial life that subsequent investigation has shown me that my first impression as to a legal question was wrong."[40] Harlan's biographer speculates that a heavy dose of political partisanship entered into his decision and basically excuses it by saying that it was a period of "partisan excess" in which party loyalty overcame scruples. Thus the precedent established in *Coy* was avoided.

The interrelationship between state and federal law is always grist for the litigation mill. An 1881 case involving the Evansville National Bank demonstrates this point. Under a federal law that permitted states to tax national bank shares—but only as long as they were not taxed to a level greater than that of other investments—an Indiana law levied taxes on national bank shares without allowing a deduction for the shareholder's debts, even though it allowed such a deduction for other moneyed capital. The federal court, speaking through Justice Harlan, held that the Indiana law imposed greater burdens on national bank shares that on other investments and found the Indiana law unconstitutional.[41]

The Judiciary Act of 1789 and its several modifications, changes and amendments included a habeas corpus remedy only for prisoners and persons held in *federal* custody. Before the Civil War, only a relatively small number of people fit this category. The greater number by far was held in state custody under state law. The 1867 habeas corpus act created a federal remedy in federal courts for state prisoners and persons held in state custody who claimed their *federal* constitutional rights were being violated. From that day until this, one of the most important functions of U.S. districts courts has been to hear petitions for habeas corpus relief by state prisoners. It represents a mammoth part of the dockets of U.S. district courts. It commenced while David Davis was the circuit justice in Indiana and became more important during the tenure of John Marshall Harlan I.

Each of the three Supreme Court justices who rode the federal circuit in Indiana had a moment of brilliance that must be remembered, although only one such moment had an Indiana connection. John McLean joined Justice Benjamin Curtis in an extended masterful dissent in *Dred Scott*. David Davis authored a majority opinion in *Ex parte Milligan* that remains viable to this day and has come back to the front burner of attention. Justice Harlan wrote a far-sighted dissent in *Plessy v. Ferguson*,[42] stating that the Constitution of the United States was color blind.

The Founders who wrote Article III of the Constitution, as well as the Judiciary Act of 1789, believed that it was important for the nation to feel the presence of both the Supreme Court of the United States and its members. The process of circuit riding was an arduous one, and most of the early Supreme Court justices disliked it intensely and complained about it loudly.

In the post–Civil War period, the work load of the Supreme Court had become inordinately difficult to manage. This created the push for creation of permanent intermediate federal appeals courts, culminating in the Evarts Act of 1891, which was signed into law by President Benjamin Harrison. The three Supreme Court justices who came to Indiana throughout a major portion of the nineteenth century handled their judicial tasks here with competence and with diligence. They certainly fulfilled the aspiration of the Founders to mingle among the local lawyers and litigants in carrying out the federal judicial functions.

These remarkable men came to Indiana to conduct federal circuit court between 1837 and 1891. In spite of outward personality differences, they had much in common. Each had been a Whig and became a Republican, and also flirted with minor parties including Free Soil, Know-nothing, and Labor. Davis eventually left the Republican Party. One thirsted for the presidency, and all at one time were deeply involved with presidential politics. One literally secured the presidential nomination of Abraham Lincoln in Chicago in 1860 and ended his public career a heartbeat from that office, remaining president pro tempore of the U.S. Senate. Each was a highly competent professional who understood what happened in trial courtrooms. The Founders' idea of having the federal judiciary represented in the center of the nation was well served when John McLean, David Davis, and John Marshall Harlan I came to Indiana.

Notes

1. Joshua Glick, "On the Road: The Supreme Court and the History of Circuit Riding," *Cardozo Law Review* 24 (April 2003): 1753, 1806.

2. John Bartlow Martin, *Indiana: An Interpretation* (New York: Knopf, 1947; repr. Bloomington: Indiana University Press, 1992), 33–34.

3. R. Carlyle Buley, *The Old Northwest Pioneer Period, 1815–1840* (Indianapolis: Indiana Historical Society, 1950), 2:573. This book was awarded the Pulitzer Prize in History in 1950.

4. Henry J. Bourguignon, "The Federal Key to the Judiciary Act of 1789," *South Carolina Law Review* 46 (1994–95): 647, 690–91.

5. 2 Reg. Deb. 931, 932 (1826). Also recorded in Glick, "On the Road," 1800.

6. Carl. B. Swisher, *The Taney Period, 1836–64*, vol. 5 of History of the Supreme Court of the United States (New York: Macmillan, 1974), 248–74.

7. Jean Edward Smith, *John Marshall: Definer of a Nation* (New York: H. Holt, 1996), 503.

8. Vallette v. Whitewater Valley Canal Co., 28 F. Cas. 926 (C.C.D. Ind. 1847) (No. 16,820).

9. Wallace v. Dewey, 29 F. Cas. 74 (C.C.D. Ind. 1845) (No. 17,099).

10. Buley, *Old Northwest*, 1:240–314.

11. Coffeen v. Brunton, 5 F. Cas. 1184 (C.C.D. Ind. 1849) (No. 2,946).

12. U.S. v. Taylor, 28 F. Cas. 24 (C.C.D. Ind. 1845) (No. 16,440).

13. Scott v. Sandford, 60 U.S. (19 How.) 393 (1857).

14. Vaughan v. Williams, 28 F. Cas. 1115 (C.C.D. Ind. 1840) (No. 16,903). This case and the whole issue of slave transit are discussed in Paul Finkelman, *An Imperfect Union: Slavery, Federalism, and Comity* (Chapel Hill: University of North Carolina Press, 1981).

15. Ray v. Donnell, 20 F. Cas. 325 (C.C.D. Ind. 1849) (No. 11,590).

16. Norris v. Newton, 18 F. Cas. 322 (C.C.D. Ind. 1850) (No. 10,307). See also Allen

Sharp, "Free at Last: How the Powell Fugitive Slave Family Became and Stayed Free," *Supreme Court Historical Society Quarterly* 17, no. 1 (1996): 7–19; and Allen Sharp, "The Transcontinental Career of Edwin Crocker," *Traces of Indiana and Midwestern History* 9 (Fall 1997): 23–29. Also see Paul Finkelman, "Fugitive Slaves, Midwestern Racial Tolerance, and the Value of 'Justice Delayed,'" 78 *Iowa Law Review* (October 1992): 89–144.

17. Prigg v. Pennsylvania, 41 U.S. (16 Pet.) 539 (1842). Also see Paul Finkelman, "Story Telling on the Supreme Court: *Prigg v. Pennsylvania* and Justice Joseph Story's Judicial Nationalism," *Supreme Court Review* (1994): 247–94.

18. The case actually went to the U.S. Supreme Court on the narrow issue of whether Norris could sue for a $500 penalty under the Fugitive Slave Act of 1793, which had been superseded by the 1850 law while the case was being litigated. See Finkelman, "Fugitive Slaves."

19. Williamson v. New Albany R. Co., 30 F. Cas. 12 (C.C.D. Ind. 1857) (No. 17,753).

20. A comprehensive view is found in James W. Ely Jr., *Railroads and American Law* (Lawrence: University Press of Kansas, 2001).

21. Swisher, *Supreme Court,* 823. See also 47.

22. David M. Silver, *Lincoln's Supreme Court* (Urbana: University of Illinois Press, 1956), 167–84.

23. Willard L. King, *Lincoln's Manager, David Davis* (Cambridge, Mass.: Harvard University Press, 1960), 210.

24. Ibid.

25. Ex parte Milligan, 71 U.S. (4 Wall.) 2 (1866).

26. William Dudley Foulke, *The Life of Oliver P. Morton, Including His Important Speeches* (Indianapolis: Bowen-Merrill, 1899), 428.

27. Under the Circuit Court Act of 1802 (2 Stat. 156), district judges also rode circuit with the Supreme Court justice assigned to a state; thus McDonald and Davis constituted the federal circuit court for Indiana.

28. Ex parte Milligan, 71 U.S. at 118–19.

29. King, *Lincoln's Manager,* 210.

30. Ex parte Robinson, 20 F. Cas. 961 (C.C.D. Ind. 1870) (No. 11,932).

31. May v. Johnson County, 16 F. Cas. 1218 (C.C.D. Ind. 1872) (No. 9,334).

32. Harry J. Sievers, *Benjamin Harrison: Hoosier Statesman* (Newtown, Conn.: American Political Biography Press, 1959), 202.

33. The 1792 law delineating presidential succession to the president pro tempore of the Senate was still in effect during this period. See 1 Stat. 239 (1792).

34. Watson v. Jones, 80 U.S. (13 Wall.) 679 (1872).

35. Emma Lou Thornbrough, *Indiana in the Civil War Era, 1850–1880* (Indianapolis: Indiana Historical Bureau, 1965), 318.

36. Pittsburg C. & St. L. Ry. Co. v. Columbus C. & I. C. Ry. Co., 19 F. Cas. 772 (C.C.D. Ind. 1879) (No. 11,197).

37. In re Coy, 31 F. 794 (1887).

38. Ex parte Coy, 127 U.S. 731 (1888).

39. It is unclear how Harlan could appoint the U.S. attorney, normally an executive prerogative. But he used this language several times in a letter to Dudley, for

example, "I must appoint a Democrat of acknowledged integrity." Quoted in Loren P. Beth, *John Marshall Harlan: The Last Whig Justice* (Lexington: University Press of Kentucky, 1992), 153.

40. Beth, *John Marshall Harlan*, 153 (citing Harlan to Claypool, January 21, 1889, John Marshall Harlan Papers, Library of Congress).

41. Evansville Nat'l. Bank v. Britton, 8 F. 867 (C.C.D. Ind. 1881).

42. "Our Constitution is color-blind, and neither knows nor tolerates classes among citizens." Plessy v. Ferguson, 163 U.S. 537, 559 (1896) (Harlan, J., dissenting).

APPENDIX

HISTORY OF OFFICIAL INDIANA STATUTES

Territorial Government

By the Ordinance of 1787 (the Northwest Ordinance) the Congress of the United States established a government for the Northwest Territory, an area encompassing what later became the state of Indiana. The principal officials of the territorial government were a governor, a secretary, and three judges. The ordinance empowered the governor and judges to adopt such laws of the original states as were necessary for governing the territory, subject to the disapproval of Congress.

It also provided that:

> So soon as there shall be five thousand free male inhabitants of full age in the district upon giving proof thereof to the governor, they shall receive authority, . . . to elect representatives from their counties or townships to represent them in the general assembly . . .

The population of the Northwest Territory reached the required number in 1798 and Governor Arthur St. Clair issued a proclamation on October 29, 1798 calling for the election of representatives. The General Assembly met in Cincinnati, Ohio from September 16 to December 19, 1799 and passed forty-five bills, eleven of which were vetoed by the governor.

These statutes and prior territorial laws were published, by authority, by Carpenter & Findlay, of Cincinnati, Ohio, in a volume entitled:

Laws of the Territory of the United States, North West of the River Ohio; Passed at the First Session of the General Assembly, Begun and Held at Cincinnati, on Monday, the Sixteenth Day of September, A.D. One Thousand, Seven Hundred and Ninety-nine Also, Certain Laws Enacted by the Governor and Judges of the Territory, from the Commencement of the Government to December, One Thousand, Seven Hundred and Ninety-Two; With an Appendix, containing Resolutions, the Ordinance of Congress for the Government of the Territory, the Constitution of the United States, and the Law Respecting Fugitives. Vol.I.

An act of Congress entitled "An ACT to divide the territory of the United States northwest of the Ohio, into two separate governments", approved by the president on May 7, 1800, established the Indiana Territory as a separate governmental unit. The act also provided for a territorial government similar to that of the Northwest Territory with legislative authority vested in an appointed governor and three appointed judges. However, the act also provided that a legislative assembly was to be formed

> . . . whenever satisfactory evidence shall be given to the governor . . . that such is the wish of a majority of the free-holders, notwithstanding there may not be . . . five thousand free male inhabitants of the age of twenty-one years and upwards . . .

On August 4, 1804, Governor William Henry Harrison issued a proclamation directing the sheriffs to hold an election upon the question of "going into the second or representative grade of Government". The vote being favorable on December 5, 1804, Governor Harrison issued a proclamation establishing a representative government. The first General Assembly of the Indiana Territory met on July 29, 1805.

Revision of 1807

The first statute revision began a year later when, by resolution of the 1806 General Assembly, John Rice Jones and John Johnson were appointed to revise the laws in effect in the territory. Chapter 98 of the Acts of 1807 adopted the revision, with alterations and amendments, and repealed all territorial laws enacted before 1807; it also provided:

> . . . that those laws so revised, altered and amended, shall, with the Laws passed at this Session of the Legislature, be the only statute Laws in force in this territory.

After this session, therefore, the body of statutory law in Indiana consisted of the Revised Statutes of 1807 and the acts passed by the 1807 assembly. The General Assembly met seven times before Indiana was granted statehood in 1816.

The Constitution of Indiana, adopted in 1816, vested legislative authority in the General Assembly, which was to consist of a Senate and House of Representatives elected by the people. Concerning the statutes that were to govern the state, the constitution provided in Article XII, Section 4, that:

> All laws and parts of laws now in force in this Territory not inconsistent with this constitution, shall continue and remain in full force and effect, until they expire or be repealed.

After the General Assembly had met for several sessions, enacting new laws and repealing old ones, the body of Indiana statutory law began to become unwieldy and difficult to research. Acts of the General Assembly, then as now, were published annually as session laws. Without consulting each volume of the session laws and prior statutes, no one could say with certainty that the applicable statute had been located. The need to alleviate this situation became apparent to the General Assembly and resulted in the *Revised Laws of 1824*.

Revision of 1824

Chapter LXXV of the *Revised Laws of 1824* set forth the following method of statutory revision, providing that:

> . . . the Governor be, and he is hereby required, to cause to be printed by their title, and date of approval only, amongst the statutes of this General Assembly, sundry private acts which are now in force in this State, and such printing . . . shall continue such private acts in force . . . [There followed a listing of the private acts to be printed.]
>
> . . . the governor be, and he is hereby required to cause to be printed at full length, amongst the statutes of this general

> assembly, all the following statutes which are now in force in this state; and such printing shall continue the same in force, and make them a part of the statutes of this general assembly . . . [A listing of the general laws which were to be thereby continued in force followed.]
>
> All statutes and parts of statutes which have not been passed or adopted by the present General Assembly, and which have not by this act been ordered to be reprinted . . . be and the same are hereby repealed . . .

It appears that the reprinting prevented the earlier laws from being repealed but did not reenact them; if this was the effect, a conflict between a law as originally enacted and as reprinted would be resolved by reference to the original enactment. However, this method made it simple to determine what law was in effect because it eliminated all laws except those that were reprinted or newly enacted.

The 1824 revision was printed by Carpenter and Douglass of Corydon in a Volume entitled:

> *THE REVISED Laws of Indiana, Adopted and Enacted by the General Assembly at their Eighth Session. To which are Prefixed, the Declaration of Independence, the Constitution of the U.S., the Constitution of the State of Indiana, and Sundry other Documents, connected with the Political History of the Territory and State of Indiana. Arranged and Published by Authority of the General Assembly.*

The 1824 revision reduced the bulk of Indiana statutory law and provided an unambiguous source for statutory research and basis for future revision. The 1824 revision proved satisfactory for several years until subsequent legislation again resulted in an unwieldy body of statutory law.

Revision of 1831

The next revision of the laws of Indiana was accomplished by the fifteenth session of the General Assembly in 1831. The *Revised Laws of 1831,* c.LVI provided:

> That the secretary of state is hereby directed to cause to be printed alphabetically, at full length . . . all the following acts and

> joint resolutions, which are hereby declared to be and continue in force . . . [There followed a list of 54 acts.]
>
> That the secretary of state is hereby required to cause to be printed in one volume, all the acts of a general nature, which are hereby ordered to be reprinted, or which are enacted or revised at the present session of the general assembly, in alphabetical order, (except as hereinafter excepted,) and shall also cause to be re-printed in the same volume . . . the following . . . [There followed a list of Acts of Congress and the Virginia Legislature and other legal documents with a substantial effect on the State of Indiana.]
>
> All statutes and parts of statutes and joint resolutions which have not been passed or adopted at the present session of this general assembly, or which have not by this act been ordered or directed to be re-printed at full length as aforesaid, be and the same are hereby repealed . . . That such of the following enumerated acts and joint resolutions, and such parts thereof, as are now in force and unrepealed, either by the laws of this present or any previous session of this general assembly; and also all acts and parts of acts, as by any other act of the present session are declared to continue and be in force, be and the same are hereby declared to be unrepealed . . . [There followed a list of 430 special and local acts and resolutions by title.]
>
> [Certain listed types of statutes] which are not repealed or contravened by any act or joint resolution of this or any previous session of the legislature of this state, or which have not expired by their own nature and operation, are hereby excepted from any repealing clause in this act mentioned.

Unlike the *Revised Laws of 1824*, the *Revised Laws of 1831* as published did not contain all the statute law governing the State because certain local and special laws passed by previous legislatures were neither repealed, nor republished in the volume. Thus the 1831 revision lacked the convenience and completeness that characterized the 1824 revision. This consideration, in addition to the effect of passage of legislation by subsequent sessions of the General Assembly, led to the *Revised Statutes of 1838*.

Revision of 1838

There is considerable question about the preparation of the *Revised Statutes of 1838*. By joint resolution in 1837 the General Assembly resolved:

> That the judges of the supreme court of the State of Indiana be, and they are hereby appointed to revise, alter, amend, abridge, enlarge and mold the State laws of the State so as to produce a comprehensive and systematic code best suited to subserve the public interest; and said judges are hereby required to lay before the next General Assembly of the State of Indiana such revisions for their action.

However, no committee report has been found to indicate what action the judges recommended. The House and Senate Journals show that the General Assembly passed a resolution in 1837 which established a joint "Committee of Revisors" but no information concerning this committee's progress can be found.

The title page of the *Revised Statutes of 1838* states that it was published through the authorization of the 22nd General Assembly. Resolution Chapter 4 of 1838 directed the treasurer and secretary of state

> . . . to select all such acts and joint resolutions, if any, of a general nature, and not either local or private, now in force, and not included in the revised acts, of the present session, and cause the same to be printed with the revised acts.

However, no statute can be found either repealing previous law, or specifying the status of the publication. If this revision had been enacted by the General Assembly, the chapters should all have had the same effective dates. However, a majority of the chapters contain effective dates from sessions prior to the 1837-38 assembly.

Because it is impossible to establish the validity of the revision, it must be considered as an unenacted compilation and should not be relied upon as a definitive source of statute law of the day.

Revision of 1843

The 1838 revision was followed by the *Revised Statutes of 1843* which again sought to reduce the viable statute law of Indiana to a usable form. Act 1841, c.67 provided:

> That Samuel Bigger be, and he is hereby, authorized to prepare a compilation and revision of the general statute laws of this state,

> and to suggest such amendments and alterations in any of said statutes, and to propose such additional ones as he may deem proper, with a view to the adoption and enactment by the legislature, of a full and complete code of general laws; such revision to be completed and reported to the general assembly as early as possible: Provided, the same shall be reported as early as the second Monday in December, 1842.

Later, Mr. Bigger obtained authority to employ the assistance of George H. Dunn, having become satisfied that assistance was required to complete the project. The 1843 revision is of special interest because it employed a modern approach to the arrangement of laws and confronted the same type of difficulties encountered today. Mr. Bigger's and Mr. Dunn's preface to the *Revised Statutes of 1843* is informative as to the motivation for the recompilation of statutes and the difficulty involved. He describes the state of existing law as follows:

> There were numerous defects in the existing statutes. Enactments relating to the same subject were found in different acts, sometime agreeing with each other, and not unfrequently contradictory. Single sections, so long and intricate as to be almost unintelligible, very often contained provisions wholly dissimilar.

This revision used an organizational scheme of arrangement which is notably modern. It is described in the preface as follows:

> The course adopted for the purpose of securing a systematic arrangement of the various matters embraced in the statutes has been to bring together in the same chapter, under appropriate divisions, all the subjects contemplated by the title of such chapter, and nothing more; to arrange each topic in its regular connection, and to comprise but a single substantive provision in each section . . .
>
> The revised statutes are divided into four parts, each part forming a distinct act.
>
> The first embraces the boundaries, jurisdiction, divisions, civil government, and internal administration of the state.
>
> The second embraces the statutory provisions relating to the acquisition, the enjoyment, and the transmission of property, real

and personal, the domestic relations, and other matters connected with private rights.

The third has relation to courts of justice and their officers, and actions and proceedings in civil cases.

The fourth embraces crimes and punishments, and proceedings in criminal cases.

The whole is divided into chapters, articles, and sections. The chapters are numbered consecutively from the commencement to the end of the *Revised Statutes.* The sections are numbered from one progressively to the end of each chapter, without regard to the articles into which the chapter is divided. This plan was adopted for convenience, it being now only necessary, in case of any reference, to state the chapter and section. In addition to the four acts above mentioned, there is another act "concerning the repeal of statutes, and general provisions relating to the *Revised Statutes.*" This act contains some important rules in relation to the construction of the *Revised Statutes,* the meaning of various terms used therein, and the effect of certain statutes enacted at the same session of the legislature, not embraced in the revision, but printed in this volume.

Unfortunately, the effect of the *Revised Statutes of 1843* was confusion because of the inadequate system used to repeal prior statutes. Chapter 59, Section 4 repealed:

> All Acts and parts of Acts, the subjects whereof are revised and reenacted in the *Revised Statutes,* or which are repugnant to the provisions therein contained, together with the provisions of such acts as have not been revised and consolidated in these Revised Statutes . . .

In derogation of this qualified blanket repeal, the Legislature specifically stated in sections 4, 5, 7, and 9 that laws concerning the state bank, the Wabash and Erie Canal, internal improvements, fees and salaries of officers, spirituous liquors, and state prisons were to remain in effect. Furthermore, section 16 exempted from repeal 31 categories of statutory law, while two later sections specifically identified 19 statutes which were to be only partially repealed.

Examination of a law which was not printed in the *Revised Statutes of 1843,* but which was still possibly in effect because it was covered by one of the categories of exceptions, was not easy. The entire body of law from the last adequate revision (the *Revised Statutes of 1831)* had to be read, a task involving the use of many volumes of session laws. The *Revised Statutes of 1843,* therefore, became the subject of considerable criticism.

Revised Statutes of 1852

There were no further revisions of the Indiana statutes until after the adoption of the 1851 Constitution, which, with amendments, remains in effect today. As in the 1816 Constitution, the new Constitution vested legislative power in the General Assembly, which comprised a Senate and House of Representatives. However, the 1851 Constitution provided for biennial, rather than annual sessions of the General Assembly. Consequently, from 1851 to 1971, session laws were published biennially rather than annually except for the laws of special sessions. The Constitution was amended in 1970 to allow regular annual sessions.

Unlike the 1816 Constitution, the 1851 Constitution included express provisions regarding the form of bills to be introduced in the General Assembly. Every act was to be plainly worded avoiding, as far as practicable, the use of technical terms. A bill was limited to only one subject and matters properly connected therewith. The bill's title was required to reflect the bill's contents. Amendatory bills were to identify the original act as last amended and the sections amended were to be set forth at length within the amendatory bill. The Constitution of 1816 had contained none of these requirements. Statutes enacted before 1852 contained many variations in form that obscured the effect of any new law on existing statutes. This state of affairs had contributed to the need for frequent revisions of the statutes.

Recognizing a need for revision of laws, the drafters of the 1851 Constitution provided, in Article 7, Section 20, that the General Assembly should provide for the appointment of three commissioners to revise and simplify the rules of pleading and practice at its first session after the adoption of the Constitution. The General Assembly was also given the option of making it the duty of the commissioners to "reduce into a systematic code, the general statute law of the State".

The new Constitution took effect on November 1, 1851. The next session of the General Assembly, the 36th session, convened in accordance with a special provision of the Constitution, on December 1, 1851, although the first regularly scheduled session under the new Constitution would not convene until January 6, 1853.

The 36th General Assembly had considerable incentive to prepare a new revision of the Indiana statutes. The new Constitution required the major changes in legislative procedure described above and also provided that:

> All laws now in force, and not inconsistent with this Constitution, shall remain in force, until they shall expire or be repealed.

As described earlier, the *Revised Statutes of 1843* were deficient. Rather than clarifying the law, they had created a considerable amount of confusion. These changes necessitated a new revision, and a joint committee consisting of two senators and three representatives was therefore appointed to prepare it. The *Revised Statutes of 1852* were enacted in 1852 and went into effect on May 6, 1853. The *Revised Statutes of 1852,* published in two volumes, contained all the general law of the State. Chapter 92 of the *Revised Statutes of 1852* provided that "all laws not enacted at the present (36th) session of the General Assembly are repealed, except . . ." Twenty categories of exceptions follow. Among these exceptions are acts of incorporation, legalizing acts, and special acts for relief of individuals. Most of the acts exempted from repeal were either temporary or of specialized application. Thus the blanket repeal contained in the 1852 revision had the beneficial effect of that of the 1824 revision in that it left little doubt concerning which statutes were in force.

Revision of 1881

In 1881 the 52nd General Assembly, in special session, enacted Chapter 94 providing for the compilation and publication in one volume of all "the general statutes passed by the General Assembly, which are in force and of practical operation". This compilation was to contain notes:

> to show by proper reference . . . the original act, or section, the time when they went into force; and also annotations, with citations of the decisions of the Court of the state construing or affecting the different sections thereof.

Because the *Revised Statutes of 1881* were never enacted by the General Assembly they are only an unenacted compilation sanctioned by the state of Indiana. Although revision was of benefit to attorneys in 1881, it, like the 1838 revision, could not be relied upon as a definitive source of statutory law.

Indiana Code of 1971

No further revision was effected by the General Assembly until 1969, when the Indiana Legislative Council began preparing a bill for enactment of the Indiana Code of 1971.

A special agency, the Indiana Statute Revision Commission, was established to oversee the work. The Commission was formed by resolution of the Legislative Council on May 21, 1969, and existed through 1971. Its members were: Sen. Phillip E. Gutman, Chairman; Rep. Richard J. Lesniak, Vice Chairman; Sen. Martin K. Edwards; Sen. Marshall F. Kizer; Sen. Marlin K. McDaniel; Sen. Robert P. O'Bannon; Sen. Wilfrid J. Ullrich; Rep. C. Joseph Anderson; Rep. Frederick T. Bauer; Rep. John Coates Cox; Rep. Ray Richardson; Rep. James Robison; Judge Richard M. Givan; Judge George B. Davis; Prof. F. Reed Dickerson; Dean Cleon H. Foust; Lewis C. Bose; Edwin K Steers; Deputy Attorney General Patricia J. Gifford; James Quinn; and James M. Yater. The Commission's staff included: Marcia J. Oddi, Director; Margaret C. Attridge; and James F. Maguire. A comprehensive discussion of the Commission's work was prepared by its staff: Oddi and Attridge, *The Indiana Code of 1971: Its Preparation, Passage and Implications,* 5 Ind.Leg.F. 1 (1971).

The volumes of session laws enacted since the 1852 revision had reached such proportions that, as a practical matter, research of official statute law was impossible without reliance upon unofficial sources. The Indiana Code of 1971 undertook not merely an updating, but a reenactment and rearrangement of viable statutory law. The arrangement was designed to accommodate new legislation in order to prolong the life of the Code and simplify future revision. Thus the viable statutes were divided into 35 major categories or Titles. Related bodies of law within these categories were further broken down into articles. Articles were divided into chapters, with each chapter usually corresponding to a prior act of the General Assembly. Chapters were divided into sections which corresponded to sections of prior acts. Not only were the laws rearranged, but new citations were adopted to reflect the arrangement. The citation form was a four-part numeric system with the first number designating the title, the second designating the article, the third designating the chapter, and the fourth designating the section. This system was designed to be particularly adaptable to computerized data retrieval methods and to ensure that the General Assembly could accurately pinpoint legislation which it proposed to amend. The Indiana Code of 1971 was enacted by the General Assembly on January 22, 1971. Additionally, the 1971 Code contained a provision repealing every statute enacted before 1971 (with certain specified exceptions). As an enacted Code, the Indiana Code of 1971 was intended to have the status of past enacted revisions and thus provide a clear and unambiguous statement of Indiana statute law.

The Supreme Court of Indiana discussed the Indiana Code of 1971 in *State ex rel. Pearcy v. Criminal Court of Marion County,* (1971) 257 Ind. 178, 274 N.E.2d 519. The Court's opinion in the case stated that the 1971 Code had official status, and that citations to its provisions were sufficient to satisfy constitutional requirements for legislation; however, it refused to recognize the repeal and replacement of prior session laws by the 1971 Code. Citations to its provisions were treated as alternate citations to the session laws from which the Code provisions were derived. The Court's opinion was based on the requirements then found in Article 4, Section 19 of the Indiana Constitution that each act be confined to "one subject and matters properly connected therewith". The General Assembly had been aware of this requirement, but acted on the premise that the Code was covered by an exception to the requirement for "original enactments of codifications of laws"; however, the Court construed the exception narrowly and found that the Code did not fall within its sweep.

Indiana Code

The decision in the *Pearcy* case posed a problem for the legislature. While there was now an official organized structure for the statutes, and Code citations could be used instead of more cumbersome session law citations, the contents of the Indiana Code of 1971 could not be relied upon as *the law.* In addition, the status of nonviable statutes which had been intentionally excluded from the Indiana Code of 1971 in order that they be repealed was left in doubt.

The response of the legislature was to propose an amendment to the Indiana Constitution. The amendment, ratified by the electorate at the 1974 November election, rewrote Article 4, Section 19. Among other changes, it broadened the exception to the one-subject-matter requirement to permit "an act for the codification, revision or rearrangement of laws".

The new Indiana Code, enacted by the General Assembly and signed into law on January 21, 1976, was very similar to the Indiana Code of 1971, retaining virtually the same arrangement and citation system. The bill for its enactment was prepared from the computerized data base used to prepare the Indiana Code of 1971, updated to reflect intervening action by the General Assembly. With the enactment of the Indiana Code, Indiana had an official enacted body of statutory law and an unambiguous source of reference for future legislative action.

The first official edition of the Indiana Code was published later in 1976 by West Publishing Company under the direction of the Indiana Legislative Council. The 1976 Edition contained not only the provisions of the Code as enacted but also all enactments of the 1976 regular session of the General Assembly affecting the Code. The 1976 Edition was updated annually by bound cumulative supplements published from 1977 to 1981. The 1982 Edition of the Code, also published by West Publishing Company, contained all enactments affecting the Code through the 1982 regular session of the General Assembly. The 1982 Edition was updated annually by bound cumulative supplements published from 1983 to 1987. The 1988 Edition of the Code, published by The Banks-Baldwin Law Publishing Company, contained all enactments affecting the Code through the 1988 regular session of the General Assembly. The 1988 Edition was updated annually by bound cumulative supplements published from 1989 to 1992. The 1993 Edition of the Code, published by West Publishing Company, contains all enactments affecting the Code through the 1993 regular session and first special session of the General Assembly. The 1993 Edition was updated by bound cumulative supplements published in 1994, 1995, 1996, and 1997. The 1998 Edition of the Code, published by West Group, contains all enactments affecting the Code through the 1998 regular session of the General Assembly. The 1998 Edition of the Code was updated annually by bound cumulative supplements published in 1999 through 2001. The Office of Code Revision of the Legislative Services Agency published the 2002 and 2003 bound cumulative supplements. The 2004 Edition of the Code, published by the Office of Code Revision of the Legislative Services Agency, contains all enactments affecting the Code through the 2004 regular session of the General Assembly.

—*Indiana Legislative Council*

CONTRIBUTORS

JOHN G. BAKER has been a judge on the Indiana Court of Appeals since 1989. He previously served as a trial judge for Monroe County (Bloomington) from 1976 until his appointment to the appellate bench. He has served as an adjunct professor for twenty-five years in both the Indiana University School of Law and the School for Public and Environmental Affairs. Judge Baker earned an A.B. in history from Indiana University in 1968 and a J.D. from Indiana University School of Law–Bloomington in 1971. He received an LL.M. in judicial process from the University of Virginia in 1995. Before assuming the trial bench, he was a partner in the firm of Baker, Barnhart and Andrews in Bloomington and was a captain in the U.S. Army Reserve.

PATRICK BAUDE is the Ralph F. Fuchs Professor of Law and Public Service at Indiana University Bloomington. He received an A.B. and a J.D. from the University of Kansas and an LL.M. from Harvard University. He has taught constitutional law at Bloomington since 1968 and writes on the subjects of federal court power and state constitutional law.

DAVID J. BODENHAMER is a professor of history and the executive director of the Polis Center at Indiana University–Purdue University, Indianapolis. He is the author or editor of seven books, including *Fair Trial: Rights of the Accused in American History* and *The Bill of Rights in Modern America* (with James W. Ely Jr.), and of more than two dozen book chapters and journal articles.

SUSAN K. CARPENTER has served as public defender of Indiana since 1981. The Office of the Public Defender of Indiana represents indigent convicted and sentenced prison inmates in state postconviction relief actions. She earned an A.B. in English language and literature (*magna cum laude*) from Smith College and a J.D. from Indiana University School of Law–Bloomington.

AMY ELSON is a Ph.D. student in history at Indiana University Bloomington.

NANCY GETTINGER currently represents the LaPorte County Department of Child Services in LaPorte, Indiana. She earned a J.D. (*cum laude*) from Indiana University School of Law–Indianapolis in 1996 and has been admitted to the practice of law in both Georgia and Indiana. She served as director of the Indiana Office of Guardian ad Litem/Court Appointed Special Advocates from 1999 to 2002.

MICHAEL GROSSBERG is a professor of history and law at Indiana University Bloomington and the editor of the *American Historical Review.* His research focuses on the relationship between law and society in American history, particularly the intersection of law and the family. He has written a number of books and articles on legal and social history and currently is working on a history of child protection in the United States, as well as coediting *The Cambridge History of Law in the United States.*

SHEILA SUESS KENNEDY is an associate professor of law and public policy at the School of Public and Environmental Affairs at Indiana University–Purdue University Indianapolis. She is also a member of IUPUI's Philanthropic Studies faculty and an adjunct professor of political science. Kennedy is the author of three books, *Free Expression in America: A Documentary History, Pickin' Fights with Thunderstorms: A Love Story, What's a Nice Republican Girl Like Me Doing at the ACLU?* and is coeditor of a fourth, *To Market, To Market: Reinventing Indianapolis.* She has published numerous articles in scholarly journals and law reviews and is a regular columnist for the *Indianapolis Star* and a frequent contributor to other periodicals.

JAMES H. MADISON is the Thomas and Kathryn Miller Professor of History and former chair of the Department of History, Indiana University Bloomington. Among his publications are *The Indiana Way: A State History; Eli Lilly: A Life;* and *A Lynching in the Heartland: Race and Memory in America.*

JOHN R. MALEY is a partner with Barnes & Thornburg LLP, Indiana's largest law firm, where he concentrates on appellate, litigation, and employment matters. He received a B.A. from the University of Notre Dame, an MBA from Indiana University, and a J.D. (*summa cum laude*) from the Indiana University School of Law–Indianapolis. He served as a law clerk to the Honorable Larry J. McKinney, judge, U.S. District Court for the Southern District of Indiana. In addition, he has served as president of the Indianapolis Bar Association, chair of the IBA's Indiana Bar Review course, and chair of the local rules committees for the Southern District of Indiana and the Marion County courts.

ROBERT J. MALEY was a sole practitioner in Richmond, with over fifty years of practice. He received a B.S. and a J.D. from the University of Notre Dame, then began his career as a law clerk to the Honorable Luther Swygert, judge, U.S. District Court for the Northern District of Indiana.

From 1957, he maintained a general practice in Richmond. He served in many professional and civic leadership capacities, including president of the Indiana Board of Law Examiners. He died in 2005. Robert Maley and John Maley, above, are father and son.

MARTHA MCCARTHY is a chancellor's professor at Indiana University Bloomington and directs the High School Survey of Student Engagement. She received a Ph.D. from the University of Florida and she specializes in education law and policy. Previously chair of the Educational Leadership Program and director of the Indiana Education Policy Center, she has also been a public school teacher and administrator. She has authored or coauthored several books and more than two hundred articles on students' and teachers' rights, church-state relations, equity issues, school privatization, leadership preparation programs, and education reform efforts. Among her recent books is *Public School Law: Teachers' and Students' Rights,* 5th ed. (with Nelda H. Cambron-McCabe and Stephen B. Thomas). She has served as president of the Education Law Association and the University Council for Educational Administration.

VIRGINIA DILL MCCARTY is a partner in the Indianapolis law firm of Landman & Beatty. She received a B.A. from Indiana University, an LL.B. (*cum laude*) from Indiana University School of Law–Indianapolis and an honorary LL.D. from Indiana University and Indiana Central College (now University of Indianapolis). She was a leader of the women's movement in Indiana in the 1970s and the first woman in the country to be appointed U.S. attorney by the president of the United States for a full four-year term. Her current practice is commercial real estate law and civil rights law.

ELIZABETH R. OSBORN is the assistant to Indiana Chief Justice Randall T. Shepard for court history and public education. She received her Ph.D. in U.S. history from Indiana University in 2004; her dissertation examines the influence of culture and gender on constitution making in antebellum Indiana, Kentucky, and Ohio. Before joining the staff of the Indiana Supreme Court, she taught at Indiana University–Purdue University Indianapolis and served as a teaching consultant at Indiana University Bloomington.

GEORGE T. PATTON JR. is the chair of the Appellate Group and a partner in the Litigation Group of Bose McKinney & Evans LLP. He earned an A.B. (*cum laude*) from Wabash College in 1984 and a J.D. (*cum laude*) from Indiana University Bloomington in 1987. He is the author of *Appellate Procedure,* 3d ed. His law review articles have been cited by the Indiana Supreme Court, the Indiana Court of Appeals, and the U.S. Court of Appeals for the Seventh

Circuit. His appellate work has resulted in more than eighty-five published opinions. Patton also has contributed to *The Brief: The Attorney's Guide to the Seventh Circuit Court of Appeals.* He is a speaker for civic, professional, legal, and judicial groups on constitutional and appellate practice.

MARGRET G. ROBB is a judge on the Indiana Court of Appeals, serving there since 1998. She graduated from Purdue University, receiving a B.S. in 1970 and an M.S. in 1972, and from Indiana University School of Law–Indianapolis where she earned a J.D. in 1978 (*magna cum laude*). She practiced law in Lafayette, Indiana, and was a bankruptcy trustee prior to her appointment to the court. She chairs the supreme court task forces on family courts and local court rules and was a member of the Indiana Board of Law Examiners. Judge Robb has served the Indiana State Bar Association, the Fellows of the Indiana Bar Foundation, the Indianapolis Bar Association, Indianapolis Bar Foundation, and the National Association of Women Judges in numerous capacities and was chair of Governor Bowen's Commission on the Status of Women. She was a recipient of the Indiana State Bar Association's award "Celebrating 100 Years of Women in the Legal Profession," the 2001 Maynard K. Hine distinguished alumni award, and the 2004 Ball State University's Women of Achievement award.

ALLEN SHARP is a federal district court judge for the Northern District of Indiana. He has spent thirty-five years as a state and federal judge. He has a bachelor's degree from George Washington University and a law degree from Indiana University School of Law–Bloomington. He also has a master's degree in history from Butler University. Judge Sharp teaches constitutional history regularly at Butler University, Indiana University South Bend, and Milligan College in Tennessee. He recently authored major articles for the *Journal of Supreme Court History* on presidents who argued cases before the Supreme Court as lawyers and on Supreme Court justices who had presidential ambitions.

RANDALL T. SHEPARD is chief justice of the Indiana Supreme Court. He is president of the Conference of Chief Justices, representing all the states and territories. Shepard graduated *cum laude* from Princeton University, earned his law degree at Yale, and received an LL.M. from the University of Virginia. He has published more than forty articles, including "The Importance of Legal History for Modern Lawyering," in various scholarly journals. Shepard is trustee emeritus of the National Trust for Historic Preservation, trustee of the Indiana Historical Society, and former chair of Historic Landmarks Foundation of Indiana.

REBECCA S. SHOEMAKER is a professor of history at Indiana State University in Terre Haute, Indiana. Her most recent publication is *The White Court: Justices, Rulings and Legacy,* published in 2004. She has authored numerous other articles on topics in constitutional and political history.

RAN ZHANG is a Ph.D. student in educational policy studies at Indiana University Indianapolis. Her area of concentration is educational leadership. She received her undergraduate degree from Peking University, People's Republic of China, with majors in both law and economics.

INDEX

Endnotes are indicated by the letter n and note number following the page number(s).